Reading Germany

READING GERMANY

Literature and Consumer Culture in Germany before 1933

Gideon Reuveni

Translated by
Ruth Morris

Berghahn Books
New York • Oxford

First published in 2006 by

Berghahn Books

www.berghahnbooks.com

Library of Congress Cataloging-in-Publication Data

Reuveni, Gideon.
Reading Germany : literature and consumer culture in Germany before 1933 / Gideon Reuveni.
p. cm.
Includes bibliographical references and index.
ISBN 1-84545-087-6 (alk. paper)
1. Consumption (Economics)—Germany—History—20th century. 2. Books and reading—Germany—History—20th century. 3. Literature and society—Germany—History—20th century. 4. Material culture—Germany—History—20th century. I. Title.

HC290.5.C6R48 2005
306.3'0943--dc22

2005048204

British Library Cataloguing in Publication Data

A catalogue record for this book is available from the British Library.

Printed in the United States on acid-free paper

ISBN 1-84545-087-6 hardback

CONTENTS

List of Illustrations

List of Tables

List of Figures

Acknowledgments

It gives me great pleasure to express my appreciation for those who have contributed to the making of this book. It all began as a doctoral dissertation for the Hebrew University of Jerusalem. I would like to thank my adviser, Moshe Zimmermann, who guided my way through German history and taught me that good scholarship is, above all else, about asking questions and seeking new readings of the past. His invaluable knowledge, support, and patience revealed to me the true meaning of the *Doktorvater* tradition. I also received support and encouragement from the other members of my dissertation committee: Steven Aschheim, Jakob Hessing, and Dan Diner. I would like to thank Wolfgang Schieder, who assisted me during my three years in Germany. I am indebted to Oded Heilbronner, who helped shape the project in its early stages. Our meetings in Jerusalem, Freiburg, Göttingin, Leipzig, and Munich motivated me to pursue this research. Different versions of the manuscript (as a whole or in part) were read by Alon Confino, Dan Diner, Anthony Kauders, and Daniel Purdy. While they do not necessarily agree with me, I am grateful for their comments and suggestions. They have helped me to refine and formulate my ideas.

This book would never have been written without the generous support I received from the following institutions. The Deutscher Akademischer Austauschdienst (DAAD) furnished me with a dissertation research fellowship in 1996/1997. Grants from the Koebner Center for German History at the Hebrew University Jerusalem and the student-exchange program between the Hebrew University and the University of Munich provided the necessary funding to complete my research.

This book was originally written in Hebrew. The text was translated by Ruth Morris. Her meticulous and vigilant work revealed new layers in the text and forced me to reformulate many of my arguments. The translation was made possible by the generous grants I received from the Koebner Center for German History at the Hebrew University of Jerusalem, the DAAD, and the Safaho Foundation for the History of the Book in Tel Aviv. I would also like to thank Antje C. Naujoks, David Rees, Matthias Schmidt, and especially my wife, Inga Harenborg, for their help in editing the text.

The research on this book brought me to different archives and libraries throughout Germany. There I encountered friendly and helpful staff members. Due to their support, what initially seemed an arduous task, turned out to be a joyful learning and discovering experience. I am especially grateful for the assistance I received from Hermann Staub in the Archiv und Bibliothek des Börsenvereins des Deutschen Buchhandels and Carole Steineck of the Deutsches Buch- und Schriftmuseum in Leipzig.

During my period of stay in Germany I made many friends, whom I am unable to fully name here. Without their help and encouragement this book would not have been written.

My two sons, Itamar and Yaron, were born while I was working on the final version of this book. To them and to Inga, my wife, I already owe so much.

Finally I would like to thanks my parents, Rivka and Avraham Reuveni, who, although initially observed my growing interest in Germany with great suspicion, eventually encouraged and supported my becoming a historian of German history. This book is dedicated to them.

INTRODUCTION

In Umberto Eco's famous book *The Name of the Rose,* the erudite Franciscan monk William of Baskerville investigates a number of mysterious deaths inside a cloistered monastery in northern Italy.[1] His inquiries have revealed that these are not deaths from natural causes, but a series of murders. Lacking any clues as to motive, means, or method, William has no choice other than to pursue as many directions as possible in the hope that one of them will lead to the malefactor. The key to solving the triple mystery lies in reading. After energetic inquiries, William by chance discovers the murder weapon—the second book of Aristotle's *Poetics,* whose pages have been anointed with poison. Given this finding, the method by which the murders were committed is also revealed: reading. All of which points to the motive for the murders—limiting knowledge by ensuring that the book would be hidden away so nobody would be able to read it. And the murderer? The murderer was the elderly monk Jorge, who when he lost his sight had to give up the coveted position of head librarian in the monastery library.

To a large extent, Eco's novel reflects the special status that reading enjoys in Western culture, which perceives reading as the touchstone of human progress.[2] In the novel, Eco highlights reading's transformative status as an activity with the capacity to change agendas. As William explains at the end of the book, the elderly monk Brother Jorge "feared the second book of Aristotle because it perhaps really teaches how to distort the face of every truth so that we would not become slaves of our ghosts."[3] This approach sees reading as an activity with the capacity to refine and cultivate mankind, but it does not ignore the destructive potential of reading as an activity able to distort reality and encourage barbarism. Essentially, it embodies Western culture's ambivalent attitude to human "progress."

One of the most striking expressions of this straightforward binary opposition is the way that Western culture perceives Germany today. The contrast between the cultured Germany—"the country of poets and philosophers"—and the barbaric Germany—"the country of judges and murderers"—serves as a yardstick by which Germany and its history in modern times are examined and measured. Even historical research still finds it difficult to rid itself of the fetters of this antagonistic schema, and not infrequently the impression is that "German history" is a mystery that historians struggle to solve like detectives faced with a difficult murder case.[4] This is a dominant tendency in studies of German culture, especially in research into reading culture in Germany prior to the iconic year of 1933.

Like Eco's elderly Brother Jorge, these studies assume that reading is not just the expression of refinement and high culture, but an activity which confused the minds of the German reading public and prepared the ground for the legitimization of the Nazi regime's murderous policies. In other words, here reading is perceived not as a neutral skill that simply reflects positions and mindsets, but rather as a causal activity with the ability to shape outlooks and influence readers' behavioral patterns. It is in this vein that Anton Kaes argues in one of the few articles to have appeared so far on reading culture in post–World War I Germany, that the mass circulation of irrational and anti-democratic articles paved the way for the mass support for Nazi policies a few years later.[5] This approach, establishing a link between the popularity of anti-democratic, nationalist, and antisemitic writings and the Nazi Party's rise to power, is shared by many scholars who have studied various aspects of the issue of these writings in Germany.

Additional evidence available to researchers shows, however, that in the 1920s there was wide dissemination of publications which were light-years away from the nationalist and antisemitic literature that allegedly paved the way for the Nazi regime's ascendancy. Erich Maria Remarque's anti-war book *All Quiet on the Western Front,* which first appeared at the beginning of 1929 and became the first best seller in Germany, is perhaps the best example of the popularity of pacifist literature during the Weimar period. By the end of 1929, more than 900,000 copies of the book had been printed—a hitherto unprecedented print run. Thomas Mann's monumental novel *Buddenbrooks* was one of the best-selling postwar novels. Up to 1933, it sold over a million copies in its discounted edition, priced at RM 2.85.[6] In the field of historical literature, the most popular books were those in the category of belletristic historical works by such Jewish liberal authors as Emil Ludwig, Stefan Zweig, and Werner Hegemann. In journalism, enormous circulations were achieved by many publications put out by publishing houses owned by Jews, many of them liberals who supported the Republic. The *Berliner Illustrierte Zeitung,* published by Ullstein, was one of the most successful of these newspapers. At the end of the 1920s, its circulation exceeded a million and a half copies, making it the best-selling illustrated paper in Germany. Estimates based on the publishing company's figures indicate that in the 1920s, total monthly circulation figures for the Ullstein papers were around four million copies, including nine hundred thousand for the daily papers.

What do these contradictory figures teach us? Was German society imbued with an extreme nationalism and antisemitic ideology that penetrated it through the reading of anti-democratic and racist literature? Or, as other figures show, was it instead imbued with more tolerant thinking, disseminated through works of literature and journalism emanating from authors and publishers with moderate and liberal positions? Which, then, was the more popular type of material? How can we determine what was more popular? And what can be learned from this popularity concerning the influence of these writings? To a large extent, these questions and the problematic nature of the issues which they raise are grounded in the hypothesis that reading is an activity capable of shaping values and influencing patterns of behavior, and that the study of popular reading material can provide indications about the positions and explain the behavior—particularly of a political nature—of readers in a variety of situations in the past.

This approach, which sees reading as a formative activity—or, more accurately, what would appear to be a discrepancy between this approach to reading and the success of reading material with a liberal and sometimes even pacifist bent during the Weimar period—constituted the background to my interest in the reading phenomenon in the period prior to the Nazis' assumption of power. I was troubled by the following basic question: is the discrepancy between the view of reading as a formative activity and the popularity of writings with a liberal bent a result of the dearth of studies about the culture of reading in pre-1933 Germany, or rather of this very attitude to reading, which is not so much based on empirical investigation of the phenomenon of reading but rather embodies an implicit or explicit desire on the part of all writers to leave their stamp on their readers' worlds? As I wrestled with this question, I identified many flaws in previous studies of reading culture in Germany. The weaknesses and simplistic nature of the formative approach to reading became increasingly clear. Jonathan Rose has listed five key weaknesses or flaws, one or more of which have affected virtually every attempt to investigate the way in which texts influence nonprofessional readers. The first flaw is the tendency to see practically any body of literature as political, in the sense that it influences readers' political awareness. The second flaw involves the approach that maintains that the influence of a given text is determined by its circulation. The third entails the assumption that the audience for popular culture is larger than the target audience for high culture and therefore more accurately reflects the positions and views prevalent among the masses. The fourth flaw contends that high culture tends to strengthen the acceptance of the existing social and political order. And the last flaw asserts that the literary canon is determined solely by the elite, meaning that normal readers are either unfamiliar with this canon or are forced to accept it.[7]

Rose does not, however, simply highlight the flaws of reading research: he also cautions against those approaches that tend to ascribe to readers the status of a passive audience which has no mind of its own and is in constant danger of being manipulated. In Rose's approach, reading is perceived as an autonomous activity which confers on the reader a status equal to that of the publisher. Consequently, in order to know how certain publications influenced readers and their worlds, it is not enough to simply take note of circulation figures and the extent of various works' popularity. Instead, the disparate messages hidden in texts must be revealed, and the reactions of their actual readers must be discovered. To be sure one has to be aware of the risk that the meaning that the author imparted to the text, or that was read into it by a particular critic, is not necessarily the message that nonprofessional readers of the text took from it. In other words, reading must not be considered simply the acquired skill of deciphering a message which appears in print, but rather as a creative activity capable of conveying meaning.

Reading, then, has been shown to be a complex social activity embodying a range of social, economic, political, and cultural interests as well as being an area where an unremitting struggle is waged between various bodies and individuals in order to shape it and determine its social status and significance.[8] Against this background, reading can clearly no longer be viewed within the sole framework of the narrow political milieu as an activity reflecting or shaping political positions, but rather must be evaluated in a broader social context reflecting an eclectic range of aspects drawn from the social experience as well as readers' daily lives.

The first challenge to confront me when I came to design my study was how to go about finding such a framework. It was only during the writing process that I realized that the framework I needed for a new angle on reading and its social context was located in the nexus between intellectual and material culture, or, in the terms in which this question is formulated in the context of this research, between reading culture and consumer culture. This question forms the focus of the present book, which examines the relationship between reading and consumption and evaluates the significance of this relationship in the period prior to 1933. It will be seen that removing the reading phenomenon from the narrow political context in whose framework it is normally examined and placing it in a broader social setting—that of the emerging new consumer culture in Germany—will present reading culture and its social significance in a new light. This investigative method will help to reveal new aspects of reading culture in Germany, provide insights into its complex social nature, and above all highlight the importance of social processes relating to the emergence of consumer culture in Germany, which, unlike the situation elsewhere, has not previously been the subject of proper historical research.[9] This method has a dual task. First, it will seek to address a field which has so far been given short shrift by historical studies, and will aim to bring out its special significance in the German context. Second, although the present study is not informed by a comparative perspective, its approach will, as appropriate, identify connections between reading and consumption in Germany and similar developments in other societies, since the German situation was not a unique phenomenon. The present study might in this way be able to provide the groundwork for future comparative research.

* * *

In the course of the last third of the twentieth century, historians began to look more and more at the phenomenon of reading. In order to reveal the varied faces of the reading phenomenon as it has developed throughout history, research has largely sought to disclose a variety of ways in which printed matter has been used, as well as structural aspects relating to the activity of reading. Using wide-ranging sources such as statistical data, collections of laws, wills, and property inventories, inventions and technological improvements, pictures of readers and furniture for reading, catalogues of private and public libraries, evidence about the process of acquiring reading skills, and lists of loans and readers' reports, historians have traced developments in reading. In addition, they have identified and traced the usage of various contrasting forms and ways of reading such as silent reading, and reading out loud, public (communal) readings and private reading, and the intensive reading of a given corpus of writings and extensive reading of a wide range of publications. In this way they have managed to reveal the process by which reading has been democratized in the modern era.[10]

Research into reading has not simply revealed the history of reading as an activity with a history. Many studies of reading hypothesize that reading is not merely an activity with the ability to disclose the information available to a given society during a particular period, but can also indicate the way that individuals, social groups, and societies perceive the reality that impinged upon them in the past, and how they steer a course through it. "If we could understand how he [the reader] has read," writes Robert Darnton, one of the leading historians of the history of reading, "we could come closer to understanding how he made sense of life; and in that way, the historical way, we might even satisfy some of our own craving for meaning."[11] Some historians of reading even claim that studying the transformation in ways of reading could provide a fresh perspective on major changes—cultural, religious, and political—that Western societies encountered from antiquity to the present.[12] This research approach, which sees reading as a creative activity that conveys meaning, is especially productive when applied to reading studies in the modern period, i.e., that time when reading became an activity with broad-based economic and social foundations, taking place in the individual domain and belonging to the daily routine of all social classes. Most studies of the history of reading carried out to date, however, still focus on the period up to the twentieth century. This tendency is particularly manifest in the area of reading studies in and about Germany.

In his seminal article on the validation of the history of reading, historian Rolf Engelsing has argued that unlike France, with its manifestly political revolution, and England, whose revolution was economic and commercial in nature, in Germany a reading revolution occurred during the transition period between the eighteenth and nineteenth centuries.[13] The essence of this revolution was the shift from the intensive reading of a defined corpus of texts to the extensive reading of an eclectic range of texts. The terms that Engelsing coined in order to validate the history of reading would appear not only to have dictated the nature of research into reading in Germany as well as elsewhere, but also to describe the actual research situation in this area in Germany, typified as it is by a whole host of studies.

One of the main causes for this abundance of research in Germany is the process of institutionalized interest in the area of reading, which began as early as the pre–World War II period. During the 1920s, in addition to two institutes looking at different aspects of book studies, no fewer than twelve different research institutes were set up in Germany to examine the press. During the period following World War II, it was mainly the Wolfenbüttel Circle and various institutes which provided training in the area of the book trade, librarianship, and journalism that were responsible for undertaking research in this field.[14]

Among the many works to emerge from these research institutes, the most outstanding are those of Rolf Engelsing, Rudolf Schenda, and Erich Schön, whose studies are far more than narrow historical monographs. Rudolf Schenda studied the emergence of popular literature in Germany "in the long nineteenth century," from 1770 to 1910. Schenda primarily addressed questions such as how many and what kinds of things people read. He analyzed different kinds of popular reading material, sparing no effort to smash the myth which ascribed the status of the "people of the book" to the Germans.[15] The 1970s and early 1980s witnessed an upsurge in research into popular literature and entertainment in Germany, particularly on the part of German Studies scholars.[16] However, these research endeavors concentrated primarily on analyzing the works themselves, rather than on their readers and hence on reading as such.

On the other hand, social historian Rolf Engelsing focused on analyzing the social aspect of the reading activity. Engelsing was more interested in the question of *who* was doing the reading, and less in such issues as the quantity and nature of reading material. In a series of articles published in the 1960s and the early 1970s, Engelsing showed how from the end of the eighteenth century onward reading began to penetrate the daily routines of different social strata, and how this development affected their lifestyles.[17]

Unlike Schenda and Engelsing, Erich Schön focused on the act of reading itself and the changes which took place in the form and mode of reading in the course of the eighteenth century. Based on an analysis of pictures of readers and reading furniture, Schön showed that beginning in the eighteenth century, physical contact with books shrank and reading became an activity of the eyes, with readers' bodies remaining static. According to Schön, the eighteenth century was not only the period when a new form of reading came into being, but also when the very concept of literature (*Literaturbegriff*) as we know it today was created. He viewed this development as symbolizing a change in the status of reading itself, as it was transformed from a purposive activity to an activity in its own right.[18]

Scholars also looked in particular at the aspect of reading habits of certain social groups, especially of the working classes. Particularly important here is the work of historian Dieter Langewiesche, who approached reading mainly as a means of assuming social control and a way of integrating workers into the ruling bourgeois culture.[19]

Two American historians made important contributions to research into the reading habits of German society. In his study on the colportage trade, Richard Fullerton investigated the process by which reading was commercialized, showing how in the second half of the nineteenth century this method of distributing reading material widened the gap between popular reading culture, "low culture," and the reading culture of society's educated classes, which became "high culture."[20]

Gary Stark studied a number of neoconservative publishing houses that acted as cultural entrepreneurs, showing how these publishers promoted German nationalism at the beginning of the twentieth century.[21] His book remains the only integrative study undertaken so far of a number of publishing houses that qualified as "cultural publishers" (*Kulturverlage*). These publishing houses, which came into being in the last decade of the nineteenth century in Germany, represented a new type of publisher, seeing their role as not just to distribute reading material, but also to organize and initiate culture. Modern German culture—Neutralism, Expressionism, Impressionism, Dadaism, as well as folk literature—owed its very existence to these programmatic publishing houses.

Unlike these studies, which focused on the period prior to the beginning of the twentieth century and primarily addressed the classical questions such as who was reading what and how, the present book concentrates on reading itself as a social and cultural phenomenon. It will deal less with reading habits, focusing instead more on examining both the role and the social and cultural significance of reading in German society in the first third of the twentieth century.

* * *

Even though German sociologists and economists such as Georg Simmel, Max Weber, Werner Sombart, Karl Bücher, Friedrich Tönnies, and others were looking as early as the turn of the nineteenth century with keen interest at the changes the new consumer culture brought in its wake, historical research in this area in Germany, still in its infancy, primarily concentrates on the post–World War II period.[22] This is illustrated by the case of a lexicon of basic historical terms (*Geschichtliche Grundbegriffe*), today considered one of the essential books for historical research in Germany, in which the term "consumption" is not listed as a separate entry. In contrast to this relative neglect of consumption by German historical research, in countries such as England, France, and the United States the field has become an inseparable part of the pantheon of subjects for historical research. How, then, does the present study relate to and perceive consumer culture?

Studies of consumer culture no longer see consumption as simply the final, trivial link in the process that begins with production, or as a function of an economic approach that seeks to increase economic growth by expanding private purchasing power. Rather, consumption is seen as part of a culture that shapes the horizon of expectations and provides a set of concepts by means of which an individual defines and navigates his or her way in society. One of the primary hypotheses that led to the change in views of consumption sees demand as having the capacity to control supply. This hypothesis has led a number of historians to conclude that the industrial revolution, at least in part, is the result of an earlier consumer revolution.[23] But even if we cannot decide whether demand precedes supply or vice versa, this approach to consumption has liberated research once and for all from the view of consumers as a passive audience subject to manipulation by manufacturers. Instead, it highlights the autonomous nature and cultural significance of the act of consumption.

The contention of this approach to consumer culture, therefore, is that "consumer culture is about continuous self-creation through the accessibility of things which are themselves presented as new, modish, faddish, or fashionable, always improved and improving."[24] Following this approach, consumption is perceived as an aggregate of processes of manufacturing, buying, and using various products and services. In other words, consumption is no longer interpreted as an activity that is given or conveys a purely social message, but as an approach by means of which social reality is to be interpreted. Need is a key concept in this approach. It is no longer perceived as something passive desirous of its wants being satisfied, but rather, as defined by Colin Campbell in his book *The Romantic Ethic and the Spirit of Modern Consumerism,* as a dynamic process "[that is] characterized by insatiability which arises out of basic inexhaustibility of wants themselves, which forever arise, phoenix-like, from the ashes of their predecessors."[25] Consumer culture encourages the constant generation of new needs, thereby promoting consumption itself as an all-purpose criterion. The most salient expression of this dynamic is revealed with the exposure of the changing symbolic significance of objects in the framework of consumer culture.

True, in *Das Kapital* Karl Marx drew attention to "the peculiar circumstance that the use-value of objects is realized without exchange, by means of a direct relation between the objects and man, while on the other hand their value is realized only by exchange, that is, by means of a social process."[26] However, only within the conceptual framework of consumer culture did the symbolic status and social significance of "objects" (*die Dinge*) move away from Marx's "peculiar circumstance" (*sonderbarer Umstand*) and become an intimate part of the "social process."

It has mainly been anthropologists such as Mary Douglas, Arjun Appadurai, and Gareth McCracken who have shown how, in the framework of consumption, the status of objects looms much larger than their exchange value and their functional purpose. These researchers have argued that objects have a social life which makes their consumption and ownership a socially significant declarative act.[27] As the psychologist Mihaly Csikszentmihalyi eloquently puts it:

> men and women make order in their selves (i.e. "retrieve their identity") by first creating and then interacting with the material world. The nature of that transaction will determine, to a great extent, the kind of person that emerges. Thus the things that surround us are inseparable from who we are. The material objects we use are not just tools we can pick up and discard at our convenience; they constitute the framework of experience that gives order to our otherwise shapeless selves.[28]

This approach has informed historical research on consumption, and today it tends to see consumption as an arena in which a struggle is being played out between symbols by means of which various social groups try to give expression to their own values and unique identities.[29] Moreover, it also affected our understanding of the nature of modernity. In contrast to the approach based on the writings of Max Weber which views modernity as a process of demystification and disenchantment of the social world, a prevailing approach especially in the field of culture studies today corroborates with Walter Benjamin's notion that under the conditions of capitalism, industrialization had also brought about re-enchantment of the social life. For Benjamin, as Susan Buck-Morss reconstructs his argument, the "threatening and alluring face" of myth was alive and everywhere in the modern city. "It peered out of wall posters advertising 'toothpaste for giants,' and whispered its presence in the most rationalized urban plans."[30] Consumption accordingly is not conceived, as Raymond Williams noted, as "sensibly materialist" but profoundly idealist, offering emotional and spiritual rather than utilitarian gratifications.[31]

This consumer culture studies point of view also teaches that the process by which society tenderizing in the modern era is inextricably linked to the fragmentation of society. Consumer culture generates a sphere in which, although everybody operates according to the same rules, individual consumers nevertheless have the ability to create and express their own unique identities. The range of consumer patterns and the varied symbolic meaning of objects, as well as the emphasis on consumers' freedom of choice, are the main components which have made consumption an area where consumers can shake off the shackles of social conventions and enjoy a world that will meet their demands and desires.

Another salient expression of this antagonistic process of standardization/heterogenization can be found in the world of print. On the one hand, reading—as an activity that deciphers printed symbols—has contributed to the process of standardization and homogenization of society.[32] On the other hand, the world of print has enabled every single interest group to express its unique identity. Taking this further, it can be contended that reading—an activity taking place in the private domain, where the reader has more or less full control over what reading material to choose and how to interpret or react to it—has become a sphere in which readers are free to shape the horizon of their expectations and to realize their most heartfelt desires. What are the implications of this comparison between reading and consumption?

So far, we have drawn a comparison between the act of reading and the way in which research today views the act of consumption. Both reading and consumption are perceived as activities which should enjoy an autonomous status not dictated by the manufacturing process alone. Is this similarity purely coincidental? What is the link between reading culture and consumer culture, and what is its significance?

The apparent similarity between reading and consumption may well be the upshot of vogues in research that, whether consciously or not, tend to relate to separate phenomena in similar fashion. Perhaps this link is the result of a third factor that is expressed equally in both areas. A no less logical possibility is that such a similarity is not random, but rather the result of a direct link between these two phenomena, to which research has so far not ascribed any special significance. The primary mission of the present study is therefore to examine whether a nexus in fact exists between reading and consumption, and if so, to investigate its nature. Looking at the act of reading in the context of consumer culture will allow us better to describe the nature and scope of consumer culture in general, and to identify some of the main ways in which it became an integral part of the daily routines of social groups in different parts of Germany until 1933.

The nexus between reading and consumption will be examined here from two different angles. First, we will examine the process by which reading became commercialized. This involves seeing reading as an acquired skill that needs both a basis and suitable motivation so as to nurture people's desire for it. Perhaps the most significant development in the process of increasing demand for reading and making it one of the daily needs of all social classes was the improvement in printing technology that took place from the mid-fifteenth century onward. Printing not only improved the graphic quality of publications and made possible their distribution to an unlimited audience of readers, but also introduced the principle of mass production: the larger the total number of copies, the smaller the relative investment in the production of individual copies. The development of printing therefore marks the beginning of the era of technical reproduction, as Walter Benjamin has dubbed it.[33]

The discrepancy between the unlimited possibilities of producing reading material and the limited demand for it led to persistent attempts to foster demand for reading. These attempts contributed significantly to the commercialization of print and to the development of marketing and distribution techniques. They show that modern reading depended upon a specific set of (consumption-oriented) values becoming acceptable and comprehensible among sufficient groups of people so that the sales of reading material can be made. Thus by presenting this aspect of reading we will be able to examine the forces of supply-and-demand and profit-and-loss at work in the world of print.

Second, we will examine two main ways in which reading as a medium nurtures new needs and encourages the consumer culture. First, the ability to read enables broad social groups to learn about behavioral patterns and lifestyles which they aspire to adopt or from which they wish to distance themselves. Especially from the end of the nineteenth century onward, during the period when reading penetrated the routines of all social strata, reading became an activity that contributed to the process of modernizing daily life and disseminating the values of consumer culture. Second, consumption—as an arena of the struggle between symbols—took place almost entirely in the imaginary consumer world. The deciphering of printed signs became an activity capable of nurturing the imaginative ability required for this struggle. But this is not all: the hypothesis that I present in this book contends that the printed world became an area in which the symbols and images of the world of the new consumer culture developed, and that reading was a form of consumption through the eyes.

These two aspects will therefore be the focus of the analysis in this book, which will show how closely consumption and reading interacted. We will see that the process by which consumer culture became commercialized contributed to the dissemination of reading, and that, conversely, reading and the world of print encouraged consumption and helped to shape and reproduce its values. We will also discuss what contemporary observers considered to be the problematic effects of these interactions. Yet, in contrast to hitherto research on culture and social criticism of this period which is still very much preoccupied with the Frankfurt School and those who in some way or another were associated with it, our discussion will concentrate on a much more praxis oriented discourse of mainly publishers, booksellers, librarians, and educators rather than on the high theoretical works of notable intellectuals such as Walter Benjamin, Theodor W. Adorno, or even Siegfried Kracauer, whose writings became influential after the Second World War.[34] This shift in emphasis is not only based on the notion that despite their Marxist leanings the Frankfurt School of Critical Theory should be placed within the broader context of the attempts of the educated bourgeoisie classes (*Bildungsbürgertum*) to explain what they perceived as the demise of their civilization in the face of the advance of new cultural forms. It will also facilitate a much more multifarious and differentiated approach to the phenomenon of "culture industry," a concept developed by Theodor W. Adorno and Max Horkheimer who in their work entirely neglect the ways in which the commercialization of culture provided opportunities for all kinds of individual and collective creativity and decoding.[35]

* * *

Our discussion will begin and end by analyzing various aspects of the discourse on the situation of reading culture in Germany following World War I. The other chapters of the book will address further, particularly structural, aspects of reading culture and its relationship with consumer culture.

The first chapter will focus on the sense of crisis which characterized the discourse on book culture in the wake of World War I. We will examine the various explanations advanced for the "book crisis," as it was known in contemporary debates, and how the sense of crisis involved the distinction between the bourgeoisie's intellectual and economic capital as two separate and mutually antagonistic domains. This chapter will present the claim that far from reflecting some failure in the development of book-reading culture, the feeling of "crisis" actually resulted from its success in becoming part of the daily routines of broad sectors of the German population.

Chapter two tests this thesis of "reading's success story" by examining the household budgets of various social groups before, during, and after the war. It will become clear that beginning at the end of the nineteenth century, reading budgets—particularly of the deprived social strata—started to increase. Especially during the war years and the immediate postwar period, household account books indicate that in both relative and absolute terms, more resources were allocated for the consumption of reading material than before the war. This tendency coincided with the economic trend reflected in postwar household account books toward a reduction in outlay on the bare necessities—food, clothing, and housing—and an increase in spending on cultural needs in general. This chapter will not only try to identify this upward tendency in the consumption of reading material, but will also present the thesis that reading itself helped to increase consumption and change the structure of household expenditure.

The third and fourth chapters will seek to provide a foundation for this thesis, by examining how reading and the consumer culture were closely intertwined. We will look first at the relationship between reading and consumption in the case of newspapers and magazines, and how this connection gave birth to the hierarchical separation of newspapers from books. Book reading was perceived as an expression of refined culture, self-restraint, and a pyramidal social order at whose apex was the educated male bourgeoisie, while newspaper reading, and above all magazine reading, were associated with the creation of the faceless mass society and an unbridled obsession with consumption. After discussing the various manifestations of this approach, we will examine book-reading culture and the way in which it fitted into consumer culture.

These chapters will also examine the various ways of distributing newspapers and books, publicity for reading, and a number of book and newspaper designs. We will see that books and newspapers were not simply products that were distributed like any other commodity, and reading was not just an activity in competition with other recreational activities and media. In fact, the world of print was a very particular sphere in which the world of symbols and images of the new consumer culture developed. Nor did this process escape the attention of contemporary players, who tried—with research into reading habits and corresponding legislation—to control reading and shape the demand for it.

The final chapter will present a number of these contemporaneous studies on reading, which investigated the reading habits of women, laborers, and youth. The interest in the reading habits of these social groups was not random, but rather the upshot of an outlook that saw women, workers, and youth as the weak links in the social order at whose apex the stratum of educated male bourgeois individuals set itself. The chapter will conclude with an analysis of a number of aspects involving the struggle against pulp and trashy literature. This struggle became a mechanism by means of which the bourgeois social strata—who actually drove forward the process of commercialization and reaped most of the benefits of its success—sought to come to grips with the rise of the new consumer culture.

The main innovation in the present study lies in its placing of reading culture within the emergence of consumer culture, a process which has sought to reinterpret a range of sources, old and new alike, which support it. This approach will show that, notwithstanding the rise of new media from the beginning of the twentieth century onward, reading was emphatically not a vanishing phenomenon. On the contrary: reading adapted and flourished during this period. I will argue that the sense of a crisis in reading culture following the First World War was in fact the result of reading's success in changing from a skill perceived as the birthright of a relatively narrow stratum of readers to an activity in which all social classes participated. This change in the status of reading was not just the result of the effort to improve the German people's educational and cultural level (*Bildung*); rather, it was primarily an upshot of the process by which the world of print was commercialized. This process, to use here John Thompson's terms, represented in many ways the emergence of new centers and networks of symbolic power which were based primarily on principles of commodity production and were generally outside the direct control of the authorities and social elites, but which they sought to use to their advantage and at times also to suppress.[36]

Reading pointed the way to the paradise of abundance and comfort aspired to by all. But this period, characterized as it was by economic hardship and political instability, also witnessed a constant widening of the gap between the world of print as a "virtual" area in which the world of symbols and images of the new consumer culture developed, and the daily realities of most social strata.[37] In the German context of the 1920s, this was a fateful and ominous trend.

Notes

1. Umberto Eco, *The Name of the Rose,* translated by William Weaver (London: Pan Books, 1984).
2. On the significance of literacy: Walter Ong, *Orality and Literacy* (London: Methuen, 1982); Jack Goody, *Literacy and the Traditional Society* (Cambridge: Cambridge University Press, 1968); idem, *The Domestication of the Savage Mind* (Cambridge: Cambridge University Press, 1977); David R. Olsen, *The World on Paper: The Conceptual and Cognitive Implication of Writing and Reading* (Cambridge: Cambridge University Press, 1996). For a critic of this approach: Brain Street, ed., *Cross Cultural Approaches to Literacy* (Cambridge: Cambridge University Press, 1993).
3. Eco, *The Name of the Rose,* 431.
4. For a evoking attempt to offer an alternative approach to German History which makes the instability of the German condition to the pivotal concern of historical construction see, Konrad H. Jarausch and Michael Geyer, *Shattered Past: Reconstructing German Histories* (Princeton: Princeton University Press, 2003).
5. Anton Kaes, "Schreiben und Lesen in der Weimarer Republik" in: Bernard Weyergraf, ed., *Literatur der Weimarer Republik 1918–1933* (Munich: dtv, 1995), 64.
6. Donald Ray Richards, *The German Bestseller in the 20th Century. A Complete Biography and Analysis 1915–1940* (Bern: Lang, 1967); Kornelia Vogt-Praclik, *Bestseller in der Weimarer Republik 1925–1930. Eine Untersuchung* (Herzberg: Verlag Traugott Bautz, 1987).
7. Jonathan Rose, "Rereading the English Common Reader: A Preface to the History of Audiences," *Journal of the History of Ideas,* 53 (1992), 48.
8. On this notion see also John B. Thompson, *The Media and Modernity: A Social Theory of the Media* (Stanford: Stanford University Press, 1995).
9. Alon Confino, "Consumer Culture in Need of Attention: German Culture Studies and the Commercialization of the Past" in: Scott Denham, Irene Kacandes, & Jonathan Petropoulos, eds., *A User's Guide to German Cultural Studies* (Michigan: University of Michigan Press, 1997), 181–188; idem, and Rudi Koshar, "Regimes of Consumer Culture: New Narratives in Twentieth Century German History," *German History* 19 (2001), 134–161.
10. For overviews on this research see for example: James Smith Allen, *In the Public Eye: A History of Reading in Modern France 1800–1940* (Princeton: Princeton University Press, 1991); Guglielmo Cavallo and Roger Chartier, eds., *A History of Reading in the West,* translated by Lydia G. Cochrane (Amherst: University of Massachusetts Press, 1999); David Finkelstein, ed., *The Book History Reader* (London: Routledge, 2001); James Raven, "New Reading History, Print Culture and Identification of Change: The Case of Eighteenth Century England," *Social History* 23 (1998), 268–287; Robert Darnton, "History of Reading," in: Peter Burke (ed.), *New Perspectives on Historical Writing* (Oxford: Oxford University Press 1986), 140–168; Roger Chartier, "Ist Geschichte des Lesens möglich? Vom Buch

zum lesen: Einige Hypothesen," in: Brigitte Schlieben-Lange, ed., *Lesen—Historisch* (Göttingen: Vandenhoeck, & Ruprecht, 1985), 250–273; idem, "Text, Print, Reading," in: Lynn Hunt, ed., *The New Cultural History* (Berkeley: University of California Press, 1987), 154–175; Rolf Engelsing, "Das Thema Lesergeschichte," *Jahrbuch für Internationale Germanistik* 12 (1980), 168–178; Georg Jaeger, "Historische Lese(r)forschung," in: Arnold Werner, Wolfgang Dittrich, and Bernhard Zelle, eds., *Die Erforschung der Buch- und Bibliotheksgeschichte in Deutschland* (Wiesbaden: Harrassowitz, 1987), 485–507; Werner Behrnes, Klaus F. Geiger, Ernst Rehermann, Reidel Heinrich, and Brigitte Schmutzler, "Planskizzen zu einer Sozialgeschichte des Lesens," *Zeitschrift für Volkskunde* 72 (1976), 1–27.

11. Darton, History of Reading, 162.
12. Guglielmo Cavallo and Roger Chartier, eds., *A History of Reading in the West.*
13. Rolf Engelsing, "Die Perioden der Lesergeschichte in der Neuzeit," in: idem, *Zur Sozialgeschichte deutscher Mittel und Unterschichten* (Göttingen: Vandenhoeck & Ruprecht, 1973); on similar developments in American context: David Hall, "The Use of Literacy in New England 1600–1850," in: David Hall, Richard Brown, and John Hench, eds., *Printing and Society in Early America* (Worcester: American Antiquarit Society, 1981), 1–47. For a critique of this thesis see Guglielmo Cavallo and Roger Chartier, eds., *A History of Reading in the West*, 25; as well as Reinhard Wittmann, "Was there a Reading Revolution at the End of the Eighteenth Century?" in: Guglielmo Cavallo and Roger Chartier, eds., *A History of Reading in the West*, 284–312.
14. For a comprehensive bibliography see the different volumes of: *Wolfenbütteler Bibliographie zur Geschichte des Buchwesens in deutschen Sprachgebieten 1840–1980* (Munich: Saur, 1990ff.); *Bibliographie der Buch- und Bibliotheksgeschichte* (Bad Iburg: Bibliographischer Verlag, 1982ff.).
15. Rudolf Schenda, *Volk ohne Buch. Studien zur Sozialgeschichte der populären Lesestoffe 1770–1910* (Frankfurt a.M.: Vittorio, 1970).
16. For these works see for example Paul Hainer, *Bibliographie deutschsprachiger Veröffentlichungen über Unterhaltungs- und Trivialliteratur* (Munich: K.G. Saur, 1980).
17. Rolf Engelsing, *Der Bürger als Leser. Lesergeschichte in Deutschland 1500–1800* (Stuttgart: J.B. Metzlersche, 1974); idem, *Zur Sozialgeschichte deutscher Mittel und Unterschichten* (Göttingen: Vandenhoeck & Ruprecht, 1973).
18. Erich Schön, *Der Verlust der Sinnlichkeit oder die Verwandlungen des Lesers* (Stuttgart: Klett-Cotta, 1987).
19. Dietrich Langewiesche, *Zur Freizeit des Arbeiters* (Stuttgart: Cotta, 1980); idem, and Klaus Schoenhoven "Arbeiterbibliotheken und Arbeiterlektüre im Wilhelminischen Deutschland," *Archiv für Sozialgeschichte* 16 (1976), 132–204; Hans-Josef Steinberg, "Workers Libraries," *History Workshop* (1976); idem, "Was sollten die Arbeiter lesen und was haben sie gelesen? Ein Beitrag zur sozialistischen Arbeiterbildung in Deutschland," *Wolfenbütteler Notizen zur Buchgeschichte* 21 (1996), 128–132; Lynn Abrams, "From Control to Commercialization: the Triumph of Mass Entertainment in Germany 1900–1925?" *German History* 8 (1990), 279–293; Peter Vodesk, Öffentliche und Arbeiterbibliotheken (Berlin: Deutscher Bibliothekverband, 1975); Felicitas Marwinski, *Sozialdemokratie und Volksbildung. Leben und Wirkung Gustav Hennig als Bibliothekar* (Munich: K.G. Saur, 1994); John Philip Short, "Everyman's Colonial Library: Imperialism and Working-Class Readers in Leipzig, 1890–1914," *German History* 21 (2003), 445–475.
20. Roland Fullerton, "Creating a Mass Book Market in Germany: The Story of the Colporteur Novel 1870–1890," *Journal of Social History* 10 (1977), 265–284; idem, "Toward a Commercial Popular Culture in Germany: The Development of Pamphlet Fiction 1871–1914," *Journal of Social History* 12 (1979), 489–513.
21. Gary D. Stark, *Entrepreneurs of Ideology: Neoconservative Publishers in Germany 1880–1933* (Chapel Hill: The University of North Carolina Press, 1981).
22. See for example: Axel Schildt, *Moderne Zeiten. Freizeit. Massenmedien und "Zeitgeist" in der Bundesrepublik der 50er Jahre* (Hamburg Christians, 1995); Michael Wildt, *Am Beginn*

der Konsumgesellschaft (Hamburg: Ergebnisse Verlag, 1994); idem, *Vom kleinen Wohlstand. Eine Konsumgeschichte der Fünfziger Jahre* (Frankfurt a.M.: Fischer, 1996); Erica Carter, *How German is She? Postwar West German Reconstruction and Consuming Woman* (Michigan: The University of Michigan Press, 1997); Jennifer Loehlin, *From Rugs to Riches: Housework, Consumption and Modernity in Germany* (Oxford: Berg, 1999).

23. Niel Mckendrick, John Brewer and J.H. Plumb, *The Birth of Consumer Society: The Commercialization of Eighteenth Century England* (Bloomington: Indiana University Press, 1982); for further literature: Lisa Tiersten, "Redefining Consumer Culture: Recent Literature on Consumption and the Bourgeoisie in West Europe," *Radical History* Review 57 (1993), 116–159; Jean-Christophe Agnew, "Coming up for air: consumer culture in historical perspective," in: John Brewer and Roy Porter, eds., *Consumption and the World of Goods* (London: Routledge, 1993), 19–40; Paul Glennie, "Consumption within Historical Studies," in: Daniel Miller, ed., *Acknowledging Consumption: A Review of New Studies* (London: Routledge, 1995), 164–203; Peter N. Stearns, "Stages of Consumerism: Recent Work on the Issues of Periodization," *Journal of Modern History* 69 (1997), 102–117.
24. Don Slater, *Consumer Culture & Modernity* (Oxford: Polity Press, 1997), 10.
25. Colin Campbell, *The Romantic Ethic and the Spirit of Modern Consumerism* (Oxford: Basil Blackwell, 1987), 37.
26. Karl Marx, *The Capital* (Online version of the English edition of 1887 as edited by Friedrich Engels: http://csf.colorado.edu/psn/marx/Archive/1867-C1/).
27. Grant McCracken, *Culture and Consumption* (Bloomington: Indiana University Press, 1988), Mary Douglas & Baron Isherwood, *The World of Goods* (London: Routledge, 1996); Arjun Appadurai, ed., *The Social Life of Things* (Cambridge: Cambridge University Press, 1986).
28. Mihaly Csikszentmihalyi and Eugene Rochberg-Halton, *The Meaning of Things: Domestic Symbols and the Self* (Cambridge: Cambridge University Press, 1981), 16.
29. One of the most notable representatives of this approach is Pierre Bourdieu, who explores in his work how various consumer goods are used by specific groups to demarcate their distinctive way of living, and to mark themselves off from others. See especially, Pierre Bourdieu, *Distinction: A Social Critique of the Judgement of Taste*, translated by Richard Nice (London: Routledge & Kegan, 1984).
30. Susan Buck-Morss, *The Dialectics of Seeing: Walter Benjamin and the Arcades Project* (Cambridge, Mass.: The MIT Press, 1989), 254.
31. Raymond Williams, *Problems in Materialism and Culture* (London: Verso, 1980), 185.
32. On this process: John B. Thompson, *The Media and Modernity*; Benedict Anderson, *Imagined Communities* (London: Verso, 1983); Laurel Brake, Bill Bell, and David Finkelstein, eds., *Nineteenth-Century Media and the Construction of Identities* (Houndmills: Palgrave, 2000).
33. Walter Benjamin, "Das Kunstwerk im Zeitalter seiner technischen Reproduzierbarkeit," in: idem, *Lesezeichen* (Leipzig: Reclam, 1970), 373–414.
34. On the history of this school of thought and its influence, see for instance: Martin Jay, *The Dialectical Imagination: A History of the Frankfurt School and the Institute of Social Research, 1923–1950* (Boston: Little, Brown and Company, 1973); Russell A. Berman, *Modern Culture and Critical Theory: Art, Politics, and the Legacy of the Frankfurt School* (Madison: University of Wisconsin Press, 1989); Rolf Wiggershaus, *The Frankfurt School: Its History, Theories, and Political Significance*, translated by Michael Robertson (Cambridge, Mass.: MIT Press, 1994); Ronald Jeremiah Schindler, *The Frankfurt School Critique of Capitalist Culture: A Critical Theory for Post-Democratic Society and Its Re-Education* (Aldershot: Ashgate, 1996).
35. According to Adorno and Horkheimer, modern culture is now produced on a rational and exploitative basis and for mass sale. In this process culture, or what is now culture industry, has lost all oppositional content and all critical distance from capitalist society with which it now totally identifies. On this see: Max Horkheimer and Theodor Adorno, *Dialektik der Aufklärung* (Frankfurt am Main: S. Fischer, 1964), especially 129–176. For an

overview of the critics of the concept of culture industry: Deborah Cook, *The Culture Industry Revisited: Theodor W. Adorno on Mass Culture* (Lanham: Rowman & Littlefield, 1996).

36. John B. Thompson, *The Media and Modernity,* 53 and 56.
37. In this context it is important to mention Reinhart Koselleck's characteristic of modern time consciousness in terms of the increasing difference between the "space of experience" and the "horizon of expectations." According to this notion modernity was experienced in day-to-day life as the gap between past and present as well as the continuously shifting horizon of expectations associated with the future. Reinhart Koselleck, *Futures Past: On the Semantics of Historical Time,* translated by Keith Tribe (Cambridge, Mass.: MIT Press, 1985), especially ch. 15. In many ways Koselleck's analysis calls to mind Walter Benjamin's distinction between time-space (*Zeitraum*) and time dream (*Zeit-traum*); on this see Susan Buck-Morss, *The Dialectics of Seeing,* 272; cf. also Helga Nowotny, *Time: The Modern and Postmodern Experience,* translated by Neville Plaice (Cambridge: Polity Press, 1994).

Chapter I

Reading as a Barometer of German Society after the First World War

In the 1920s, the term "book crisis" was central to discussions about the situation of books and reading. As in many other areas, in these discussions too the recent World War I was regarded as a watershed which was referred to in terms of "before" and "after." True, the feeling that books were not selling and that book-reading culture was disappearing—feelings which epitomized the awareness of a "book crisis"—was not a new perception which typified the postwar period. However, as we will see, in the wake of World War I, the collapse of the imperial German political order and the popularity of the new media—films, the gramophone, and the radio—this sense of a crisis affecting books acquired new dimensions.

Examining reading culture from the point of view of its contemporaries serves a threefold purpose. First, it reveals some characteristics of book culture in the period after World War I which have so far received scant scholarly attention; and second, it shows how the group of cultured people and readers of books known as the "educated bourgeoisie" viewed the particular reality of the period. We will see that, after World War I, reading was viewed as a barometer of German society, and the prevailing sense of the critical situation of the book was not only related to economic hardships, political tensions, a feeling of cultural decline, and structural problems in the book trade: first and foremost it constituted part of the discourse concerning the social changes which occurred in Germany after the war.

Third, given the dominance of the notion of crisis, the question arises whether the "book crisis" was the subjective feeling of a restricted group of people connected with books, or whether it represented a genuine situation, evidence of which may be found in the realities of the period. At odds with the contemporaneous notion that books were in crisis, there is actually much evidence to the effect that the book market in general, and book reading in particular, flourished after World War I. This discrepancy between the perceived status of books and their actual situation will serve as the basis for the main argument of this chapter. In contrast to the discourse of the period, which saw the "book crisis" as something objective, the claim I will be making is that the "book crisis," insofar as it existed at all, did not express a disappearance of reading culture, but rather reflected the bourgeoisie's accomplishment in managing to popularize that culture.[1] From this point of view, the sense of a "book crisis" not only reflected the success of the bourgeoisie, which had set itself the goal of spreading reading culture throughout all levels of society and imposing its values and lifestyle on the society of the period, but also was one of the conflicting manifestations of modernity.[2]

The Three-Way Boundaries of the "Book Crisis"

It should come as no surprise that during a period of economic hardship, social instability, armed clashes between rival political forces, and uncertainty about the nature of the future political system, the book market's attitudes on the one hand also emphasized the chaos and anarchic situation in which it found itself, while on the other hand simultaneously expressing the hope that its situation would improve in the future.

Cutthroat competition, overproduction of titles, high prices, the popularity of pulp and trashy literature, and economic hardships which led to the decline of libraries, research institutes, and readerships were the dominant elements in the chaotic picture of the German book trade market in the postwar period.

As indicated by numerous references to the situation of the book trade market during these years, books were regarded as the bedrock of culture, of education (*Bildung*), and of scientific research. As such, books were considered the very fundament of nation-building and an instrument in the struggle against other peoples.[3] As a result, the difficulties with which the German book trade market was struggling were viewed not only as a matter for book dealers, but also as part of a general crisis—social, political, economic, and cultural—affecting Germany in the wake of the World War. As Wilhelm Moufang warned in 1921, as long as German books were beyond the reach of the reading public in Germany and abroad, and at a time when Germany's former enemies—and here he meant France in particular—were continuing to invest in and perfect their propaganda machinery, Germany was at grave risk of economic and cultural impoverishment, and of being increasingly isolated in the world.[4]

The link between the book trade market and what happened to Germany in the immediate postwar period is also reflected in the plans and proposals to deal with the hardships which had overtaken this area. The key word in these discussions was "socialization."[5]

The Socialization of the Book Trade

In the period immediately following the November Revolution, the term "socialization" became an incantation, particularly in the left-wing camp, for a solution to all of Germany's economic and social woes. At the center of the idea of socialization was the shift from an economy based on private ownership and free competition to an economy where the means of production would be subject to common ownership operating according to a centralized economic program.[6] The desire for socialization not only reflected the interests of those political groups whose goal was to turn Germany into a society based on the principles of Socialism, but also of an approach, shared also by a number of industrialists, which saw common ownership of the means of production as a possible solution to rescuing Germany from the economic and social plight in which it had become embroiled following the World War.[7] To be specific, the term socialization was not necessarily tantamount to the nationalization (*Verstaatlichung*) of the means of production, but rather in most cases proposed common public ownership (*Vergesellschaftung*), with the goal of "rationalizing" economic life. Proposals for socialization were made in a number of domains, from insurance and health via transport, electricity, and water, to a range of industrial enterprises: coal, steel, the chemical industries. The book trade market was not excluded from such proposals.

In a lecture given by Walther Borgius to the Bund des neues Vaterlands convention in December 1918 on the approaches and aims of socialization, for the first time a detailed proposal was outlined for socializing the book trade market.[8] In essence, Borgius suggested organizing the publishing houses by their areas of specialization in a central publishing house (*Zentralverlag*), in parallel to organizing the consumers in a cooperative (*Genossenschaft*), which would make possible a direct link between the manufacturer, in this case the publishing house, and the consumer, and would operate to the benefit of their mutual interests. In this way Borgius tried to offer a cure for the malady affecting the current system, with competition between the various publishing houses resulting in uncontrolled publishing and the excess production of titles, and the intermediate or wholesale trade (*Zwischenhandel*) preventing any reduction in book prices and excessively complicating the running of the book trade market.

According to Borgius's proposal, therefore, merging publishers into a single central publishing house and dropping the system of wholesale trading, to be replaced by the direct marketing of books from publisher to reader, would not only reduce the economic risks of book publishing and increase the control exercised over the number of titles published; these steps would also significantly reduce the price to the consumer and improve German books' ability to compete on the international book market.

Borgius's proposal focused on the nonfiction area. This was characterized by a distinct target audience, who because of their interest in a specific book or books normally change from readers to buyers. The socialization of the book market was therefore intended to guarantee the continued existence of science and culture in Germany by protecting the interests of the stratum of consumers of nonfiction works—academics, members of the liberal professions, functionaries, and students—whose ranks constituted the hard core of the "educated bourgeoisie" (*Bildungsbürgertum*).[9]

Moreover, Borgius argued that the area of belles lettres, where readers were primarily interested in being entertained, presents a different kind of challenge. Since the target audience of belletristic literature basically encompassed the entire public, which had available to it a range of possible ways of obtaining reading material, the problem posed by this area does not relate to the need to improve the distribution system or reduce the price of belletristic works, but rather is how to perfect control of it. Unlike the area of nonfiction, where he rejected any attempt at nationalization and imposing a State monopoly on systems of producing and distributing reading material, in the case of belletristic literature Borgius called for nationalization of the lending libraries and the bookshops at railway stations, which were the main distribution agents for what was defined as pulp and trashy literature (*Schund- and Schmutzliteratur*). In this way Borgius hoped to step up the supervision of popular reading material and to encourage the reading of what he considered good literature.

Against this background, it can readily be seen that the goal of socialization was not just to guarantee the economic existence of the book market, by changing its confused and disorganized distribution structure—the "chaotische, unorganisierte Gestaltung des Absatzes"—but also to protect the interests of German society's educated classes by reducing book prices and maintaining the quality of publications, so that the book trade market would be able to offer the German people, as defined by Walter Dette in his proposal for socialization, the best, purest, and noblest literature — "dem Volke das Beste, Reinste und Edelste zu bieten."[10]

The proposals for the socialization of the book market attracted great attention and sparked a stormy debate both among people in the book trade and in the academic world generally, which engaged in intensive debate on the various proposals for socialization. Most of the criticism agreed with Borgius's diagnosis of the book market's plight, and even accepted the need to reform it. However, the overwhelming majority rejected the socialization solution, arguing either that it was misguided or that it was unsuitable for the German book market.

Most of the attacks on the idea of socialization came from people associated with the Börsenverein des Deutschen Buchhandels (Bv)—the German booksellers' umbrella organization—who saw it as a threat to their organization's very existence. Apart from the ad hominem criticism directed at Walther Borgius and the presenting of socialization as an unrealistic utopia, fundamental arguments were also advanced against the very idea of socialization. These primarily attacked the proposal of setting up a central publishing house, as well as the link that was made between the plight affecting the book market and the free competition between publishers and the bookshops.

In two programmatic articles published in 1919 in the *Börsenblatt des deutschen Buchhandels,* Eduard Ackerman and Otto Riebcke, two prominent members of the Bv, did their best to present the drawbacks of the idea of socialization so as to set out the Börsenverein's position on the issue.[11] Scrapping the wholesale book trade, Riebcke argued, and creating a direct link between the publisher and readers might indeed reduce the risks involved in book publishing. Furthermore, by shortening the path between the publisher and the reader's bookshelf and considerably reducing the outlay required to publish reading material, it would also become possible to reduce book prices. However, because this distribution method was based on a direct ratio between the number of publications and the number of readers, it would make it impossible to expand readerships. The bookshops all over Germany and the publicity given to a book, mainly through the medium of bookshop windows, were not only a tool in the distribution of reading material, but also a means of attracting potential readers. According to this approach, therefore, the preventing of competition between publishers and bookshops alike might not only lead to the book market becoming a rigid rather than a fluid affair, but would also eliminate books' educational vocation and exacerbate the gaps between different social classes. Another argument advanced by Riebcke was that if socialization's mission was to protect the interests of the educated middle classes, then how during a period of such major economic hardship could it set itself the goal of scrapping jobs which constituted a source of income for this very stratum?

In contrast to Riebcke, who focused on the social implications of implementing the idea of socialization, Ackermann attacked its economic justification. He argued that greater resources would be required to finance the socialization reform of the book market than estimated by Borgius.[12] However, apart from the various financial difficulties, Ackermann argued that the sole book publisher approach would make it necessary to set up a vast administrative apparatus, which would make the operating of the book market extremely cumbersome and result in a mechanical state of mind, with a concomitant disinclination to work and a curtailment in creative freedom on the part of authors and publishers alike, whose personalities played a cardinal role in determining the nature and vitality of the book market.[13] As Gerhard Menz enlarged on this point in 1920, cultural life needed freedom, not central economic planning. Accordingly, he concluded that despite the difficulties affecting the current system and the danger that certain elements were exploiting it in order to circulate what was defined as inferior literature, it was still to be preferred.[14]

The purpose of socialization, therefore, may have been to safeguard the interests of the middle classes by rationalizing the book trade market and improving the quality of publications. However, its critics feared that it would spawn a despotic body which would exercise absolute control over the book market and on which there would be absolute dependence on the part of both readers (who would only be able to read what that body offered them) and authors (who would be obliged to publish via that body only).[15] Even the supporters of the idea of socialization were aware of this danger. For example, Julius Bunzel—who was convinced that the future would lie with cooperative undertakings—argued that because of the nature of the book market, the process of socialization should be located in a readers' organization and not a body of publishers, as suggested, for example, by Borgius and Walter Dette. In Bunzel's opinion, what made the book market unique relative to other areas could not simply be limited to the difficulty of defining who were the producers—authors or publishers—but necessarily also involved the status of books themselves, which were far from being commodities that could be controlled like any other products. Hence merging numerous publishing houses into a single central publisher and attempting to control the production of books would result in more harm than good for the book market specifically, and German culture in general.[16]

The various criticisms directed at the socialization proposals reflected the fear of Communism gaining control over Germany and the concern of book dealers, most of whom were organized in the Bv, Germany's book dealers' association, that they would lose their influence over the book trade market. Most of those in favor of socialization also agreed that socializing the book market should be made conditional on the socialization of the entire German economy. For these reasons, and after the Socialization Commission, set up by the German government to examine the various possibilities of socialization, had in its 1921 Bill rejected the proposal to socialize the reading material market (apparently because of the fear on the part of the commission's members that socialization would turn into censorship), and in the wake of pressure by people from the book trade, the debate over socialization began to dissipate as early as 1921. In the Börsenblatt's index for 1922, all we find under the term "socialization" is a reference to the socialization of school textbooks, and from 1923 onward this term is entirely absent from its index.

Like the arguments for and against the socialization of the book market, the emphasis on the book market's economic plight and the danger that this situation posed for the future of Germany showed that during this period reading was perceived as a national resource, with efforts being required to both foster and oversee it. Nonetheless, awareness of the crisis from which the book market was suffering at the time was not perceived as a result of a loss of interest in reading, but rather as the upshot of the difficulty of distributing books, the causes of which were variously identified as being the rampant economic hardships and political chaos, which primarily impacted on the middle classes' purchasing power; or, as argued by the proponents of the socialization idea, the flawed structure of the book trade market.

The fear of Germany being isolated, of the country becoming an impoverished failed satellite state of its former foes, on the one hand, and the hope that the window of opportunity which had opened up after the World War could be exploited in order to renew and change the face of German society and the German state, on the other hand, were therefore the key components which influenced attitudes to the situation of the book trade market in the period immediately following World War I. In the 1920s, no fundamental changes occurred in the difficulties plaguing the book trade market and the perception of books and reading. The essence of the plight of the book trade market remained the problem of distributing books, and in this period also its causes were identified with the general conditions which had come about in Germany in the wake of World War I and/or in the structure of the book trade market itself. However, in this respect the 1920s can be divided into two stages. At the beginning of the decade the crisis affecting the book trade market was primarily ascribed to the struggle over Germany's political future and the economic hardships of the time, which were bankrupting publishers and bookshops alike and at the same time drastically eating into the reading public's purchasing power. In contrast, in the second half of the 1920s—a period when statistics indicate a record number of publications as well as bookshops and publishers, the attitude which saw the difficulties affecting the book market as a reflection of social changes modifying the face of German society became more dominant. This is one of the things that we gather from the stormy debates that took place in the second half of the 1920s under the heading of the "book crisis."

The Book as Commodity

The debate over the "book crisis" issue flared up in 1927 in the wake of the publication of Edmund Winterhoff's doctoral dissertation on the crisis of the book market.[17] In his introductory chapter Winterhoff asserted that one of the basic problems of the book trade was its refusal to consider books as a product which, like many other products, behaves according to the laws of supply and demand of the free market. The printing press and its technological perfection in the course of the nineteenth century had made the book a typical mass-produced item: the investment needed for its manufacture can be slashed by reproducing it on a massive scale. As a result, in order for a book to be a product in which it is economically worthwhile to invest, publishers must try to increase the print runs of the publications they produce. According to this approach, the large number of new titles published every year in Germany, and the increase in the number of shops and publishers constituted proof of the fact that booksellers in Germany failed to grasp the nature of books as a commodity. Winterhoff argued that the book industry should concentrate on maximizing the number of copies printed by it of every edition of existing books, rather than on publishing new titles. Putting it another way, Winterhoff was saying that the book trade market's plight was the result of the extensive production of titles with the concomitant neglecting of intensive production of existing titles. It was this tendency, he argued, which was making books an expensive product inaccessible to a goodly proportion of potential book readers.

According to this approach, making the book trade market subject to the free trade laws of supply and demand would not only increase the profit which could be made from books, for authors and publishers alike, but would also make them cheaper for consumers. However, in Winterhoff's opinion the crisis affecting the book trade market was not solely the result of a conceptual error which prevented the book dealers from relating to books as a product like any other product: it also tied in with this market's flawed structure, which prevented it from becoming a profitable business. Winterhoff identified the Bv's control of the book trade market, using the method of fixed book prices, as the main factor behind the crisis of the book trade market.

Winterhoff, therefore, like Borgius and Dette before him, ascribed responsibility for the crisis of the book trade market to its flawed structure. However, unlike the socialization proposals which viewed the crisis as the upshot of the mismatch between the book trade market and the conditions created in Germany in the wake of the World War and considered that its solution was to provide increased supervision of the market by applying economic planning and concentrating control over it in a single body, Winterhoff made the link between the book trade market crisis and structural factors whose roots lay in the prewar period. He called for rationalization of the book trade market by liberalizing rather than regulating it. In Winterhoff's opinion, abolishing the system of fixed retail prices and opening up the book trade market to free competition were the only ways of saving the book trade from the crisis currently engulfing it.[18]

As Winterhoff himself acknowledged, the analysis of the book trade market and proposals for reforming it were based on the arguments of Karl Bücher, whose book on the book trade and science ("Der deutsche Buchhandel und die Wissenschaft") sparked a lively debate among book circles in Germany when it appeared in 1903.[19] References to Bücher's arguments were not only designed to reinforce arguments about the nexus between the structure of the book trade market and the crisis affecting it: they also sought to show that long-term factors lay behind this crisis, not originating exclusively in the World War and Germany's postwar situation. This argument was one of the key reasons for the stormy discussion which erupted among the ranks of book dealers following the publication of Winterhoff's doctorate. Two particularly crucial reactions were the detailed comments by Gerhard Menz, then editor-in-chief of the German book trade organization's journal, the Börsenblatt für den deutschen Buchhandel and professor of book trade studies (Buchhandelbetrieb) at the Leipzig Commercial College, and Paul Nitschmann, a cofounder of the Bookshop Owners' Guild (Buchhändlergilde) and member of the Bv board.[20]

Menz and Nitschmann argued that it was unacceptable and illogical to ascribe all the ills of the book trade market to a single cause—the cartelization of the book trade market by means of fixed book prices. However, their criticism not only involved an attack on Winterhoff's monocausal analysis, which in their opinion ignored many other factors which had helped to bring about the crisis affecting the book trade market: they also argued that Winterhoff was blaming the wrong element for the crisis. In their view, Winterhoff's mistake was that he was ascribing the crisis of the book trade market to book prices only. In other words, if Winterhoff had compared the price of books with the price of other products, he would have discovered that the relative rise in book prices, compared with the prewar period, was far more moderate than the rise in prices of other products. Menz and Nitschmann asserted that Winterhoff was uncritically assuming that reducing the cost of books and releasing them from the fetters of the fixed price system would guarantee that they would sell. Thus Nitschmann argued that from the theoretical point of view it would be correct to assume that the larger the print run of each edition of a particular book, the lower the price of each copy. However, from the practical point of view, it turned out that once a publishing house had a successful author, it had no interest in rushing to reduce the price of an individual copy, irrespective of the number of copies that it printed of that author's book.

Moreover, in the absence of fixed retail prices, bookshops would have to set a book's price themselves, based on its sales and the price that they themselves paid for it. But as Menz and Nitschmann asked in the light of this state of affairs, what guarantee is there that this situation will make it easier to reduce book prices? In addition, not only does this situation threaten to wipe out large numbers of bookshops and publishers who will be unable to cope with the cutthroat competition, in addition to increasing the cartelization of the book market in the wake of the growth of powerful combines: it is also likely to alter the nature of reading material itself. The proportion of nonfiction works, which do not sell widely, will drop further, with a concomitant increase in the sales of works of fiction, particularly those considered less refined. This is precisely the situation which the Bv wanted to avoid by means of the system of fixed retail prices for books. The purpose of this method, therefore, was to safeguard the economic livelihoods of bookshops and publishing houses, while at the same time maintaining the quality of the reading material sold by them. In addition, for Menz and Nitschmann the fact that bookshops and publishing houses were not interested in changing this system was proof positive that the crisis was not rooted in the structure of the book trade market. Menz also drew attention to the fact that Winterhoff himself emphasized that the war and the economic hardships had utterly changed the conditions in which the book trade market operated. Given this state of affairs, asked Gerhard Menz, how could responsibility for the increasingly dire crisis be attached to a form of organization which for so many decades had had a positive influence on the book trade market? To which Nitschmann added a further argument, to the effect that Winterhoff, the economist, was wrongly assuming that a book was a commodity which lent itself to mass production like any other product. Unlike cigarettes, a bar of chocolate, or items of clothing which were based on the principle of repeat purchases, a book was a product which was generally bought just once. Even the keenest book lover would not buy books the same way that a smoker makes repeat purchases of his favorite brand of cigarettes. A reader will always wish to try a new book, and even the biggest consumers of books, such as libraries and research institutes, generally buy just one copy of each book. The fact that it is possible to mass produce books was therefore viewed as incidental rather than something capable of affecting a book's one-off use. According to this approach, the book trade would never be just a "business," nor was it at liberty to become such.[21]

Winterhoff's book was perceived, therefore, as proof of the world war's influence as a factor that helped to precipitate the book crisis, and in particular as proof of the uniqueness of books as a commodity situated between the material and the intellectual worlds and which could not be related to solely by means of categories borrowed from the economic sphere. Winterhoff's opponents certainly did not imagine that less than two years after his book was published, a new debate would erupt over the causes of the book crisis, in which of all things book dealers would be accused of ignoring the intellectual dimension of books.

The Book Trade's Intellectual Vocation

The very title of Rudolf Borchardt's lecture—"The Present Situation's Responsibilities in Respect of Literature" (*Die Aufgaben der Zeit gegenüber der Literatur*)—which he delivered on 8 February 1929 in Bremen, intimates his position concerning the factors involved in and the nature of the crisis affecting books.[22] Borchardt had no desire to address the political, social, and cultural responsibilities of contemporary literature; rather, his argument was that the present situation was duty-bound to do something for the sake of literature, i.e., for the sake of German cultural and intellectual life, of which in his opinion literature was the very heart. If nothing was done in the next few years to save intellectual life in Germany, Borchardt warned at the beginning of his lecture, Germany would become a culturally fifth-rate nation. One of the most unmistakable indicators of the deterioration in the German intellect was the situation of books in Germany, which Borchardt summarized in the aphorism: "The people which buys the fewest books prints the most."[23]

Borchardt considered the main signs of the book crisis to be the inroads into the public's purchasing power, the flawed structure of the book trade market, and the mismatch between reading material and the readership's tastes. However, unlike the views examined above, which laid responsibility for the crisis primarily at the feet of the economic hardships and the structure of the book trade market, Borchardt saw the book crisis as part of Germany's national and educational crisis of the intellect (*nationale Bildungskrisis*) which went all the way back to the last decade of the nineteenth century. He argued that the reading public was alienated from classical German literature, the reason being the change in the nature of the book trade market as a result of the processes of modernization.

According to Borchardt, the traditional publishing houses were universalist by nature: in other words, their target audience was the entire people, and they also published a broad assortment of works, from light fiction via magazines to nonfiction and German literary classics. Not only did this situation make it possible to effectively control the publication of reading material, it also enabled the publishing houses to promote quality books which do not normally sell widely, as well as to maintain a balance between the different areas of publishing and the hierarchical relationship between them. There was a similar situation in bookshops. In the past, said Borchardt, nostalgically recalling his childhood days in Eastern Prussia, the shop which sold books also offered a variety of other printed items, stationery, sweets, and a wide range of other products. Books were therefore just one component of an economic setting which made a living from selling a varied array of products. This situation enabled the shop to maintain a form of literature intended for not particularly large groups of readers requiring high-caliber works. Such people came from the ranks of functionaries, officers, scholars, and property owners in the town and its environs. As a result, the retail outlet which "also" sold books (*Auchbuchhandel*) served a variety of needs. It became a meeting place for different social groups, making possible the dissemination of classical German literature.

Unlike the situation in France and above all in England, where according to Borchardt the universalist structure of publishers and bookshops had been maintained, in Germany from the 1890s onward an extreme change occurred in the nature of publishers and distribution agents. The key process to understanding this change was the professionalization and specialization of the book trade market, which upset the balance between the different areas of publishing and turned the book trade into a business designed for financial profit rather than nurturing the intellect (*Bildung*) or Germany's national interest. For the book trade, the flourishing of naturalism and modern literature during these years embodied the essence of this development. In particular, the founding of publishing houses and bookshops specializing in the publication and distribution of modern literature led to the increased publishing of belletristic material, the elimination of universalist publishing houses, and the complete and utter commercialization of the domain of reading. This situation became even more pronounced after the war. Germany's defeat, the political upheavals, and the everyday struggle to survive in the postwar conditions heightened the aimlessness of the general public. However, German literature in particular, and intellectual life in general, one of whose tasks was, according to Borchardt, to provide the German nation with guidance and leadership in the special conditions engulfing it, was no longer capable of rescuing it from its plight. One of the key reasons for this state of affairs was the fact that the book trade market had maintained its prewar character, and was continuing to swamp the public with modern literature. Borchardt also argued that the reading public had changed its nature after the world war. The main factor in this shift was the quickened pace of development of the education system toward the end of the nineteenth century. Borchardt estimated 90 percent of readers in the postwar period to be new "arrivals" on the reading market. This generation of readers, drawn primarily from the working classes, had been educated in the transitional period spanning the end of the nineteenth century and the beginning of the twentieth, when the vogue was for modern literature, and they no longer had an understanding of what was "good" German classical literature. The inevitable result of this situation was the loss of the public's faith in the book trade market.

In Borchardt's view, the flood of publications, the uncontrolled desire for innovation, and all the other characteristics of the high-speed modernization of the book trade market resulted in the undermining of the book trade's authority and a concomitant public backlash against it. Although most members of this reading public were by now unfamiliar with good German literature, they were still able to identify the vapidity of most of the new works published. The most salient expression of this situation was the fact that the publishing houses continued to issue works even though the public had simply stopped buying books.

Given his perception of the nature of the German publishing business and the factors responsible for the crisis affecting German books, Borchardt outlined a number of proposals for dealing with the crisis. Essentially he called for action in five fields: 1. A return to the model of universalist publishing houses and reversing the trend toward specialized publishers and bookshops. 2. The merging of bookshops in small and medium-size towns, and a return to books to be sold through the "also a bookshop" trade (*Auchbuchhandel*). 3. Setting up a network of lending libraries (*Leihbibliotheken*) to be financed by the book industry and to disseminate reading material which would meet the needs of the reading public. 4. Founding a new literary journal to review intellectual life in Germany and provide book recommendations. 5. Borchardt's last and most original proposal was to proscribe modern literature—including his own—for a number of years, and to return to what he considered to be the classics of German literature.

It should come as no surprise that Borchardt's lecture attracted great attention precisely from those circles which were ideologically closest to him. A particularly intense reaction to Borchardt's analysis and observations came from the young book dealers movement (*Jungbuchhandel*), whose roots went back to the nineteenth turn-of-the-century youth movements.[24] Exceptionally, the April 1930 issue of the young book dealers' circular (*Jungbuchhandel-Rundbriefe*), coming in the midst of a series of booklets examining professional issues in the book trade, was given over in its entirety to analyzing Borchardt's lecture.[25] The issue's fifteen articles presented positions of professionals from a range of fields: literature, librarianship, education, and the book trade, as well as people with a range of political leanings, from the Social Democrat historian of literature Alfred Kleinberg, through the National Liberal Paul Fechter, to the National Conservative pedagogue Ernest Füge. This diversity was intended to show that the publication had no intention of becoming an anti-Borchardt polemic, wishing instead to offer a carefully considered analysis of his arguments which, in the opinion of the issue's editor, Gerhard Schönfelder, had not been adequately considered by the book dealers' guild.

In the introductory article to this special number, Max Niederlechner, a book dealer from Berlin and a friend of Borchardt's, sought to praise Borchardt's qualities as an intellectual and to explain the source of his conservative positions and the public reaction to them. Niederlechner presented Borchardt as a Don Quixote of German conservatism. He explained that Borchardt, as a conservative of Jewish descent, was in a special position—rejected by the German Right because of his Jewish origins, and by the Left because of his conservatism. This state of affairs provided the backdrop to the social criticism of Borchardt and the reaction to it. In other words, Borchardt was unable to accept the current period and the current period was unable to accept him. According to Niederlechner, this paradox was the essence of Borchardt's tragic situation. However, Niederlechner's call to show understanding for Borchardt's situation failed to prevent him from being made the butt of criticism throughout the entire publication. This vilification of Borchardt focused on four main points. The first and main point concerned his idealistic view of German classical literature and its importance for the German people. For example, Alfred Kleinberg and Hans Hoffman attacked Borchardt's basic attitude to the nexus between the status of classical German literature and the contemporary intellectual crisis. Kleinberg argued that the reason for the rift between the German people and German literature was not the popularity of modern literature or changes in the nature of the book trade market, but rather lay in the elitist and apolitical nature of classical German literature itself. He explained that developments in Germany were very different from the situation in England, where the intellectuals were closely involved in the country's social and political affairs, a trend reflected in the English literary canon, whose subject matter was the "general destiny of the nation" (*Gesamtschicksal der Nation*). According to Kleinberg, the German situation had led to the development of the ideal of "the isolated intellectual," who was utterly aloof from day-to-day existence and contemporary social and political issues. The upshot was that classical German literature reflected the world of this narrow class within the German people—the bourgeoisie—and by its very nature it was unable to play the role assigned to it by Borchardt. Hans Hoffman, director of the Leipzig Municipal Library, drew on his experience in the field in asserting that classical literature no longer satisfied the needs of the modern reader, and that in order for literature to influence members of the general public, it had to take account of their social situation. Ernst Füge, a National Conservative with a background in education, concurred with this statement, arguing that cultural flowering could not be expected in a period of economic adversity. Kleinberg, speaking from his historical point of view, and Füge and Hoffman, with their practical experience, therefore argued that society, or more precisely the people or nation, was to be preferred over literature or the intellect. This standpoint constituted the primary difference between Borchardt and his critics, the bedrock for rejection of his positions. In a similar vein we can also identify the second point of criticism, attacking Borchardt's sentimental attitude to the nineteenth century and his dogmatic rejection of the present. For example Fritz Klatt, a progressive educator, argued that Borchardt was completely ignoring the possibilities that the modern world offered the educational system. He also argued that never had so many possibilities been available for spreading culture and broadening the educated public in Germany. And Hans Bott, editor of the *Jungbuchhandel-Rundbriefe*, argued that in every generation similar arguments are advanced about the woes of the present and the wonders of the past, and that the difference between Borchardt's pessimism and the outlook of the younger generation lies in the fact that the latter do not see the present as a chaotic situation, but rather as a transitional era during which the forces of progress and tradition jockey for position as a new culture emerges.

A third point of criticism concerned the comparison between Germany and France and England. Two articles on the situation of the book market in France and England tried to show that in these countries, the situation was no better than in Germany. The last point discussed in this issue, mainly in the form of Gerhard Menz's article, related to the question of the book dealers' responsibility for the book crisis and Borchardt's proposals as to how to solve it. Publishing, Menz explained, was duplication and distribution ("Verlegen is Verfielfältigen und Verbreiten"), and the publisher is the entrepreneur who finances these activities. Hence if the publisher wishes to continue publishing, it is up to him to ensure that his investment produces returns. Economic considerations therefore restrict publishing's freedom, making it necessary for the sector to be attentive to the readership's preferences and feelings during any particular period. Nevertheless, Menz makes the point that in terms of publishers' economic interests, it is preferable for there to be continuity in readers' tastes, rather than a situation where the public's taste follows the whims of ever-changing fashions. Also, despite the power ascribed to distributors and advertisers, Menz argued forcefully that the book trade neither determined public taste nor was responsible for producing literature. He made the point that every epoch deserves the literature that it gets. Given this description of the situation, returning to universal publishing or calling for the proscription of modern literature would not be able to change the nature of literature or the prevailing situation. Menz concluded his arguments by stating that the basic mistake made by most criticism of book dealers—apparently referring here to Borchardt and Winterhoff alike—was that not only did this confuse the symptoms with the causes of the book market's plight, but it also selected one of the symptoms at random and made it the sole cause of the book trade market's troubles.

The reactions to Borchardt's lecture may be viewed as a pivotal point for describing the different groups on the German Right at the time. They illustrate not just contemporaneous intellectual diversity, but also the centrality of the generational component as a factor in its divided nature. For example, we gather that the up-and-coming generation of German book dealers had developed a distinctive outlook, combining a feeling of national mission, the "Lebensreform" (life-reforming) ideas of the turn-of-the-century youth movements, ways of thinking borrowed from the socialist world of ideas and categories, and an attempt to use technological innovation in order to strengthen the position of the book trade market.[26]

The debate sparked by Borchardt's lecture and Winterhoff's book was therefore indicative of the special status of the book trade. On the one hand, the book trade was accused of neglecting its intellectual mission and being inclined to commercialize culture. On the other hand, it was being called upon to rationalize the book trade market on the basis of an approach which viewed books as products, which like many other products obeyed the free market's laws of supply and demand. This form of discussion shows the ascendancy of the "midway mentality," referring to the more or less natural tendency to locate books midway between the intellectual world (culture) and the material world (economics) when talking about how people relate to books. Nevertheless, it must not be forgotten that the goal of Winterhoff and Borchardt, like Borgius before them, was to restore the position of books and make them a fundamental part of German social and cultural life. While the debates which raged over their writings testified to the sharp divisions of opinion over the reasons for the crisis and how to solve it, they also pointed to a dominant approach which ascribed to books a special status in cultural and social life, and wished to rescue them from the crisis in which they were engulfed.

What then was the "book crisis"? Was this nothing more than an expression of the plight of the book trade market, unable to adapt itself to the adverse economic and social realities of the postwar period, or did it reflect an intellectual and cultural crisis which boiled down to the decline of reading culture?

The following discussion will show how, beginning in the mid-1920s, the dominant thinking about the causes of the book crisis did not relate solely to Germany's economic plight, or the prevalent sense of a cultural decline, but was first and foremost part of an ongoing dialogue about the social changes taking place in Germany in the wake of the world war. Keywords in this debate were the "disintegration of the bourgeoisie" (*Auflösung des Bürgertums*), "proletarianization" (*Proletarisierung*), and German society's uniformization as a mass society (*Vermassung*). The use of these terms expressed the sense of changes in social stratification as well as the far-reaching transformation of lifestyles in postwar Germany. However, while these discussions to some extent reflect a genuine change in the realities of life following the world war, they mainly reflect the fear of a loss of cultural hegemony on the part of those groups of "book people" in German society who saw it as their mission to provide the German people with intellectual and cultural leadership. We will refer to these groups as the "educated bourgeoisie."

The Disintegration of the Bourgeoisie

In 1926, an article appeared by publisher Samuel Fischer, entitled "Comments on the Book Crisis," in which he stated in an oft quoted sentence:

> People practice sports, dance, spend their evening hours by the radio, in the cinema, every single hour outside their jobs is filled solid and nobody has the time to read books.[27]

According to this approach, the problems that books were having in reaching readers were not solely an outcome of economic hardships impoverishing the middle classes, or the structural defects of the book market: they were also ascribed to the loss of the general public's interest in reading, in the face of the highly attractive new media and entertainment resources. The loss of interest in books was therefore perceived as an inseparable part of the process of the disintegration of the bourgeoisie itself, which constituted the traditional target audience for books.[28]

Books, according to the laments of numerous publishers and bookshop owners, had become a seasonal product, with interest growing as Christmas approached and readerships being available only for best sellers that everybody talked about for a short while and that were soon forgotten. This situation was not only reflected in an ever shorter "shelf life" for books, but also in the nexus between the overproduction of titles and what was considered the public's addiction to novelty (*Novitaetensucht*).

Picture 1: The book vs. books

An illustration of this is supplied by the results of the 1928 survey that Willy Haas, editor of the journal called *Die Literarische Welt,* made of a number of Leipzig's best-known publishers—Reclam, Insel, Felix Meiner, E. Seeman, Paul List, and Ferdinand Hirt. They were asked whether Germany's book trade market was in crisis. Results indicated that there was no particular sales crisis on the book trade market. In other words, the publishers did not report a significant drop in the sales of their publications.[29] However, Haas did not consider this finding a reason for optimism. He explained that the book situation had not yet reached a critical stage because publishers were taking every possible step to prevent the deterioration of book sales. Librarian Max Wieser explained that the modern economy, with its mass production–based methods, could not afford any stoppages if it wished to guarantee its continued existence. This principle applied equally to the production of books. In other words, books had to be published in order to keep the printing houses, publishers, and bookshops going. As a result, Wieser even went so far as to observe that, instead of writers queuing up at publishers' doors as in the past, the publishers were actively looking for authors.[30] According to this approach, books had changed from a subject which up to the world war had shaped contemporary culture and tastes, into an object, any interest in which was determined by fleeting fashions following the world war. Another way of expressing this is to say that the "reading craze" (*Lesewut*) and "obsession with reading" (*Lesesucht*)—expressions which primarily designated the reading of women and youth in the late eighteenth and early nineteenth centuries—had given way to "reading weariness" (*Lesemüdigkeit*), which was perceived as reflecting the disintegration of the bourgeoisie.[31]

The change in the status of books and reading was perceived as an upshot of the world war, and in particular of the wave of Americanization which reshaped attitudes to life (*Lebensauffassung*) and changed public tastes.[32] The undermining of the State's authority, changes in women's status and the weakening of family structures, the rise of the employee class, intergenerational conflicts, demands for rationalization in many areas of society, the growing popularity of sport, dancing, films, and the radio, and the idealization of America were just some of the issues addressed in the intense debates about Germany's situation and the changes affecting German society in the wake of the world war.

Thus for example in his 1925 study book about the German book trade, Gerhard Menz argued that one of the destructive results of the world war was the change in the makeup of those working in the book trade market, i.e., the fact that more women had begun working in book selling. In Menz's view, this tendency was weakening the book trade, proving that men's presence in the sector was indispensable, at least in managerial positions.[33] Book dealer Hans Semm went so far as to call upon book dealers not to employ women. He asserted that women took advantage of their apprenticeships to make some easy pocket money and find themselves a husband, and that most of them had no interest whatsoever in remaining in the sector, instead viewing it as a temporary occupation only. Against this background Semm warned bookshop owners not to yield to the temptation to employ women as cheap labor.[34]

Such arguments are indicative of the difficulty which men above all had in accepting the social reality where a process of redefinition was taking place in male/female role allocation.[35] However, despite the vital nature of these changes, most references to the position of books—particularly by people in the book trade—focused on the reading public and the changes affecting it in the wake of the world war, and less on book dealers and the impact that social changes were bringing about in the structure and nature of the book trade.

For example, Samuel Fischer explained that the world war and the subsequent economic suffering had impoverished the bourgeoisie and destroyed the bourgeois social fabric, which had been the bedrock of German intellectual and cultural life. The collapse of the bourgeois associations which had represented the interests of various groups within the middle classes, organized cultural and leisure activities, and generally acted as a central component in the process of society building and social communication, was identified as one of the key processes which had changed the face of German society following the world war. In the light of this state of affairs, the loss of interest in reading and the change in the nature of books graphically illustrated these changes. The literary associations, evenings of readings, libraries, and drama associations were more than mere means of disseminating culture and knowledge: in fact, they were responsible for creating a feeling of shared German culture (*Gemeinschaftsgefühl deutscher Kultur*), and it was these associations which made reading into a social event, and concomitantly books a means of forging bonds between people. An educator by the name of Adolf Waas even commented that the undermining of the status of the family, the basic framework of bourgeois society, also influenced the nature and social function of book reading. He argued that while in the prewar era the bourgeois family had routinely got together in the evenings for communal book readings, the world war and the subsequent economic hardships had made such social book readings a rarity.[36] In contrast, Siegfried Kracauer considered the reason for the diminution in book-reading culture to lie in the postwar growth of the employee class, in other words the transition from the old bourgeoisie to the new middle classes. He explained that the employee class, which owed its very existence to bourgeois capitalism, was striving to distance itself from the working class and its culture, but at the same time was being prevented from joining the ranks of the old propertied and educated *Bürgertum*. The upshot was the emergence of a new stratum, lacking a cultural home, which sought to tread a third way between the old bourgeois class and the working class. This situation led to this group taking refuge in the new recreational culture in the form of films, the gramophone, radio, and sport.[37]

Picture 2: Book and sport: The increasing spread of sports need not diminish the consumption of books

Some even argued that the very activity of book reading had changed its nature as a result: instead of a tranquil pastime, deriving pleasure from books' artistic qualities, in terms of both form and substance, reading was now a purposive activity, designed to provide the reader with the requisite information as quickly as possible. Publisher Friedrich Oldenbourg explained this change as resulting from the rapid development of the daily press at the end of the nineteenth century.[38] The world war and the immediate postwar period, when newspapers were the main source of information about what was happening on the battlefront and the home front alike, accelerated this development, increasing the public's dependence on the daily press. It became clear that despite fears that the press would adversely impact on book sales, its influence affected how books were read rather than their distribution. It was argued that books were now read like newspapers—quickly and for a purpose; they began to be passed on from one person to the next, like papers and magazines, and were rarely read more than once by the same person.[39]

The change in the nature of the activity of reading was also reflected in shorter average book lengths, and even more so in the growing demand for works with more pictures and less text. The demand for more illustrations and fewer words was ascribed to the popularity of films, proving that a picture could convey a larger quantity of information at higher speeds, as well as the growing popularity of the radio, which showed that the spoken word was more influential than its written counterpart.[40] Librarian Max Wieser asked whether books still suited the modern mentality as a means of education, enlightenment, and artistic expression. He predicted that in the future, books would no longer play such a central role in society as they had in the past three hundred years, from the sixteenth century onward.[41]

The popularity of films, the radio, and the gramophone was therefore indicative of the end of the monopoly hitherto enjoyed by the written word as a repository of human knowledge and the transition from a reading and writing culture, where books were the primary means of mediating between man and his environment, to a seeing and hearing culture, which perceived reality through the new representational media. In a 1928 article, Johannes Molzahn exhorted his readers with cause, "Nicht mehr lesen! Sehen!" (*Stop Reading! Look!*).[42]

According to contemporary reports, not only did book reading change its nature, but also books themselves underwent a transformation in the wake of the world war. Books were no longer perceived merely as contents: their very form also played an important role in determining their social status and role. The type of binding, as well as the quality of the paper and printing all determined a book's status. Books formed an inseparable part of the contents and furnishings of every self-respecting bourgeois home, with the book cabinet—at least according to the books on etiquette which maintained their standing throughout the Weimar period—occupying pride of place in the drawing room in which guests were received.[43] However, the value attached to a book's form was not just an expression of the importance of aesthetic values in the bourgeois lifestyle: it was also intended to prevent books from being turned into products, whose technical reproduction would negate their unique aesthetic distinctiveness and their mission as a bridge between the worlds of the mind and of matter. After the world war, as a result of the economic hardships and above all the paper shortage at the beginning of the 1920s, publishers were forced to make do with inferior paper and printing quality. This situation inevitably impacted negatively on books' aesthetic distinctiveness and their role as a symbol of a particular social class.[44]

The transition from a pattern of tranquil rereading in groups to one-time, high-speed, and purposive reading, concurrent with the loss of books' aesthetic distinctiveness was therefore perceived as an expression of the transformations which affected German society itself in the wake of the world war. In his 1926 article publisher Reinhard Piper explained this change as follows: a book is intended for an individual whose decision as to whether to come into contact with it depends solely on his or her personal taste. Consequently, for Piper the loss of interest in reading following the world war symbolized the transition between the bourgeois world of values, centered round the individual's freedom of choice, and the mass society in which the individual, addicted to films and the radio whose audience is the anonymous mass or multitude, renounces his or her autonomous will and unique personality.[45]

The "book crisis" was therefore understood as a state of weariness with reading and a change in the status and nature of books as a result of the process of disintegration of the bourgeoisie, or alternatively as part of the process through which proletarianization occurred and German society became a mass society.

The Process of Proletarianization of German Society

Against the background of the discussions about socialization proposals and the tribulations of intellectual life, in 1921 Alfred Weber identified with disquiet the process of the proletarianization of intellectual life. In his famous lecture about the tribulations of intellectual work that he gave at the meeting marking the fiftieth anniversary of the Association for Social Policy (*Verein für Sozialpolitik*), he described the vanishing of intellectuals who had a benefactor (*Rentenintellektuelle*) and were therefore free of economic worries, and the emergence of the working intellectuals (*Arbeitsintellektuelle*), who were forced to adapt to the forces of the free market.[46] This change, to a large extent, was indicative of the shift from an era in which culture was able to remain aloof from all economic or commercial considerations, to a period in which the economy governed everything.[47] The process of proletarianization was perceived not merely as part of the process of change in social stratification in which more and more people found themselves living proletarian existences (*proletarische Existenzen*), or a political process of increasing influence by workers' parties, but also as part of the change in values and lifestyles dominating German society. The essence of this process was the way that increasingly, economic primacy prevailed over cultural primacy.

In the lecture that Karl Mennicke, a religious Socialist figure, gave to the young book dealers in Potsdam in 1928, he argued that the materialist nature of the process of proletarianization was the upshot of the social status of the working class. Mennicke explained that just as the interests of the bourgeois class ascendant in the seventeenth and eighteenth century had forced it to act against the feudal social order, so in the modern industrial age the working class was fighting the bourgeoisie for its living space. The bourgeoisie's struggle for emancipation constituted the background to the development of liberal ideology, while the old elites defended themselves by means of conservative ideologies. The working classes also had their own ideology—Socialism. However, according to Mennicke, the tragic difference between these ideologies lay in the fact that while the liberal and conservative ideologies had evolved during a time when these groups were at an advanced stage of their historical development, and were an expression of the mind's ongoing attempt to overcome matter, the Socialist ideology reflected the working class's hopeless situation and focused solely on this aspect of its existence.[48]

The dwindling demand for reading material of a high intellectual caliber, the growing demand for popular reading material, and above all the tendency toward the commercialization of culture were considered the distinctive characteristics of this process of proletarianization. By way of illustration, Hans Thomas, the pen name of Hans Zehrer, who since 1929 had been editor of the German New Right's magazine, *Die Tat* ("The Deed"), and the ideologist of the group which gathered around him, highlighted the change in the status of the bourgeoisie, the book trade's traditional target audience. He argued that this public was undergoing a rapid process of proletarianization, or as Zehrer put it in his characteristic style:

> Your buying circles are changing. Readers' intellectual demands are dwindling. The scourge of proletarianization and vulgarization is spreading at the speed of light and supporting the tendency, already present, to a flattening and general leveling out.[49]

The economic impoverishment of the middle classes, the destruction of bourgeois patterns of organization, the blurring of class distinctions, the undermining of the bourgeois world of values, as well as the tendency to commercialize culture were, therefore, the main characteristics of the process whereby the bourgeoisie disintegrated and German society became proletarianized. These processes were also corroborated on a statistical basis. A 1930 study by the Bavarian Statistics Office, for example, found that after the world war, the German people's social classes had not reverted to "closed boxes."[50] Those groups which were viewed as being "weak links" in the bourgeois social order and particularly vulnerable to the influence of the new media, fleeting fashions, and pulp fiction were the workers, women, and youth. The close study of these groups' reading patterns as well as their leisure and recreational behavior, together with the 1926 legislation to protect youth against pulp and trashy writings' (*Gesetz zur Bewahrung der Jugend vor Schund- und Schmutzschriften*), were all salient expressions of this attitude. The final chapter of this work will examine this issue in depth.

The process of the disintegration of the bourgeoisie involved two main aspects: it was an expression of the body blow dealt to the cultural hegemony of the bourgeoisie, or more precisely its group of educated males, which attached supreme importance in its world to reading, and in particular to book reading; at the same time the process of the disintegration of the bourgeoisie was an expression of the change of character of the bourgeoisie itself. In this context, a central position is occupied by criticism of the young generation of academics in the Weimar Republic, about whom it was said that they had stopped reading books and become ignoramuses, unfamiliar with the subtleties and complexities of German culture. Walter Hofmann, for example, the head of Leipzig's municipal libraries, reported

Picture 3: Hippopotamus in the library: Down with intellect! The coming generation will live in strength and beauty

that in 1921 he was contacted by the Rector of Leipzig University, Richard Schmidt, who asked him to assist the university to set up a library intended to help to improve the general education of the city's students. Schmidt, it was argued, was cognizant of the danger that there would develop in Germany a generation of narrowly specialized academics with a keen interest only in sports and current events, who as Max Weber defined it, would become specialists without spirit (*Fachmensch ohne Geist*).[51] It is noteworthy in this connection that at least in the pages of *Die Tat*, whose articles were written by representatives of the younger generation of the German New Right, blame for this development was ascribed to the universities themselves. The argument was that the latter had become a production line for turning out doctorates.[52] The reasons for this criticism were, undoubtedly, ideological, tying in with this group's anti-bourgeois stance.[53] But even if the charges levelled against the young academics—the hard core of the educated bourgeoisie—claiming that they were neglecting book reading were far-fetched, there was a prevalent feeling that middle-class men and women, the traditional target group of the book trade market, were neglecting reading, and in particular book reading.

The Struggle for Cultural Hegemony and the Democratization of Reading

The positions of books and of book reading were therefore considered a barometer of the changes taking place in German society in the wake of the world war, and as reflecting, explicitly or implicitly, the fear of loss of control over it. However, while such attitudes on the part of liberal and left-wing publishers like Samuel Fischer, Reinhold Piper, or Kurt Wolf stressed the danger of the process of the disintegration of the bourgeoisie and the rise of the faceless mass society, expressing their fears about the loss of hegemony by the bourgeois lifestyle and social order, in New Right circles there was no vision of any danger accompanying the flourishing of the new leisure culture or the emergence of the mass society: rather, the concern there was about the difficulties of developing an elite capable of leading German society and the German people.

For instance, the publisher of *Die Tat*, Eugen Diederichs, argued in his Reichstag address on the occasion of German Book Day on 22 March 1929 that the bourgeois elite, with its roots in the universities and the property owners, was no longer capable of leading the German people. In his opinion, a new intellectual stratum should have emerged in Germany, whose feeling of responsibility and loyalty to traditional values and German culture would unite all groups and classes (*Stände*) making up the German people into a single community.[54]

Hans Zehrer, in his 1931 article about the chaos of books ("Das Chaos der Bücher"), even explained that the process of the proletarianization of

German society did not just tie in with the growing primacy of the economy over the primacy of the intellect, but was also part of the process of Germany's democratization. In Zehrer's view, this process had eliminated the stratum of the German cultural elite, and led to disorientation and chaos in Germany's intellectual life overall, and the book trade market in particular. Following the world war, he accordingly argued, Germany was lacking in an elite leadership class as well as the masses to recognize such a group. Identifying the malaises of industrial society and the danger of class rule, Hans Freyer, one of the New Right's prominent intellectuals, called for a "revolution from the right."[55]

Against this backdrop, the problem facing Diederichs, Zehrer, Freyer, and others of the same ilk, who aspired to the end of the bourgeois era, was not confined solely to the problem of generating a new intellectual elite, but also involved how to find ways to enable such a leadership class to impose its concepts on and control German society. Zehrer, who admitted in his article on the chaos of the book trade that there was a problem entailed in acknowledging that the same economic principles which determine potato-eating habits apply equally to the book market, made the process of commercialization, or as he dubbed it capitalization (*Kapitalisierung*) of intellectual life into the starting point of his position. The commercialization of the intellect is a process initiated by the bourgeoisie, and in Zehrer's thought it formed part of his arguments against the bourgeoisie and, concomitantly, a means that could be used by the new intellectual elite in order to impose its concepts on society. As a result, unlike Borchardt, he did not call for the book trade market to be restored to its nineteenth century ideal situation, whether real or imaginary; instead, far closer to the socialization proposals of the early 1920s, he proposed strengthening control over the book trade market by means of the central economic planning of intellectual life. However, his proposals had nothing at all in common with the socialization proposals of the early 1920s, which were largely advanced by left-wing circles, at least in the sense that Zehrer saw the nationalization of means of production and central economic planning as a typical German economic principle. For Zehrer and his circle, socialization, if we can use this term here, was a way of achieving cultural hegemony and social discipline.

Zehrer's nationalist and socialist outlook was not limited to the limited group of *Die Tat* writers, as research tends to assume. In the 1920s the socialist idea apparently underwent a process of legitimation, making it acceptable even in circles which were traditionally hostile to it. For example, in a 1928 article Thomas Mann referred to the need for a new synthesis, a German "third way" combining the conservative right and the revolutionary left:

> What is required, what could finally be German, would be an alliance and a pact of the conservative idea of culture with the revolutionary thinking about society, between Greece and Moscow.[56]

These ideas had an effect on the book dealers. One group which was particularly close to the *Tat* circle, which undoubtedly had the ability to make a contribution to the dissemination of the idea of combining German nationalism with the idea of Socialism, was that of the young book dealers. The immediate source of the young book dealers' circles was the Launsteiner Kreise, founded by publisher Eugen Diederichs in 1922. This took its name from Launstein Castle in the Franconian forest where its members gathered. These encounters, which took place in the bosom of nature and drew their inspiration from the life-reforming movements of the early twentieth century, were designed to increase book dealers' professional awareness as well as their social-national mission. At first, this was a restricted group of people from the world of books—publishers, librarians, educators, writers, and editors—who were supposed to meet once a year in order to exchange ideas about current political, economic, and cultural issues and their impact on the book trade market. As early as the second meeting in January 1923, held under the watchword of "Youth movement—Education of the people" (*Jugendbewegung—Volksbildung*), a call was issued to set up a professional training body for the up-and-coming generation of book dealers, which would not only provide a new form for the professional training of book dealers but would also provide new contents—hailed as professional education along the same lines as education for people (*Berufsbildung als Menschenbildung*). This call provided the background to the setting up of the summer academy, whose goal was to provide a place where younger and older book dealers alike could get together for a week or two, both studying and enjoying walks in the beautiful surroundings, with the aim of providing the younger book dealers with the tools for tackling the mission facing the book trade of the future, i.e., in a world of rapid technological change controlled by economic forces. The model for the summer academy was taken from the English Fabian movement and the German *Volkshochschule* or adult education classes. The first attempt to run the academy took place in 1923, but it was not until 1925, after the Bv began to support it, that the academy managed to achieve a solid footing and become a success story. In 1924 Hans Bott, who in addition to Diederichs, considered the father of the young book dealers' movement, was its key figure, set up the first local study group or *Arbeitsgemeinschaft* of young book dealers in Karlsruhe. Bott's study group soon became a model for how young book dealers could organize themselves in other German cities, acting as the basic organizational unit of the movement which began to acquire influence in book trade circles in those years. In 1925 Bott, using private funding, also established the movement's circular, known as the *Jungbuchhandel-Rundbriefe,* which examined issues involving the relationship between the educational system and book dealers, the training to be received by book dealers and their role in society. In 1931 after the journal changed its name to *Die neue Stand,* the young book dealers redefined their mission, stating that their primary goal was to combat the process of intellectual and economic proletarianization and find a solution to the social issue.

At the same time as the social involvement to which the book dealers' movement had committed itself, Hans Bott declared that politically speaking, the young book dealers' movement was independent but not neutral.[57] What this meant was that as Bott saw it, the young book dealers were supposed to be members of a variety of political parties and trade associations, so as to overcome party political divisions, with the goal of creating a movement which would be apolitical, deliberately combining both the socialist and the national components. We learn about the political significance of this endeavor in an article by Friedrich Uhlig, who together with the editor of *Der neue Stand*, Gerhard Schönfelder, was an assistant to Professor Gerhard Menz at the school for book trade studies (*Lehrstuhl für Buchhandelsbetriebslehre*). In the first part of this article, which was intended to act as a kind of guide to the contemporary book publishing scene as well as to reveal publishing houses' political tendencies, Uhlig explained that the November 1918 Revolution did not denote the victory of the socialist idea, but rather, the victory of bourgeois liberalism and the democratic state: in other words, the victory of a political regime which did not have the welfare of the people as one of its guiding principles, instead defending the narrow vested interests of different interest groups in German society. In Uhlig's opinion, the most salient expression of this victory was the triumph of economic patterns of thought and the party-political splintering characteristic of the period. Moreover, according to Uhlig, in their ferocious political struggles, the parties were ignoring the young generation—the wartime generation—with its strong national awareness and revolutionary outlook. This generation was searching for an overall solution to the adversities with which it was beset, and it found this in the blending of the national and socialist elements as a new basis for community life. This combination, as a solution to the problems of the time, was also adopted by Adolf Hitler. However, in Uhlig's opinion, when Hitler's National Socialist movement joined the political system, it became a political party like any other and hence part of the struggle between the different interest groups. As a result, he did not recognize the National Socialist Party as a force able to respond to the needs of the young generation. In Uhlig's view, the generation of the world war had far better options available to it than the Nazi Party in the form of nonparliamentary organizations and associations such as the Kampfgemeinschaft revolutionärer Nationalsozialisten, Wehrwolf, Oberland, Das kämpfende Landvolk, and the Bündische Jugend. These organizations were not part of the Nazi Party, and were faithful to the founding values and ideas of the national-socialist movement.[58] Or as Uhlig concluded:

> These battling young people, workers and farmers, are rallying under the banner of the black flag. "The black front is the front of the conservative revolution."[59]

As yet, research has not looked in depth at the young book dealers and their ties with the *Tat* circle, the different groups of religious Socialists and the other groups which might be classified under the term of "the conservative revolution." A key figure in this story will undoubtedly be Eugen Diederichs, publisher of *Die Tat* (whose subtitle from 1913 to 1929 was "The Social-Religious Monthly for German Culture"), the father of the young book dealers' movement, and whose publishing house issued Hans Freyer's book "The Right-Wing Revolution."[60] Research efforts to try to disclose the relationships between the young book dealers and the various groups and individuals who belonged to the Right during this period would undoubtedly contribute greatly to our understanding of the nature, scope, and influence of the ideological environment out of which the Nazi movement evolved.

For our current purposes, it is important to highlight one of the basic components in the young book dealers' outlook, as expressed for them by Carl Mennicke, the religious Socialist. In his 1928 address to a study group of young book dealers in Potsdam, Mennicke identified the presence of a rift (*Kluft*) in German society between the educated classes and the general public—only among Catholics was this rift not so significant. Mennicke explained this situation by claiming that the Catholic Church had managed to maintain its position as a religious and spiritual leadership, as well as its character as a unifying body embracing the educated and uneducated alike. As a result, he asserted, in order for the educated Protestant classes generally and the book dealers specifically to successfully overcome the rift between educated circles and other social classes, and to be capable of representing the interests of broad-based social strata, as well as influencing them, they had to acknowledge the changes that had taken place in German society in the wake of the war. Mennicke therefore called on the Book Dealers' Guild not to be "bourgeois," but to acknowledge the process of the blurring of social differences and be prepared to become part of it.[61]

Since the young book dealers, the *Tat* circle members, and even certain parts of religious Socialism came to terms with the processes by which mass society was being created as an irreversible situation, they wanted to study how best to use the range of tools available to them in modern society in order to maintain the book trade's status and strengthen the influence of books. This meant that these circles understood that it was precisely in a society undergoing a high-speed process in which social differences were being blurred (*Umschmelzungsprozess*) and a mass society was emerging that the control of modern technology and the awareness of the social situation of the simple man also made it possible for the narrow stratum of intellectuals to impose their outlook on broad-based strata of society; or to put it slightly differently, that would enable such a stratum to create a "historical bloc" and achieve cultural hegemony within such a society. Gramsci from the right? A totally reasonable possibility. However, whether this approach by the New Right can be characterized as Gramscian or as something completely different, it was certainly not a new phenomenon on the German intellectual scene.

World War I was not what made people aware of the social transformations and the change in the nature and lifestyle of German society, nor what led to a recognition of the dangers and possibilities that modern technology offered the book trade. As will be shown below, this history also contributed to the sense of a "book crisis" following the world war, and it is vital for an understanding of the nature and significance of this crisis.

Sources of the Feeling of a "Book Crisis"

As early as the prewar period, and especially in the transitional period at the turn of the century, we see the flourishing of a form of literature which highlighted the process of degeneration of the bourgeoisie, in particular in its urban form, and criticism of modern society, concurrently with diverse efforts to reform and inject new life into the form and style of bourgeois existence. These two phenomena are interrelated, and to a large extent constituted part of the reaction of the bourgeoisie, and in particular of its younger generation, to the contemporary processes of accelerating modernization.

The definition of certain writings as pulp and trash, and the lively public discussion of ways of combating this phenomenon, in particular from the last decade of the nineteenth century onward, were perceived at the time as an expression of the transformations taking place in German society. The struggle against these writings reflected the feeling of disappointment on the part of the educated bourgeoisie, who had hoped that education and enlightenment would not only help to shape and improve the cultural level of wide-ranging sectors of German society, but would also help to bridge the social divide and strengthen national awareness. This was reflected by one of the key mottoes of the German educational movement at the time, "Volksbildung als Volks-bildung"[62] (education of the people as nation-building). In contrast the male, educated bourgeoisie saw social rifts as widening, together with moral deterioration and above all a loss of its influence over society. One of the expressions of this state of affairs was the attempt to combat cheap literature by reducing the cost of what was considered good literature. The *Kulturverlag* cultural publishing houses set up in Germany beginning in the last decade of the nineteenth century are one of the most important manifestations of this development.

These "cultural publishing houses" were an example of the new type of publishing house, which did not see its role as merely distributing reading material but rather viewed itself as organizing and promoting culture. The publisher as an organizer was no longer a random collector and publisher of writings; instead, a conscious effort was made to publish a particular kind of writing, based on the publisher's personal taste. The publishing house consequently became a kind of commercial brand, conveying a given literary image. The publishing houses of Samuel Fischer, Insel, Ernest Rowohlt, Eugen Diederichs, Kurt Wolf, Bondy, Albert Langen, and Bruno Cassirer are just a few examples of this phenomenon. Modern German literature—neutralism, Expressionism, Impressionism, Dadaism, and even *voelkisch* literature—owed its existence to these programmatic publishing houses.

By combining the commercial and intellectual component, books' economic capital and cultural capital, these publishing houses sought to act as a kind of "third way" between the arrogant approach, particularly of the old-established publishing houses which viewed quality books as the province of a select social stratum, and those publishing houses which published popular literature and market books as products like any other product, intended for as wide a public as possible. The "cultural publishing houses," which shared little in common in political terms, tried therefore to take advantage of advanced production and distribution methods in order to expand their readerships and promote cultural values.

Even though these processes indicate a shedding of the male, educated bourgeoisie's arrogant view of reading culture and an almost complete rejection of everything involving the processes of modernization and popular culture, they do not testify to any fundamental change in the view that gave culture priority over the economy or any discarding of the "midway mentality," which saw books as something located between the material world and the intellectual world. In this case the justification for making books cheaper and trying to popularize them was imparting cultural values and making intellectual capital, not financial gains. The "cultural publishing houses" tried to expand readerships by making books cheaper and adopting innovative distribution methods in order to disseminate culture, combat pulp and trashy fiction, reduce the gaps between the social strata, and strengthen national awareness in Germany.

The attempt—or more precisely the feeling of failure—to combine books' cultural capital with their economic capital and thereby generate a new popular culture, which would promote cultural values and act as a means of maintaining social order and tranquillity, provided the background to creating an awareness of a "book crisis" after the world war, largely among male, bourgeois liberal circles who espoused the slogan "Bildung macht frei" (education is liberating).

The world war was perceived as an event which constituted a rupture, tearing apart the very fabric of society and disturbing the equilibrium between the primacy of the economy and that of culture. In this sense, the assertion that the narrowly delineated bourgeois era had come to an end in the wake of the world war was more than an attempt to objectively describe the transformations which had come about in German society following the world war: it was also an admission of the bourgeoisie's failure to impose its values and lifestyle on German society. In this sense, Rudolf Borchardt's comment that the war was the collapse, the catastrophe of the new world, not the old ("Der Krieg ist der Zusammenbruch, die Katastrophe der neuen Welt gewesen und nicht der alten") is an apt description of the situation of key groups among the bourgeoisie.[63]

The Dialectic of Success

The foregoing has shown that despite the differences between the various approaches to describing the situation of German society generally, and specifically the nature and ways of solving the "book crisis," there was wide-ranging agreement about the importance of books as a basic component of German social life and culture. In other words, the conceptual system which ascribed major cultural and social importance to books and determined attitudes to them, continued to dominate, with no alternative being proposed by either Right or Left. Given this situation, it would appear that despite evidence of the transformations undergone by postwar German society, the negative impact on the bourgeois world of values was not fatal, as shown by the material that we have examined so far. The intense scrutiny to which the position of books was subjected, the fears about what would happen to books, and the quasi-natural link, which has lasted right up to our days, between reading and book reading are all proof of the control exerted by the bourgeois world of values in which reading generally, and book reading specifically, have special worth. In this sense at least, Germany did not suffer from an absence of "bourgeoiseness," as the "special path" (*Sonderweg*) thesis in its different versions tries desperately to claim.

It is possible, as Siegfried Kracauer observed, that the fact that more people found themselves reduced against their will to "proletarian" conditions of existence actually helped to strengthen the bourgeois way of life.[64] Or, as Ernst von Aster put it in 1930, while the conditions of people's existence may have become proletarian, the spirit remained bourgeois.[65]

Many in left-wing circles shared this approach. In the pages of the journal *Die Arbeit* ("Labour") in particular we find numerous references to the changes which had ostensibly taken place in the middle classes of German society following the world war. Thus sociologists such as Emil Lederer, Theodor Geiger, or Hans Tobis showed that despite the economic hardships which primarily affected men of property, and notwithstanding changes in the nature of the middle class, mainly through its expansion to include the stratum of employees who sometimes earned less than laborers and eked out a precarious economic existence, claims of a "dying middle class" (*sterbender Mittelstand*) were mistaken.[66] Moreover, economic hardship actually strengthened the value of culture, making it the key component in the construction of bourgeois identity.

The refusal to give up the characteristics of the bourgeois lifestyle, even in groups whose conditions of existence were the same as those of the working class, therefore not only emphasized the diversity of the middle classes, but also showed that the factors which determine behavioral patterns, the world of values, and class consciousness are not always economic living conditions. To put it another way, the bourgeoisie stopped being a homogenous social stratum, instead becoming a system of values and a lifestyle. This tendency did not escape the keen eyes of contemporary cultural critics, and it is reflected most saliently in discussions about the disappearance of the working class as a result of becoming a class with bourgeois characteristics, i.e., its "bourgeoisification."[67]

Theodor Geiger distinguished for example between "Verbürgerung" (becoming bourgeois), a change in actual social status, i.e., a shift from worker status to the bourgeoisie, and "bourgeoisification" (*Verbürgerlichung*), which is a change in social values, i.e., adopting bourgeois patterns of behavior and values despite an absence of change in conditions of existence and social status. Consequently he argued that since bourgeois culture is so dominant, even somebody who is a worker through and through (*Vollblutprolet*) is unable to avoid its influence.[68]

Such arguments can even be found in the cultural journal of the German Communist Party (KPD), *Linkskurve* (left-hand curve). In a 1930 article Kurt Klaber argued that one of the difficulties preventing the mass distribution of the proletarian novel among the working classes was the dominance of the bourgeois approach which saw books as objects to be owned (*Besitzobjekte*), attaching greater importance to a book's form than to its contents. This demonstrative approach to book reading led to many workers refraining from buying the proletarian books which were published as booklets with low graphic quality and at cheap prices. Klaber even pointed out that the laboring class which did not belong to the SPD or was under the sway of the Catholic Church and constituted the natural target audience for the proletarian novel, whose size he put at between one and two million, preferred to borrow light reading material from the low-cost lending libraries (*Leihbibliotheken*) and to buy expensive books with luxury bindings which they could display on their shelves or in book cabinets in their homes.[69]

Did the bourgeois world of values collapse, then, as indicated by the discussions about the crisis affecting books or, as other comments would indicate, did German society undergo a rapid process of bourgeoisification, which actually strengthened the bourgeoisie and its values? In other words, was the book crisis a subjective feeling of a narrowly defined stratum of book circles in German society, or was it an actual situation which can be corroborated by the realities of the time?[70]

The varied picture painted by contemporary material is a result of a whole range of political and social outlooks propounded by participants in discussions about the situation of books and reading in German society following World War I. However, a more in-depth examination of these issues will show that the different processes which at first sight appear to contradict each other do not necessarily do so. Analysis of the distribution methods for reading material, the place of reading in leisure activities and recreational patterns, ways of controlling reading, and reading material consumption patterns will show that reading generally, and book reading specifically, did not disappear after the world war. Furthermore, in this period reading became an inseparable part of the daily routines of all social strata, with unprecedented numbers of books being sold. Hence there was an infrastructure for reading which not only disseminated and promoted literary output, but also the bourgeois world of values and its lifestyle.

It may be said that the popularization of reading was an expression of the success of the bourgeoisie, or to be more precise of the bourgeois lifestyle, in achieving cultural hegemony in German society. However, this success, which was bound up with the change of nature and role of reading and the "midway mentality," which situated books between the economy and culture as two mutually inimical areas, also provided the backdrop to the generation of the feeling of a "book crisis."

Notes

1. The secondary Literature on the crisis of the book after the First World War, which amounts to two items, is not only descriptive in character, but also adapts the contemporary perspective of an objective crisis: Herbert G. Göpfert, "Die Buchkrise 1927–1929. Probleme der Literaturvermittlung am Ende der zwanziger Jahre," in: Paul Raabe, ed., *Das Buch in den zwanziger Jahren* (Hamburg: Hauswedell, 1978), 33–46; Berthold Brohm, "Das Buch in der Krise. Studien zur Buchhandelsgeschichte der Weimarer Republik," *Archiv für Geschichte des Buchwesen* 51 (1999), 189–331.
2. For various opinions on the paradoxical nature of modernity, cf. Georg Simmel, "Die Grossstädte und das Geistesleben," in: idem, *Das Individuum und die Freiheit* (Frankfurt am Main: Fischer, 1993); Jeffrey Herf, *Reactionary Modernism* (Cambridge: Cambridge University Press, 1984); Zygmut Bauman, *Modernity and Ambivalence* (New York: Cornell University Press, 1991); Thomas Nipperdey, "Probleme der Modernisierung in Deutschland" in: idem, *Nachdenken über die deutsche Geschichte* (Munich: dtv, 1986), 52–72.
3. Stefan Wanart, *Um die Zukunft des deutschen Buches* (Freiburg i.B: Ernst Guenther Verlag, 1920); Wilhelm Moufang, *Die gegenwärtige Lage des deutschen Buchwesen. Eine Darstellung der Spannung und Reformbewegung am Buchmarkt* (Munich: J. Sweizer Verlag, 1921); Felix Meiner, *Warum sind die Bücher so teuer?* (Leipzig: Verlag des Deutschen Verlagvereins, 1920); Wolfgang Boehm, "Die kulturelle Bedeutung des deutschen Buchhandels und seine wirtschaftliche Lage," Ph.D. diss., University of Frankfurt a.M., 1922.
4. Wilhelm Moufang, "Die kulturpolitische Krisis des deutschen Buches," Hochland 19 (1921/22), 216–227.
5. Karl Bücher, *Die Sozialisierung* (Tübingen: J.C.B. Mohr, 1919); Wilhelm Röpke, "Sozialisierung," in: Ludwig Elster, Adolf Weber, and Friedrich Wieser, eds., *Handwörterbuch der* Staatswissenschaft, vol. 7 (Jena: Gustav Fische Verlag, 1926), 567–578; Eduard Heimann, "Sozialisierung," *Neue Blätter für Sozialismus* 1 (1930), 12–28; Emil Lederer, "Probleme der Sozialisierung," in: idem, *Kapitalismus, Klassenstruktur und Probleme der Demokratie in Deutschland 1910–1940* (Göttingen: Vandenhoeck & Ruprecht, 1979), 155–172.

6. Alfred Amonn, *Die Hauptprobleme der Sozialisierung* (Leipzig: Quelle & Meyer, 1920), 5–13.
7. Gerald Feldman, *The Great Disorder: Politics, Economics, and Society in the German Inflation 1914–1924* (Oxford: Oxford University Press, 1997), 138.
8. Walther Borgius, "Zur Sozialisierung des Buchwesens," in: Hermann Beck, ed., *Wege und Ziele der Sozialisierung* (Berlin: Verlag Neues Vaterland, 1919), 122–161.
9. He estimated this group's total numbers within the territory of the Reich as three hundert thousand individuals. Borgius, Zur Sozialisierung, 141.
10. Walter Dette, *Die Sozialisierung der Buchproduktion und des Buchhandels* (Hannover: Banas & Dette, 1919), 7.
11. Eduard Ackermann, "Zur Sozialisierung des Buchwesens," *Börsenblatt für den Deutschen Buchhandel* 86 (1919), 835–838; Otto Riebcke, "Gedanken zur Sozialisierung des Buchwesens," *Börsenblatt für den Deutschen Buchhandel* 88 (1919), 813–815, 817–820.
12. According to Borgius's estimates, eighteen million marks would be a sufficient basic capital to implement the reform, while Ackermann reckoned that at least half a billion marks would be needed.
13. Gerhard Menz, *Der Deutsche Buchhandel* (Gotha: Flamberg Verlag, 1925), 22–37.
14. Gerhard Menz, "Zur Frage der Sozialisierung des Buchhandels," *Börsenblatt für den Deutschen Buchhandel* 163 (1920), 84.
15. Leopold v. Weise, "Die Sozialisierung des Literaturverlages," in: Ludwig Sinzheimer, ed., *Die geistige Arbeit. Schriften des Vereins für Sozialpolitik* (Munich: Duncker & Humblot, 1922), 385–414.
16. Julius Bunzel, "Die Sozialisierung des Verlages," in: Ludwig Sinzheimer, ed., *Die geistige Arbeit* (Munich: Duncke & Humbolt, 1922), 415–437.
17. Edmund Winterhoff, *Die Krisis im Deutschen Buchhandel* (Karlsruhe: Verlag G. Braun, 1927).
18. Reinhard Wittmann, "Streifzüge zur Geschichte des festen Ladenpreises für Bücher," *Buchhandelsgeschichte* 13 (1976), 385–392.
19. On this controversy cf. Thorsten Grieser, "Der >>Bücher Streit<< des deutschen Buchhandels in Jahr 1903," *Archiv für Buchhandelsgeschichte* 48 (1996), 17–28; Hartmut Zwahr, "Inszenierte Lebenswelt. Jahrhundertfeiern zum Gedenken an die Erfindung der Buchdruckkunst. Buchwerbe, Buchhandel und Wissenschaft," *Geschichte und Gesellschaft* 22 (1996), 5–19.
20. Gerhard Menz, "Die Krisis im deutschen Buchhandel," *Börsenblatt für den Deutschen Buchhandel* 94 (1927), 961–966, 1172–1174, 1313–1316; Paul Nitschmann, *Die Krisis im Deutschen Buchhandel* (Berlin: Verlag der Deutschen Buchhändler, 1928).
21. For a detailed discussion of the issue of books as products, to a large extent representing the official stance of the Börsenverein, as argued by Menz: Gerhard Menz, "Das Buch als Ware und Wirtschaftsfaktor," *Archiv für Buchgewerbe und Gebrauchsgraphik* 67 (1930), 445–459.
22. Rudolf Borchardt, "Die Aufgabe der Zeit gegenüber der Literatur," in: idem, *Reden* (Stuttgart: Ernst Klett Verlag, 1955), 345–396. On the Brochard controversy: Herbert G. Göpfert, "Die Aufgabe der Zeit gegenüber der Literatur. Rudolf Broschardt und der Buchhandel," in: Werner Adrian, ed., *Das Buch in der dynamischen Gesellschaft* (Trier: Spee Verlag, 1970), 123–131; Gisela Bruchner, "Rudolf Brochardt und der Buchhandel. Ein Beitrag zur Situation des deutschen Buchhandels in den letzten Jahren der Weimarer Republik," *Archiv für Geschichte des Buchwesens* 14 (1974), 286–348; Gerhard Schuster, "Rudolf Borchardt und der Insel Verlag," *Buchhandelsgeschichte* 10 (1982), 97–114.
23. Brochardt, Die Aufgabe, 359.
24. Research on the young book dealers is extremely scanty. The following discussion will show the importance of the younger book dealers for the New Right in Germany. This will simply serve to increase the need for a monograph addressing this issue in depth. For further literature: Gerhard Schönfeld, "Zur Geschichte des deutschen Jungbuchhandels," *Der neue Stand* 2 (1932), 34–37; Hans Köster, "Jugendbewegung—Lauensteiner

Kreis—Anfänge des Jungbuchhandels," *Börsenblatt für den Deutschen Buchhandel* 29 (1966), 757–763; Harry Fauth, "Zur Geschichte des Jungbuchhandels in Deutschland 1923–1933," in: Karl-Heinz Kalhöfer and Helmuth Rötzsch, eds., *Beiträge zur Geschichte des Buchwesens,* vol. IV (Leipzig: VEB Fachverlag, 1969), 163–187.

25. All following quotations are taken from *Jungbuchhändler-Rundbriefe* 16 (1930) which was titled: *Buch der Zeit. Kritik der Zeit. Volk der Zeit. Auseinandersetzung mit Rudolf Borchardt.*
26. On this nexus see: Louis Dupeux, *Nationalbolschewismus in Deutschland 1919– 1933. Kommunistische Strategie und Konservative Dynamik* (Frankfurt a.M.: Büchergilde Gutenberg, 1985); Christoph H. Werth, *Sozialismus und Nation. Die deutsche Ideologiediskussion zwischen 1918 und 1945* (Opladen: Westdeutscher Verlag, 1996).
27. Samuel Fischer, "Bemerkungen zur Bücherkrise," in: Friedrich Pfäffin, ed., *S. Fischer Verlag von der Gründung bis zur Rückkehr aus dem Exil* (Marbach: Ausstellungskatalog, 1985), 357–360, here 357.
28. For a later version of the thesis of the disintegration of the bourgeoisie, constituting a specific form of the thesis of Germany's special path in history, see in particular: Hans Mommsen, "Die Auflösung des Bürgertums seit dem späten 19. Jhr.," in: Jürgen Kocka, ed., *Bürger und Bürgerlichkeit im 19. Jahrhundert* (Göttingen: Vandenhoeck & Ruprecht, 1987), 288–315; Konrad H. Jarausch, "Die Krise des deutschen Bildungsbürgertums im ersten Drittel des 20. Jhrs.," in: Jürgen Kocka, ed., *Bildungsbürgertum im 19. Jahrhundert. Politischer Einfluß und gesellschaftliche Formation* (Stuttgart: Klett Cotta, 1989), 180–206; Horst Möller, "Bürgertum und bürgerlich-liberale Bewegung nach 1918," in: Lothar Gall, ed., *Bürgertum und bürgerlich-liberale Bewegung in Mitteleuropa seit dem 18. Jahrhundert* (Munich: Oldenbourg, 1997), 243–342.
29. Willy Haas, "Gibt es eine Krise im deutschen Buchwesen? Gespräche mit den bedeutendsten Leipziger Verlegern," *Literarische Welt* 5 (1929), 135–136, 145, 152, 160, 168.
30. Max Wieser, "Die geistige Krisis des Buches und die Volksbibliotheken," *Preußische Jahrbücher* 191 (1923), 182–201, here 190–191. It is interesting to note here that a few years later Siegfried Kracauer in his famous essay "The Mass Ornament" made similar observations about the nature of capitalist production as an end in itself. Siegfried Kracauer, "The Mass Ornament," (first published in 1928), in: Anton Kaes, Martin Jay, and Edward Dimendberg, eds., *The Weimar Sourcebook* (Berkeley: University of California Press, 1994), 404–407.
31. Anton Kaes, "Schreiben und Lesen in der Weimarer Republik," in: Bernhard Wyergraf, ed., *Literatur der Weimarer Republik 1918–1933* (Munich: Hanser Verlag, 1995), 38–64.
32. Adolf Halbfeld, *Amerika und Amerikanismus* (Jena: Diederich, 1927); Alf Lüdtke, Inge Marßolek and Adelheid v. Saldern, eds., *Amerikanisierung. Traum und Alptraum im Deutschland des 20. Jahrhunderts* (Stuttgart: Franz Steiner Verlag, 1996); Frank Becker, *Amerikanismus in Weimar. Sportsymbole und politische Kultur 1918–1933* (Wiesbaden: DUT, 1993); Dan Diner, *Verkehrte Welten. Antiamerikanismus in Deutschland* (Frankfurt a.M.: Eichborn, 1993).
33. Menz, *Der Deutsche Buchhandel*, 169. On this issue cf. Gerhard Schönfeld, "Die soziale Frage im Buchhandel," *Jungbuchhändler-Rundbriefe.* Sonderhefte: Die soziale Frage 16 (1930), 10–22; Susanne Suhr, *Die weiblichen Angestellten* (Berlin: Zentralverband der Angestellten, 1930); Werner Adrian, "Frauen im Buchhandel. Eine Dokumentation zur Geschichte einer fast lautlosen Emanzipation," *Archiv für Geschichte des Buchwesens* 48 (1998), 147–247.
34. Hans Semm, "Einiges über die Lehrlingsausbildung," *Buchhändlergilde-Blatt* 7/8 (1926), 89.
35. For a general survey of this issue cf. Karen Hagemann, *Frauenalltag und Männerpolitik. Alltagsleben und gesellschaftliches Handeln von Arbeiterfrauen in der Weimarer Republik* (Bonn: Dietz Verlag, 1990); Renate Bridenthal, Atina Grossmann, and Marion Kaplan, eds., *When Biology becomes Destiny: Women in Weimar and Nazi Germany* (New York: Monthly Review, 1984); Ute Frevert, *Women in German History* (Oxford: Berg, 1988).
36. Adolf Waas, "Lesekreise," *Volksbildungsarchiv* 10 (1923), 144.
37. Siegfried Kracauer, *Die Angestellten* (Frankfurt a.M.: Suhrkamp, 1971).

38. Friedrich Oldenbourg, "Über die Zukunft des Buches," in: idem, *Buch und Bildung* (Munich: Becksche Verlagbuchhandlung, 1925), 92.
39. Fritz Klatt, "Die Rolle des Buches in der Gegenwart," *Jungbuchhändler-Rundbrief* 1 (1926), 1; Friedrich M. Huebner, "Buchgewerbe und die neue Zeit—Geistige Grundlage," *Archiv für Buchgewerbe und Gebrauchsgraphik* 64 (1927), 299–309.
40. Friedrich Oldenbourg, "Die geistige Krisis und das Buch," *Börsenblatt für den Deutschen Buchhandel* 257 (1927), 1213–1219.
41. Max Wieser, "Die geistige Krisis des Buches," 184.
42. Johannes Molzahn, "Nicht mehr Lesen! Sehen!," *Das Kunstblatt* 12 (1928), 78–82, reprinted as *"Stop Reading! Look!"* in: Anton Kaes, Martin Jay, and Edward Dimendberg, eds., *The Weimar Sourcebook.* The most comprehensive account of the political significance of the new media was Horkheimer and Adorno's famous essay on the cultural industry (*Kulturindustrie*) in which, from the perspective of their exile in America at the height of the Second World War, they drew attention to the destructive influence of the new media and their contribution to the success of Nazism in Germany. Max Horkheimer and Theodor Adorno, *Dialektik der Aufklärung* (Frankfurt am Main: S. Fischer, 1964), especially 129–176. This book had much influence. For a criticism of this point of view and an attempt to break free of the influence of the essay of Horkheimer and Adorno, cf., for example, Eve Rosenhaft, "Lesewut, Kinosucht, Radiotismus: Zur (geschlechter) politischen Relevanz neuerer Massenmedien in den 1920er Jahren," in: Alf Lüdtke et al., eds., *Amerikanisierung,* 119–143. For a general survey of the changes in the media in the period of the Weimar Republic, cf. Stephan Lamb and Aanthony Phelan, "Weimar Culture: the Birth of Modernism," in: Rob Burns, ed., *German Cultural Studies* (Oxford: Oxford University Press, 1995), 53–99. A main source on the new media, the First World War experience, and their influence on people's mentalities is still Walter Benjamin's essay *Das Kunswerk im Zeitalter seiner technischenn Reproduzierbarkeit.* Useful insights can be also be found in: Paul Virilio, *War and Cinema: The Logistics of Perception,* translated by Patrick Camiller (London: Verso, 1989); Friedrich Kittler, *Grammophon, Film, Typewriter* (Berlin: Brinkmann & Bose, 1986).
43. Wolfgang Martens, "Der gute Ton und die Literatur. Anstandsbücher als Quelle für die Leseforschung," in: Herbert G. Göpfert, ed., *Buch und Leser* (Hamburg: Ernst Hauswedell & Co., 1977), 203–229.
44. On this, cf., for example, "Wie hat sich der Geschmack der Bucherkäufer seit dem Krieg Verändert?" (no author stated), *Börsenblatt für den Deutschen Buchhandel* 30 (1925), 264.
45. Reinhard Piper, "Das Buch und der Mensch von Heute," *Börsenblatt des deutschen Buchhändler* 93 (1926), 1537. On this see also Siegfried Kaucauer, "Über Erfolgsbücher und ihr Publikum," in: idem, *Der verbotene Blick* (Leipzig: Reclam, 1992), 241.
46. Alfred Weber, *Die Not der geistigen Arbeit* (Munich: Duncker & Hombolt, 1923).
47. Kurt Kersten, "Wirtschaft, Kultur, Intellektuelle," *Die Weltbühne* 19 (1923), 583–585, here 583.
48. Carl Mennicke, *Der Buchhandel in der geistigen Lage der Gegenwart* (Potsdam: R. Heidkamp, 1928), 20.
49. Hans Thomas, "Das Chaos der Bücher," *Die Tat* 23 (1931), 647.
50. Josef Nothaas, *Sozialer Auf- und Abstieg im Deutschen Volk* (Munich: J. Lindauer, 1930).
51. Leipziger Stadtbibliothek, Abt. Fach Bibliothek (197), Dienstnachlaß von Walter Hoffmann—A 17 Arbeitsberichte, 1923–1924; Max Weber, *The Protestant Ethic and the Spirit of Capitalism,* translated by Talcott Parson (New York: Charles Scribner's Sons, 1976), 182.
52. Gerhard Schönfeld, "Der Untergang der Bildung. Wirtschaft und Bildung," *Die Tat* 23 (1931), 18–34; Hans Thomas, "Akademisches Proletariat. 137000 Menschen wollen 'Doktor' werden," *Die Tat* 22 (1931), 816–823.
53. Klaus Fritzsche, *Politische Romantik und Gegenrevolution. Fluchtwege in der Krise der bürgerlichen Gesellschaft: Das Beispiel des 'Tat-Kreises'* (Frankfurt a.M.: Suhrkamp, 1976).
54. Eugen Diederichs, "Die Krisis des deutschen Buches," *Die Tat* 21 (1929), 4.

55. Hans Freyer, *Revolution von Rechts* (Jena: Diederichs, 1931).
56. Thomas Mann, "Kultur und Sozialismus" in: idem, *Gesammelte Werke* vol. XII (Frankfurt a.M.: Fischer Verlag, 1960), 649.
57. Hans Bott, "Jungbuchhandel, politische Parteien und Gewerkschaften," *Der neue Stand* 2 (1932), 229–232, here 229.
58. On these groups: Dieter Fricke, ed., *Lexikon zur Parteigeschichte. Die bürgerlichen und kleinbürgerlichen Parteien und Verbände in Deutschland 1789–1945* (Leipzig: Bibliographisches Institut, 1983); Armin Mohler, *Die Konservative Revolution* (Darmstadt: Wissenschaftliche Buchgesellschaft, 1989).
59. Friedeich Uhlig, "Der Standort der Verlage im politischen Lebensraum," *Der neue Stand* 2 (1932), 128.
60. Erich Viehöfer, "Der Verleger als Organisator. Eugen Diederichs und die bürgerlichen Reformbewegungen der Jahrhundertwende," *Archiv für Geschichte des Buchwesens* 30 (1988), 1–147; Ulf Diederichs, "Jena und Weimar als verlegerisches Programm. Über die Anfänge des Eugen Diederichs Verlag in Jena," in: Jürgen John, and Volker Wahl, eds., *Zwischen Konvention und Avantgart: Doppelstadt Jena—Weimar* (Weimar: Böhlau, 1995), 51–81; Gangolf Hübninger, ed., *Versammlungsort moderner Geister. Der Eugen Diederichs Verlag—Aufbruch ins Jahundert der Extreme* (Munich: Diederichs, 1996); idem, "Der Verleger Eugen Diederichs in Jena. Wissenschaftskritik, Lebensreform und völkische Bewegung," *Geschichte und Gesellschaft* (1996), 31–46; Irmgard Heidler, *Der Verleger Eugen Diederichs und seine Welt 1896–1930* (Wiesbaden: Harrassowitz, 1998).
61. Mennicke, *Der Buchhandel*, 40.
62. Leopold v. Wiese, ed., *Soziologie des Volksbildungswesens* (Munich: Duncker & Humbolt, 1921); Walter Hofmann, "Menschenbildung, Volksbildung, Arbeiterbildung in volkstümlichen Büchereien," *Archiv für Erwachsenenbildung* 2 (1925), 65–104; Dietrich Langewische, "<<Volksbildung<< und >>Leserlenkung<< in Deutschland von der wilhelminischen Era bis zur nationalsozialistischen Diktatur," *Internationales Archiv für Sozialgeschichte der deutschen Literatur* 14 (1989), 108–125.
63. Rudolf Borchardt, "Schöpferische Restauration," in: idem, *Reden* (Stuttgart: Ernst Klett Verlag, 1955), 245.
64. Kracauer, *Die Angestellten.*
65. Ernst v. Aster, "Die Krise der bürgerlichen Ideologie," *Die neue Rundschau* 42 (1931), 3.
66. Theodor Geiger, *Die Soziale Schichtung des deutschen Volkes* (Stuttgart: Ferdinand Enke Verlag, 1987 originally 1932); Emil Lederer, *Kapitalismus, Klassenstruktur und Probleme der Demokratie in Deutschland 1910–1940* (Göttingen: Vandenhoeck & Ruprecht, 1979); Hans Tobis, "Das Mittelstandsproblem der Nachkriegszeit und seine statistische Erfassung," Ph.D. diss., University of Frankfurt a.M., 1930.
67. Max Victor, "Verbürgerlichung des Proletariats und Proletarisierung des Mittelstandes," *Die Arbeit* 8 (1931), 17–31; Hendrik de Man, "Verbürgerlichung des Proletariats?" *Neue Blätter für Sozialismus* 1 (1930), 106–118; Goetz Briefs, "Proletariat," in: Alfred Vierkand, ed., *Handwörterbuch der Soziologie* (Stuttgart: Ehke Verlag, 1931), 441–458.
68. Theodor Geiger, "Zur Kritik der Verbürgerlichung," *Die Arbeit* 8 (1931), 534–553.
69. As proof he notes that even in proletarian bookshops in the Ruhr, for every three bound books by the author Adam Scharrer (1889–1948) one cheap copy was sold in the form of a booklet. The proletarian novel would be more widely distributed, he argued, only if workers rid themselves of the idea that a link existed between a book's form and its content, and started to believe that even a cheap pamphlet could be valuable reading. Klaber's article also provides proof of the Left's efforts to create a popular culture which would exploit political needs: Kurt Klaber, "Der proletarische Massenroman," *Linkskurve* 5 (1930), 22–25, here 23.
70. On this see: Moritz Föllmer, and Rüdiger Graf, eds., Die Krise der Weimarer Republik: Zur Kritik eines Deutungsmusters (Frankfurt a.M.: Campus Verlag, 2005).

Chapter II

READING CULTURE, READING BUDGETS, AND CONSUMER SOCIETY

Following World War I, discourse about the situation of books and reading was dominated by a sense of a crisis affecting book sales. Some attributed the causes of this crisis to the structure of the book market itself. A more widespread view blamed the crisis on the decline of book-reading culture, seeing it as an expression of social changes affecting Germany in the wake of World War I, primarily as manifested in the disintegration of the bourgeoisie. Various conflicting interpretations can be advanced concerning the extent to which this sense of a crisis affecting books was a situation for which evidence can be found in contemporary realities. What is uncontested is that book prices in the wake of World War I reached new heights. This state of affairs made books appear beyond the reach of those with average incomes for the time. On the other hand, in the 1920s book sales enjoyed a number of unprecedented successes. Given this situation, did a book crisis actually exist? Did the reading public, as many contemporary reports claim, give up reading, instead going to the cinema and sporting events, or listening to the wireless and records? These questions were raised in the chapter on the "book crisis," where we presented various questions about the validity of the thesis of the disintegration of the bourgeoisie and in particular about the existence of an objective "book crisis." In the present chapter we will examine a number of these issues. We will attempt to shed light on the position of reading among the potential and actual target audience for the book trade market. To put it another way, whether or not the "book crisis" was a situation bound up with the social changes which took place among the reading public in the wake of World War I, as was claimed by many from the limited group of book people who took part in the discussions about the situation of books and reading, this discussion must necessarily involve addressing readers themselves and examining what status reading had for them.

Who, then, were these people who made up the reading public? During the Weimar Republic period, by which time illiteracy had become a marginal phenomenon, the reading public comprised the overwhelming majority of the population. This public did not have uniform literacy skills, however. Not everybody who could put his signature on an official document or make out the meaning of street signs could necessarily read a novel, a daily newspaper, or a magazine without illustrations.[1] Notwithstanding the difficulties involved in laying down clear-cut criteria which could be used to determine the level and precise size of the reading public, we have sufficient data to allow us to assert that from the last decade of the nineteenth century onward, as a result of improvements in the educational system, increased leisure, legislation on compulsory military service, improvements in living conditions and lighting, as well as printing techniques and the distribution of reading material, the size of the German reading public increased steadily.[2]

Even if we agree to include in the reading public everyone not defined as illiterate and those not included in the professional reading public, we are still faced by a number of basic methodological difficulties relating to the status of reading among this public of readers. The main difficulty in any attempt to penetrate the "reading world" of unprofessional readers relates to the problem of sources capable of enabling such research to be undertaken. This public of readers left practically no material attesting to its reading habits or the significance that reading had for it. Moreover, most of the sources available to us which claim to present data about the reading habits of this anonymous reading public were collected by contemporaries, usually in such a way as to provide material which would either corroborate or refute a particular approach to the group being studied. In order to get round this difficulty, and so that we can look beyond the screen obscuring the various groups which made up the target audience of the commercial reading-matter market, we must find sources which relate to reading as objectively as possible. One such source, which until recently has been more or less ignored by historians, comprises household account books.[3]

Sources

Research today has available to it a fairly impressive collection from the pre– and post–World War I periods of account books kept by families from a variety of different social backgrounds and geographical areas. The source of this database is generally research carried out by contemporaries into the living expenses of families from a variety of social strata and parts of Germany and elsewhere. Such studies, which primarily focused on the poorer classes in urban parts of Germany, had a twofold purpose: to provide affluent circles with a picture of the socioeconomic situation of the weaker strata of German society, and thereby to find ways of bringing them into the mainstream of the German people. In this way, these studies quickly became part of the political and social discourse of the period, and above all a component of the growing interest in the "Social Question." Secondly, such studies formed part of the demand to rationalize households, which were considered an area for which women were responsible.[4] In this sense, they reflected the world of contemporary male-bourgeois values. They sought to develop appropriate tools for controlling and rationalizing household management, as well as to instill these tools in women and the lower orders. To this end, schools of household management were even set up, and an extensive body of literature developed in this field, designed specifically for women and the needy.[5]

Even though statistics were being collected on household expenditure as early as the end of the eighteenth century, it was not until 1907 that the first official survey was carried out of the household expenditure of needy families in the Reich by the Imperial Statistics Office, which was founded in 1872. This study, published in 1909, collected data from 31 cities, covering 3,800 families of which 960 were found to be suitable for inclusion in the final results.[6] In 1927–1928 the Reich Statistics Office carried out a similar survey of the cost of living of over 2,000 families from 56 different communities and social groups—blue-collar workers, white-collar workers, and civil servants. The results of this survey were published in their entirety in 1932.[7] These data files will constitute the main sources for the present chapter. We will also use additional figures which were largely collected by those with an academic interest in the field or by a variety of interest groups, primarily trade unions trying to highlight their members' unique socioeconomic status and in this way to promote their distinctive collective awareness relative to other sociovocational groups. In this connection it is worth making the point at this juncture that studies of living expenditure pose a fair number of methodological problems. The data available to us are neither complete nor continuous. They were collected from a small sample of the population, with an emphasis on family expenditure budgets only, mainly needy families, and generally without paying attention to the criterion of representative sampling. In addition, the methods and criteria for selecting and organizing the data varied from one survey to another. Most of the samples fail to follow up developments in living expenditure over a protracted period. Nor do they undertake comparisons with the results of other surveys. It is also important to note that keeping household accounts—a typical "bourgeois" phenomenon—and in particular participating in surveys which studied the nature of household expenditure, requires a high level of reading comprehension and corresponding arithmetical skills. Hence, the mere fact that household accounts were kept assumes that this population was part of the reading public, at least potentially, although these respondents were classified as belonging to the needy strata of society.

Notwithstanding the various limitations and drawbacks associated with the disparate data files in our possession, cost of living research is a unique source. It offers valuable information about living conditions and how families from different areas and social groups and with disparate income levels shaped their lifestyles in the past. Cost of living studies can therefore provide an extremely valuable source for investigating attitudes to reading. It can be very helpful simply to examine such questions as: Do the various surveys include expenditure on reading material? What categories did they use for such expenditure? What was the importance of expenditure on reading? And how did they interpret the data about reading expenses? Apart from these questions, the data available to us, despite their limitations, can provide us with fairly strong indications about reading material's part in the overall cost of living in the postwar years compared with the period before the war, and above all can enable us to examine the relative proportion of the reading budget compared to expenditure on new media and leisure-time pursuits such as films, radio, or sports, which were commonly seen as activities which supplanted reading.

Research into Cost-of-Living and Reading Expenditure

The foundations for research in Germany into the cost of living of private households were laid by Ernst Engel. As early as 1857, Engel drew attention to the link between the structure of domestic expenditure budgets and households' standards of living, asserting that the higher their income, the smaller the proportion spent on food, even if the amount a family spent on these items was higher in absolute terms.[8] According to this approach, standard of living was not solely a function of income levels: rather, it was reflected in the structure and nature of household expenditure. For Engel, the reduction in the proportion of expenditure on food and the concomitant proportionate increase in amounts spent on other items not related to physical needs constituted an index for a high standard of living and affluence.[9] Engel's diagnosis, which was soon dubbed "Engel's Law," was readily adopted by the world of bourgeois values, and came to influence the nature of research into household expenditure in the nineteenth and the first third of the twentieth century in Germany as well as elsewhere. The main issues examined by such studies concerned the relationship between income and expenditure, sources of income, and the structure and nature of household expenses.

The increased research interest in this set of questions in Germany in the second half of the nineteenth century can undoubtedly be ascribed to the social, economic, and political changes which took place in that country during these years. However, this area of research may also be viewed as an expression of the growing importance of consumption and leisure as the main aspects determining standards of living in German society, which during these years was setting out on its winding and tortuous path to a consumer society. Carle C. Zimmermann observed this process in 1933, showing that Engel's Law was actually only applicable to certain societies which attached major importance to values such as "progress," "culture," and "leisure."[10] Hence according to Zimmermann, references to "Engel's Law" should be dropped in favor of the category of an "Engel type," which was normally to be found in the industrialized societies of Western Europe and North America.

In the model outlined by Engel, cost of living was divided into two major, hierarchically related groups: the first group comprised outlay for physiological needs, primarily meaning expenditure for food. The second group of "other expenditure" was sometimes defined as psychological or "cultural needs," and included expenditure on taxes, health, insurance, travel, education, culture, recreation, and so on. Expenditure on housing, clothing, heating, and lighting, which in addition to spending on food comprised by far the greater part of domestic budgets, was sometimes included in one group and sometimes in the other. The relationship between these two categories of expenditure constituted one of the main indices for determining a society's level of affluence, or more precisely that of different groups in any given society. In other words, the cost-of-living structure was perceived, as Adolf Günther put it, as a yardstick of social stratification.[11] In the light of this approach, most studies pointed to differences in the cost-of-living structures of bourgeois families, where expenditure on "psychological" or "cultural" needs occupied a significant proportion of the household budget, and those of working-class families, where expenditure on "physiological needs" left only a very small proportion of the household budget to meet "other needs." The relationship between these two groups of expenses also provided an index for tracking changes in social status in Germany following World War I. Many contemporary reports, based on a comparative analysis of household account books, viewed the world war as a watershed event which reshaped cost-of-living structures, changing the consumption patterns of many social strata. Some even argued that the economic hardships during the war and the period immediately after it, which primarily affected members of the middle class, on the one hand and the improvement in workers' social welfare conditions in the wake of political changes and Germany's transformation into a welfare state, on the other, helped to narrow social gaps in Germany.[12] We will refer later to this issue of the world war's impact on consumption and the structure of cost-of-living budgets generally, and reading budgets specifically. For our current purposes it is important to remember that while detailed attention was devoted to the proportion of physiological needs, the share of "other expenses" was not similarly considered—not, at least, expenses for reading needs, which did not occupy a particularly major position in the expense budgets of any social stratum. Only a relatively small number of surveys specifically mention expenditure on reading material as a separate category. The assumption is that this situation was not simply the upshot of the relative scope of expenditure on reading material, but primarily the fruit of research focusing on the impoverished social classes and interest in the "social question," with this interest focusing on the physical and hygienic circumstances of various social groups.

Expenditure on reading material was viewed as part of those expenses not classified with subsistence-level income.[13] Such an approach is particularly manifest in those studies which chose a less neutral form of words for this part of "other expenses." For example, in Henriette Fürth's 1922 study of household expenses of the bourgeois middle classes (a follow-up to research which she published in 1907), we find reading budgets listed under the general group of "Luxuskonsum bzw. nicht unbedingt lebensnotwendige Ausgaben," together with outlay on sweets, delicacies, tobacco and cigarettes, wine, ice cream, membership fees for various associations, outings, concerts, and theater.[14] The fact that a considerable proportion of the account books, including of needy families, reported expenditure on reading material, shows that spending money on reading material had become part of overall needs for all social strata and was not a luxury enjoyed solely by a select class. But even if expenditure on reading material was considered a kind of luxury, it was certainly not classified with the "corrupting" type of luxury, such as outings and spending time at cafes, alcohol, or other sybaritic items, which were primarily related to satisfying bodily needs or, as Werner Sombart the sociologist put it, "satisfying unbridled cravings."[15] Being an activity of the mind, reading was perceived as an activity expressing refinement and self-restraint. Unlike luxuries of the corrupting type, which were the expression of illusory desires, the consumption of reading material was viewed therefore as the satisfying of genuine needs. In particular in needy groups, with limited budgets which did not allow for any great flexibility, the hypothesis was that a budget for reading, however small, substituted for expenditure on drink, smoking, and the other type of corrupting luxuries.

Under what heading in household budgets was expenditure on reading material classified? Generally, reading budgets appeared under expenses for "intellectual needs" (*geistige Bedürfnisse*). In certain cases, "intellectual needs" were linked to expenditure on education (*Erziehung und Unterricht*), while in many cases they became "intellectual and social needs" (*geistige und gesellige Bedürfnisse*), appearing in the same category as expenses for membership fees for various associations and outlay on recreational activities, such as going to the theater, cinema, or circus, holidays, and sports. In a survey carried out by the Reich Statistics Office in 1927–1928, as well as one by the Hamburg Statistics Office in 1929, which are the most detailed and systematic cost-of-living studies of the time, outlay on reading material, books, newspapers, and magazines not related to education form part of spending on culture (*Bildung*), in addition to school, kindergarten, instructional, and additional educational expenses. Such outlay was considered a form of investment in the future, or as Johannes Müller put it in his book on the statistics of culture in Germany, an investment which made possible upward social mobility.[16]

Despite the varied combinations under which we find expenditure on reading material, it is definitely possible to identify a dominant attitude to these outlays which views reading as an activity of a different cultural nature from entertainment and recreational activities, although they sometimes appear under the same expense category. In this context, it is noteworthy—and this will be a central issue below—that the data available to us do not, generally speaking, distinguish between newspaper reading and book reading.

Having so far focused on cost-of-living studies and how they deal with reading budgets, the time has now come to examine the statistics themselves and try to see what can be learned from them about the consumption patterns of German society generally, and about spending on the consumption of reading material specifically.

Consumption and Reading

A considerable number of factors, both subjective and objective, are capable of determining the nature and structure of households' cost of living. Personal taste, health status, religious denomination, technological innovations, a variety of fashions, economic structure, the political situation, or the weather are just a few of the factors which can shape the structure of household expenses. Cost-of-living research focusing on the social question generally related to four parameters as influencing cost-of-living structures: income levels, social stratification, family size, and area of residence. It is this approach which determined the collection and processing of data in the various surveys in our possession.

The main criterion for distinguishing between different social classes was based on a vocational sociological (*berufssoziologisch*) approach. It was the occupation of the husband—the "man of the family"—which determined class affiliation. In this way the bourgeois classes, which included public employees or civil servants with tenure (*Beamten*) and members of the liberal professions, were distinguished from white-collar workers (*Angestellte*) and the laboring classes. This approach, which presupposes that the area in which the husband is employed determines consumption patterns, lifestyle, and social stratification, is a hypothesis which must be proved. This is a project undertaken by Ermin Triebel, who on the basis of the analysis of over five thousand account books which were assembled from eleven different contemporary sources, reprocessed, and computerized in the 1980s, showed that even if the data are examined on the level of income, the man's job remains a primary factor that influences the private household's consumption patterns. Consequently, Triebel argued that it is possible to treat this element as a significant factor in determining social stratification.[17] Social historian Reinhard Spree, on the basis of an analysis of the same data, qualified Triebel's unequivocal conclusion.

Spree pointed out that despite different incomes, representatives of a range of vocational groups have similar consumption habits, and only at the extremes, in other words at the highest and lowest income levels, is there social homogeneity of the kind that Triebel meant.[18] Furthermore, according to Spree, the private household account books show that the more workers' income levels and living conditions improve, the greater the similarity between their consumption habits and lifestyle and those of civil servants and white-collar workers.

The cost of living of private households would appear, therefore, in many cases to be the outcome of a compromise between a desired lifestyle and given economic resources and conditions. It comes as no surprise, therefore, that low income, hard physical labor, long hours, large numbers of children, and difficult living conditions, which were generally the lot of the working classes, made it difficult to attain a large number of people's desires, while imposing dreary patterns of consumption calculated to meet basic subsistence needs.

The constant characteristic present in all the data files in our possession, spanning the prewar and postwar periods alike, indicates the relatively high proportion of expenditure on food in the overall budgets of low-income informants, i.e., blue-collar workers, compared with the relatively low proportion spent on this item by high-income groups, i.e., civil servants and white-collar workers. On the other hand, high-income groups spent relatively more on housing costs, with white- and above all blue-collar workers with low income levels not allocating large amounts of their income on these needs. For other areas, too, such as clothing, recreation, culture, and education, civil servants and white-collar workers, who generally had large incomes, tended to budget larger amounts than blue-collar workers, in both relative and absolute terms. These differences are characteristic of the structure of the budgets of laborers, white-collar workers, and civil servants in both the pre- and postwar periods. Nevertheless, a comparison of data from the prewar period with their postwar equivalents does point to a change in the structure of private households' budgets for all social strata in the wake of the world war.

The figures in Table 2.1 show that not only did a change occur in the structure of household expenditure following the world war, but there was also a tendency to increased consumption by all social strata compared with the prewar period. This change in the structure of consumption primarily consists of the reduced proportion of expenditure on necessities, in particular in the food category, compared with the increase in the proportion spent on fixed (*Pflicht*) expenses—such as taxes and insurance—and other expenditure, mainly comprising outlays on services, such as health, culture, education, recreation, and transport. This tendency can be seen not only among civil servants and above all white-collar workers, but also in the ranks of the blue-collar workers. What it means is that after the war, civil servants, white-collar workers, and blue-collar workers alike spent

Table 2.1
Real consumer expenditure: 1907 and 1927–1928 (1907 index = 100)[19]

Expenditure		Blue-collar workers 1907	Blue-collar workers 1927/8	White-collar workers 1907	White-collar workers 1927/8	Civil servants 1907	Civil servants 1927/8
Necessities	Total	100	96	100	111	100	97
	Food	100	94	100	103	100	92
	Clothing	100	123	100	129	100	103
	Housing	100	89	100	118	100	102
Fixed (*Pflicht*) expenses	Total	100	278	100	144	100	154
	Insurance	100	278	100	293	100	87
	Taxes	100	277	100	79	100	293
Miscellaneous	Total	100	129	100	256	100	128
Total expenditure	Total	100	108	100	130	100	106

larger amounts, at least in relative terms, on services, including education, culture, and recreation—categories which generally speaking also included a reading budget. Do these figures attest to an improved standard of living in the postwar period, as perhaps could be contended on the basis of Engel's Law? In the light of the household expenditure statistics collected primarily in the 1927–1928 period of relative stability, it is not possible to offer a satisfactory answer to this question. In this connection, Reinhard Spree has suggested referring to the modernization of consumption, or more precisely the inhibited modernization (*gehemmte Modernisierung*) of consumption, in particular of the lower middle classes and the impoverished strata of society—a modernization which was impeded by the economic hardships and political instability of the interwar period.[20] It is also possible to interpret these changes as an additional indication of the reduction in social gaps in Germany and an expression of the tendency toward the bourgeoisification of society and the increasing importance of consumer culture in that country. Another way of putting this is to say that the changes in the structure of household budgets are indicative of the affluent bourgeois classes' success in imposing their consumption habits, with their preference for fixed and optional expenses over necessities, on broad swaths of society including the impoverished laboring classes.

What, however, is the link between these developments and reading? The democratization of reading that began in the second half of the nineteenth century, as we will argue in subsequent chapters, did not relate solely to increased consumption generally, and specifically to the making of reading into a consumer product: rather, it was one of the factors which contributed to a change in consumption habits per se. Reading became a medium which encouraged consumption and helped to make it one of the foundations of social life at the time. However, before we can test this thesis, we must first examine the reading budgets themselves and how they changed between the pre- and postwar periods.

Reading Budgets: The Period Before the World War

The 1907 survey by Germany's Imperial Statistics Office is a primary source of data for the pre–World War I period. In it expenditure on reading material—books and newspapers—is recorded in a single category which also includes outlay on membership dues of various organizations and unions such as political parties, trade unions, religious associations, sports clubs, and so on. It is possible that one of the reasons for reading budgets being linked in one and the same category with outlay on membership dues is that payment of membership dues for a party, trade union, or cultural or sports association normally included a subscription to a magazine or access to a library. However, as we will demonstrate later, blue-collar workers tended to allocate larger amounts to membership dues for various organizations than civil servants and high-income white-collar workers. For this reason, apparently, the data of the 1907 Imperial Statistics Office survey show that the reading budget and membership dues of blue-collar workers were similar to and on low income levels even higher than the reading budgets of middle- and low-income civil servants.

This picture does not significantly change when we examine income levels which are homogeneous in socioeconomic terms: in other words, income above M 4,000 (which includes only civil servants) and below M 1,200, which only laborers received. True, expenditure on reading material increases in absolute terms as income levels go up, but as a proportion of total outlay, no significant change occurs. Furthermore, a more detailed examination of the behavior of budgets for outlay on reading material on the different income levels actually indicates that as income rises, so the reading budget shrinks in relative terms. For example, if we compare income levels which are homogeneous in socioeconomic terms, we will see that families with incomes of over 5,000 marks a year allocate 100 marks and above for annual expenditure on reading material and membership dues of various organizations. However, this amount represents just 1.71 percent of their total expenditure. In contrast, blue-collar families with incomes of below RM 1,200 spend no more than 29 marks a year for this purpose. On the other hand, this amount constitutes 2.68 percent of their total expenditure. The results of the study carried out in Breslau in 1907–1908 were similar. This study, in which data were collected from 89 families of blue-collar workers, white-collar workers, and civil servants, also indicates that as income levels decrease, so an increase occurs in the relative amounts of expenditure for reading and membership dues, but also that laborers tend to spend more on reading needs and membership dues for various organizations and associations than do white-collar workers and civil servants.[21]

It would appear therefore that this category of outlay behaves similarly to the Engel curve, which indicates that the relative proportion of food expenditure declines as income increases. It is possible that this tendency is related to the fact that reading, like food expenses, is a need which can be satisfied with modest means and hence at the highest income levels the relative proportion of this budget is small although the amounts of money used for it are large. If this hypothesis is correct, then it would appear that among the middle and lower-middle classes reading does not constitute a symbol of social status, with what are for them modest amounts being sufficient to satisfy these needs. A more logical possibility is that the factor for Engelian behavior in this category would rather be outlays on membership dues of various organizations and associations. In other words, low-income blue-collar workers tend to be more involved in the activities of various organizations, particularly trade unions and political parties, than civil servants and white-collar workers. This state of affairs may be viewed as attesting to a tendency toward the politicization of laborers as opposed to civil servants and white-collar workers.

There is no parallel pattern in the other two categories. The expenditure in the education category indicates that the larger the income, the greater the spending on education, in both absolute and relative terms. This tendency is particularly striking among civil servants. In the Reich survey, spending on education for an income level of more than 5,000 marks comprises over 7 percent of total expenditure. However, the most significant difference identified by this data is to be found in the category of outlay on recreational activities. Not only does the recreation budget indicate differences between the different income levels, but it also shows that with the same income levels, there are differences between blue-collar workers and civil servants. The latter tend to budget more for recreational activities such as theater, concerts, films, restaurant meals, holidays, outings, and so on. In the upper income brackets, where outlays on education are also the highest, we also find the greatest expenditures on recreational activities and holidays. On average the M 4,000–5,000 income bracket, for example, spends M 73.09 on recreation, or 2.59 percent of its total expenses, while those earning more than M 5,000 spend some M 175.85 a year, or 3 percent of their total outlay, on these activities.

These figures show, therefore, that it was not reading, but education and above all recreational activities which in these years were one of the main characteristics of the lifestyle of the bourgeois middle class, and it is on these items that middle- and lower-grade civil servants spent what in direct relationship to their income levels were larger amounts than the blue-collar workers, in both absolute and relative terms. On the other hand, reading and membership of various organizations played a more central role for those with low incomes, and especially laborers. The reason for this tendency may well lie in the fact that reading was a cheap pastime and that for laborers whose income was not particularly high, the associations were the only possibility of enjoying recreational and holiday activities.

Analysis of family size and the relationship between expenditure on reading material and membership dues for various organizations on the one hand, and recreational budgets on the other, reinforces the distinction outlined above. The number of children in the family is a decisive factor when it comes to educational expenses, but the figures in the 1907 Reich survey also show that in civil servants' and white-collar workers' families, irrespective of family size, there is a clear-cut preference for the recreational budget over the budget for reading and membership of various organizations. On the other hand, working-class families of whatever size spend more on reading material and membership dues for organizations and various associations than on recreational activities. A similar tendency is indicated by the figures published by Alfons Kraziza, which were collected from women readers of the popular family magazine *Nach Feierabend.* Here too, reading budgets maintain their relative share despite changes in family sizes.[22]

Great caution must of course be exercised when interpreting these findings. It must not be forgotten that the data of the 1907 Reich survey and the figures of the Breslau survey do not distinguish between expenditure on reading material and expenditure on membership dues for associations and various organizations. As income levels rise, the amounts budgeted by middle- and lower-grade civil servants for these categories become comparable, and on higher income levels even exceed the amount that blue-collar workers lay out for these purposes. In other words, since blue-collar workers tend to budget larger amounts for membership dues for associations and various organizations, it can be reasonably assumed that the actual reading budget of middle- and lower-grade civil servants is no smaller than that of blue-collar workers. This is confirmed by the data published by a Leipzig Municipal Statistics Office employee, showing his family's cost of living over a ten-year period, from 1895 to 1905. Despite the family's relatively low income, its outlay on reading material was relatively large. The average amount spent on books over the period reported on was M 23.86 a year, or 0.99 percent of total expenditure, while M 21.62 was spent annually on newspapers and magazines, representing 0.90 percent of the total. These outlays together constituted 1.90 percent of the family's total expenditure. If we add to them sums spent on membership dues for various associations, which averaged M 14.88 a year, we can see that these items comprised 2.52 percent of the family's cost of living.[23] In this case there is no doubt that this official's education and scientific work were responsible for his family's reading expenses being higher than the average in the 1907 Reich survey.

It is also interesting to note that the budget for presents, which can be assumed to include money spent on buying books too, does not indicate any significant differences in the case of people with similar incomes between middle- and lower-grade civil servants and blue-collar workers. If we take those with income levels of between M 2,000 and 3,000, these items averaged M 14 for a total of 151 working-class families. This figure represented 0.6 percent of their total expenditure, as opposed to M 10.54 or 0.4 percent of the budget of eighty eight civil servants' families. The situation changes when we take sociovocationally homogeneous income levels. Here we see that for income levels below M 2,000, the budget for presents of 361 working-class families was M 4.90 or 0.3 percent of their total outlay. On the other hand, for income levels above M 3,000 a year, 118 families of civil servants on average budgeted M 38.20, or 1 percent of their total expenditure, for presents. These figures also show therefore that for similar income levels, blue-collar workers' consumption habits did not noticeably differ from those of white-collar workers, and that it was only on homogeneous income levels that the gap between them becomes more significant. However, here too, in the absence of specific details about the nature of these outlays, it will be difficult for us to draw any conclusions. Furthermore, it is not clear why in the Reich survey only 740 families were included for the category of expenses on "newspapers, books, and membership dues" out of the 852 who kept account books for an entire year. Is this just a random state of affairs, or does it mean that only 86 percent of the survey sample actually had expenses in this category? And what about the remaining 14 percent? The data of the 1907 Reich Statistics Office survey and the Breslau survey figures are not sufficiently detailed to enable us to use them in order to draw unambiguous conclusions about reading material consumption habits. As a result, we will have to make use of other contemporary sources in order to provide a more varied picture of the situation.

The explanatory notes to the 1909 Metallurgy Industry Union survey, which collected data from the household account books of 320 of its members, claim that outlays on culture and recreational activities do not depend solely on income levels, but also reflect individual tastes and interests. Some of the account books indicate high levels of consumption of reading material, books, and newspapers, while others fail to indicate any great interest in this area. The figures from this survey underscore the idea of elasticity in expenditure on reading material.[24] A similar tendency is also identified by a survey which examined the cost of living of the families of 127 low-grade Postal and Telegraph Authority employees, from March 1912 to February 1913.[25] In this case too, the figures show that such expenditure varies from one family to another, and that it is difficult to identify a particular pattern as characterizing reading material consumption habits. This is also borne out by the household budget of the Leipzig Statistics Office employee, Karl von K…, where we can see that the amounts allocated for the purchase of reading material were not fixed, but varied from one month to the next.[26] Thus the elasticity of the reading budget, at least among civil servants and blue-collar workers with low incomes, was one of its important characteristics. According to those who carried out the cost-of-living survey of metallurgy workers, one of the reasons for this was the influence of the regional factor in shaping the recreational and cultural habits of blue-collar workers. Cultural "fare" in the big cities was available on a larger and more varied scale than in small towns or rural areas. For example, in 1908 sociologist Adolf Weber drew attention to what he called the "thirst for education" (*Bildungshunger*) of the urban middle and lower classes.[27] This propensity was reflected in expenditure on concerts, the theater, or the cinema, to which the residents of small towns and rural areas did not always have access. But did the regional component also influence the consumption of reading material so decisively?

Workers in the metallurgy sector lived mainly in urban areas and hence their expenditure on culture and recreation was relatively high. In the Metallurgy Industry Union study, outlay on reading material was classified under the heading of education, entertainment, and newspapers. On average, a metallurgy worker's family spent M 27.79, or 2.07 percent of its total budget on these items. If we add membership dues for various associations, which averaged M 34 a year or 1.86 percent of total outlay, this gives us a figure of M 71.79 or 3.93 percent of the annual total. This sum is practically the same as the average amount in the Reich Statistics Office survey under the category of disbursements on "intellectual and social needs," which was M 72.70 or 4.0 percent of blue-collar workers' total expenditure. It should be noted that expenses under this heading appeared in all the account books. However, since this category of expenses failed to distinguish between disbursements for reading material and other expenditure, we have no way of knowing what proportion was constituted by reading material. On the basis of contemporary reports, it may however be reasonably assumed that the lion's share went to the consumption of reading material.

Another cost-of-living survey that was carried out in 1910 for miners in the Saarbrücken area shows far lower figures. In this case, the outlay on social and intellectual needs of more than 92 miners' families, who kept account books for an entire year, varies between M 20 and M 23, constituting no more than 1 percent of their total cost of living.[28] The person who carried out the survey, Ernst Herbig, gave three main reasons for the low amounts spent by Saarbrücken area miners compared with the results obtained for this category in the Reich Statistics Office survey and the Metallurgy Industry Union survey. The first reason was structural: only a small proportion of the miners in the Saarbrücken area were unionized or paid membership dues to various associations. The two other surveys, and especially the metallurgy workers' survey, specifically attest to far greater involvement by blue-collar workers in the activities of organizations and various associations. The second reason was geographical, and relates to the differences between urban and rural areas. It must be remembered that the 1907 Reich Statistics Office study and the Metallurgy Industry Union study collected data primarily from Germany's urban areas. In these locations, the range of cultural offerings was far richer than in a far-flung area like Saarbrücken, where miners did not have the temptations of shows, circuses, films, or concerts. The third reason involves working-class lifestyles in rural areas. Since the men who worked in the mines lived in rural areas, they spent a considerable proportion of their free time on work around their houses and gardens. Such activities were not just profit-oriented, but also constituted a form of rest and recreation for the miners' families.

However, and here we come back to the question of the relationship between the consumption of reading material and regional differences, the relatively low outlays of the miners in the Saarbrücken area under the category of "intellectual and social needs" do not necessarily reflect differences between miners' reading-matter consumption patterns in small-scale locations and the reading habits of blue-collar workers in urban areas. According to Herbig, the miners did not make sufficient use of the many libraries dotted around between the mines, where books could be borrowed free of charge. Nevertheless, he pointed out that in most homes, the local paper was read daily, in addition to a religious weekly paper and trade union paper in the case of miners who belonged to one of the trade unions.

Herbig's observation about the reading habits of the rural population became a widely held view at the beginning of the twentieth century, receiving support from other contemporary studies too. Research carried out in the Magdeburg district village of Belsdorf, which had a population of 460, showed that almost every household took a daily paper practically every day.[29] Kraziza's data also show that the differences between reading budgets in urban and rural areas were not particularly significant, and in fact in medium-size towns larger sums were budgeted for the consumption of reading material than in the cities.[30]

In the light of these figures one should not be over-hasty in asserting that there were no differences between the reading-matter consumption habits of blue-collar workers in urban areas and those who lived in rural areas. It would appear that in the latter, more reading was done in the winter than in the summer. A study by Fritz Tangermann shows that in the winter period, large numbers of *Schauromane* were sold in the village of Belsdorf. These novels were short, cheap, easy to read, and illustrated with large numbers of color pictures. These minibooks were read enthusiastically by the village residents. The intensity of book borrowing from the small village lending library was also greater in the winter than the summer.[31] On the other hand, in urban areas no such link can be readily identified between the seasons and reading habits. In fact, the Breslau Statistics Office study indicates that expenditure under the category of "intellectual and social needs" was higher in the summer than the winter.

This was apparently a result of the fact that a wider variety of entertainment and recreational activities was available in the summer than in the winter.

Climate and the regional component were not the only factors which influenced the reading-matter consumption patterns of blue-collar workers. Reading budgets also indicate differences between different working-class groups—particularly skilled and unskilled workers. The 1907 Reich Statistics Office survey shows that skilled workers spent on average M 13.19 (0.7 percent) for educational purposes and around M 81.14 (4.3 percent) on intellectual and social needs annually, compared with unskilled laborers who spent just M 6.28 (0.4 percent) and M 59.69 (3.5 percent) for these purposes. This tendency would appear to be another reason for the difference between the Saarbrücken area miners' survey and the two other studies.

Notwithstanding the differences between reading budgets for different areas and different working-class groups, we can state unequivocally that by the turn-of-the-century transitional period, blue-collar workers can no longer be seen as a stratum to which reading culture was alien. During this period, ever larger portions of the blue-collar population became regular consumers of reading material. The fact is that working class reading budgets, like those of middle- and lower-grade civil servants, were not particularly large and contemporary reports show that these groups' reading fare consisted largely of daily papers, magazines, reading material put out by a variety of associations and organizations, as well as colportage booklets and penny dreadfuls (*Groschenheften*), which were extremely popular at the time.[32]

Reports of working-class living conditions and in particular of housing hardships in urban areas tend to reinforce the hypothesis that blue-collar workers did not belong to the book-consuming public of those years. However, this does not mean that laborers did not read books. In the course of the nineteenth century, libraries—whether commercial lending libraries or public libraries, trade union, party, church, or workers libraries—offered workers something of an alternative to buying books at bookshops.[33]

What of the affluent social strata of the bourgeoisie? A unparalleled study by Erna Meyer-Pollack, which tracked the cost of living of a district judge's family in the north of Germany for nearly twenty six years, gives us a unique glimpse into the world of a senior civil servant around the turn of the century.[34] When the observation period began, the family consisted of five people: the judge himself, his wife, and their three sons, aged four months to three years. In 1882 another son was born, and in 1890 the couple had a daughter. From 1892 onward, the sister of the judge's wife lived with the family. In the initial phases of the study, the family lived in a small provincial town in the north of Germany. After the father was appointed judge in Berlin in 1888, the family left the provinces to move into a seven-room flat in the German capital. The move to Berlin improved the family's income, but it also increased expenditure. Up to 1888 the family's average income was over M 9,341 a year, while its outgoings were around M 7,062 on average. After the family moved to Berlin, its average income swelled to over M 13,670 a year, but its expenditure shot up to an annual average of around M 13,137. According to Meyer-Pollack, apart from the difference between the high cost of big city living compared with life in a small town, another reason for the family's high level of expenses, particularly toward the end of the observation period, was the father's state of health.

Roles were firmly divided between the man of the house and the wife. The wife was responsible for the everyday running of the household, and from 1902 onward the daughter also began to help out with the running of the household's affairs. The man of the house managed financial affairs and kept the household's books. Throughout the entire observation period, the household employed a cook and a maid, and for a while there was also a nanny. In addition to the judge's precarious state of health, an additional factor that influenced the family's lifestyle and consumption habits was the father's very firm antialcohol views, a tendency which perhaps explains the family's rather frugal way of life.

To what extent this family is characteristic of the upper levels of the bourgeoisie during the turn-of-the-century period is a moot point, open to a range of interpretations. Nevertheless, it may certainly be seen as representing the narrow high-income bourgeois stratum within German society, because the family of a senior civil servant was required to observe a way of life befitting the father's profession and the family's social standing. Inter alia we learn about the nature of this lifestyle from the category of outlays "for intellectual and social needs" in the family's account books, which comprises six headings, including outlay on newspapers and books in addition to expenditure on recreational activities, postage, membership dues for various associations, and social events.

One of the decisive factors which influenced the nature of outlays "for intellectual and social needs" was the move in 1888 from the small provincial town to the capital, Berlin. Before their move, the family spent a more or less fixed amount on hospitality and social events, which was apparently sufficient to meet its social obligations. Every winter the family held one big function for the husband's professional colleagues, or alternatively hosted them in small groups. Etiquette also required the lady of the house to invite the wives of the other judges to afternoon coffee from time to time. Particularly in the first few years, the move to Berlin significantly increased outlay on social functions. This tendency is reflected especially in expenditure on drink and hackney carriages. On the other hand, Berlin offered so much socially that the family did not have to attend every single social event, and after the birth of their daughter in 1890 as well as in the wake of the husband's health troubles these expenses, in both relative and absolute terms, began to plummet toward the end of the observation period.

The move from a small town to the metropolis had a similar effect on the family's recreational expenditure on such things as plays, concerts, lectures, outings, or sports activities. In this case the difference lay not only in the greater variety offered by the German capital compared with a small provincial town, but also in the children's greater involvement in these activities. It is noteworthy that the family did not seem to be particularly interested in taking part in the activities of a variety of associations and organizations. The only expense listed under the category of associations was the mother's membership fees for the choral group (*Gesangverein*) to which she belonged.

What about the family's reading budget? We find here the same situation as for postal charges, which were not significantly affected by the move to Berlin. Furthermore, unlike outlay on social events and recreational activities, where there was an upward tendency, in absolute terms at least, after the move to Berlin we can actually identify a downward tendency in the budget for reading material expenditure, and in particular outlay on newspapers—at least insofar as the proportion of total household expenses made up by the reading budget dropped, even though the total amount allocated for newspaper consumption remained more or less fixed. This finding is supported by a comparison between the percentage of total expenditure laid out for reading material, books, and newspapers up to 1888, compared with the subsequent period. Prior to the move to Berlin, 0.89 percent of the family's total expenses went to the consumption of reading material. In contrast, during the Berlin period, the reading budget made up just 0.68 percent of its cost of living.

When the family resided in a small provincial town, it had subscriptions to the two local papers and one magazine from Berlin. Meyer-Pollack identifies three main reasons for the family's avid newspaper reading before it moved to Berlin. First, life in the tranquil surroundings of a small town increased the need for up-to-date news, and this inquisitive instinct could not be satisfied by just one local paper with its largely one-sided reports. Second, life in a small town left more time for reading than in the city. And third, apparently social life also affected reading habits. In order to be able to take part in conversations about current events at social events, it was necessary to remain abreast of a range of topics and positions, to which end it was necessary to read at least two newspapers with different outlooks. It should also be noted that the family cancelled its magazine subscription some time before it moved to Berlin, apparently in order to save both time and money after the birth of their fourth son.

The budget for buying books was largely earmarked for the husband's professional activities, and included the purchase of academic and professional books and journals. Here too we find that the largest expenses were incurred prior to the move to Berlin, and were one-off outlays involving the father's academic activities. During the Berlin period, the book-buying budget would appear to have been reduced to the bare minimum for purchasing new books. Given the family's income level, the amount of money it spent on reading material was fairly small. The figures provided by Meyer-Pollack do not indicate whether this budget also included purchases of belles lettres, and whether the wife or children used this or another budget to buy books. Nor do the figures in Meyer-Pollack's research indicate what portion of the family's budget for presents, which averaged M 676 a year, was earmarked for buying books, or whether the family received books as gifts from outside. From the description of the contents of the house, for example, we gather that the family's bookcase was in the father's study, not the living room. This fact may indicate a functional approach to books, which were not merely viewed as objects to be displayed in the living room.

The figures in Meyer-Pollack's study indicate, therefore, that at least among the haute bourgeoisie, there was no fundamental difference between the cities and the small towns in terms of reading material consumption. These figures also indicate that a set amount was set aside for newspaper reading and that there were no far-reaching changes over the years. In contrast, the book budget, which did fluctuate, depended on a variety of factors and circumstances which governed the amount allocated to purchasing books every year. This shows that newspaper reading was a basic need for which a set amount was allocated by the family, unlike outlay on books which was far more flexible. Meyer-Pollack reports that the father at least tried not to spend excessive amounts on buying books. From the figures we are unable to determine whether this rule applied to books for work only, or to books generally. One cannot of course rule out the possibility that members of the household received many books as presents, and that once the family's library reached a certain size, there was neither room nor need to expand it. However, this is another aspect about we do not have enough information.

The general impression given by inspection of this family's account books is that its lifestyle was not particularly hedonistic. Apparently the family preferred to invest its resources mainly in the needs of the household, the children's education, and travelling, and less in "social and intellectual needs." In accordance with this spending policy it made a point of not spending a single superfluous mark on the consumption of reading material.

Another study that the Reich Statistics Office published in 1911 of the cost of living of high-ranking civil servants paints a somewhat different picture.[35] In this case, two families' expenses were observed. One was the family of a senior official in the Prussian Housing Ministry, covering the period 1894–1908, while the other involved a researcher at a scientific research institute in Berlin, from 1899 to 1910. At the beginning of the observation period, the senior Prussian Housing Ministry official's family consisted of five persons, with an additional daughter being born in 1894. The mother died that same year, and the father's sister came to run the household. At first this family lived in a large city in Westphalia, but in 1899 they moved to Berlin. The family of the researcher at the academic institute is an example of a young family—the husband was aged 30, the wife 24—started in 1898, a year before the observation period began. During the observation period the couple had five children, three girls and two boys. In these studies outlay on reading material is classified under the heading of "newspapers, books, and membership dues for various associations." In both families, the expenses under this heading are higher than those of the judge's family. On average, the housing ministry official's family spent around 246 marks (3 percent) annually on these items. Although those who administered the survey identified the factor responsible for the high level of expenses relating to the consumption of reading material as being the father's disapproving attitude toward social and recreational activities, the amount laid out by the family over the entire observation period for reading and membership dues of various associations was only slightly larger than the amount it spent on recreational activities such as concerts, the theater, or outings. In this connection, attention must also be drawn to the relatively large proportion that educational expenditure represented in the family's budget. As the children grew up, this figure experienced linear growth, increasing from M 38.20 (0.4 percent) in 1897 to M 1958.70 (15.7 percent) in 1908. The reading expenditure of the academic researcher's family was also greater than the amount that the judge's family spent on reading, averaging M 291 or 5 percent a year for books, newspapers, and membership dues for various organizations. In this case the father's high level of involvement in a variety of scientific associations, through which according to the authors of the study he hoped to advance his academic career, and his research work itself were undoubtedly responsible for the high level of expenditure under these headings. In 1910, for example, the father belonged to twelve different academic associations, budgeting the amount of M 89.65 for this purpose.

In order to round off the picture obtained so far, we will now briefly present another study which for ten years followed the cost of living of a middle-class family.[36] Henriette Fürth's study examined the cost of living of the family of a businessman (*Kaufmann*) who initially had his own business, but then ran into financial difficulties and became a tenured public employee (*Beamte*). At the beginning of the observation period, the family consisted of the two parents and six children. Twins were born in 1899. Over the last two years of the observation period, the two oldest children left the parental home. The family, which throughout the observation period lived in a seven-room flat in Frankfurt am Main, initially employed two girls to help with the housework, but later, despite the birth of the twins, cut back to just one servant.

In the course of the years between 1900 and 1905, the period during which the husband became a salaried employee, the family's income averaged M 11,148 a year. The husband's salary made up 43 percent of this sum. The remainder came primarily from the work carried out by the wife, who during her youth had trained as a seamstress, and the four oldest children, who as long as they were living in the parental home contributed their share of the household expenses. Despite the family's relatively high income, it barely covered its expenses, which over this period averaged M 11,131 a year. According to Fürth, the size of the family, the father's illness in 1903 and 1904, and the hard work on the part of the wife and the children with the aim of securing a livelihood for the family, were the main components governing the structure of this family's household expenses.

Because the couple worked really hard, it was absolutely vital for them to spend lengthy periods away on holiday and recuperation. During the observation period, the couple laid out more than M 4,199 just for holidays and convalescence—some 4 percent of the household's budgeted expenditure during this period. However, the family's day-to-day difficulties in making ends meet did not prevent them from consuming products which Fürth defined as luxuries for this family, such as alcoholic beverages, ice cream, sweets, shows, concerts, swimming, ice skating, and books and newspapers.

Outlay on reading material was not fixed, and it would appear that the figure spent on this item was influenced by the family's financial situation in any particular year, and above all by the requirements of the children's schools. Although the amounts budgeted by the family for reading material are not particularly large given the fact that throughout the entire observation period at least six members of the family could read, the figures presented by Fürth show that reading was not an activity alien to the household's members. It should also be noted that the two older children's bedroom had a bookshelf, and there was a bookcase in the living room. According to Fürth, the father often went to the public library and the municipal reading rooms. He was a member of a liberal association, while the family belonged to a cultural association which from time to time organized lectures on a variety of topics. Here too we have no information about the nature of the budget for presents. However, Fürth reports that a third of the family's reading budget was earmarked for specialized literature for the requirements of the wife's work, the husband, and the children.

Despite the similarities between the families we have reviewed so far—the large number of children, and the fact that they lived in big cities and had fixed incomes with an Engel expenditure structure which allocates greater weight to fixed and optional expenses than to outlays on food—these families represent different versions of the bourgeois lifestyle. For example, although the Berlin judge's family had a higher income and fewer children, it had a more modest lifestyle than the family of the Frankfurt businessman. Although the judge's family made a point of observing all the rules of social good manners, its household account books indicate that it attached greater importance to good education for the children and household expenses than to recreational and other expenditure. A similar tendency is reflected by the cost of living of the two other Berlin families, with greater weight attached to expenditure on cultural needs generally, and reading in particular. On the other hand, the Frankfurt family did not stint on expenditure relating to the children's education. Its children did not go on to university: after completing their secondary education, they spent a while undergoing training as sales personnel and then began earning a livelihood. This family also spent less on household expenses and more on other needs such as clothing, outings, holidays, or alcohol. The fact that the wife also worked in order to contribute to the Frankfurt family's livelihood—a situation which was interpreted as reflecting economic hardship—is a further indication of the difference between the Frankfurt family and the three other families.

What about differences in the area of reading material consumption? In all the instances that we examined above, reading material consumption habits were first and foremost determined by professional requirements, particularly those of the husband. An additional factor that governed the nature of reading material consumption habits was the family's social status and the lifestyle that it was obliged to maintain, as well as the political and social interests of its different members. Reading as a leisure activity must of course be added to these factors. A comparison between the proportion of expenditure allocated to reading material by the Berlin judge's family and the Frankfurt family respectively shows that during the twenty-six years of observation, the Berlin family's reading budget made up 0.73 percent of its total budget, compared with the Frankfurt family's reading budget which, excluding textbooks, amounted to 0.53 percent of its total expenditure during the observation period. However, if we focus on the parallel time span of 1896–1906, we find that the difference in the two families' consumption of reading material is not so marked. During this period the Berlin family allocated around M 585 to the consumption of reading material compared with M 554.64 by the Frankfurt family. But while the Berlin family allocated just 0.35 percent of its total expenditure during this period to reading material, the amount budgeted by the Frankfurt family represented 0.53 percent of its total outlay. Expenditure for reading needs in the two other families was far greater. During the observation period, 2.5 percent of the Prussian housing ministry official's expenditure went toward needs relating to reading and membership dues for various organizations, while 4.65 percent of expenditure by the researcher's family was spent during the observation period for these purposes. It would appear, therefore, that even among high-level members of the bourgeoisie no uniform pattern of reading material consumption can be readily identified, with considerable differences existing between different groups within the same social class.

From the figures presented so far it will be difficult to reach any overall conclusion as to patterns of reading material consumption by different classes within German society in the pre–World War I period. Nevertheless, the data do allow us to state that by the beginning of the twentieth century at the latest, the consumption of reading material was no longer a characteristic of specific groups in German society: rather, it was an activity in which ever broader sectors of the population engaged. We have also seen that not only did social classes have flexible reading budgets, but the amounts spent for these ends were not particularly large, and the less well-off actually tended to spend relatively more of their resources on the consumption of reading material and membership of various organizations than their more affluent counterparts. In this context it is also noteworthy that while newspapers became an inseparable part of the upper middle-class lifestyle around the 1880s, as observed by Meyer-Pollaćk, for example, the private household account books indicate that within twenty years newspapers had also become a routine sight in the homes of blue-collar workers in small towns and rural areas.[37] On the other hand, when it comes to the consumption of books we can identify more significant differences between the working classes and the bourgeoisie, and between urban and rural areas. Evidence for this comes not only from the larger amounts that those with large incomes and urban residents spent under the heading detailing outlay on reading material consumption, but also from the differences between the budget for presents of those with high incomes and those who earned less. However, the impression given by the various figures is that even the educated bourgeois classes were not unlimited consumers of books, and that among all social classes this budget was extremely flexible and subject to the influence of many factors.

Given these findings, we can perhaps identify the heightened tendency at the turn of the century to reduce book prices and expand the target audience for the reading material market—as reflected for example in the establishment of cultural publishing houses (*Kulturverlage*) or the travelling and mail order book business (*Reise- und Versandbuchhandel*), as well as in the distribution of reading material to an anonymous target audience in department stores, railway stations, kiosks, or street trading—as an attempt by the reading material trade to influence the demand for reading material, and above all as a reaction to the bourgeoisie's small-scale consumption of books. In this sense, Rudolf Schenda's contention that in the pre–World War I period reading was not generally a primary need of the various strata of German society and book reading specifically was not a popular activity, even among the bourgeoisie, is undoubtedly a logical possibility for describing the contemporary situation.[38] Given this state of affairs, the longing of a variety of book circles in postwar Germany for the prewar period when "the bourgeoisie" were by all accounts avid consumers of books, was to a large extent nostalgia for a fantasy reality.

However, this is just one way of describing the reality of the period. In contrast with Schenda's "bookless people" thesis, Rolf Engelsing convincingly showed that not only did illiteracy become a marginal phenomenon at the beginning of the twentieth century, but the activity of reading, and book reading specifically, actually expanded so as to encompass society's weakest classes, as indicated by the figures from the household account books presented above, as they began to express ever more interest in it.[39] In addition, the quasi-Engelian behavior of reading budgets and outlays on membership dues for various associations, on the one hand, and the search on the part of the book trade during the immediate prewar period for ways to increase its target audience on the other hand, are salient expressions of the fact that beginning around the turn-of-the-century transition period, reading became part of all social classes' aggregate of needs. This is borne out, for example, by the department stores' insistence at the beginning of the twentieth century on trading in books at prices lower than those set for them by the publishers, despite the tooth-and-nail war waged by the German association of book dealers which set out to defend the system of fixed book prices. The department stores, as bodies operating on the basis of purely commercial considerations, would not have stocked books—mainly works for adolescents, world and German classics, popular novels, cookery books, and so on—and sold them at less than the price fixed for bookshops unless they had been convinced that the number of copies they would sell of each book would provide them with an attractive profit.[40]

Against this background, how did the world war affect reading material consumption patterns?

The World War and the Immediate Postwar Period

The feelings of national spiritual exaltation and enthusiasm for warfare with which Germany entered the hostilities in 1914 quickly dissipated in the light of the mass slaughter on the front lines and hunger on the home front. Many families, whether because their menfolk had been conscripted and sent to the front or because large numbers of businesses went bankrupt, lost their livelihood. The Allied economic blockade and Germany's wartime economy led to shortages of numerous basic consumer and food items. As a result, an ever wider divide developed between the wartime economy, for which all available resources had to be mobilized to serve the war effort on the front, and society's needs back home. This tension climaxed in the winter of 1916 as hunger became unbearable and the civilian population began to show more and more signs of opposition to and frustration with the situation confronting it.[41] This was the background to the passing of a series of regulations by the military and civil authorities. At the same time, a series of organizations came into existence to deal with the relationship between the interests of the front and the needs of the home population. One of these organizations, whose goal was to represent and defend the interests of close on ten million consumers against the military and civil authorities alike, was the War Committee for Consumer

Interests (*Kriegsausschuß für Konsumenten Interesse*—KAKI). In 1916 the organization distributed household account books to some two thousand of its members, and in this way began to collect data about the wartime consumer habits of the families of blue-collar workers, white-collar workers, and civil servants. This survey is one of the most interesting sources for examining the living conditions and consumer habits of German society during the world war. Below we will examine expenditure on reading material and a number of outlays normally associated with it under the heading of "intellectual and social needs."

The data collected in this survey reveal that while during the war, expenditure on reading material of all income levels tended to increase, other outlays tended to drop, in both absolute and relative terms. Categories which were affected particularly badly included expenditure on recreational activities and membership dues for various organizations. A deep-seated change occurred compared with the prewar situation, when the recreational budgets of high-income strata, in particular among white-collar workers and middle- and lower-grade civil servants, were larger in both relative and absolute terms than reading budgets. It is noteworthy that the KAKI figures indicate the persistence of low-income people's tendency to allocate relatively more resources to the consumption of reading material than did their high-income counterparts.

The relatively large sums earmarked for presents during these years are perhaps the most surprising aspect of the KAKI study. Perhaps it was precisely because during a period of shortages, of social and interpersonal tensions, gifts became a means of reconciling people and easing pressure. Does this mean that books were one of the beneficiaries of this tendency? This would certainly be a logical possibility. Waldemar Zimmermann, who designed the survey for KAKI, explained this tendency as resulting from the increasing demand for information about what was happening on the front lines as well as on the home front.[42] Apparently, during the wartime years reading became an important instrument in the struggle for day-to-day survival. Newspaper reading in particular became a vital point of reference both in the large cities where conditions for existing were particularly difficult, and also in the rural parts of the country, where the newspaper was practically the only way of getting information about what was happening on the front and at home alike.

What about the consumption of books? We will have a problem coming up with an answer to this question on the basis of the KAKI study alone. Zimmermann's report indicates that newspapers constituted the primary reading material at the time. This does not mean that books were not consumed during the world war. The figures of the German Book Dealers' Association on titles published, to cite another possible source, show that the number of publications during the world war dropped sharply, from 34,871 in 1913 to 14,743 in 1918. However, on the basis of these figures we are unable to say whether this tendency was the upshot of a drop in demand for books, or a result of the paper shortage and increased publishing costs. Nor do we have figures for the wartime ratio between first editions and reprints. Nevertheless, the German Book Dealers' Association figures do show that while very few nonfiction works were published during the world war, the number of belletristic works continued to undergo linear growth, from 4,045 titles in 1908, representing 14 percent of total works published, to 6,515 or 24 percent of total publications in 1920.[43] One of the factors which explains the growth of publishing activities in the area of belles lettres is the demand for reading material among the soldiers at the front. A widespread distribution network for reading material began to develop during the war in order to serve this readership. In addition to initiatives which called upon civilians to send reading material to the front, and the setting up of numerous libraries for front-line soldiers, it is particularly interesting to note the part played by two publishers, Hermann Hillger (1894) and Georg Stilke (1872), in distributing reading material on the battlefield. These two companies, which specialized in the publishing of theoretical works and the distribution of popular reading material, maintained most of the field bookshops (*Feldbuchhandlungen*) on the various fronts. This situation constituted the background to the development of much tension among book dealers and mutual recriminations about the creation of a monopoly and attempts to oust other book dealers from this market segment.

Although these reading material distribution agents were called bookshops, to begin with they concentrated on distributing newspapers only. There were two main reasons for this: first, among the troops there was major demand for up-to-date information about the situation back home. Second, newspapers were easier to transport to the front and to sell there. However, these shops soon expanded their wares, and started to distribute books too. Because these distribution agents' target audience was extremely heterogeneous, the shops tried to offer the broadest possible range of newspapers and books so as to meet the diverse needs of soldiers with different reading habits and tastes. But it was not just the content of books which had to adjust to suit the new readership. The form of books also had to adapt to the situation and needs of soldiers on the battlefield. In order to convince the troops to invest in buying books, the bookshops had to offer a range of cheap, easily transportable books.[44] In this sense the world war played a significant role in improving and developing the distribution methods for reading material. It contributed greatly to a change in attitudes to the forms of books, the possibilities of distributing reading material, and the nature of the target audience of the book trade market.

The world war was a factor which speeded up the intensity of reading as an activity, and it increased demand for reading material, newspapers and books alike. Moreover, if there were still some doubts in the prewar period, the world war showed indubitably that reading had become one of the basic needs of day-to-day existence in contemporary German society.

This tendency did not come to a sudden halt in the immediate postwar period. This is graphically illustrated, inter alia, by another study by Henriette Fürth examining postwar changes in the cost of living structure of the family from Frankfurt which she had studied prior to the world war. The figures that Fürth presented show that expenditure on the consumption of reading material was the only outlay in the category defined by Fürth as "expenditure on luxuries or expenditure not vital for subsistence," which after the world war made up an increasing proportion of total household expenses. In this context it is noteworthy that the only group of expenses to maintain their relative share of total expenditure in the postwar period was that of membership dues for various organizations, apparently because of the father's political activities.[45]

Additional figures from the summer of 1920, presented by Gerald Feldman and Martin Niehuss, support the perception that the increased consumption of reading material persisted after the world war. In this case the data describe the cost of living of two families, each consisting of five people, of a civil servant and a railway worker in a medium-size town. In both families, expenditure on reading material was greater, in relative terms, than that of the Frankfurt family, although their incomes were smaller. These figures would seem to provide support for a pattern in which the lower the income levels, the higher the relative proportion of expenditure on reading material.[46]

The sources we have used cannot tell us whether it was only the tumultuous political events and economic hardships which contributed in the immediate postwar period to the increased consumption of reading material. We can surmise that during this turbulent period, not only were written texts a means of preserving and transmitting information, an arena of political struggles, and a tool for negotiating the contemporary realities; they were also of importance to leisure and recreational activities, as a medium for escaping from the painful circumstances of the period. These would appear to be the main factors which contributed to the increased consumption of reading material during the world war and in the period immediately following it. It must also be pointed out that political considerations also encouraged the consumption of reading material, and especially of newspapers, which were viewed as a paramount means of propaganda.

Against this backdrop, what happened to the consumption of reading material in the course of the 1920s, at a time when reading had to compete with the new media and leisure opportunities which were becoming ever more popular?

The Second Half of the 1920s

Generally, historical research views the period between the hyperinflation of 1923 and the major economic crisis of 1929 as a relatively stable period—

the "golden years" of Weimar culture. During these years extremely detailed and systematic surveys were carried out of the consumption habits of various groups in German society, and one of the aspects examined was attitudes to reading material consumption patterns.

We will examine the data from this period from two main viewpoints. The first will attempt to analyze the developments in reading material consumption patterns relative to the period prior to the world war. The second will examine reading material expenditure compared with other spending on items such as the cinema, radio, and sports. The main database of this period is the Reich Statistics Office survey which was carried out in 1927–1928 and published in 1932.[47]

The first question to be addressed in the light of the figures in Table 2.2 is whether expenditure on reading material after the world war was higher or lower than in the period before the war. The different methods used for collecting data, as well as the change in the value of the currency and its purchasing power, make it impossible to provide a precise answer to this question. For example, a comparison of the data from the 1927–1928 Reich survey with those of the 1907 Reich survey shows that in 1907 larger sums—in both relative and absolute terms—were spent under the category including outlay on reading material. However, unlike the 1907 Reich survey, where figures on reading material consumption were recorded in a single category together with expenditure on membership dues for various organizations, in the 1927–1928 survey these expenses were recorded in separate categories. Combining the two categories of expenditure will show that total outlay on the consumption of reading material and mem-

Table 2.2

Spending on books, newspapers and magazines by family, 1927–1928

	Blue-collar workers (896)			White-collar workers (546)			Civil servants (489)		
	No. of cases	RM	Percent	No. of cases	RM	Percent	No. of cases	RM	Percent
Under 2500	83	29.30	1.3	—	—	—	—	—	—
2500–3000	252	32.92	1.2	—	—	—	—	—	—
Under 3000	—	—	—	36	35.36	1.3	28	32.41	1.2
3000–3600	292	37.80	1.2	87	44.96	1.4	68	40.43	1.2
3600–4300	177	41.85	1.1	133	51.45	1.3	96	47.39	1.2
4300–5100	84	52.31	1.0	131	60.78	1.3	81	66.32	1.4
5100–6100	—	—	—	83	71.00	1.3	81	73.65	1.3
6100–7300	—	—	—	76	102.50	1.3	79	86.73	1.3
7300–10,000	—	—	—	—	—	—	40	130.15	1.6
10,000+	—	—	—	—	—	—	25	153.33	1.3
Total	888	37.76	1.1	546	61.67	1.3	498	71.16	1.3

bership dues for various organizations was larger, in relative and absolute terms, than spending for these purposes during the prewar period. Thus if during the period before the world war the worker's family spent on average M 51.47 on this category, or around 2.80 percent of its total outlay, in the 1927–1928 survey the working class family spent RM 112.93 in a year on these items, or 3.39 percent of its total expenditure. The amounts that middle- and lower-grade civil servants' families laid out on this category during the period prior to the world war averaged M 66.88, or 2.09 percent of their total expenditure. On the other hand, according to the 1927–1928 survey the white-collar worker's family spent on average RM 121.66 or 2.58 percent on these items, while the civil servant's family spent an average of RM 121.16 (2.26 percent of their total expenditure) on the consumption of reading material and membership dues for various organizations. In other words, even if we have a problem determining whether this growth is only the result of higher prices for reading material and membership dues for various organizations, or whether it is also the upshot of increased consumption of reading material and greater involvement in the activities of various organizations, particularly professional and political organizations, or a combination of these two factors, it can definitely be stated that following the world war—at least in terms of the relative position of outlay on reading material in total expenditure—no reduction occurred in this category of spending. Moreover, there are reasonable grounds for assuming that the tendency of increased consumption of reading material which began during the prewar period and strengthened during the war and the immediate postwar period, also continued in the second half of the 1920s.

One of the main processes which strengthens this hypothesis is the change which occurred in the structure of private household expenses after the world war: in other words, the increase in fixed and optional expenses, and the reduction in expenditure on necessities, primarily food. Contemporary observers were also aware of this trend. They too argued that since there was no increase in average wages during this period, at least not in real terms, and the cost of food products did not decline, the change in the structure of private household expenditure had to be related to adjustments affecting education, culture, and leisure, primarily among the less affluent classes. A great deal of support can be found for this argument in household account books. Figures collected between 1925 and 1929 in Hamburg show, for example, that taking outlay on the consumption of reading material, membership dues for various organizations, and recreational activities per individual consumer (*Vollperson*) as 100 in Hamburg in 1925, in 1926 the corresponding figure was 107, 121 in 1927, and 147 in 1928, reaching 168 in 1929.[48] Similar trends are indicated by many other surveys of the period which were carried out by a variety of professional associations. Despite the political instability, and economic hardships of the time, many families preferred to skimp on necessities so that they could spend larger amounts on education, culture, and recreational activities.[49]

It must be emphasized that the 1927–1928 Reich study classified reading material expenditure as a subcategory, together with outlay on schooling and other training activities, of the category of cultural (*Bildung*) expenditure. The reading budget made up by far the larger part of this category—around 70 percent for blue-collar workers, white-collar workers, and civil servants, particularly with middle and lower salary levels. As income levels went up, even though the reading budget grew in absolute terms, it fell drastically in relative terms compared with the other expenses in this category. The data of the Hamburg study, which focused on needy families, show that the relative and absolute proportion of expenditure on reading material was higher in all social groups than other expenditure in the category of culture. It is possible that this relationship between the reading budget and educational spending is a result of the State's growing involvement in educational matters which released many families, particularly needy ones, from the economic burden of educating children and the concern for their future occupational prospects. However, this means that the tendency for large sums to be allocated to purposes defined as education and culture, particularly among white-collar workers and needy laborers, was in fact tantamount to increased reading budgets.

The processes and factors which also determined the nature and size of reading budgets originated in the prewar period. The tempestuous events during and immediately after the world war, as we have seen above, increased dependency on the written text and increased the consumption of reading material. This development, we would contend, was accelerated during the 1920s by the social policy of the Weimar Republic, which shortened the working day, introduced the compulsory education act, and improved workers' social welfare conditions. The inflation and unemployment of the late 1920s also contributed to increased reading activities, and in particular, as Gary Cross has shown, to the strengthening of the culture of work and spend.[50] Cost of living studies themselves, which were primarily interested in the relation between income and expenditure and especially in the structure and nature of private household expenditure, are a manifest expression of this pattern. The hyperinflation of the early 1920s, which showed that the value of money is a result of its purchasing power; the massive unemployment, which made work the difference between a self-respecting life and humiliation; and the social welfare policy which set itself the goal of improving workers' living conditions, inter alia by increasing leisure and strengthening their purchasing power, were processes which contributed to the idealization of consumption. The interwar period symbolized not only the beginning of the era of the short working day and the flourishing of the leisure and recreational culture, but primarily the transformation of consumption itself into the essence of work and of recreational activities. According to this approach, during these years consumption became a mindset which shaped a lifestyle, norms, and behavior, as well as introducing concepts which society used to interpret the reality surrounding it.[51]

What about reading budgets? Although it will be difficult for us to evaluate the rate at which spending on the consumption of reading material increased during these years, there is no reason whatsoever to assume that the growing importance of consumption in the 1920s and the change in the actual structure of consumption were not connected to the ever greater consumption of reading material at the time. In other words, the growing amounts allocated to the consumption of knowledge, culture, and leisure attest to increased consumption of reading material. Moreover reading itself, and this is a hypothesis which the household account books cannot support on their own, was a medium through which consumption could be encouraged and dependence on consumption legitimized. Substantiating this hypothesis will be something which we will address in the next two chapters.

Postwar reading budgets themselves behaved fairly similarly on all income levels and for all socioeconomic groups. In other words, outlay on reading material, in absolute terms, increased in direct proportion to income levels, while their relative position in total expenditure remained more or less fixed, at least among white-collar workers and civil servants. This situation testifies to the importance of reading among all social groups and for all income levels, and was indicative of the fact that reading in the period after the world war became one of the basic needs of day-to-day existence for all social strata. In this sense the 1920s continued the trend toward reading's expanded and reinforced status, which had begun as early as the prewar period.

The figures that we have examined from the prewar period show that at least among society's affluent strata, there were no significant differences between the consumption patterns for reading material in the big cities and smaller-scale locations, and sometimes the latter actually consumed more reading material than their bigger counterparts. Apparently this situation did not change in the wake of the world war. Data collected by the *Allgemeine freie Angestelltenbund* (AfA-Bund) association of white-collar workers, for example, show that white-collar workers spent more on newspapers and magazines in the provinces than in the big cities.[52] Among blue-collar workers the situation was somewhat different. A survey carried out among building laborers in 1929 shows that in terms of the proportion of spending on newspapers and books, there was no difference in terms of the size of the locality. However, the survey results also show that not only were the sums budgeted by building workers in the big cities for reading material needs greater than those spent in smaller locations, but in the big cities more families incurred expenditure on the consumption of reading material than in the small towns.

Other figures collected from among the families of agricultural workers in 1927 indicate that just 48 of the 130 families which took part in the survey bought a daily paper on a regular basis during the observation year. This survey's data also show that in the outlying districts of East Prussia and northwest Germany, agricultural workers consumed less reading material than their counterparts in the center and south of Germany, where agricultural workers tended to read more.[53] The building trades association survey also showed that in eastern Germany, especially East Prussia, which was an agricultural area where there were also few companies involved in the distribution of reading material, building laborers spent less on reading material than in other parts of Germany, where the proportion of total income constituted by reading budgets was similar to the average of the 1927–1928 Reich survey, i.e., 1.2 percent of total household expenses.[54]

Notwithstanding differences between consumption patterns of laborers from different occupational fields and parts of the country, as well as between the different socioeconomic groups, it can definitely be stated that in the late 1920s, even blue-collar workers tended to consume more reading material than in the prewar period, and in this sense laborers formed part of the overall trend which characterized the consumption patterns of German society during those years. Nevertheless, as in the prewar period, the impression is that the amounts budgeted for the consumption of reading material by all income levels, by all social groups, and in the various parts of the country were not particularly large.

The information available to us indicates that even in the 1920s, the reading menu of a goodly part of German society, especially those with low incomes, largely consisted of newspapers and magazines. In this sense, German society's reading material consumption patterns did not differ greatly from the situation in other countries. One of the reasons we know this is a study, published in 1933, comparing the cost of living of working-class families in a number of big cities worldwide. The cost-of-living figures collected from one hundred workers at the Ford plant in Detroit indicate, for example, that while each family spent on average $12.09 a year on buying a daily paper, forty eight families reported expenditure of just $3.04 on buying magazines, and only seven families reported spending money to buy books, totalling $2.88.[55]

As we have seen in the discussion about the book crisis, in the 1920s many critics charged that the reason for the limited consumption of books was their high price to the consumer. In 1927, the average retail shop price (*Ladenpreis*) for a book in Germany was RM 5.55. This meant that even in the second half of the 1920s, books were a product which on the whole could only be afforded by the well-off. In addition, not only was purchasing a book a relatively expensive business even for people with average incomes, but just having somewhere to keep a book and being able to read it required the presence of conditions such as a place to store books, quiet surroundings, heating, suitable lighting, and free time. Broad sections of the German populace did not yet enjoy such conditions during this time.

Despite the momentum enjoyed in the 1920s by the construction of low-cost housing and the drop in rents, the housing problem was still one that affected vast numbers of the population, particularly among the laboring classes. Overcrowding and a shortage of both beds and stoves were just some of the difficulties that typified the dire housing situation in the 1920s.[56] A study carried out by Heinrich Kautz, in which he examined the living conditions of twelve hundred miners' and steel industry families in a typical working-class community in the Ruhr, indicates that most of the houses did not have enough beds for all family members, and that it was standard for at least two people to share a bed. The same applied to heating. The ratio between the number of stoves and the number of rooms was 1:3: normally there was a stove in the kitchen, which was also used for cooking purposes.[57] Logically, it can be assumed that in such conditions it would be difficult, to say the least, to enjoy reading a book in a relaxed atmosphere in one's own home. Nevertheless, according to Kautz 16 percent of the working-class families had a bookshelf in their homes, while 10 percent of them owned a bookcase. This study also indicates that in addition to furnishings such as a sofa, a large mirror, a folding table, or a flower vase, a bookshelf and bookcase were included in the house contents which constituted the furnishings of the parlor (*gute Stube*) in blue-collar workers' houses. Kautz also argued that after the world war, a change occurred in the style of furnishing the parlor in many laborers' houses, as they replaced the dresser (*Vertikow*) with a bookcase. A survey carried out by a research group headed by Erich Fromm between 1929 and 1931 with the goal of investigating the mental world of blue- and white-collar workers of different age groups and with different political outlooks, also identified the dominance of the approach which saw book reading as a criterion of refinement in the lower-middle and working classes. In response to the question, "Do you have a favorite book?", most respondents—white- and blue-collar alike—indicated books which were generally considered works of cultural value.[58] Moreover, we also have evidence from household account books showing that low-paid workers bought books, even if the sums they laid out for this purpose were not particularly large.

It should be borne in mind that in the 1920s a positive explosion took place in ways of distributing books and newspapers, in an attempt to expand the target audience of reading material consumers. In addition to department stores offering books at tempting prices, the early 1920s witnessed the founding of book clubs (*Buchgemeinschaften*), while at the end of the decade the *Volksausgaben* or popular editions, selling at the magic price of RM 2.85, began to dominate the book market. The public libraries and commercial lending libraries were also very popular during this period. We will discuss these and other distribution methods in the coming chapters.

It would appear that despite the relatively high average price of books in the 1920s, nothing lay beyond the reach of low-income groups. The popularity of the various agents who distributed reading material in the 1920s and the possibility of buying or borrowing books at a relatively low price proves that far from books vanishing, perhaps for the first time they became part of the reading menu of broader groups of readers than in the past. In this sense, the figures about reading budgets, most of which do not distinguish between spending on buying books and expenditure on newspapers and magazines, should be interpreted with great caution. It is possible that the position of books in the reading consumption basket was actually greater than the picture painted by the household account books. In the light of all of this, how did the consumption of reading material compare with the new media and leisure-time pursuits such as films, radio, or sport?

The data from the 1927–1928 Reich survey (Table 2.3) show clearly that for all income levels and socioeconomic groups, expenditure on reading material is significantly higher, in both relative and absolute terms, than the average for the new media and leisure-time pursuits. Even among white-collar workers, who were considered the main target audience of the new media and leisure-time pursuits, there is an unmistakable preference for expenditure on reading. A similar picture is also provided by the figures from the Hamburg Statistics Office. While in the Reich survey 100 percent of the civil servants and 99 percent of the working-class families reported expenditure in the reading category, just 58 percent of the working-class families reported expenditure on the cinema, 20 percent on the radio, and 52 percent on sports. Among white-collar workers, 66 percent of the families which took part in the survey reported expenditure on the cinema, 43 percent on the radio, and 65 percent on sports. In the case of civil servants' families, 64 percent recorded expenditure on the cinema, 39 percent on the radio, and 68 percent on sports. According to the association of white-collar workers, the AfA-Bund, the adult family members, i.e., the married couple, went to the cinema or the theater once every two months on average, and only half of the 462 families which took part in this survey had a radio in the house during the 1928–1931 observation period.[59] Given these figures, were the new media and leisure-time pursuits as influential in the 1920s as is conventionally and insistently claimed—a claim which lies in the 1920s themselves?

Karl Christian Führer posed this question in an article which he published in the *Historische Zeitschrift* journal in 1996. Based on an analysis of a broad range of sources, he showed that during the Weimar Republic period the cinema, radio, or sports could not be considered to be a culture of the masses or alternatively a mass culture whose primary characteristics are individualization, standardization, and homogenization. According to Führer—and this contention is borne out by most of the private household account books—these were activities which were primarily to be found in the big cities and among the prosperous social classes.[60]

Table 2.3
Expenditure on reading material compared with outlay on cinema, radio, and sports

Income	Cinema		Radio		Sports		Newspapers and books	
	RM	Percent	RM	Percent	RM	Percent	RM	Percent
Blue-collar workers								
Below 2500	2.59	0.1	1.42	0.1	1.72	0.1	29.30	1.3
2500–3000	2.65	0.1	5.01	0.2	2.92	0.1	32.92	1.2
3000–3600	4.06	0.1	7.07	0.2	3.25	0.1	37.0	1.2
3000–3600	4.82	0.1	6.07	0.2	5.56	0.2	41.85	1.1
3600–4300	11.69	0.2	19.24	0.4	13.48	0.3	52.31	1.0
Average	4.38	0.1	6.89	0.2	4.43	0.1	37.76	1.1
White-collar workers								
Below 3000	3.70	0.1	7.01	0.3	1.23	0.1	35.36	1.3
3000–3600	4.26	0.1	9.65	0.3	6.51	0.2	44.96	1.4
3600–4300	5.47	0.1	17.57	0.4	7.60	0.2	51.45	1.3
4300–5100	6.15	0.1	19.82	0.5	13.04	0.3	60.78	1.3
5100–6100	4.81	0.1	36.11	0.7	13.58	0.2	71.00	1.3
6100 and above	11.46	0.1	35.17	0.5	29.32	0.4	102.50	1.3
Average	6.06	0.1	21.42	0.5	12.25	0.2	61.67	1.3
Civil servants								
Below 3000	2.41	0.1	9.80	0.4	3.80	0.2	32.41	1.2
3000–3600	2.95	0.1	5.04	0.1	4.28	0.1	40.43	1.2
3600–4300	3.82	0.1	12.80	0.3	5.67	0.1	47.39	1.2
4300–5100	4.73	0.1	18.13	0.4	11.51	0.2	66.32	1.4
5100–6100	6.58	0.1	26.18	0.5	13.85	0.3	73.65	1.3
6100–7300	6.25	0.1	34.02	0.6	15.89	0.2	86.73	1.3
7300–10000	4.45	0.1	23.11	0.3	36.17	0.4	130.15	1.6
10,000 and above	7.69	0.1	18.89	0.1	45.33	0.4	153.33	1.3
Average	4.85	0.1	19.12	0.3	13.72	0.2	71.16	1.3

Irrespective of whether we accept Führer's position according to which the new media and leisure-time pursuits were widespread only among a certain sector of German society and in the 1920s were activities which constituted a status symbol for the prosperous parts of society, and had still not become popular culture; or whether we argue that during those years films, radio, and sports had just begun their process of popularization, the figures available to us show that the claim frequently advanced in the 1920s, to the effect that the new media and leisure-time pursuits were eating into the expenditure on reading generally, and book reading in particular, does not hold water in light of the sources available to us. Not only were the sums of money spent on the consumption of reading material at the end of the 1920s significantly larger than expenditure on the cinema, radio, or sports; we have no proof whatsoever to the effect that such spending came at the expense of reading budgets. In addition, the figures we have show that the larger the sums spent on the cinema, radio, and sports, the more money was allocated for the consumption of reading material. We therefore conclude that the competition with the new media and leisure-time pursuits did not adversely affect the consumption of reading material, but actually increased it. The radio scripts and the literary programs on the radio, the many magazines which developed around the new media and the new leisure-time patterns, or the initiative (eventually blocked by the German Book Dealers' Association) on the part of a number of book dealers who had noticed that films based on books increased sales of the latter, to set up an organization of bookshops in the cinemas, are just a few examples of the way in which the new media and leisure-time pursuits contributed to the distribution of reading material.[61]

The figures which we have presented so far have shown that in the 1920s, the trend of continuing consumption of reading material persisted, and that the new media and leisure-time pursuits did not harm the distribution of reading material: on the contrary, they would appear to encourage and increase it. In this sense, reading became an integral part of the new consumer and leisure culture, and in the 1920s as well it remained the most common leisure activity for all social classes. Thus the contention that a nexus exists between the process of the disintegration of the bourgeoisie and the abandoning of reading does not hold water in the light of the figures from the household account books. Furthermore, the bourgeois classes—civil servants and white-collar workers alike—which allocated larger sums for the consumption of reading material than during the prewar period, and the ever greater consumption of reading material among the working classes, actually indicate a general tendency towards a strengthening of reading among all social strata.

The household account books and additional evidence from the period also make it clear that the reading menu consisted largely of newspapers and magazines, during both the pre- and postwar periods. The household account books do not provide us with details about the nature and content of reading material. However, the considerable outlay on membership dues for various unions and organizations, particularly among the low-waged, indicates that in addition to a daily paper or light magazines, reading material with a pronounced political character also formed part of these classes' reading menu. On the other hand, the sources on which we have drawn cannot provide a reply to the question of differences between the consumption habits of different groups by gender, generation, region, and religion. Despite the limitations of the sources used above, based on them we can state that, from the transition period around the turn of the century reading, or more precisely the consumption of reading material, was an object to which ever broader parts of German society devoted more and more resources. We would hypothesize that this state of affairs was helped not only by the tempestuous events during and following the world war, which increased dependence on reading as a means of transmitting knowledge, the unique value which was ascribed to reading as an expression of refinement and a skill through which education could be acquired, or reading's function as a time-passing recreational activity; but also by the ever-increasing importance of consumption in German society, primarily beginning in the last third of the nineteenth century. As of these years we witness attempts to improve the distribution systems for reading material and a change in attitudes to its target audience. These changes turned books, newspapers, and magazines into products intended for mass consumption.

What is the connection between these processes? Was this tendency of commercializing reading just a reaction to the sluggish demand for reading material among the traditional target audience of the reading material trade, a situation which forced it to seek out new markets; or was it an expression of the growing demand for reading material among new classes of readers, spurring dealers to distribute a wider range of reading material to a broader public than in the past? Irrespective of whether one alternative is more correct than the other, or both are equally applicable, these two possibilities point to a link between reading culture and consumer culture. This process, and in particular the fear of its ramifications, played a key role in generating an awareness of the critical situation of books in the wake of the world war. Nevertheless, the claims of overproduction of books, the discussions of the issue of book prices, the fear that books had lost their buying public, as well as the "midway mentality" which separated economics and culture and located books in the "halfway house" between them—these are just a few examples of the fact that even among "book people," "consumption" had become a catchall yardstick.

In conclusion, an analysis of household account books shows that the public of reading material consumers comprised all classes and social groups, and that in the 1920s the audience of readers, in practice, was larger and more varied than that for films, radio, or sports. It was reading which was the mass phenomenon of the period, and as such it was able to influence or at least reflect the patterns of behavior and lifestyles of broad social strata. Given this situation, the question is whether reading can be related to as an activity which contributed to the standardization and homogenization—or alternatively the heterogenization and individualization—of German society during these years. In the next chapters, which will examine how reading material was distributed and the link between reading and consumer culture, we will try to address this question. We will see that reading culture dovetailed neatly with the new consumer culture, which it also helped to promote. It will be our contention that the paper-swamped world to a large extent became an area where there developed a world of images and symbols of the new consumer culture, as well as providing a striking reflection of the complex and antagonistic nature of this culture.

Notes

1. David Vincent, *The Rise of Mass Literacy* (Malden: Polity Press, 2000).
2. Rolf Engelsing, *Analphabetentum und Lektüre* (Stuttgart: J.B. Metzler, 1973); Wolfgang Langenbucher, "Die Demokratisierung des Lesens in der zweiten Leserevolution," in: Hubert G. Göpfter, ed., *Lesen und Leben* (Frankfurt a.M.: Buchhändler Vereinigung, 1975), 12–35; Karl-Ernst Jeismann, "Zur Bedeutung der Bildung im 19. Jahrhundert," in: idem, and Peter Lundgreen, eds., *Handwörterbuch der deutschen Bildungsgeschichte*, vol. III. (Munich: C.H. Beck, 1987), 1–21.
3. Toni Pierenkemper, ed., *Haushalt und Verbrauch in Historischer Perspektive. Zum Wandel des privaten Verbrauchs in Deutschland im 19. und 20. Jahrhundert* (St. Katharinen: Scripta Mercaturae Verlag, 1987); idem, "Das Rechnungsbuch der Hausfrau und was wir daraus lernen können," *Geschichte und Gesellschaft* 14 (1988), 38–63; Rudolf Braun, "Einleitende Bemerkungen zum Problem der historischen Lebensstandardforschung," in: Werner Conze, and Ulrich Engelherdt, eds., *Arbeiter im Industrialisierungsprozess* (Stuttgart: Klett Cotta, 1979), 128–135.
4. Ernst Engel, *Rechnungsbuch der Hausfrau und seine Bedeutung im Wirtschaftsleben der Nation* (Berlin: Verlag von Leonahrd Simon, 1882); Rolf Engelsing, "Probleme der Lebenshaltung in Deutschland im 18. und 19. Jahrhundert," in: idem, *Zur Sozialgeschichte deutscher Mittel- und Unterschichten* (Göttingen: Vandenhoeck & Ruprecht, 1973).
5. On this: Lotte Panofski, "Die Lebenshaltung der Kohlenbergwerksarbeiter in deutsch und in polnisch Oberschlesien," Ph.D. diss., University of Cologne, 1931; Albrecht Sommer, *Lehre vom Privathaushalt* (Berlin: Junker und Dünnhaupt Verlag, 1931); Erna Meyer, *Der neue Haushalt. Ein Wegweiser zu wirtschaftlicher Hausführung* (Stuttgart: Franckh'sche Verlagshandlung, 1927); Warren G. Breckmann, "Disciplining Consumption: The Debate about Luxury in Wilhelmine Germany, 1890–1914," *Journal of Social History* 24 (1990–1991), 485–505.
6. Dieter Dowe, ed., *Erhebung von Wirtschaftsrechnungen minderbemittelter Familien im Deutschen Reich (erst 1909). 320 Haushaltungsrechnungen von Metallarbeitern* (first published in 1909) (Bonn: Dietz Verlag, 1981).
7. *Die Lebenshaltung von 2000 Arbeiter- Angestellten- und Beamtenhaushaltungen. Erhebung von Wirtschaftsrechnung im Deutschen Reich vom Jahre 1927/8.* Einzelschriften zur Statistik des Deutschen Reiches (Berlin: Hobbing Verlag, 1932). In 1937, another official survey was carried out by the Reich Statistics Office, with data being collected from eight hundred locations. The study covered some three thousand families with monthly incomes of under RM 150. Partial survey results were published in 1939, with the remainder being processed and republished in 1960 only.
8. Ernst Engel, *Lebenskosten belgischer Arbeiter Familien* (Dresden: C. Heinrich, 1895).
9. Ernst Engel, *Werth des Menschen* (Berlin: Verlag von Leonhard Simon, 1883).
10. Carle C. Zimmerman, "Ernst Engel's Law of Expenditures for Food," *The Quarterly Journal of Economics* 47 (1932–1933), 78–101.
11. Adolf Günther, "Die Folgen des Krieges für Einkommen und Lebenshaltung der mittleren Volksschichten Deutschlands," in: Rudolf Meerwarth, Adolf Günther, and Waldemar Zimmermann, *Die Einwirkung des Kriegs auf Bevölkerungsbewegung, Einkommen und Lebenshaltung in Deutschland* (Stuttgart: Deutsche Verlag, 1932), 127.
12. Reihard Spree, "Klassen und Schichtenbildung im Spiegel des Konsumentenverhaltens individueller Haushalte zu Beginn des 20. Jahrhunderts—Eine clusteranalytische Untersuchung," in: Toni Pierenkemper, ed., *Haushalt und Verbrauch in historischer Perspektive. Zum Wandel des privaten Verbrauchs in Deutschlands im 19. und 20. Jahrhundert* (St. Katharinen: Scripta Mercaturae Verlag, 1987), 56–81; Armin Triebel, "Vom Konsum der Klasse zur Vielfalt der Stile: Haushaltbudgetgierung seit der ersten Hälfte des 20. Jahrhunderts," *Historical Social Reaserch* 22 (1997), 81–105.
13. Stephan Leibfried, "Existenzminimum und Fürsorgerichtsätze in der Weimarer Republik," *Jahrbuch der Sozialarbeit* 4 (1981), 469–523.

14. Henriette Fürth, *Der Haushalt vor und nach dem Krieg. Dargestellt an Hand eines mittelbürgerlichen Budgets* (Jena: Gustav Fischer, 1922), 23.
15. Werner Sombart, *Liebe, Luxus und Kapitalismus. Über die Entstehung der modernen Welt aus dem Geist der Verschwendung* (Berlin: Wagenbach, 1992), 85–89.
16. Johannes Müller, *Deutsche Kulturstatistik* (Jena: Gustav Fischer, 1928), 7.
17. Armin Triebel, "*Zwei Klassen und die Vielfalt des Konsums. Haushaltsbuetierung bei abhängig Erwerbstätigen in Deutschland im ersten Drittel des 20. Jahrhundert,*" 2 vol. Ph.D. diss., Free University of Berlin, 1991.
18. Spree, Klassen und Schichtenbildung.
19. Spree, Klassen und Schichtenbildung, 51.
20. Reinhard Spree, "Modernisierung des Konsumverhaltens deutscher Mittel- und Unterschichten während der Zwischenkriegzeit," *Zeitschrift für Soziologie* 14 (1985), 400–410.
21. "Breslauer Haushaltungsrechnungen aus den Jahren 1907 und 1908," *Breslauer Statistik* XXX (1912), 152–264; Gerhard Albrecht, "Breslauer Haushaltsrechnungen," *Concordia. Zeitschrift der Zentralstelle für Volkswohlfahrt* 12 (1912), 417–419.
22. Alfons Kraziza, *259 deutsche Haushaltungsbücher geführt von Abonnenten der Zeitschrift "Nach Feierabend" in den Jahren 1911–1913* (Leipzig: Verlag Bernhard Meyer, 1915), 78.
23. Karl von K.... "Wirtschaftsrechnungen," *Zeitschrift für die Gesamte Staatswissenschaft* 62 (1906), 710–738.
24. Dieter Dowe, Erhebungen von Wirtschaftsrechnungen von Metallarbeiter (first published 1909) (Bonn: Dietz, 1981).
25. Ludwig Heyden, *Wirtschaftsrechnungen von unteren Post- und Telegraphenbeamten* (Berlin: Verband der unteren Post- und Telegraphenbeamten, 1916).
26. Karl von K., Wirtschaftsrechnungen.
27. Adolf Weber, *Die Großstadt und ihre sozialen Probleme* (Leipzig: Quellen & Meyer, 1908), 20; cf. also: Georg Simmel, "Die Großstädte und das Geistesleben," in: idem, *Das Individuum und die Freiheit* (Frankfurt a.M.: S. Fischer, 1993).
28. Ernst Herbig, "Wirtschaftsrechnungen Saarbrücker Bergleute," *Zeitschrift für das Berg- Hütten- und Salinenwesen im Preußischen Staate* 60 (1912), 451–613.
29. Fritz Tangermann, "Die Landgemeinde Belsdorf am Anfang des 20. Jahrhunderts," Ph.D. diss., University of Leipzig (1905), 98.
30. Ksrziza, *259 deutsche* Haushaltungsbücher, 158.
31. Tangermann, Die Landgemeinde Belsdorf.
32. Rudolf Schenda, *Volk ohne Buch. Studien zur Sozialgeschichte der populären Lesestoffe 1770–1910* (Frankfurt a.M.., Vittorio, 1970); idem, *Die Lesestoffe der kleinen Leute* (Munich: C.H. Beck, 1976); Roland Fullerton, "Creating a Mass Book Market in Germany: The Story of the Colporteur Novel 1870–1890," *Journal of Social History* 11 (1977), 265–284; idem, "Toward a Commercial Popular Culture in Germany: The Development of Pamphlet Fiction, 1871–1914," *Journal of Social History* 13 (1979), 489–513.
33. Dieter Langewiesche, and Karl Schönhoven, "Arbeiterbibliotheken und Arbeiterlektüre im Wilhelminischen Deutschland," *Archiv für Sozialgeschichte* 16 (1976), 191–194; Peter Vodosek, *Arbeitsbibliotheken und öffentliche Bibliotheken. Zur Geschichte ihrer Beziehungen von der ersten Hälften des 19. Jahrhunderts bis 1933* (Berlin: Dt. Bibliotheksverband, 1975); Frank Heidenreich, *Arbeiterkulturbewegung und Sozialdemokratie in Sachsen vor 1933* (Köln: Böhlau, 1996).
34. Erna Meyer-Pollack, "Der Haushalt eines höheren Beamten in den Jahren 1880 bis 1906," in: Franz Eulenburg, ed., *Kosten der Lebenshaltung in deutschen Großstädten. Ost- und Norddeutschland* (Munich: Duncker & Humblot, 1915), 1–92.
35. "Zwei Wirtschaftsrechnungen von Familien höherer Beamter" *Sonderhefte 3 Reichs-Arbeitsblatt* (1911).
36. Henritte Fürth, *Ein mittelbürgerliches Budget über einen zehnjährigen Zeitraum* (Jena: Gustav Fischer Verlag, 1907).
37. Meyer-Pollack, Der Haushalt, 65.
38. Schenda, *Volk ohne Buch,* ch. VII.

39. Engelsing, *Analphabetentum und Lektüre*, 135.
40. Käthe Lux, *Studien über die Entwicklung der Warenhäuser in Deutschland* (Jena: Gustav Fischer Verlag, 1910), 94–142; Rudi Klotzbach, "Deutsche Warenhäuser als Buchhändler," Ph.D. diss., University of Leipzig, 1932; "Verkauf von Büchern in Warenhäusern," in: Sächsische Staatsarchiv Leipzig, Börsenverein des Deutschen Buchhändlers zu Leipzig, Findbuch, No. 785.
41. Gerald Feldmann, *The Great Disorder. Politics, Economics and Society in German Inflation 1914–1924* (Oxford: Oxford University Press, 1993); idem, *Army, Industry and Labour in Germany 1914–1928* (Princeton: Princeton University Press, 1966); Jürgen Kocka, *Klassengesellschaft im Krieg. Deutsche Sozialgeschichte 1914–1918* (Göttingen: Vandenhoeck & Ruprecht, 1973); Volker Ullrich, *Kriegsalltag. Hamburg im Ersten Weltkrieg* (Cologne: Promet Verlag, 1982).
42. Waldemar Zimmermann, "Die Veränderungen der Einkommens- und Lebensverhältnisse der Deutschen Arbeiter durch den Krieg," in: Rudolf Meerwarth, Adolf Günther, and Waldemar Zimmermann, *Die Einwirkung des Krieges auf Bevölkerungsbewegung, Einkommen und Lebenshaltung in Deutschland* (Stuttgart: Deutsche Verlag, 1932), 436.
43. Ernst Umlauff, *Beiträge zur Statistik des Deutschen Buchhandels* (Leipzig: Verlag des Börsenvereins der Deutschen Buchhändler, 1934), 78.
44. Birgit Welt, "Bücher ins Feld! Die literarische Versorgung der Soldaten im Ersten Weltkrieg," *Buchhandelsgeschichte* 10 (1995), 1–16; Inge Ehringhaus, *Die Lektüre unserer Frontsoldaten im Weltkrieg* (Berlin: Junker und Dünnhaupt, 1941); Bertold Hack, "Der Bahnhofsbuchhandel vor und im 1. Weltkrieg," *Der neue Vertrieb* 551 (1972), 1–28.
45. Henriette Fürth, *Der Haushalt vor und nach dem Krieg*, 22.
46. Gerald Feldman and Martin Niehuss, "Haushaltsrechnungen aus der Inflationszeit. Material und Interpretationen," in: Gerald Feldman, ed., *Die Anpassung an die Inflation* (Berlin: Walter de Gruzter, 1986), 265–277.
47. Cf. also Ute Schneider, "Lektürebudgets in Privathaushalten der zwanziger Jahre," *Gutenberg Jahrbuch* 10 (1996), 341–351.
48. "Die Lebenshaltung der wirtschaftlich schwachen Bevölkerung in Hamburg in den Jahren 1925 bis 1929, insbesondere im Jahr 1927," in: *Statistische Mitteilungen über den hamburgischen Staat* No. 26 (1931), 35.
49. Herbert Eichmann, "Darstellung und Analyse der Strukturwandlungen des Massenverbrauchs in Deutschland," Ph.D. diss., University Münster, 1955; Sandra J. Coyner, "Class Consciousness and Consumption: The New Middle Class during the Weimar Republic," *Journal of Social History* 10 (1977), 310–331.
50. Gary Cross, *Time and Money. The Making of Consumer Culture* (London: Routledge, 1993), 13.
51. Rudy Koshar, ed., *Histories of Leisure* (Oxford: Berg, 2002); Richard Butsch, ed., *For Fun and Profit. The Transformation of Leisure into Consumption* (Philadelphia, Tempel University Press, 1990); Martha Olney, *Buy Now Pay Later* (Chapel Hill: The University of North Carolinia Press, 1991); Don Slater, *Consumer Culture & Modernity* (Cambridge: Polity Press, 1997).
52. *Was verbrauchen die Angestellten? Ergebnisse der dreijährigen Haushaltungsstatistik des Allgemeinen Freien Angestelltenbundes* (Berlin: Freier Volksverlag, 1931), 60.
53. Max Hofer, *Die Lebenshaltung des Landarbeiters. Wirtschaftsrechnungen von 130 Landarbeiterfamilien* (Berlin: Landvolk Verlag, 1930), 72 and 91; cf. with Wilhelm Bernier, *Die Lebenshaltung, Lohn und Arbeitsverhältnisse von 145 deutschen Landarbeiterfamilien* (Berlin: Enckehaus, 1931).
54. *Die Lebenshaltung der Bauarbeiter nach Wirtschaftsrechnungen aus dem Jahre 1929* (Berlin: Deutscher Bauwerksbund, 1931), 114–115.
55. *Beitrag zur Frage der internationalen Gegenüberstellung der Lebenshaltungskosten* (Genf: Internationales Arbeitsamt, 1933), 198; for the situation in England: Richard Hoggart, *The Uses of Literacy. Aspects of Working Class Life, with Special References to Publications and Entertainments* (London: Chatto and Windus, 1957).
56. Helene Wesel, *Lebenshaltung aus Fürsorge und aus Erwerbstätigkeit* (Berlin: R. Müller, 1931).

57. Heinrich Kautz, "Die Industriefamilie als Wirtschaftsverband," in: Theodor Bauer, ed., *Sozialrechtliches Jahrbuch* Vol. II (Mannheim: J. Beusheimer, 1931), 183–210.
58. Erich Fromm, *Arbeiter und Angestellte am Vorabend des Dritten Reiches. Eine sozialpsychologische Untersuchung* (Munich: Dtv, 1983), 150–157.
59. *Was verbrauchen, 30;* cf. also Otto Suhr, *Die Lebenshaltung der Angestellten* (Berlin: Freier Volksverlag, 1928), 24.
60. Karl Christian Führer, "Auf dem Weg zur 'Massenkultur'? Kino und Rundfunk in der Weimarer Republik," *Historische Zeitschrift* 262 (1996), pp. 329–381; idem, "A Medium of Modernity? Broadcasting in Weimar Germany 1923–1932," *The Journal of Modern History* 69 (1997), 722–753.
61. Stephan Füssell, "Das Buch in der Medienkonkurrenz der zwanziger Jahre," *Gutenberg Jahrbuch* 10 (1996), 322–340; Wolfram Wessels, "Die Neuen Medien und die Literatur," in: Bernhard Weyergraf, ed., *Literatur der Weimarer Republik 1918–1933* (Munich: Hanser Verlag, 1995), 65–98; Eve Rosenhaft, "Lesewut, Kinosucht, Radiotismus: Zur (geschlechter-) politischen Relevanz neuerer Massenmedien in den 1920'er Jahren," in: Alf Lüdtke, Inge Marßolek, and Adelheid v. Saldern, eds., *Amerikanisierung. Traum und Alptraum im Deutschland des 20. Jahrhunderts* (Stuttgart: Franz Steiner Verlag, 1996), 119–143; Paul F. Lazarfeld, *Radio and the Printed Page* (New York: Arno Press, 1971, first published 1940).

Chapter III

From the Commercialization of Reading to Commercializing Reading

Consumption is far more than an act that relates to a particular socioeconomic structure, or the last, minor link in a process which begins with production. Rather, as argued by several researchers into consumer culture, the act of consumption is what determines production, and as such it constitutes one of the central factors that propel forward the process of modernization. According to this approach, logically and historically the Industrial Revolution is the outcome of a consumer revolution which preceded it or was at the very least a significant factor in its development.[1] But even if we cannot decide which came first—demand or supply—or whether supply determines demand or vice versa, it would appear that the transition, according to Georg Simmel, between a barter economy and a cash economy or, in Rolf Engelsing's terms, between the autarchic private household and one based on the income-versus-expenditure formula,[2] turned consumption into a culture that molded the norms of social behavior and dictated the set of concepts through which individuals interpret the reality to which they are subject, as well as the limits of individuals' expectations and visions in society.[3] Against this background, the advanced social legislation, as well as the inflation and unemployment of the 1920s were factors which reinforced rather than weakened the consumer ethos.[4] From this point of view, the trend highlighted in the chapter on reading budgets, involving an increase in the consumption of reading material, formed part of the overall tendency toward greater commercialization and an increase in consumption on all fronts—a tendency which began to pick up speed in Germany at the end of the nineteenth century. However, the presentation on reading budgets also outlined a more compelling argument, to the effect that reading was not just part of this process, but actually contributed to its acceleration.

The process by which the reading public expanded and reading became the norm among all social classes made reading one of the key elements that contributed to the process of modernization of everyday life. In this sense, reading was an activity which had the power to contribute to the process of standardization and homogenization of society. At the same time, it could also bring about an awareness of social disparities and feelings of frustration based on an inability to make wishes come true. But there was more: the process of democratization of reading, and the way that it became an intimate activity belonging to the private domain, made it practically impossible to control. Questions such as: Does somebody read? What has a person read? How does that person read? Or what kind of reaction is there to reading material? are issues over which there is no control. For this reason, reading cannot be considered a neutral medium that mediates between, or is used as a tool by, groups with different vested interests—political, cultural, or economic—to manipulate broad-based social strata, but rather must be viewed as an autonomous activity in which the public of readers has a status equal to that of those who publish reading material. What we will be contending here is that reading became an activity with the potential to foster new needs and mold the expectations of broad sectors of the population. Furthermore, the autonomous and intimate nature of reading shows it to have been an activity which enabled readers to express their diverse desires, sometimes irrespective of their specific social status.

Thus the need for a medium which would address the general public of individuals, combined with the technological developments which made both the manufacturing and the distribution processes better and cheaper, led to the creation of a diverse reading culture which not only served different cultural, commercial, and political interests, but also blurred social differences. At the same time it also awakened and provided an expression of the unique consciousness of individuals, social groups, and the entire spectrum of areas of interest, vested and otherwise. As will be shown below, these conflicting characteristics of reading culture played a key role in determining hierarchical attitudes to it. Book reading was considered an expression of refinement, self-restraint, and a pyramid-shaped social order at whose apex there stood the educated male bourgeoisie, while the reading of newspapers and, primarily, magazines was associated with the creation of a faceless mass society and an unbridled addiction to consumption.[5] The present chapter will trace the process responsible for the emergence of this hierarchical view of reading—in other words, the way that reading became part of and contributed to the development of the new consumer culture, which started to become a dominant force in Germany in particular in the wake of World War I. We will first describe the different methods of distribution for newspapers and magazines, showing how the process of commercializing the distribution of reading material changed attitudes regarding target audiences for newspapers and magazines. We will then try to see how this process of commercialization penetrated the reading culture itself and turned it into one of the key agents of the new consumer culture. The end of this chapter will discuss reactions to this process as expressed in criticism of newspaper reading and the differentiation between book reading and newspaper reading.

The Commercialization of Reading

During the eighteenth century, newspapers and magazines began to consolidate their position as a key means of conveying information as well as agents in the dissemination of values and lifestyles among disparate social groups.[6] It would be difficult, for example, to imagine the Enlightenment movement, whose moral and educational nature encouraged the distribution of reading material, without the existence of its periodicals. At first these publications appeared in Latin, and were intended primarily for a learned male audience. However, once the newspapers and periodicals began to appear in German, their target audience also expanded. This process was associated with the emergence of new types of newspapers. Salient examples of this development include the light entertainment magazines (*Unterhaltungszeitschriften*), the homiletic weeklies, and the fashion magazines which began to appear in Germany in the second half of the eighteenth century.[7] Unlike many other contemporary publications, these journals no longer targeted the educated male populace, but rather the bourgeoisie, and in particular the women of the bourgeoisie.[8] In the course of the nineteenth century, we observe a strengthening of this tendency toward the broadening of newspapers' target audience, which Habermas saw as an expression of structural change in the bourgeois public sphere.[9] Beginning in the 1830s, the political press also started to become a more dominant force in Germany. In addition to technological advances and the development of trade, other factors which spurred newspapers to look for new groups of readers included the growing demand for democratization, the idea of nationalism, the easing of censorship, and the elimination of various taxes on newspapers following the 1848 revolutions and above all after the unification of Germany. Both newspapers and magazines were now able to discover their magnetic power as a medium capable of attracting a large audience.

This development is aptly illustrated by the family magazines (*Familienblätter*). These periodicals not only presented the family ideal: they also addressed a variety of issues relating to family life, with the goal of showing every member of the household how to contribute to family happiness. *Die Gartenlaube*, founded in 1853, is perhaps the best known of these periodicals, whose readership was primarily made up of women. Over twenty years, the *Gartenlaube*'s circulation expanded from 5,000 in 1854 to 460,000 in 1873, with various estimates putting its actual readership at two million.[10] However, it was not until the end of the nineteenth century, following the establishment of the German nation-state, the removal of various limits on the distribution of newspapers, the reduction in the price of paper, and the improvement of printing techniques, lighting, the media, and transport, that the breakthrough was made to the mass distribution of reading material generally, and of newspapers and magazines specifically. During these years we note the rapid development of a dense distribution network for newspapers and periodicals. This development is one of the most striking expressions of the process of popularization of reading culture. Furthermore, as will be seen below, not only did the improvement and expansion of reading-matter distribution techniques demonstrate a new perception of the target audience for reading material, reinforcing economic ways of thinking about reading culture: they also made the distribution points for reading material into "sites" where readers from different social groups, irrespective of their specific social status, could meet and move freely.[11] From the beginning of the twentieth century onward, "reading sites," i.e., the distribution points of reading material where the paths of readers from different social strata crossed, became an integral part of the modern, primarily urban, landscape. This development was reflected most conspicuously by distribution methods such as bookshops at railway stations, as well as kiosks and street newspaper vendors. These methods for distributing reading material constituted part of the process by which the consumer society came into its own, acting as landmarks that helped readers to navigate their way through the developing space of modern life.

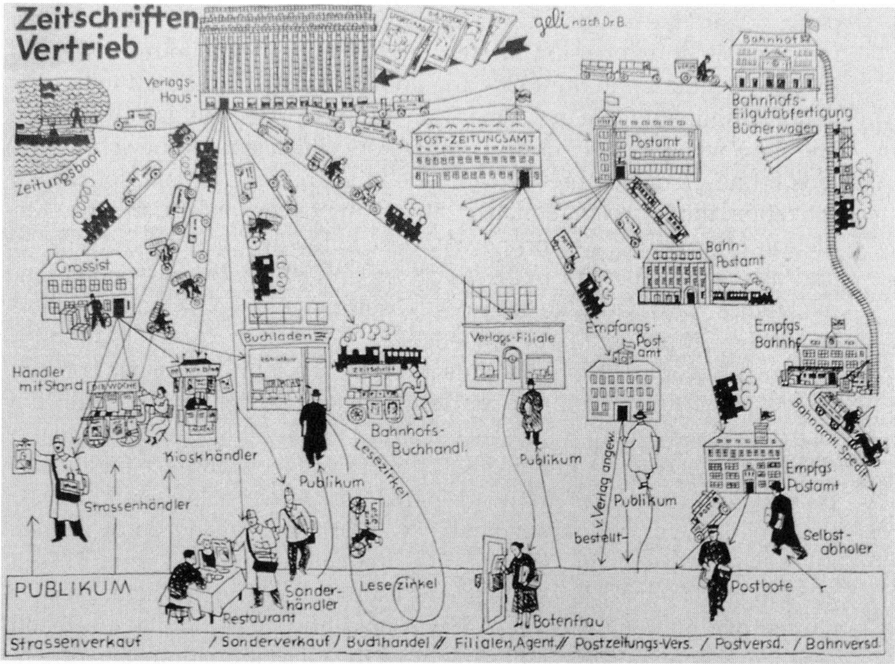

Picture 4: Dissemination network of newspapers

Book Peddling (*Kolportagehandel*)

In addition to bookshops, which were considered the primary distribution channels for reading material, in the course of the nineteenth century other—in part new—outlets for reading material developed apace.[12] Unlike the bookshops, whose traditional target audience was the affluent bourgeoisie, these other distribution agents saw the whole of society as their potential target audience. The book peddling trade (*Kolportagehandel*), or as it preferred to call itself the "book and newspaper trade" (*Buch- und Zeitschriftenhandel*), is perhaps the best known and best documented example of this development.[13]

In contrast to the bookshops, whose "bourgeois" target audience had to come to a shop in order to buy reading material, the "book and newspaper trade" turned this marketing method on its head, thereby presenting an innovative view of the target audience for reading material. Rather than waiting for buyers to come to the shop, the book-peddling companies sent their representatives out, mainly to the small towns and rural areas. These salesmen then went from house to house, distributing catalogues and samples of reading material, normally to the women who spent most of their time at home, and getting them to take out subscriptions to newspapers, magazines, encyclopedias, cheap novels, and other printed matter. The "book and newspaper trade" comprised two main divisions, differentiated by the reading material distributed by them and their methods of payment. The "traveling and mail order book business" specialized in distributing encyclopedias, dictionaries, and classical literature whose high price forced salesmen to adopt the "buy now, pay later" system for books. For example, between 1885 and 1893, traveling book salesmen distributed a total of 143,000 copies of Meyer's Comprehensive Encyclopedia (*Meyers Großes Konservationslexikon*) for a total of 24.51 million marks, as well as 38,000 copies of Meyer's Compact Encyclopaedia for a total of 900,000 marks.[14] In contrast, the magazine trade, which made up most of this business, focused on the distribution of newspapers and magazines for which customers were asked to pay cash when they took out a subscription.

The agents' vested interest in getting subscribers to sign, and the fact that they came to the reader's front door and had a personal link with subscribers, were also factors which convinced many publishing houses to use this marketing method. Another aspect was the fact that, in addition to companies which specialized in distributing reading material using the direct marketing method, there were emerging publishers whose publications were not available in the shops, only through signing a deal with the publisher or his representatives. From the middle of the nineteenth century onward, the number of companies involved in this kind of business increased steadily. In 1869 there were 219 companies involved in this domain; by 1875 their numbers had swelled to 854 (589 shops, 193 publishers, 72 shops and publishers combined), and in 1890 the figure increased further to 1,183 (998 shops, 135 publishers, and 60 combined). The number of those employed in this field in the 1890s has been estimated at 26,000, and at the end of the 1920s at 38,000 individuals.[15]

The so-called book and newspaper trade managed to expand the target audience for reading material well beyond those social classes who frequented the bookshops, quickly becoming one of the biggest distribution agents of reading material. In 1932 it was estimated that the turnover of this commercial sector was around 150 million marks—around a quarter of the total turnover of the entire book trade market.[16] However, since the "book and newspaper trade" specialized in the distribution of popular reading material, and the motivation which drove its distribution agents was financial gain, this trade was accused of distributing pulp and trashy fiction. As in other similar cases, those involved in the book and newspaper trade argued that they were not responsible for generating the demand for such dubious reading material, but simply distributed it. Or as the literary historian Rudolf Schenda put it, the "book and newspaper trade was not the mother of the demand for pulp fiction, merely its nanny."[17] Emil Niewöhner, in his 1934 book on the origins of the "book and newspaper trade," even argued that the importance of the latter was in fact to be found in its contribution to expanding readerships and increasing the public's growing dependence on reading. According to Niewöhner, increasing the consumption of reading material and generating the need to read would actually pave the path to improving this readership's reading tastes.[18]

This pragmatic approach to the issue of distributing what were considered inferior works was widespread among other agents involved in disseminating reading material that was popular with broad sectors of society. What is interesting in this approach, which distinguished between reading as a neutral activity that deciphers symbols printed on paper and reading material as such, is that it saw the purpose of disseminating reading material as being to foster and increase dependence on reading, from the outset relinquishing any pretension to determining on readers' behalf what they were allowed to or should read. According to this approach, increasing dependence on reading by turning the reading public into a public of consumers of reading would also help advance attempts to improve the reading tastes of the general public. Consumption, therefore, was here perceived as an activity with the potential to spur readers on to try new reading experiences, which might make them more selective and discriminating, and not as an activity which blunts the minds of a mass readership. This optimistic view of consumption was one of the fundamental constituents driving the process of commercialization of reading forward, and it also helped to make reading into a commercializing activity. However, the "book and newspaper trade" did not enjoy an unchallenged status in the area of distributing reading material generally, and journals and magazines specifically. The "magazine subscription club" (*Lesezirkel*) that came into being at the beginning of the eighteenth century continued throughout the nineteenth and twentieth centuries to retain its position as an important distribution agent, primarily for the family magazines and illustrated weeklies.[19]

The "Magazine Subscription Club" (*Lesezirkel*)

The "magazine subscription club" or "reading circle" distributed reading material using the subscription system. However, in contrast to the conventional subscription system, under which the paper became readers' property, the "magazine subscription club" operated according to an entirely different principle. The journals and magazines remained the property of those who promoted the "magazine subscription club": in return for payment, they were lent to subscribers. For their part, readers undertook to return the reading material to the club after a specified time. In this way, the material could be circulated to other magazine subscription club subscribers. This method allowed readers to enjoy reading a wide range of magazines at a lower cost than buying them outright or subscribing personally to each individual magazine. This system of distribution, based on recognition of the fact that a magazine loses its value once it has been read, operated according to the principle of "recycling reading"—if we can so dub the principle underlying this distribution method. Thus instead of being thrown away after being read, magazines enjoyed an extended life cycle, being exchanged between readers and read over and over again until there was no further demand for them. In certain cases, journals' life cycles were so long that publications that came out at Christmas only reached the last subscribers at Easter.

At a time when a journal was an expensive item and reading an activity engaged in by a select class of the literate, the magazine subscription club was a convenient and cheap way of supplying the growing demand for reading material. It formed part of the activities of the reading societies (*Lesegesellschaften*), the lending libraries (*Leihbibliotheken*), and the reading rooms (*Lesekabinette*) which in the course of the eighteenth century became extremely popular with the up-and-coming bourgeoisie.[20] Thus the magazine subscription club was a typical *bürgerlich* phenomenon, which operated on a commercial footing. However, as the price of journals and magazines went down significantly and the possibilities of obtaining reading material increased, the magazine subscription club became a phenomenon characteristic specifically of the less affluent parts of society. It was in particular in the small towns and rural areas of Germany where it was still relatively difficult to obtain reading material, and the demand for an up-to-date copy of each journal was not particularly great, that this method of distribution was extremely successful. In addition, the principle of "recycling reading" actually had many advantages for guest houses, hairdressers, doctors' surgeries, lawyers' offices: in short, anywhere with waiting rooms for a random public drawn from all social strata. In those locations, it was important to avoid accumulating magazines which would age rapidly and become out of date. The magazine subscription club solved this problem. It also offered subscribers journals which were in demand, rebound in order to help preserve them. This way of distributing journals shows how disparate social groups could read the same journals and magazines. Thus an entire range of social strata participated in popular reading culture which was not, therefore, the exclusive province of the weakest or most vulnerable social groups as is often thought. Bookshops at railway stations, which will be examined below, are yet another example which gives credence to this thesis.

At the end of the nineteenth century, Germany had some twelve hundred companies involved in distributing periodicals using the magazine subscription club method. For most of them, a thousand or so, this was an ancillary activity. During the first third of the twentieth century, and in particular during the period of economic upheaval of the 1920s, this method of distribution was further refined, until in 1937 it was estimated that Germany had some three to four hundred companies that specialized in distributing periodicals using the magazine subscription club method.[21]

During the transitional period between the nineteenth and twentieth centuries, many companies started to offer "magazine subscription club" services as a way of advertising. Since the magazine subscription club rebound the journals—on average, nine to ten issues were included in a single volume—it could add advertisements (*Inseraten*) to the new volume, or they could be stuck on the cover. This tendency led to clashes with the publishing houses, which complained that the magazine subscription club companies were changing the magazines' external appearance. Publishers were not, however, just afraid that their bargaining power with advertisers would be weakened: they also argued that the principle of "recycling reading" would make it impossible to increase magazines' print runs. On the other hand, publishers knew that the principle of recycling reading extended the magazine's life span, maintaining its advertising power over an extended period. This situation, which the publishers were able to exploit when bargaining with their various advertisers, reflects the disparity between the number of copies of a particular paper printed and the actual size of its readership. In other words, the print run of a particular newspaper or magazine cannot be the sole indicator of its popularity. As a result, when evaluating the popularity of a particular publication, in addition to the number of copies printed it is necessary to take into account other factors, including methods of distribution and the locales where it is read.

The Mail

In addition to the "book and newspaper trade" and the "magazine subscription clubs," the mail, particularly after the unification of Germany in 1871, became a key distribution method for newspapers and magazines. Not only did the postal network help to maintain contact between the publishing houses and the various agents who distributed the reading material; it also mediated between the publishers and their readers. In this case, the publishers bypassed the services of the wholesale trade, instead themselves signing up subscribers, normally through female sales agents (*Botenfrauen*), with the newspapers being mailed directly to readers' homes.[22] Thus since the postal service acted as a body linking publishers and readers, it had a clear vested interest in expanding readerships and encouraging the consumption of newspapers and magazines. This situation was manifestly reflected in the fact that postal agencies in various areas themselves organized magazine subscription clubs (*Lesezirkel*) and passed the papers around between their readers.

According to official German Postal Authority figures, in 1871 a total of 203 million copies of newspapers were sent by mail; in 1900 this figure rose to 1,176 million, peaking in 1921 at 2,733 million newspapers and magazines. It would appear that the main factors which led to a drop in the number of papers sent by mail during the 1920s were the increase in postage costs and competition with alternative methods of distribution. In 1932, the number of papers sent by mail plummeted to 1,590 million, with figures in the 1930s remaining steady at around 1,600 million.[23] The postal service was therefore the primary distributor of newspapers and magazines. However, this was no neutral distributor of reading material. As an official authority, the postal service was a patent example of the State's diverse vested interests in increasing consumption generally, and in the case under consideration the consumption of papers and magazines specifically.

Railway Bookshops

The development of the German railway network in the second half of the nineteenth century was another significant factor which contributed to the distribution of reading material. The length of track and the number of people using Germany's railway system experienced linear growth in the nineteenth century. In 1880 the railways carried 0.145 billion passengers. In 1900 their numbers reached 0.627 billion; by 1910 the figure was 1.121 billion, and in 1925 the number of passengers reached 2.1 billion.[24] The development of the railways not only facilitated the transfer of information and goods between different areas; it also led to the creation of a new readership—the traveling public. The railways, and in particular the railway station, became a meeting place for people drawn from all social strata. These people needed information about destinations, and in particular reading material in order to help deal with the tedium of railway journeys.[25] Identifying this tendency, bookseller Carl Schmitt began selling papers at the Heidelberg railway station as early as 1854. In 1876 he sold the prestigious university bookshop owned by him in order to devote himself full-time to the bookshop at the railway station. Within two years he opened branches at other stations in the state of Baden. Soon shops and stalls selling reading material were introduced at other railway stations throughout Germany, normally by publishers and highly respected bookshops in search of new and profitable channels for distributing reading material. An example is the Brockhaus publishing house, which in the 1870s started to organize the selling of reading material at railway stations in the city of Leipzig. But the most famous and important company to become involved in the business of selling reading material at railway stations was the George Stilke publishing house (1872), which specialized in law and jurisprudence books and also brought out the important National Liberal periodical, *Preußische Jahrbücher*. In 1882 Stilke was awarded the concession to sell reading material at the city of Berlin's railway stations, and it quickly extended its operations to railway stations all over Northern Germany. According to various estimates, Stilke Publishers owned some 40 percent of the bookshops at railway stations throughout Germany.[26]

Around the turn of the century, the number of companies involved in distributing reading material at railway stations throughout the entire country was estimated at around 200, a figure which was thought to be around 250 in the postwar period. According to German Railways (*Reichsbahngesellschaft*) statistics, some 800–900 of its railway stations apparently had sales outlets for reading material.[27] In 1931 the turnover of railway station bookshops was estimated at RM 22,995,990, a figure which was apparently lower than this commercial sector's real turnover. During the 1920s the pages of the official newspaper of railway bookshops, *Der Bahnhofbuchhandel*, frequently reflected far more complaints about the unrealistic rents that the railway administration charged bookshops at railway stations than claims about travellers giving up reading or declining revenues from sales of reading material as the factors threatening the economic survival of these shops.

Although originally rail passengers came primarily from the affluent classes, the first railway bookshops concentrated on selling cheap reading material considered to be light reading. Apart from timetables, maps, pictures, and postcards, these shops and mobile vending stalls primarily offered newspapers, magazines, and entertaining, light fiction.[28] These bookshops, which saw themselves as a politically neutral body serving an anonymous target audience irrespective of religion, class, or political views, and as being required to meet Mr. Everyman's reading needs, sought to apply the broadest possible common denominator in serving the diverse public that frequented the railway stations. This stance was also encouraged by the leases between the Railway Administration and the railway bookshops, forbidding the latter to sell writings of a party political nature or what was considered immoral literature. That was the reason why, for instance, the distribution of socialist newspapers in railway stations was forbidden until November 1918. The German State questioned the loyalty and affiliation of socialist as well as other groups, especially Catholic ones. These groups were even considered to be "Reichsfeinde" (enemies of the State), and the exclusion of socialist literature from the public sphere was just one of the measures taken against them. In this sense, the "depoliticization" of the reading material in railway stations not only contributed to the view that the travelling public comprised reading-material consumers whom one did not have to educate; it also facilitated the process of nation-state building in Germany, whereby citizens were to become loyal patriots devoid of particular loyalties, let alone revolutionary sympathies.

When it came to choosing the reading material offered for sale at the railway stations, the main criterion was therefore its shelf life, in two main senses. Since the commercial space available at railway stations was limited and rents were high, reading material at most railway stations was sold from small vending kiosks and mobile stalls, or was handled by itinerant sellers who went from one platform and carriage to the next carrying reading material. As a result of these constraints, railway bookshops concentrated primarily on distributing newspapers and magazines, and less on selling books, which were generally heavy and bulky. In addition, sales followed the principle of "everything on display is for sale." This approach meant that readers were free to choose for themselves, without the help or recommendation of a sales assistant. Managers therefore made a point of displaying their wares in such a way as to attract potential customers, who could choose their favorite reading material. This approach was also reflected in the choice of assistants at railway shops. Generally they were not experienced bookshop personnel, expected to direct readers to a particular type of reading material, but rather ordinary employees with no special training in the book trade.

Beyond the technical and conceptual constraints affecting the railway station bookshops, the demand for reading material was the main factor that influenced the range of works distributed by them. For this reason, different locations offered different selections, depending on the nature of the region and travelers' needs. For example, at the major railway stations and in tourist areas with large numbers of international travelers, bookshops distributed many newspapers and magazines in foreign languages as well as a great deal of literature and information about the area served by the railway station. Despite differences between stations in different areas, however, contemporary reports indicate that what most of the traveling public wanted to find on sale at railway stations were newspapers, easy-to-read magazines, detective stories, family novels, and adventure stories which were enjoyable to read, cheap, and not too heavy to take with them on a trip. It appears that the traveling public's reading tastes were influenced not only by factors such as sex, age, social status, or educational level, but also by the actual train journey: or as expressed in contemporary terms, "by the psychology of the travelling public." Apart from the fact that travelling by train, particularly in the cheaper classes, was not particularly comfortable and it was difficult to concentrate sufficiently to read difficult works, railway travel was not considered time to devote to sophisticated culture or improving the mind (*Bildung*). Perusal of the etiquette books of the period, many of which devoted a chapter to the etiquette of travelling, shows that travelling by train was time which could be spent talking and resting, apart from reading. Train travel was therefore seen as a period of time to be taken advantage of in order to recharge one's batteries before arriving at one's destination. If passengers—the erudite and the non-erudite alike—wanted to read during their train trip, their requirements were for something light and enjoyable which would help pass the time that they were "en route" as quickly as possible.

As a result, neither the railway station bookshops nor the "book and newspaper trade" had pretentious cultural and educational goals. Rather, they operated on the basis of the principle of supply and demand. In other words, they tried to fit in with the varied range of people who frequented railway stations so as to meet their special reading needs. As indicated above, in order to achieve this goal the railway station bookshops adopted a marketing strategy of displaying their reading material to the reading public, enabling them to pick up whatever took their fancy. This marketing approach underscored readers' freedom of choice in two main ways. First of all, it did not seek to impose itself, instead leaving the decision of what to read up to the readers themselves. Second, this approach turned bookshops at railway stations into a kind of space where readers from diverse social backgrounds could move freely, at least with their eyes, without any feeling whatsoever of being bound by their social status outside the railway station.

These characteristics of railway station bookshops, despite the fact that their lease with the railways prohibited the distribution of literature which was considered immoral, apparently played an important role in creating a public image of the railway station bookshop as one of the main distribution channels for trashy literature. Some books on etiquette even recommended travellers to equip themselves with reading material from home for their journey and to refrain from buying reading material at railway stations. This attitude to railway station bookshops is also reflected in the oft-repeated demands for stepped-up monitoring of the reading material distributed at railway stations. Friedrich Avenarius, the publisher of the influential magazine *Der Kunstwart* ("Arts Sentinel") and founder of the Dürerbund organization, one of whose guiding principles was "art for the people," in 1913 proposed the establishment of a body to monitor the distribution of reading material at railway stations. Avenarius suggested that a central body be set up to centralize ways of dealing with and monitoring reading material for the masses. Until they were approved by this body such works, which were to cost no more than one mark, would not be cleared for distribution at railway bookshops and other locations—schools, bars, newsstands, and so on—frequented by the potential target audience for such cheap reading material.[29] Avenarius's idea received valuable support from Jacques Bettenhausen of Dresden, who owned one of Germany's biggest chains of railway station bookshops. Apparently, Bettenhausen hoped to obtain exclusive control over such a monitoring body for popular reading material, giving him a monopoly, as was the case in France and England, in the area of distributing reading material at Germany's railway stations. Although Avenarius's initiative was only a proposal, it triggered a storm of protest among businessmen with railway station bookshops and led to the intervention of the booksellers' umbrella organization, the Bv, which fiercely opposed any attempt to interfere with the book trade on the part of elements external to the booksellers' organization. The failure of Avenarius's initiative did not prevent demands for supervision of the reading material sold by bookshops at railway stations being voiced once again after the war. Walther Borgius, in his famous proposal to make the book trade part of the public sector, demanded that the bookshops at railway stations be nationalized in order to improve their regulation.[30] In 1919, the issue of monitoring railway station bookshops was the subject of a parliamentary debate, and in the 1920s a government commission was even established to examine the possibilities of regulating these shops.[31]

Hence the bookshops at railway stations were not just places which supplied reading material in order to combat the tedium of traveling. Their widespread distribution, their diverse target audience, and the wide range of information offered by them made them something of a reference point in the space of modern life, helping the traveling public to successfully navigate the station on arrival or departure. The newsstand was another distribution agent for newspapers and magazines playing the same role.

Kiosks

In addition to the "book and newspaper trade" and the magazine subscription club, which specialized in the distribution of subscriptions for reading material predominantly in rural areas and small towns, and the railway station bookshops which operated in urban areas, around the turn of the century new distribution methods began to develop in the large cities to enable newspapers and magazines to be sold directly from kiosks and in the street.[32]

The desire to set up kiosks at centrally located street corners of the major cities as sales points, primarily of newspapers and magazines, was apparently part of an attempt designed partially to prevent and partially to regulate the street sales of newspapers and magazines. Sociologist Werner Sombart compared this phenomenon to the spread of gonorrhea in large cities, even going so far as to demand its eradication from the urban public space.[33] However, the institutionalization of street sales of newspapers by installing special structures for this purpose not only provided a response to the demand to purge public space of this "ugly and insanitary" phenomenon of street trading, but also embodied a hierarchical approach to the public space—an approach which preferred "inside" (fabricated spaces) to "outside" (open areas).[34] One result of this approach was to make public space and the individual's location within it something of an index of social identity. As structures intended for the selling of reading material, kiosks were therefore part of this process of arranging public life in a hierarchical spatial setting which strove to create an "aesthetic" and "sanitary" public space.

The word "kiosk" comes from the Persian kuš via the Turkish "köşk," meaning an open pavilion built in the oriental style. However, despite the fact that kiosks in Germany lacked any stylistic affinity with their oriental origins, the kiosk was a kind of compromise which was acceptable to large numbers of communities, both aesthetically and in terms of proper social order.[35] As a sales point for reading material, the kiosk quickly became an inseparable part of the urban landscape, not only as a distribution point for reading material but also as part of advertising's domination of urban public space. Unlike the bookshops at railway stations, whose advertising areas belonged to the railway company, kiosks could rent out their available surface areas for advertising purposes.[36] In addition, in the second half of the 1920s, when radios were still the exclusive province of the affluent classes only, many kiosks began playing them to passersby, in this way helping to popularize broadcasting among social strata for whom at the time this was an unattainable luxury. However, kiosks not only contributed to the organization of urban public space, the distribution of reading material, the expansion of advertising space in the cities, and the popularization of the new media: especially after World War I, they also played an important social function. In the 1920s, the granting of concessions to open kiosks formed part of a social policy designed to solve the very real plight of ex-soldiers, and above all of those crippled in the war, by creating jobs suitable for them. In this way the authorities tried to compensate demobilized soldiers for having served their country, and to a large extent to assuage the feelings of bitterness of many of them who found it difficult to integrate into civilian life after the war.

Hence kiosks were locations where manifest cultural, commercial, and social interests met, and they became a tool for maintaining order and good taste in society. The most extreme expression of this tendency can be found in the postwar period when large numbers of kiosks were established. It would therefore appear that, of all times, it was during these years of economic upheaval and political crises that an approach was adopted which viewed consumption as an instrument for preserving social tranquillity and encouraged the authorities' increasing involvement in shaping the public space. This development is most saliently expressed in attitudes to the street, as an area where public life is conducted. The street now became an object, belonging to the community, which could now rent it out, both as a means of supervising and controlling public order, and also, like any other capitalist, in order to make a profit. At the same time, the authorities' increasing intervention in shaping public space also marks the beginning of the process of privatizing public space and entrusting it to private circles, normally for commercial purposes, such as in the case of kiosks. From this point of view, the State's increasing ability to act as a force in organizing and regulating society may be viewed as part of the process by which the consumer society came into being.

However, the kiosk as a meeting place for the interests of disparate social forces not only reflected diverse social changes, but also embodied alterations in how newspapers were distributed, with the shift from circulation to subscribers to direct sales. The most manifest expression of this process, which gained momentum around the turn of the century, was the selling of newspapers in street trading.[37]

Street Selling of Newspapers

The principle behind street trading asserted that in order to persuade the public to buy reading material, readers could not be expected to come to the sales point, whether shops or kiosks: instead, reading material had to be brought to those locations where the public passed by so that they could not ignore reading material which was offered for sale under their very noses, as it were. The argument was that readers should not be made responsible for motivating consumption, which should be perceived as a field for which responsibility lay with sellers and the goods offered for sale to passersby. By adopting the direct approach to consumers, whether by situating newspaper selling points in as many places as possible—on pavements, in stairwells, at the entrance to public locations, at tram stops, and so forth—or by moving among people, waving newspapers and calling out their names in the street, in cafés and bars, street sellers tried to heighten awareness of newspapers and hence increase purchases. The selling of newspapers and magazines in the street was not only a tool for distributing reading material, but also a means of advertising which helped to make passersby aware of the existence of newspapers and magazines. Accordingly, more and more publishers began to make use of this distribution method, whether by sending their own vendors out to the streets and public places, or through distribution agents who performed this work on behalf of the publishing houses. At the beginning of the 1920s, the city of Berlin alone had between thirty and forty companies involved in this distribution sector. Unlike subscription-based distribution, which was generally intended for a defined public of readers, every day street sellers approached an undefined public with the goal of selling as many copies of newspapers as possible. As a result, street selling had the potential to significantly expand print runs. Contributing factors included both the vendors as well as breaking news, which increased interest in the papers reporting the story. Hence street sales of newspapers were flexible and far more responsive to the fluctuating needs of their readership than subscription-based distribution methods.

This method of distribution was first used in Berlin by Ullstein, perhaps Germany's biggest newspaper publisher before the Nazis assumed power. In 1904, dissatisfied with the circulation of one of its morning papers, *Berliner Zeitung*, until then sold by subscription only, Ullstein decided to adopt the American model and to sell papers in the street. In 1905 the August Scherl publishing house, Ullstein's largest competitor in Berlin, also began to sell its papers in the street, and the trend soon engulfed Rudolf Mosse as well, who together with Ullstein and Scherl dominated the German newspaper market.[38]

By the postwar period, newspaper street vendors were selling practically the entire range of newspapers, not just the gutter press (*Boulevardblätter*) with which this distribution system was normally identified. As important a daily paper as the *Frankfurter Zeitung* was distributed primarily by direct sales, in shops, in kiosks, and in the street, and not by subscription. Even such manifestly political papers as the SPD's *Vorwärts,* the KPD's *Rote Fahnen,* the NSDAP's *Der Völkische Beobachter,* or the Nationalist-Conservative paper of the Catholic Central Party, *Germania,* and the *Deutsche Zeitung* of the conservative German right (Deutsche Volkspartei) were sold in the streets of the major cities.[39] In the 1920s, the illustrated weeklies, sports papers, glossy magazines, cinema, fashion, and crossword puzzle magazines had enormous circulations. They no longer sold any copies worth speaking of on a subscription basis. Instead, their sales took place primarily at various outlets in shops, kiosks, and the street. At the end of the 1920s, the radio magazines became an important source of income for street newspaper vendors, with some two million copies of this kind of publication being sold every week in German cities.

The transition from a subscription-based distribution system to direct sales of newspapers was also related to a change in their appearance. This development was principally reflected on the front page of daily papers. The pages of advertisements were banished to the back of the paper, headlines became far bigger and more prominent, and more photographs were used. By adopting these changes, newspapers tried to create a less staid front page which would attract the attention of passersby. This visual revolution in the area of newspaper design formed part of developments in commercial aesthetics, which used spectacular design and visual elements such as color, light, and shape in an attempt to attract potential consumers. This was part of the general process of enhanced visual appeal in the modern age.[40]

Notwithstanding the advantages that street sales of newspapers offered publishers, the latter did not hasten to give up the economic security given them by a fixed readership who took out subscriptions. This situation formed the backdrop to a permanent disagreement between the publishers, who saw street trade as a means of obtaining new subscribers, and the street dealers, who argued that subscription-based distribution prevented newspaper circulation figures from growing and harmed potential profits. As for readers, they could now enjoy the best of all worlds. They could have a paper delivered to their home, and in addition they could purchase on the streets a paper which they might perhaps not wish to have delivered to their home address. But not only did street trade offer readers a varied range of papers and magazines at practically all hours of the day or night: it also meant that readers did not have to make the effort to go to newspaper outlets, thereby making buying newspapers a less time-consuming business.

When trying to understand the phenomenon of street sales of newspapers the key word is therefore "speed." This was reflected in the swiftness with which the paper came off the presses and reached its readers, as well as the actual action of "consuming" the papers.[41] It is not at all surprising therefore that this distribution method could exist only in locations where "the street" and public locales had begun to occupy a more central position in people's everyday routines, places where there was large-scale demand for up-to-date information and speed had become one of the characteristics of lifestyles—the large cities. These changes in lifestyles and the very pace of people's existence also became central themes in how life was perceived in Germany's big cities from the turn of the century onward. For example, as one of the street vendors' specialized magazines noted, the home had become a place where people spent less and less time, while life outside the home—at school, at the workplace, at cafés, in parks and on the way to and from these locations—was coming to fill more and more of people's time. The modern woman, too, it was argued, "who goes out to work," no longer spends as much time at home as in the past. Large cities were therefore perceived as having a tempo and way of life in complete contrast to the typical pace of life in small towns or rural areas characterized, as Georg Simmel put it, by slowness, simplicity, and their uniform, stable way of life.[42] Viewed against this background, the newspaper street trade was a telling expression of big-city life, just as attempts to fight it were part of efforts to regulate and perhaps also to hold back the acceleration in the pace of life.

Sell where? Sell when? Sell how? Sell what? And who was allowed to sell? These were just a few of the questions that the authorities considered

Picture 5: The fastest newspaper. An advertisement for the Ullstein daily B.Z. am Mittag

as they attempted to set behavioral norms in this area of commercial endeavor. In some cities a ban was introduced on newspaper vendors shouting their wares in order to attract the attention of passersby. Frequently vendors had to be aged at least sixteen, and precise definitions were laid down about the permitted areas and hours for selling newspapers in the street. Despite the restrictions imposed on this form of trading as well as efforts to ban it, the number of those involved in selling newspapers in the street increased steadily. In 1871 Berlin had seventeen or twenty street newspaper vendors. Most of them sold papers at the city's railway stations before the Stilke company was awarded the concession to sell papers there in 1882. In the 1880s there were already several hundred newspaper vendors in Berlin's streets, and in the period between 1900 and the outbreak of the world war, estimates put their numbers as swelling to close on 2,000. In 1920, 1,957 people (1,119 men and 838 women) were registered in Berlin as engaging in the licensed selling of newspapers and magazines in the capital's streets.[43] In 1929, the number of those whose lawful occupation was newspaper street vendor totaled 3,700.[44] During the world war which, as we saw in the chapter on reading budgets, increased dependence on newspapers as a cardinal source of information about events on the front lines and the home front alike, this phenomenon of street sales of newspapers spread to other large cities in Germany such as Hamburg, Frankfurt, Leipzig, Breslau, Cologne, and Munich.

A number of factors contributed to the flourishing of this commercial sector after the world war. The first is the increased reliance on newspaper reading during the war, and the reinforcement of this trend in the turbulent postwar years. Political events, inflation, and increased interest in sports events, betting, and the stock exchange heightened demand for up-to-date information on the one hand, and for entertainment on the other hand.[45] The street sales of newspapers and magazines could meet these needs extremely quickly and efficiently. The second factor was the precarious economic situation, which made many people wary of long-term financial commitments. As a result they preferred to give up their subscriptions and to buy a newspaper only when they were able to pay for it, using a range of outlets. The third factor was encouragement by the publishing houses themselves, which had identified the economic potential of this phenomenon. And fourth, no major outlay was needed to become involved in the street selling of newspapers. As a result, this commercial field was an occupation ideally suited to the weaker strata of urban society, involving a relatively high proportion of women, old people, children, and handicapped individuals. In the postwar period, these categories expanded to include large numbers of disabled ex-soldiers, and at the end of the 1920s the unemployed. This would appear to be the reason why the authorities in the Twenties displayed a relatively tolerant attitude toward this phenomenon, and for their part the publishing companies took advantage of this situation in order to increase their profits.[46]

At the end of the 1920s, as indicated by many articles in the street vendors' specialist press, the street selling of newspapers and magazines suffered a major crisis. On the one hand, the economic hardships had adversely affected the buying power of the reading public, who were buying fewer papers than in the past. On the other hand, the large numbers of jobless, who hoped to find a temporary solution to their plight in selling papers in the street, significantly increased the numbers of those involved in this trade. This situation made an attempt to make a living from selling papers in the street almost impossible. The increased competition and reduced profits from sales of papers were also factors which forced many newspaper street vendors to begin selling books and reading material other than newspapers and magazines. This step was even justified in the pages of the street vendors' specialist press: it was argued that the selling of newspapers and magazines in bookshops and other outlets which in principle were not supposed to distribute reading material was eating into street newspaper vendors' livelihoods, and this gave them the right to diversify the reading material distributed by them.

In conclusion it may therefore be said that the street selling of newspapers is a manifest example of how the varied interests of the authorities, advertisers, distributors, and consumers could be combined. This combination not only promoted the cultural model of creating a special sphere to reflect the system of values that we identify with consumer culture, it also turned into a mechanism which made it easier to cope with the everyday misery of life during the exceptional period in the wake of World War I. In view of all this, it appears that despite the struggle against the phenomenon of selling newspapers in the street, whether via outright prohibition or via its institutionalization through kiosks, the various elements which fought against the newspaper vendors did not so much fear a situation in which there was a place for everything as they wanted everything to have its place.

Direct or Subscriber-Base Marketing

Although in the 1920s the direct selling of newspapers and magazines was a thriving phenomenon, Otto Groth wrote in 1930 that in contrast to countries such as France and the USA, where direct sales of newspapers were more or less the norm, Germany remained a country of subscribers.[47] Following his mentor Karl Bücher, Groth saw this situation as reflecting differences in lifestyles between Germany on the one hand, and France and the USA on the other, where the hunger for sensation and fast pace of life had changed the face of newspapers. Or as Karl Bücher himself described the difference between subscription papers and papers sold directly:

> The editor of a subscription paper is like the vicar who every Sunday stands in the pulpit before the same congregation, while the editor of a newspaper sold retail is like the virtuoso performer who plays his violin today before the music connoisseurs of this city and tomorrow of that city and has to please all equally.[48]

But beyond all speculation concerning the differences in mentality and norms of social behavior between the direct-selling countries and the subscription countries—Germany, Austria, Switzerland, and Holland—there were also more pragmatic reasons which contributed to maintaining the vitality of the subscription-based distribution system in Germany. True, the publishing houses were aware that it was impossible to significantly expand newspapers' circulation figures when print runs were determined by subscriber numbers. However, this distribution method did limit the economic risk associated with publishing for an undefined audience which on any particular day could decide to buy the competing paper, or not to buy a paper at all. The economic hardships of the 1920s and the extreme fluctuations during those years in the circulation figures of direct-sale papers actually increased the need for economic security, with the result that the subscription-based distribution system was not dropped. Consequently, publishers viewed direct selling mainly as a way of increasing their subscriber base, even making sure that the price of a single copy would always be cheaper for subscribers than for direct-sale customers.

In addition, over and above the fact that publishers tried to make subscriptions economically worthwhile, the tooth-and-nail competition for readers, between publishing houses as well as the different newspaper distribution agents, created a whole range of means designed to entice the reading public to take out subscriptions. Magazine subscription clubs offered gifts and many benefits such as books, diaries, weekend excursions, tickets to the theater and cinema, sporting events, and so on in order to entice readers to take out subscriptions with them. Many publishers even offered a month's free subscription to the paper or free legal advice for subscribers. In addition, many daily papers began to include supplements on a range of topics in an effort to attract the attention of readers from different social groups with varied areas of interest.[49] Advertisements and posters were also a standard means of increasing awareness of a particular newspaper.[50] But among the various methods that they used to ensnare subscribers, the "insurance paper" or alternatively "subscriber insurance" as a publicity means for newspapers deserves special attention.[51] The insurance magazines are a striking example of integration between bodies with manifest commercial interests and newspapers, as well as the way that the newspaper-reading culture encouraged patterns of economic thinking and the dissemination of values considered *bürgerlich*, like reading and insurance, among a diverse readership.

Insurance Newspapers

Invented in England at the beginning of the 1880s, insurance newspapers soon began to appear in France and beginning in the 1890s in Germany too. In 1911, Germany had as many as 297 insurance newspapers, 69 of which were weeklies, 36 specialist, and 192 daily publications covering the entire political spectrum. That year the number of insured persons, excluding their families, was estimated at 5.5 million, and the amount paid out under the insurance for subscribers' claims exceeded three million marks. From May 1901 onward, the insurance newspapers, like the whole of the private insurance sector, came under government supervision.

What exactly is an insurance newspaper? The term designates a newspaper which seeks to attract the largest possible number of readers through insurance coverage enjoyed by them because they are subscribers, or in the case of "subscribers' insurance," insurance enjoyed by virtue of being a subscriber, for example, to a "magazine subscription club." In other words, that paper's publisher or distribution companies offered subscribers insurance as a benefit, bearing the cost themselves. Sometimes the publishers themselves were the insurers (a form of insurance called *"unbeaufsichtigt"*—unsupervised), but in most cases they insured subscribers with the various insurance companies (a form of insurance called *"beaufsichtigt"*—supervised). This insurance/newspaper arrangement was not just a means of tempting readers to take out a subscription: it was also supposed to establish a lasting association between the readership and the newspaper, so that it would not be worth readers' while to cancel their subscription. The three main types of insurance which were designed to achieve this goal were accident insurance, death insurance, and personal liability insurance (*Haftpflichtversicherung*). Readers thus enjoyed cheap insurance, with payments being made on a regular basis, covering all types of damage and all subscribers. They also avoided the painful bureaucratic process of filling out lengthy forms, medical examinations, meetings with insurance agents, and so on—aspects normally associated with signing an insurance agreement with a private company.

Germany's most famous insurance newspaper was the family weekly called *Nach Feierabend* ("After Hours"), founded as an insurance newspaper in 1899. In 1914 the paper's readership topped the million mark. *Nach Feierabend*'s stunning success showed that insurance as an advertising medium was particularly suitable for newspapers which were not associated with a particular region or party, and which sought to attract the broadest possible social spectrum. After the world war, the number of publications which became "insurance newspapers" practically doubled, from 69 in 1913 to 118 in 1928.[52] Women's and fashion papers were responsible for most of this upsurge. It would appear that for many women who joined the labor market in the 1920s, the combination of insurance and fashion papers was irresistible. Seemingly, the desire to keep abreast of the most up-to-date fashion developments and women's need to enhance their economic security and independence were the main reasons for the success of "insurance newspapers" among their female readership. Another factor was at work too: normally a wife's insurance through the insurance papers was part of her husband's insurance, and so the possibility for women of obtaining insurance without their husbands' assistance for the most part became a declarative act symbolizing women's emancipation. However, this link between the paper and insurance was not only a solution which met the needs of the "new woman" in the postwar period. During a period of economic hard times and political instability, the insurance newspaper became practically the only way for wider social circles than in the past to acquire insurance.

The insurance newspapers were therefore viewed as an original and practical idea for publishers, who acquired a faithful body of subscribers and readers, primarily from less affluent circles, for whom insurance was now in reach. However, this situation also presented publishers and distribution agents with a new dilemma. The insurance/paper connection was intended to increase a newspaper's subscriber base. At the same time, since the publishers and distribution agents either assumed the costs of the insurance or were associated with the insurance companies which bore this charge, they looked for their subscribers among a public with a low level of risk, in other words among the bourgeoisie or white-collar workers. Erwin Fink, for example, in his 1916 doctoral dissertation on "subscription insurance," advised the Social Democratic papers to stay away from insurance as an advertising medium since the readership of these papers belonged to a population with a high risk level.[53]

The insurance newspapers therefore found themselves in a situation where, on the one hand, they were very attractive to working-class readers, in whom they were not particularly interested; while on the other hand, for the *Bürgertum* the insurance offered by these papers was not always sufficiently attractive. There is no way of knowing to what extent this conflict limited subscriptions. However, there are grounds for assuming that in most cases, the desire to increase the number of subscribers outweighed the fear of having to make insurance payouts. This finding is supported by two main reference points. First of all, insurance is perceived as a social benefit not to be withheld from working-class people in high-risk jobs. This was one of the reasons why, from 1914 onward, even a Social Democratic newspaper like the *Münchener Post* became an insurance newspaper. Second, despite the fact that the insurance newspapers had a basic preference for the bourgeoisie and white-collar subscribers, they did not want to relinquish their working-class readership. This is one of the implications of the payouts totaling 1,700,000 marks which were made in 1912 to 114,780 subscribers of one of the biggest insurance newspapers published in Leipzig. Of the thirty four professional categories of the paper's subscribers, the biggest group (ca. 20 percent) of those who received payouts belonged to the working class. A similar picture is provided by figures from the Nürnberger Lebensversicherungsbank, the largest insurance company in the field of Germany's insurance newspapers. The company's statistics in the postwar period indicate that for every 1,000 instances in which it paid out compensation for accidents, 236 involved women and 764 men, of whom 596 were manual workers or artisans (*Handwerker*), 54 worked in transport, 106 in mining, 75 in farming, and

169 were self-employed or engaged in trade and clerical duties. In 1913, the National Supervisory Office for Private Insurance examined insurance newspapers and noted:

> Subscriber insurance has undoubtedly proven to be an effective means in many respects for making the blessings of insurance coverage available to some extent to broad sectors of the population, thereby contributing to the consolidation of economic circumstances of the working classes and tradesmen. Private accident insurance is mainly intended only for more affluent circles; generally speaking, companies do not consider the accident insurance of broad circles of the working population a worthwhile business, and many of them avoid it. Here, subscriber accident insurance has clearly filled a gap.[54]

The "gap" referred to in the government report clearly grew during World War I and the postwar period.

During the war, many newspapers also began to insure subscribers against the risk of death on the battlefield. During this period, compensation was paid out to at least fifty thousand families of war casualties. During the postwar period as well, the newspapers continued to insure disabled war veterans, who were considered a group with a particularly high level of risk. During the years of rampant inflation, this kind of insurance, with its straightforward paperwork and weekly payments method, which enabled it to adjust payments to the fluctuating value of the currency, demonstrated an amazing ability to survive. Compared with the normal types of insurance, which practically collapsed in the conditions created in postwar Germany, the insurance newspapers also became an attractive alternative for the middle classes who were interested in continuing to insure themselves as in the past. Devaluation, the associated crumbling of the value of savings, political instability, and unemployment increased the need for economic security for the future that was offered by insurance. However, during this period of economic adversity and political instability many found it impossible to invest in private insurance.[55] The newspaper/insurance combination therefore provided a satisfactory response to the need to increase economic security and the desire to avoid tying up additional funds in insurance. This state of affairs also meant that during this period, private insurance was no longer viewed as a luxury intended for select social circles, instead becoming a phenomenon of the people, embracing all strata of society. The insurance newspapers' very success also shows how newspaper reading was an inseparable part of day-to-day routine existence in the 1920s, rather than a special expense and something distinct from daily budgets.

Growing demand for information and entertainment, combined with a longing for the security provided by insurance, therefore guaranteed the success of the insurance newspapers in the 1920s. Most of those insured in Germany, who mainly had accident and death policies, were covered through the insurance newspapers. According to conservative estimates, in 1931 between 12 and 15 million people were insured through the insurance newspapers, with payouts totaling between 25 and 30 million marks every year. In 1929, the Nürnberger Lebensversicherungsbank on its own gave insurance coverage to some 5.3 million people through insurance newspapers, and in 1928 it paid out compensation totaling 8.7 Reichsmarks.[56] It would appear, therefore, that the insurance newspapers' popularity during these years does not simply attest to the way in which during this period of material and moral bankruptcy society dealt with the difficulties of daily existence, but also demonstrates how reading was an integral part of this process.

As in other similar circumstances, the insurance newspapers' success also generated disagreement over the nature of this phenomenon and how to relate to it. The supporters of the insurance newspapers highlighted the insurance newspapers' role as agents in disseminating the *bürgerlich* world of values. The expansion of readerships and the circulation among the working classes of publications with cultural and practical values were just some of the arguments advanced in support of the insurance newspapers. In addition, it was claimed that the insurance newspapers helped to disseminate the idea of insurance among social classes whose ethic had not previously included worrying about the future. According to this approach, among these social classes insurance as a social value strengthened their feeling of responsibility for their relatives and society, making them better citizens. Hence the combination of newspapers and insurance was viewed by the supporters of the insurance newspapers as a manifest expression of *Bürgerlichkeit,* as well as part of the attempt to impose it on German society.

In contrast, the critics of the insurance newspapers saw the combination of newspapers and insurance as mixing things which were downright incompatible—chalk and cheese, as it were—in a blend just as harmful to insurance as to newspapers and reading culture. On the one hand, the insurance companies were afraid that the use of insurance as a means of gaining publicity for newspapers would undermine the status of insurance. The proponents of this view pointed out that reducing the cost of insurance and making it available as a benefit to newspaper subscribers convinced many people to try the fly-by-night insurance policies of the insurance newspapers instead of insuring themselves directly with the insurance companies' solid and reliable form of insurance. Going further, the critics of the insurance newspapers argued that publishers should concentrate on newspapers, not insurance, a field which had nothing to do with their field of expertise. On the other hand, insurance newspapers were also seen as an element which was threatening to change the German newspaper scene. The local and political press in particular, although itself making use of insurance as a publicity gimmick, feared that the success of insurance as a means of advertising these more widely distributed and apolitical publications would impact negatively on their own circulation figures. What is more, not only were the insurance newspapers perceived as undermining the distribution of reading material, blunting readers' opinions, and contributing to the process of making German society into a society of the masses, but it was also feared that the newspaper/insurance combination would undermine the status of newspapers, making them a tool in the service of insurance.

The use of reading material as a means of advertising various products and businesses was not exclusive to the insurance sector. Thus in the 1920s many companies published so-called company magazines (*Hauszeitschriften*), either for internal use and a restricted target audience of the company's workforce, or for advertising purposes and a broad-based target audience.[57] For example, the Berlin gas company accompanied its customers' gas bill with a fourteen page monthly magazine called "Die Pause" (*The Break*), published by itself. In 1926, the Stollwerk chocolate company in Cologne also began publishing a magazine, called "Stollwerk Post," which it distributed to its customers. Like any other magazine, these magazines contained articles, stories, crosswords, and advertisements, as well as information about the company issuing them. However, the most salient examples of this tendency to use reading material as sales promotion material were those newspapers and magazines which were not considered to be "company magazines."

Commercializing Reading

Demand for a means of keeping abreast of events and conveying information to as many people as possible constituted the common basis for the development of advertising and newspapers alike, as well as the combination of the two. Research studies cite material indicating that from the very earliest stages of the development of the press at the end of the sixteenth century, newspapers published assorted advertisements.[58] However, the importance of this combination of newspapers and advertising as one of the means of addressing social and economic relations is expressed most saliently in the "information gazettes" (*Intelligenzblätter*) which began to appear in the German states at the end of the seventeenth century.[59] Announcements about births, deaths, and marriages, market opening hours, information about prices, "wanted" advertisements, notices about lost property, information about loans, and buying and selling offers were just some of the advertisements which appeared in these papers. In addition, these information gazettes also published notices to the public by the authorities, news, essays, and articles about a whole range of subjects. Most of the information gazettes were owned by the authorities or closely controlled by them. The authorities were not only interested in making the information gazettes their mouthpiece, but also sought to use them in order to have a monopoly over the conveying of information in as many areas as possible, so as to strengthen their supervision and control of social and economic life.[60] Additionally, the authorities saw information gazettes as a source of revenue for the state coffers. However, even though the absolute state invested resources in an attempt to nationalize the advertising field, it was unable to prevent the various political newspapers and magazines issued by private circles from publishing advertisements. For Karl Bücher, this situation was not only a result of the growing need for advertising in a society undergoing an ever faster pace of urbanization and commercialization, but also an expression of the hostility to the State traditional in Germany.[61]

These information gazettes began to disappear from the German press scene at the beginning of the nineteenth century, finally making their official exit in 1850 after legislation abolishing the State's monopoly on advertising in Prussia.[62] The Napoleonic conquests and, following them, the 1848 uprisings, the involvement and growing interest of extremely broad strata of society in the political process, and above all the heightened pace of development of trade and industry from the end of the eighteenth century onward were key factors in the democratization of the domain of advertising in Germany. However, it was not until the last third of the nineteenth century, after Germany's unification and the repeal in 1874 of legislation requiring deposits to be lodged on the founding of magazines which accepted advertisements, as well as the repeal of taxes on advertising and the special taxation proportional to the size of the issue levied on newspapers accepting advertisements, that the go-ahead was given for the major breakthrough by newspapers in Germany. These changes were reflected not only in the increased importance of advertising as a means of addressing social and economic relationships by mediating between supply and demand, but also in the nature and appearance of the advertising itself.

Up to the beginning of the nineteenth century, advertising appeared primarily as a text by means of which people, normally private individuals or official bodies, sought to promote various interests. At this time newspapers carried a wide range of advertisements for products and especially diverse services offered by craftsmen, musicians, doctors, or university lecturers. During this period, however, when newspapers were the province of a relatively narrow social class of the literate and a paper circulated within a given area only, these were casual advertisements of a manifestly personal and regional nature. Generally the various products advertised in newspapers were not on sale in the local markets but were offered on a one-off basis only. Even the appearance of advertisements, including the size and shape of the letters, was uniform, and there was no difference in terms of graphics between them and the other parts of the paper. One of the first areas to try to break out of the local and personal framework offered by the local press of the period and to achieve new ways of graphically presenting publicity was the book trade. Advertisements for books, as well as publicity for lotteries, appeared with increasing frequency in eighteenth century newspapers. In 1740 100 percent of the advertisements in the Berlin paper the *Vossische Zeitung* were for books. By 1765, the percentage of advertisements publicizing books had dropped to 53 percent, occupying 41 percent of the advertising space in the paper. In 1860 only 12 percent of advertisements, which took up 8 percent of the advertising space, were for books. But in the same year, books were still the most common commodity to be advertised in the paper, occupying the largest proportion of its advertising space.[63] Book dealers not only tended to use newspaper advertising in order to promote their sales: they also listened to readers' requirements and tried to adapt their publications to demand and to the changing fashions of the time. By way of illustration, in 1831 the fear of a cholera outbreak is reflected in an advertising campaign in the contemporary press for books dealing with this subject.[64]

There were two main factors behind publishers' intensive use of advertising in newspapers. First of all, many papers were owned by publishing houses, and it was only natural for them to use their own resources in order to promote the sales of their other publications. Second, since books, which were the first products which could be mass produced, were not protected prior to mid-nineteenth century copyright legislation, publishers looked for the fastest way to find as large a clientele as possible before other publishers started to publish the book as well.[65] Advertisements for books in the eighteenth and early nineteenth century were therefore one of the earliest expressions of the commercial (modern) use of publicity.[66] As early as the eighteenth century, book publishers, and particularly books as products, were responsible for determining the nature of the use of advertising as a means of promoting commercial interests. However, this state of affairs was for the most part consigned to the sidelines of public discourse as the process of commercialization expanded and the relative place of book advertising shrank in the course of the nineteenth century.

Beginning in the 1820s, both the nature and the look of advertising started to change. At first it was still textual in nature, the main variables being the size and form of the letters. Then illustrations began to creep into advertisements, which beginning in the 1890s became colorful spectacles combining textual and above all complex visual elements. In the postwar period, primarily under the influence of the "truth in advertising" principle, the use of photography increasingly came to influence the graphic design of advertisements.[67] This visual revolution not only showed that pictures were the most effective way of conveying messages quickly: it made advertising into a dynamic field which used a whole range of approaches to attract the reading public's attention by all and any means available. For example, instead of the casual advertising of a particular product in one local paper, at the end of the nineteenth century protracted advertising campaigns were introduced for different products in a number of papers at the same time. It was during this period that commercial brand names made their first appearance. In the wake of these changes, even the use of the written word underwent fundamental modifications. Instead of written words being intended solely to convey a message or information about a given product, they became part of a product's image and attempts to increase awareness of it. Advertising slogans and "advertising poems" (*Reklamegedichte*), which were extremely popular at the beginning of the twentieth century, are salient illustrations of this change, which also indicates how advertising tried to infiltrate readers' daily routines through the use of language.

However, the rise of new commercial advertising did not mark the disappearance of the old form of advertisements. As the use of commercial advertising increased, so did the contrast between the "small ad" as a text used primarily to serve the needs of the "little man" in a particular area and commercial advertisements, with their lush and unique graphic appearance targeting as wide an audience as possible on a supralocal level. "Small ads" were mainly to be found on the newspaper's advertisements page, and constituted a source of income for newspaper publishers as well as an indication of the paper's popularity with its readership.[68] In this connection, it is particularly interesting to note the position of "personals," most of which were written in a form of coded language (chiffre ads). These became a tool for satisfying supply and demand in the area of relationships between the sexes, and their numbers rose constantly from the end of the nineteenth century onward. These advertisements, generally camouflaged under the category of "offers of marriage," reflected the demand for casual sexual affairs as well as homosexual relationships.[69]

What is more, the existence of a medium which directly reached broad sectors of society convinced a whole range of parties with specific interests to use newspapers in order to promote these. For example, before the war the German animal welfare society decided that instead of organizing information campaigns using meetings and lectures, which would be attended by a few hundred people at most, it should invest in conveying information by means of advertising in newspapers with far larger audiences.[70] However, changes in the advertising sphere were primarily an upshot of the advent of mass production and increasing competition between producers and sellers, who began to allocate more and more resources to advertising, combined with the reduction in the price of newsprint. The latter development was in particular a result of the use of cellulose to produce paper, as well as increasingly sophisticated printing techniques which rendered possible a significant increase in print runs and led to breakthroughs in the graphic design of advertisements. The use of color photographs and eye-catching lettering now enabled advertisers to promise their readerships a veritable paradise of comfort and happiness. Commercial advertising became a guide to the promised land of the consumer society and was viewed as the driving force behind the economy of the modern market.

This qualitative change—in the nature and design of advertising—was also bound up with a quantitative change in the number of advertisements and the frequency with which they appeared in the press. In the course of the nineteenth century we see a constant increase in the number of advertisements in newspapers, as well as in the numbers of newspapers and magazines themselves. In 1816 the *Leipziger Tageblatt*, for instance, carried 28 different types of advertisements. By 1860 the same paper was already carrying 48 different fields of advertising.[71] The same year, 57 different advertising domains were to be found in the *Vossische Zeitung*, which had 16 pages of editorial material compared with 56 pages of advertising. In 1848, the *Münchner Neuesten Nachrichten* published some 14,000 advertising orders (*Anzeigenaufträge*). By 1900, this figure had climbed to 331,450, swelling to 476,400 in 1920.[72] This development in the realm of advertising is further reflected in the creation of a new form of newspaper, centered round advertising—the so-called "*Generalanzeigerpresse*," or advertising press. The *Generalanzeigerpresse* papers began to appear in Germany in the 1880s, operating on the basis of the mass production principle, which enabled the cost of individual issues to be slashed proportional to the newspaper's print run.[73] True, such attempts involved increased printing costs, with a concomitant increase in the economic risks associated with publishing the paper.[74] However, this was a calculated risk, since the paper was now targeting a wider readership as well as more advertisers than in the past. In order to reach the largest possible audience, reducing the cost of an individual copy of the paper was not enough. It was also necessary to induce the public to read the paper. The main approaches used by these papers in their attempts to gain popularity among as broad a readership as possible included publishing articles and stories about the daily lives of the simple man and sensationalist descriptions of accidents, disasters, and courtroom reports, combined with a substantial reduction in the price of "small ads" for private individuals, mainly by introducing a system of charging by the word. Increased circulation figures were not only intended to increase profits from sales, but also constituted a factor in dealings between newspapers and advertisers. In other words, the larger a paper's circulation, the higher the price that the newspaper's owners could demand for its advertising space. Hence a dependency developed between the papers and the advertisers, as Wilhelm Naumann put it, with the "text acting as an advertisement that increased print runs and the print run acting as publicity for the advertisement."[75]

When it came to magazines, this tendency was even more marked. The light entertainment papers (*Unterhaltungsblätter*), and in particular the illustrated weeklies which began appearing in Germany in the 1890s, were published in unprecedented print runs, opening up new horizons for advertisers. Thanks to increasingly sophisticated printing and photographic techniques, papers' graphic quality improved vastly. Advertisers were swept away on a wave of enthusiasm, enjoying the ability to publish advertisements covering entire pages and to try out new methods of graphic representation in their publicity campaigns.[76] The entire range of distribution methods was applied to the illustrated weeklies as well, guaranteeing them large-scale readerships. In addition, many publishers bound the weeklies and offered them for resale as bound volumes, an activity which also extended these publications' life span.

Germany's most widely distributed illustrated weekly was the *Berliner Illustrierte*, which first appeared in 1891 and in 1894 was acquired by Ullstein Publishers. In 1894 the weekly had a print run of 14,000; by 1902 this figure had already shot up to 100,000, and before the war its circulation was estimated at close to one million. In 1927 the magazine's print run exceeded 1.7 million copies, with 14,671,000 kilos of paper being required to print it. At the same time the cost of a single page advertisement was 11,520 Reichsmark.[77] Unprecedented circulation figures were also achieved by the fashion papers, which as Erna Lehmann showed in 1914 were closely associated with the textile industry.[78] Thus, as argued by Max Weber in his paper to a 1910 conference of sociologists, the press now had two main kinds of customers—the readers and the producers (advertisers)—and it tried to earn from both.[79]

But newspaper advertising not only cut the cost of publishing papers and encouraged their mass distribution: it also contributed to creating the conditions which made it possible to increase the actual numbers of newspapers and magazines published. In other words, newspaper publishing became a profitable line of business that attracted large numbers of entrepreneurs. Furthermore, political parties, as well as myriad trade union groups, companies, associations, and also different interest groups or people with a variety of sexual orientations were all interested in issuing their own publications. Thus newspapers became a key element in structuring the unique identity of interest groups and a whole range of organizations. As a result, the number of magazines and newspapers grew constantly.[80] In the span of one hundred years, a nineteenfold increase occurred in the number of magazines and newspapers, from 371 in 1826 to 7,303 in 1930. Especially from the end of the nineteenth century onward, many newspapers were established in Germany. For example, of the 2,900 papers published in 1916, 47 percent (1,376) were founded between 1871 and 1900. This tendency continued in the postwar period. Research carried out by the Berlin-based Press Research Institute indicates that ca. 20 percent of the daily papers published in Prussia in 1930 were founded between 1918 and 1930. The total print run of daily papers in Germany in 1932 was around twenty six million copies. In the magazine field the situation was similar. Every year following the beginning of the twentieth century saw the founding of around two hundred new journals in Germany, a tendency which continued in the postwar period. Around one-fifth of the magazines published in 1928 were founded after the world war, with Gerhard Menz estimating the same year that one magazine was published in

Germany for every ten thousand inhabitants, with one copy for every two people.[81]

The increased competition between the newspapers and the reading public's wide-ranging needs was also one of the factors which encouraged the search for new markets for reading material as well as new ways of distribution. In particular during the postwar period, after the establishment of the Weimar Republic and at a time of heightened competition with other advertising methods and new media, this tendency toward the fragmentation of the newspaper scene was reinforced. The splitting of political parties resulted in a broad spectrum of the political press unprecedented in Germany's history.[82] At the end of the 1920s Germany had ninety eight different papers put out by the independent trade unions alone (*freigewerkschaftliche Blätter*), with total print runs of 6,971,700 copies.[83] Even in the area of magazines defined as nonpolitical, the spectrum was vast. A total of 301 magazines for sports, in addition to 227 illustrated and light entertainment magazines, 175 different women's and fashion magazines, 67 magazines for youngsters, and 58 radio and broadcasting magazines made up just part of the range of magazines published in Germany in 1931. The gamut covered by magazines was so complex that in addition to the general catalogues of the press, at the end of the 1920s catalogues began to appear specializing in certain kinds of publications.

In contrast to the tendency (particularly by magazines) to specialize, the daily press, political and nonpolitical alike, began to acquire a universalist character, covering an extremely broad range of spheres. In addition, some newspapers were interested in attracting as broad a readership as possible, while others targeted a more defined circle. A newspaper thus became an expression of a particular lifestyle and part of the image of diverse social groups. In this sense, the press is a manifest example of the fact that the "mass media" not only contribute to social homogenization and standardization, but also reflect the heterogenization and fragmentation of modern society.

As a result of these developments, the question of differences between the different newspapers and magazines and their respective influence was no longer a purely academic issue, but rather one with practical implications. Advertisers wanted to know where they should place their orders in order to ensure maximum impact for their publicity.[84] The increasing professionalization of the advertising sector, as reflected in such things as the founding of agencies specializing in advertising, is a manifest expression of this new demand in the publicity domain. In 1855 a bookseller called Ferdinand Haasenstein set up Germany's first advertising agency in the town of Altona. The same year Ernest Litfaß, a printer and bookseller, installed the first "advertising columns" in the city of Berlin. To this day these are still known in German as *Litfaßsäule*—Litfass columns. In 1864 another advertising agency was opened by G.L. Daube in the city of Frankfurt am Main. Later the agency was bought up by August Scherl's publishing house. Publisher Rudolf Mosse founded his first advertising agency in Berlin in 1867: by 1932 this had grown to fifteen branches in Germany, and twenty abroad. In 1928 it was estimated that Germany had two thousand advertising agencies and fifteen different professional advertising and marketing associations.[85]

Initially the advertising agencies concentrated on acting as intermediaries between newspapers and advertisers. Toward the end of the nineteenth century they also began to provide advice to entrepreneurs on advertising matters, developing into businesses offering an entire range of publicity-related services. A significant part of the large advertising agencies' activities involved the issuing of catalogues of newspapers and magazines designed to provide a kind of guide to the complexities of the world of the press. Beginning in the 1890s magazines such as *Die Reklame* (1891), *Propaganda* (1897), or *Moderne Reklame* (1902) were founded specifically for those involved in the advertising field. They constituted part of the efforts to organize advertisers in their own interest-based associations.

The professionalization of the advertising field was also reflected in the attention paid to it by the academic world, normally as part of research into the press. Even as early as the prewar period, large numbers of studies were published about this area, and in 1914 Karl Bücher founded the first press research institute at the University of Leipzig. However, it was not until after the war that academic interest in these phenomena became institutionalized. By 1930 Germany had as many as twelve institutes researching the press, and lectures on the press and advertising were given at many universities and commercial colleges.[86] The founding of these institutes in postwar Germany was no coincidence. One of the decisive factors in their establishment was not only the process of accelerated commercialization, but the war itself, or rather its lessons. One of the purposes in setting up these research institutes was to improve Germany's propaganda machinery, whose weaknesses had been exposed in the course of the war when confronted with the propaganda machinery of Germany's foes. However, although this particular aspect demonstrates that the importance of the press and advertising in shaping public opinion was recognized at the time, discussion of this area does not fall within the scope of the present work.

Advertising therefore had to adapt itself to the different types of newspapers in accordance with each paper's specific style and target audience, and it became an inseparable part of the paper's image. In fact, from the end of the nineteenth century onward there were practically no newspapers or magazines which did not carry advertisements. Even the political and religious press, financed by the political parties and the religious establishment respectively, could not avoid publishing advertisements. For instance, despite Ferdinand Lassalle's call in 1863 for an advertisement-free press, August Bebel stated at the 1892 SPD Party Conference in Berlin that it was no longer possible to charge low prices for the party's publications without accepting commercial advertising.[87] This acknowledgment of the importance of advertising is also reflected, among other things, in the relative proportion of income derived from advertising in an important Social Democratic newspaper such as *Vorwärts* ("Forwards"), which increased from 17 percent of the paper's total revenues in 1892 to 33 percent in 1912. In another Social Democratic newspaper—the *Leipziger Volksblatt*—advertising-based income was far greater. In 1902 44 percent of the paper's income came from advertising; in 1913 this source made up 50 percent of the paper's revenues, and after the war and the hyperinflation during which the paper's income from advertising declined, advertising still made up 58 percent of its income in 1924.

In 1908, in connection with a proposal to impose a special tax on income derived from advertising, it was estimated that income from advertisements in daily newspapers amounted to some 185,846 million marks, and 226,456 million marks in magazines.[88] In 1930, it was estimated that the sales turnover of advertising space in the daily press was around one billion Reichsmarks, and two billion RM in magazines. Hence advertising was a vital source of income for the existence of newspapers, in certain cases comprising up two-thirds of their revenue. In other words, from the end of the nineteenth century onward, the press was actually unable to survive without advertising.

Recognition of the importance of advertising as a source of income for newspapers was also one of the reasons why newspaper owners invested great effort in combating the approach—still prevalent in the 1920s—to the effect that a solid business did not need to advertise in newspapers. To a large extent this attitude was a reaction to the perception of advertising as a necessary condition for the existence of the free market economy and a symbol of modernity. Yet despite this reluctance to use advertising, at least from the turn of the nineteenth century onward the dependence between advertising and newspapers became a fact of economic life.

One of the most salient expressions of this state of affairs was the separation of editorial pages and advertising pages in newspapers on the one hand, and the blurring of the boundaries between them on the other hand. From the early twentieth century onward we can see increasing attention being paid to the issue of disguised advertising, primarily by means of editorials in the daily press which were written on behalf of and with the financing of commercial undertakings; or alternatively by the publishing of commercial advertisements in the form of articles on the advertising pages. In magazines, and particularly in the fashion, light entertainment, and sports weeklies, it was even harder to distinguish between advertising and editorial material. Not only did these magazines blur the boundaries between articles and advertisements: they themselves actually acted as a form of distribution agent for lifestyles and preferences. The fashion papers, for example, not only presented the latest fashions in words and pictures: they also distributed patterns which became extremely popular, particularly among less affluent circles who lacked the resources to buy fashionable ready-made models in shops and department stores. In her 1914 doctorate, Erna Lehmann estimated that every year the fashion papers distributed some six million such patterns. The enormous success of these patterns shows not only how the fashion papers encouraged the consumption of clothing items and various fashion items, but also how they marketed the fashions themselves.[89]

The fear that advertising pages would displace the pages of editorial material also proved unfounded. It became clear that both the advertising pages and the editorial pages expanded significantly as the dependence between papers and advertising increased. For example, in 1894 the *Berliner Illustrierte* had 12 pages; by 1902 it had grown to 16 pages, and by 1927 it had swelled to 48 pages. Emil Dovifat gives the example of one of the weekend editions of a large daily newspaper in Berlin: of the paper's 79 pages, 25.5 were given over to editorial material and 53.5 to advertising, including 17 pages of small ads. A random examination of the weekday paper showed that of the 20 pages in the issue, 8.25 were text and the remainder advertisements.[90] Compared with the papers of the early nineteenth century with their 2–4 pages, the daily papers in the 1920s were so packed with reading material that Kurt Loele, editor of the magazine for railway station bookshops, voiced fears about modern newspapers being so bulky and unwieldy that they were no longer suitable for railway reading.[91]

Statistics from the immediate postwar period indicate a decline in the revenue that newspapers derived from advertising. The income figures for one of the daily papers published in the south of Germany indicate that in 1913, the ratio between advertising income and sales revenues was 73:27, with the bulk derived from advertising. However, by 1922 the situation had reversed: the figures were 28:72, with most of the paper's income coming from sales. Later in the 1920s the advertising-to-sales ratio stabilized, with about half of most newspapers' income being generated by advertising. Contemporary commentators linked this tendency primarily to the inflation and economic hardships of that period, which significantly increased newspapers' advertising costs and adversely affected readers' purchasing power. However, even if newspapers' revenues from advertising during the postwar period were down on figures from the prewar years, recognition of the importance of advertising, and in particular of commercial advertising, as a vital source of income for the press actually grew. During these years even public bodies such as the railway company and the postal authority began to rent out advertising space. Outdoor ads were placed almost everywhere. As Janet Ward in her very stimulating study *Weimar Surfaces* has noted: "the old Wilhelmine decorations that were religiously removed from buildings' facades in the radical architectural face-lifts of the functionalist 1920s *Neu Bauen* … were … reapplied and redecorated … in the service of technologically amplified 'light advertising' (Lichtreklame)."[92] Advertising also began to gain a foothold in the cinema. Unlike countries such as England, France, Austria, and Switzerland which banned commercial advertising on the radio, in Germany advertisements were carried by this medium as well.[93] In addition, company magazines (*Hauszeitschriften*) began to appear in the 1920s. These papers, put out by commercial companies, quickly proliferated. Overall, steady growth occurred in the numbers of newspapers and magazines published in the 1920s. In other words, despite reports about newspapers' declining incomes from advertising, increased numbers of newspapers meant constant growth in advertising space.

The newspaper owners therefore found themselves fighting on two fronts during the period of commercialization, economic adversity, and increasing popularity of the new media. On the one hand they had to fight for their readership; on the other, the struggle for the attention of the advertising public grew ever more desperate. This situation resulted in increased levels of "self-advertising" by newspapers, which used both advertising and editorial pages for this purpose.[94] The economic hardships of the times even led to some papers beginning in the 1920s to require payment in return for publishing reviews of theater and concert performances and so forth on the editorial pages. The increasing use of the "insurance papers" discussed above was also part of this development, showing the extent to which the period was dominated by economic patterns of thought. The facts of life that engulfed the German press in the wake of the world war forced it therefore to try out a broad range of approaches in order to survive in the increasingly cutthroat competition and economic adversity. These steps reinforced the process of commercialization of the press rather than obstructing it. However, the newspaper was not just a promoter generating advertising space: it also played a key role in the process of commercialization and the inculcation of new consumer culture values in everyday lifestyles.

The process of the commercialization of newspaper distribution examined in the first part of this chapter was one of the main expressions of the change in the target audience's attitude to reading material. This process contributed to the increased dependence on reading among all social groups in all parts of Germany. Targeting the broadest possible audiences and striving to meet the reading tastes of readers from a broad range of social strata and groups is therefore symbolic of the victory of a commercial way of thinking which views readers as a reservoir of potential consumers who are to be nurtured equally. The emergence of this approach played a key role in the evolution of modern consumer culture. The distribution methods outlined above patently reflected this tendency. They blurred traditional social differences, becoming sites where the paths of members of disparate social groups crossed. The distribution of newspapers and magazines in locales where a broad spectrum of social strata met, such as railway stations, kiosks, waiting rooms, and the streets, also showed that no single social class was responsible for the popularity enjoyed by newspapers and magazines. Rather, this phenomenon was generated by readers from the entire social spectrum. In addition, the marketing strategies of these distribution agents and their widespread use turned such "reading sites" into a means which helped readers to navigate their way through the evolving space of modern life. At railway stations, at kiosks, and through street vendors it was possible to immediately obtain a broad range of printed up-to-date information, and to satisfy a variety of requirements which did not necessarily match a particular reader's given social status. The increasingly visual appeal to readers in efforts to maximize newspaper and magazine sales, and in particular the broad range of reading materials, which offered far greater complexity and variety than the surroundings in which they were located, also showed that these "reading sites" were not only an integral part of the modern-urban-consumer space, but also helped to reproduce it.

Reading material itself also underwent an accelerated process of commercialization. In particular the combination of newspapers and advertising made reading an essential means for handling supply/demand relationships in a range of social domains. Both the world war and the years that followed it were times of increasing demand for information and entertainment to distract people from what was going on. This tendency boosted demand for newspapers among broader social classes than in the past. In this way the press also helped to reinforce these ways of thinking in terms of supply and demand, buying and selling, and a market economy operating under conditions of free competition to attract the attention of an anonymous target audience. What was unique to newspapers, therefore, was that they not only became a product which was traded in like any other product, but reading them actually encouraged this process of commercialization.

Newspapers targeted individuals. The phenomenon of the *Lesegesellschaften* (reading societies), one of the bourgeoisie's key institutions in the late eighteenth and early nineteenth centuries when newspapers were still read out in groups, began to vanish with the approaching twentieth century. In their stead came the silent and individual reading of a newspaper. The etiquette books of the period, which decried the offensive practice of joint newspaper reading, whether by peeking over a newspaper reader's shoulder or reading a paper out loud, reveal this tendency.[95] The wide range of magazines and newspapers, on the one hand, and the many different kinds of advertisements, on the other hand, also helped to reinforce the awareness of a reader's freedom of choice and the individualization of reading. Furthermore, the dependence between advertising pages and editorial pages made advertisements an inseparable part of a newspaper's nature and image, as well as an essential component in its existence. Given this situation, not only did readers have to make a study of and come to grips with the choice of newspapers and magazines on offer, as well as being able to distinguish between advertising and editorial material: they also learned in this way to identify themselves as consumers. As a result, the editorial pages of newspapers, which marketed information and entertainment, and especially the magazines and commercial advertisements helped to strengthen this perception of readers as consumers.

These developments also impacted on how newspapers were read. Not only was reading a purposeful activity with the goal of obtaining information and entertainment: it also became an activity capable of arousing readers' curiosity and stimulating their imaginations.[96] Both the editorial and the advertising pages used a whole range of approaches in their attempts to attract readers' attention. This was the reason, for example, why the graphic appearance of the editorial pages, which determined the paper's distinguishing commercial characteristic and constituted part of what made it unique, became more important. The *Generalanzeiger* papers, for example, some of which continued to publish their advertising columns before the editorial pages as late as the 1920s, reversed the order in which the different parts of the paper appeared. Various efforts were also made to inject new life into the newspaper's appearance so as to make it more spectacular and easier to read. Many papers even encouraged readers to play an active role in the actual writing of the paper. Readers' letters are perhaps the most striking example of this tendency. It is noteworthy that readers' involvement in writing the paper was particularly dominant in the local press.[97] A parallel development can be found in advertising. Viktor Mataja reports on a number of newspapers in Germany and Austria which ran advertising competitions in which readers were asked to choose what they considered the most attractive and effective advertisements. Some advertisers even involved readers in the actual advertising process by running competitions in which a cash prize was promised for those readers who suggested a brand name or advertising slogan for a particular product.[98] The *Berliner Morgenpost* daily paper, owned by Ullstein Publishers, distributed as a gift to readers a card game called "Da haben Sie den Salt!" (loosely translated as "What a mess!"), in which readers had to put together a number of advertisements for the paper's small ads listings. From the instructions accompanying this card game we gather that the motivation for developing the game was to draw readers' attention to the problems of designing a suitable advertisement. All of these examples bear witness to the process of commercialization of reading, and even more so to the ways in which this process was able to permeate readers' daily routines.

Hence the combination of advertising and newspapers not only contributed to the distribution of newspapers themselves or to encouraging the consumption of a range of products and services: it marketed consumption itself as a lifestyle leading to the Shangri-La of modern society. Reading became a form of "consumption through the eyes." In this sense, leafing through the pages of a newspaper became a form of flâneurie (loitering, aimless strolling) with the eyes. It was very similar to window-shopping where consumption "through the eyes" involves looking at shop or department store windows, which played a significant role in changing consumption from a purposeful activity to a purpose or end in its own right.[99] But even if "just looking" was not always, as in department stores, a prelude to "just buying," newspaper and magazine reading was an activity through which readers learned to be consumers.[100] The printed world was the quintessential domain in which there developed the world of symbols and images of modern consumer culture, and reading became an activity by means of which readers navigated their way in the evolving world of supply and demand of goods and services. Moreover, unlike department stores, which were a manifestly big-city phenomenon, newspapers and magazines reached all social groups in all areas, urban and rural alike. Newspaper and magazine reading was therefore of decisive importance in the modernization process of daily life and the fostering of consumer culture.

Consequently, any attempt to tackle the issue of sources of knowledge about the act of consumption or about the ways in which the consumer culture permeated daily life cannot and must not ignore the place of reading, especially newspaper reading, in this process.[101] In other words, while the press played a key role in creating the "public sphere" in the course of the eighteenth century, it played no less significant a role in the process of creating modern consumer culture as we know it from at least the last decade of the nineteenth century onward. This process did not escape the keen eyes of contemporary observers. The rest of this chapter will examine a number of aspects of the criticism directed at it.

Criticism of Reading: Newspaper Reading vs. Book Reading

Criticism of the newspaper/advertising alliance had an openly moralistic character. From church circles to newspaper owners themselves, complaints were heard about misleading advertising, the use of advertisements in order to deceive, and above all about advertising which was in bad taste and violated moral values.[102] The separation of editorial and advertising pages, as one of the arguments went, removed the responsibility for the contents of advertisements from the newspaper owners, so that it became possible to publish large numbers of indecent and deceptive advertisements (*Schmutz- und Schwindelinserate*). The Newspaper Owners' Association and Advertisers Association did call on their members to increase control over the advertisements published by them. However, notwithstanding these efforts the press was perceived as being willing, out of avarice, to publish all kinds of advertisements. A frequently advanced argument was that the publishing of advertisements had become the primary purpose of the press, to which even the editorial pages were subordinate. Walter Benjamin, who studied this process of commercialization in depth, went even further, stating that it "is practically impossible to write about the history of information without relating to the history of corruption in the press."[103] The commercialization of the press was, therefore, perceived as a process that adversely affected the freedom of the press and the newspapers' duty to represent the public interest.[104]

The separation between the editorial and advertising pages and the discussion about their relationship was therefore an inseparable part of the view that culture and economics, i.e., mind and matter, were two separate and mutually antagonistic areas. The newspapers, in this light, were required to determine the guiding principle that underlay their operations: the economic or the cultural. The emergence of this dilemma—a paper's economic capital vs. its cultural capital—also constituted the background to the oft-repeated demand that responsibility for publishing advertisements be shifted from the newspapers to the control of the local communities or the State. Ferdinand Lassalle, Heinrich von Treitschke, Max Weber, Karl Bücher, and Werner Sombart were just a few of the "team" of critics who warned against the process of commercialization of the press and raised their voices in support of the idea of a monopoly over advertising as a means of blocking this commercialization. Renouncing the cultural ambitions of the press and instead focusing on making economic capital was just one dimension of this criticism. Other aspects also subjected to the spotlight of critical scrutiny included newspaper readerships and newspaper reading itself.

Picture 6: The advertiser vs. newspaper (the advertiser knocks down the editor of the advertisements while the publisher and chief editor are watching sweating)

As Karl Bücher wrote, for example, in 1923, in Germany's large cities, it became a custom (*Sitte*) to spend every single free moment reading the paper. At cafés, in doctors' or lawyers' waiting rooms, in trams—all that was to be seen were people's heads buried in the pages of a newspaper.[105] People became so dependent on the paper, Hans Traub added, that many of them were afraid not to read a newspaper. In his view, the specific form of this addiction varied from one person to the next. Some would skim the entire paper; others would read certain parts only; while yet others would read the whole paper from cover to cover.[106] Walter Benjamin connected this development to the changed textuality, declaring that "the newspaper is read more in the vertical than in the horizontal plane, while film and advertisement force the printed word entirely into dictatorial perpendicular."[107] According to this approach, newspaper reading became an activity in which the eyes automatically fed the brain, instead of the brain directing the eyes when reading. The mechanization of reading was viewed therefore as a component in the manipulation of readers. Addiction, mechanization, and manipulation were perceived as the primary characteristics of newspaper reading. In this light, it is no wonder that those who were considered to be the primary victims of this kind of reading were women, workers, and youth. As an illustration, the data collected in 1927 by Rudolf Seyffert, professor of business studies at the University of Cologne, about the degree of intensity of reading the advertising pages in the daily press indicated that in a sample of 1,732 respondents (1,331 men and 401 women) 35 percent read the advertising pages regularly, 56 percent read them occasionally, and 9 percent never read them. However, this study also showed that of the fifteen different vocational groups into which the survey respondents were divided, workers read the advertising pages with the greatest intensity, with 63 percent of them reading the advertising pages on a regular basis.[108]

Specifically, contemporary research identified women as the group of readers most devoted to advertising. The various published guidelines on advertising even drew advertisers' attention to the importance of women as consumers generally, not just in the area of female items. Women were perceived as those who did the shopping in every family, and hence it was suggested that advertisers focus their advertisements on them.[109] Overall, females were viewed as a group which could be easily influenced. The fact that most shoplifting in department stores was done by bourgeois women was explained by the claim that women were easily swayed.[110] Victor Mataja, for instance, explained that newspaper advertising was particularly effective among women because many of them felt uncomfortable in the public domain, preferring to view advertisements in the privacy of their own homes rather than looking at advertising posters in the streets. In his eyes, this tendency was also one of the reasons why newspapers had retained their status as an extremely effective means of advertising, despite the popularity of the new media.[111] The world war, which increased dependence on the newspapers as a means of conveying information, as well as the subsequent political changes, especially following the granting of votes to women, also encouraged more women than in the past to read daily newspapers. In other words, the postwar period marked the end of the days when it was the householder's role to read the paper and update the members of his household on the latest news. The party political press in particular tried to attract women readers. Many newspapers began offering supplements designed specifically for women and to deliberately target both sexes. Women's inclusion in the readership of daily papers also tied in with the process of commercialization of the newspapers. It was conventionally argued that this new readership wanted more advertising, more stories, and fewer erudite articles and politics in the daily press.[112]

Discussions about newspaper reading were therefore part of contemporary discourse about the process of the making of a mass society, one of whose chief characteristics was a way of relating to social reality based on gender/class. Specifically, the emergence of a faceless society of the masses was perceived as a process in which the male/bourgeois subject, who assumed full responsibility for how he lived his life, disappeared, to be replaced by the (female/working class) *Massenmensch*—the common man or woman, mere gullible objects at the mercy of fads which determined their way of life for them.[113] In support of this argument, Otto Groth admitted in his famous book on newspapers, "*Die Zeitung*," that he was constantly astonished anew to discover the lack of discernment on the part of readers. Karl Jaspers summarized this view as follows:

> In order to make sales, the instinct of millions must be gratified: the upshot of sensationalism, dullness for the mind, avoiding making any demands on the reader is a situation where everything is trivialized and brutalized.[114]

This schizophrenic attitude—which treats readers as a mindless mass, addicted to all kinds of manipulations, while at the same time dictating the nature and content of the publications and being responsible for the fragmentation of the newspaper scene (a state of affairs which contemporaries dubbed the "dictatorship of the readers"[115]), which views reading as an activity that contributes to discipline and social tranquility, and at the same time an activity capable of stirring up political and social tensions—was not only a characteristic of discourse about newspaper reading: it was also one of the manifest characteristics of discourse about modern consumer society.[116]

How reading/consumption were related to therefore to a large extent reflects the complex nature of the *Bürgertum* itself, and shows that this was not an interest group hewn from a single block. In this connection it is particularly interesting to note the status of publishers, caught as they were between two worlds. It was the publishers who propelled forward the process of commercialization of reading, and it was they who enjoyed its fruits. Some of them, as shown by the exposition so far, did indeed maintain the optimistic attitude to consumption, in the hope that increasing demand for reading material would also pave the way to an improvement in most readers' reading list. However, many of them subscribed to the view that perceived culture as lying beyond all economic or commercial considerations, and readers as a faceless mass whose taste was to be molded. This ambivalent situation also constituted the backdrop to the generation of the hierarchical approach to reading, distinguishing as it did between newspaper reading and book reading.[117] In other words, newspaper reading was bound up with the creation of the faceless, mass society and unbridled addiction to consumption, and it symbolized the victory of economic patterns of thought over cultural values. In contrast, book reading was perceived as an expression of self-restraint, refinement, and a pyramid-shaped social order at whose apex stood the male, educated *Bürgertum*. Nevertheless, this hierarchical separation between book reading and newspaper reading does not mean that book-reading culture was remote from the process of commercialization and the rise of the new consumer culture.[118] As outlined above, the first commercial advertisements were for books, and the domain of advertising was closely connected with the book trade. Books became articles symbolic of refined culture and education, and were perceived as luxuries of the non-corrupting variety which belonged in every self-respecting *bürgerlich* home. It would appear, therefore, that book-reading culture also formed part of the process by which the consumer society emerged. The next chapter will examine a number of aspects of this process, together with the relationship between book culture and the new consumer culture.

Notes

1. John Brewer, Niel McKendrick, and John H. Plumb, *The Birth of Consumer Society: The Commercialization of Eighteenth Century England* (Bloomington: Indiana University Press, 1982); Ben Fine, and Ellen Leopold, "Consumerism and Industrial Revolution," *Social History* 15 (1990), 151–179.
2. Georg Simmel, *Philosophie des Geldes* (Munich: Duncker & Humblot, 1930); Rolf Engelsing, "Probleme der Lebenshaltung in Deutschland im 18. und 19. Jahrhundert," in: idem, *Zur Sozialgeschichte deutscher Mittel- und Unterschichten* (Göttingen: Vandenhoeck & Ruprecht, 1973), 11–25.
3. Don Slater, *Consumer Culture & Modernity* (Cambridge: Polity Press, 1997); Lisa Tiersten, "Redefining Consumer Culture: Recent Literature on Consumption and the Bourgeoisie in West Europe," *Radical History Review* 57 (1993), 116–159; Jean-Christophe Agnew, "Coming up for Air: Consumer Culture in Historical Perspective," in: John Brewer, and Roy Porter, eds., *Consumption and the World of Goods* (London: Routledge, 1993), 19–40; Paul Glennie, "Consumption within Historical Studies," in: Daniel Miller, ed., *Acknowledging Consumption: A Review of New Studies* (London: Routledge, 1995), 164–203; Peter N. Stearns, "Stages of Consumerism: Recent Work on the Issues of Periodization," *Journal of Modern History* 69 (1997), 102–117.

4. Gary Cross, *Time and Money: The Making of Consumer Culture* (London: Routledge, 1993).
5. Morag Shiach, *Discourse on Popular Culture* (Cambridge: Polity Press, 1989), 71–100.
6. On the History of Newspapers in Germany see: Otto Groth, *Die Zeitung* (Mannheim: Bensleimer, 1930); Karl Schottenloher, and Johannes Binkowski, *Flugblatt und Zeitung. Ein Wegweiser durch das gedruckte Tagesschriftum* (Munich: Klinkhardt & Biermann, 1985, originally 1922); Irene Jentsch, "Zur Geschichte des Zeitunglesens in Deutschland am Ende des 18. Jahrhunderts," Ph.D. diss., University of Leipzig, 1937; Margot Lindemann, *Deutsche Presse bis 1815* (Berlin: Colloquium Verlag, 1969); Karl Bömer, Bibliographisches Handbuch der Zeitungswissenschaft (Leipzig: Otto Harrassowitz, 1929); Kurt Koszyk, *Vorläufer der Massenpresse* (Munich: Wilhelm Goldmann Verlag, 1972); idem, *Deutsche Presse im 19. Jahrhundert* (Berlin: Colloquium Verlag, 1966).
7. On the history of Journals: Joachim Kirchner, *Die Grundlage des deutschen Zeitschriftenwesens* (Leipzig K.W. Hiersmann, 1928); idem, *Das deutsche Zeitschriftenwesen: Seine Geschichte und sein Wesen* (Wiesbaden: Harrassowitz, 1962); Gerhard Menz, *Die Zeitschrift* (Stuttgart: C.E. Poeschel Verlag, 1928).
8. On this development: Erna Lehmann, "Die Entwicklung und Bedeutung der modernen deutschen Modepresse," Ph.D. diss., University of Heidelberg, 1914; Lore Krempel, *Die deutsche Modezeitschrift* (Coburg: Tagblatt Haus, 1935); Karen Heinz, "Schick, selbst mit beschränkten Mittel! Die Anleitung zur alltäglichen Distinktion in einer Modezeitschrift der Weimarer Republik," *Werkstatt Geschichte* 7 (1994), 9–17. Edith Rosenbrock, *Die Anfänge des Modebildes in den deutschen Zeitschriften* (Charlottenburg: Rudolf Lorentz Verlag, 1942); Wolfgang Martens, *Die Botschaft der Tugend. Die Aufklärung im Spiegel der deutscher moralischen Wochenschriften* (Stuttgart: J.B. Metzlersche Verlagsbuchhandlung, 1968); Ute Schneider, *Der moralische Charakter. Ein Mittel aufklärerischer Menschendarstellung in den frühen deutschen Wochenschriften* (Stuttgart: Akademische Verlag, 1976); Wolfgang Martens, "Leserezepte fürs Frauenzimmer. Die Frauenzimmerbibliotheken der deutschen moralischen Wochenschrift," *Archiv für Geschichte des Buchwesens* 15 (1975), 1143–1200.
9. Jürgen Habermas, *Strukturwandel der Öffentlichkeit* (Frankfurt a.M.: Suhrkamp, 1990); For different interpretation of Habermas argument: Carig Calhoun, ed., *Habermas and the Public Sphere* (Cambridge, Mass.: MIT Press, 1992).
10. Ernst Lehmann, *Einführung in die Zeitschriftenkunde* (Leipzig: Verlag Karl W. Hiersemann, 1936); Anne-Susanne Rischk, *Die Lyrik in der Gartenlaube 1853–1903* (Frankfurt a.M.: Peter Lang, 1982); Heidemarie Gruppe, *Volk zwischen Politik und Idylle in der Gartenlaube* (Frankfurt a.M.: Peter Lang Verlag, 1976); Annette Seybold, "Erzählliteratur in der konservativen Presse 1892–1914," Ph.D. diss., University of Frankfurt a.M., 1987.
11. On reading and urban life see also the volume: Malcolm Gee, and Tim Kirk, eds., *Printed Matters: Printing, Publishing and Urban Culture in Europe in the Modern Period* (Aldershot: Ashgate, 2002), and Peter Fritzsche, Reading Berlin 1900 (Cambridge, Mass.: Harvard University Press, 1996).
12. Karl Bücher, "Der Zeitungsvertrieb," in: idem, *Gesammelte Aufsätze zur Zeitungskunde* (Tübingen: Verlag der H. Laupp'schen, 1926), 193–233; Oswald Kohut, *Zeitung und Zeitschriften als Handelsgut* (Berlin: Verlag Waldheim, 1930); Wilhelm Heidelberg, "Der Vertrieb," *Die Reklame* 22 (1929), 899–902.
13. Ernst Drahn, *Geschichte des deutschen Buch- und Zeitschriftenhandels* (Berlin: Central Vereine Deutscher Buch und Zeitschriftenhändler, 1914); Franz Jahn, "Der deutsche Kolportagebuchhandel," Ph.D. diss., University of Würzburg, 1928; Emil Niewöhner, *Geschichte und Probleme des Zeitschriftenbuchhandels* (Dresden: Zahn & Nasch, 1932); idem, *Der Reise- und Versandbuchandel* (Dresden: Zahn & Nasch, 1933); idem, *Der deutsche Zeitschriftenbuchhandel* (Stuttgart: Poeschel Verlag, 1934); Fridrich Elsner, *Beiträge und Dokumente zur Geschichte des werbenden Buch- und Zeitschriftenhandels* 2 vol. (Cologne: Verband vom werbenden Buch- und Zeitschriftenhandel e.V., 1961).
14. Albert Martino, *Die Deutsche Leihbibliothek* (Wiesbaden: Harrassowitz, 1990), 565.
15. Ernst Drahn, "Die Bedeutung des Buch- und Zeitschriftenhandels innerhalb des Gesamtbuchhandels," in: idem, *Zwei Vorträge. Bericht über die 44 Mitgliederversammlung des Re-*

ichsverbandes Deutscher Buch und Zeitschriftenhändler 19 u. 20 Juni München (Berlin: Verlag des Reichsverbandes Deutschen Buch und Zeitschriftenhändler, 1932), 5.

16. Drahn, Die Bedeutung des Buch, 49 and 72.
17. Rudolf Schenda, *Volk ohne Buch. Studien zur Sozialgeschichte der populären Lesestoffe 1770–1910* (Frankfurt a.M., Vittorio, 1970), 270.
18. Niewöhner, *Der deutsche Zeitschriftenbuchhandel,* 51.
19. Karl Felske, *75 Jahre Verband Deutscher Lesezirkel 1908 bis 1983* (Düsseldorf: Verband Deutscher Lesezirkel, 1983); idem, ed., *Die deutschen Lesezirkel* (Düsseldorf: Verband Deutscher Lesezirkel, 1969); Georg Jäger, "Die deutsche Leihbibliothek im 19. Jahrhundert. Verbreitung—Organisation—Verfall," *Internationales Archiv für Sozialgeschichte der deutschen Literatur* 2 (1977), 106–109.
20. Otto Dann, ed., *Lesegesellschaft und bürgerliche Emanzipation* (Munich: Beck, 1981); idem, ed., *Vereinswesen und Bürgerliche Gesellschaft in Deutschland* (Munich: Oldenbourg, 1984).
21. Erich Berger, "Vertrieb und Werbung," *Die Reklame* 24 (1932), 192.
22. Otto Groth, *Die Zeitung* vol. 3 (Mannheim: J. Bensheimer, 1930), 35–70; Karl Botz, "*Zeitungsvertrieb der Deutschen Reichspost,*" Ph.D. diss., University of Mannheim, 1933; *Der Vertrieb von Zeitung und Zeitschriften durch die Deutsche Bundespost* (Berlin: Berliner Formula-Verlag, 1955).
23. Karl Sautter, *Geschichte der Deutschen Post* (Frankfurt a.M., 1951), 593.
24. *10 Jahre Deutsche Reichsbahn* (Berlin: Hoppented, 1934), 4; cf. also *Hundert Jahre deutsche Eisenbahn. Jubiläumsschrift zum hundertjährigen Bestehen der deutschen Eisenbahn* (Berlin: Deutsche Reichsbahn, 1935).
25. Wofgang Schivelbusch, *Geschichte der Eisenbahnreise. Zur Industralisierung von Raum und Zeit im 19 Jahrhundert* (Frankfurt a.M.: Fischer, 1981); Dieter Vorsteher, "Bildungsreise unter Dampf," in: Hermman Bausinger, Klaus Beyer, and Gottfried Kroff, eds., *Reisekultur. Von der Pilgerfahrt zum modernen Tourismus* (Munich: C.H. Beck, 1991), 304–311; Joseph Roth, "Reiselektüre," original 1931 in: idem, *Werke* vol. 3 (Cologne: Kiepenheuer & Wirtsch, 1976), 347–348.
26. Richard Leibl, "Die geschichtliche Entwicklung des deutschen Bahnhofsbuchhandels," *Der Vertrieb,* no. 24, 25, 26, 37 (1937), no. 15, 16 (1938), and no. 24 (1939); Bertold Hack, "Marginalien, Nachrichten und Dokumente aus der Geschichte des Bahnhofsbuchhandels bis zum Ersten Weltkrieg," *Der neue Vertrieb* 17 (1965), 2–15; idem, "Der Bahnhofsbuchhandel vor und im 1. Weltkrieg," *Der neue Vertrieb* 24 (1972), 1–28; Ernst Heimeran, "50 Jahresfeier des Verbandes Deutscher Bahnhofsbuchhändler" in: idem, *Von Büchern und Büchermachen* (Munich: Verlag Dokumentation, 1968), 151–172; Karl Fuchs, "Die gewerberechtliche Behandlung der Bahnhofsbuchhandlung," Ph.D. diss., University of Cologne, 1936; Siegfried Frehoff, *Der Bahnhofbuchhandel in Deutschland* (Mainz: Magisterarbeit, 1982); Oskar Häring, ed., *Stilke, Georg 1872–1922* (Berlin: Stilke Verlag, 1922); Wissel, von K., "Jahrhundertjubiläum Georg Stilke," *Börsenblatt für den Deutschen Buchhandel* 27 (1971), 3086–3087; Karl Schmitt, *Unsere Firmengeschichte 1841–1966* (Heidelberg: Schmitt & Co., 1966); Annemarie Meiner, *100 Jahre Theodor Ackermann* (Munich: Theodor Ackermann, 1965); *August Vaternahm 1874–1974 Bahnhofsbuchhandel* (Kassel: Selbs Verlag, 1974).
27. "Niederschrift über die Besprechung von 26. März. 1925 über Schund- und Schmutzschriften auf den Bahnhöfen" in: Geheimes Staatsarchiv Preußischer Kulturbesitz. Rep. 77, Tit 2772 Bd. 1 No. 8, 123.
28. Christiane Haug, "Das halbe Geschäft beruht auf Eisenbahnstationen... Zur Entstehungsgeschichte der Eisenbahnbibliotheken im 19. Jahrhundert," *Internationales Archiv für Sozialgeschichte der deutschen Literatur* 23 (1998), 70–117; R.M.S. Hall, "Railway Publishing," *Publishing History* 22 (1987), 43–72.
29. Bertold Hack, "Vom Bahnhofsbuchhandel unter besonderer Berücksichtigung des Zensur Problem," in: Günther Pflug, Brita Eckert, and Heiz Friesenhahn, eds., *Bibliothek- Buch - Geschichte* (Frankfurt a.M.: Vittorik Klostermann, 1977), 269–279.
30. Walther Borgius,"Zur Sozialisierung des Buchwesens," in: Hermann Beck, ed., *Wege und Ziele der Sozialisierung* (Berlin: Verlag Neues Vaterland, 1919), 122–161.

31. "Bekämpfung der Schund- und Schmutzschriften auf Bahnhöfen, in Zeitungskiosken und im Straßenhandel," Geheimes Staatsarchiv Preußischer Kulturbesitz. Rep. 77, Tit 2772 No. 8, 8a.
32. Although already in 1974 Rudolf Schenda drew attention to the kiosks as outlets for the distribution of reading material, there has not yet been any further research on the history of kiosks in Germany. Rudolf Schenda, "Das Kioskheft," in: Alfred Clemens Baumgärtner, ed., *Lesen—Ein Handbuch* (Hamburg: Verlag für Buchhandel Forschung, 1974), 40–43. Some valuable references on the history of kiosks could also be found in the unpublished Ph.D. dissertation of Elisabeth Naumann, "Der Kiosk. Entdeckung an einem trivialen Ort. Von Lustpavilion zum kleinen Konsumtempel," Ph.D. diss., Free University of Berlin, 1999, which is a sociological study on contemporary kiosks.
33. Werner Sombart, *Der moderne Kapitalismus*, vol. 2 (Munich: Duncker & Humblot, 1927), 360.
34. On the relationship between 'inside' and 'outside' see especially, Richard Sennett, *The Conscience of the Eye. The Design and Social Life of Cities* (New York: Alfred A. Knopf, 1990).
35. The kiosks became so much a natural part of the urban landscape that when, in the 1920s, the proposal was made in Cologne to close the kiosks and transfer the trade in newspapers and journals to mixed businesses, it raised a stormy controversy and the matter was quickly taken off the city's agenda.
36. Franz Joest, "Deutsche Bahnhof-Plakat-Reklame" in: Paul Ruben, ed., *Die Reklame und ihre Kunst und Wissenschaft* (Berlin: Hermann Paetel, 1914), 191–206.
37. As in the case of kiosks, the literature on the sale of reading material in the street is by no means abundant. The basis for our account is two professional street-vendors' journals, and the monograph: Otto Nahnsen, *Der Straßenhandel mit Zeitungen und Druckschriften in Berlin* (Essen: Verlag der wirtschaftlichen Nachrichten aus der Rurbezirk, 1922).
38. Ullstein, at the end of the 1920s, had 600 vendors in the street, Scherl had 500, and Mosse 300. On the major newspaper publishers in Berlin: Peter De Mendelsohn, *Zeitungsstadt Berlin. Menschen und Mächte in der Geschichte der Deutschen Presse* (Berlin: Ullstein, 1959).
39. On the political newspapers see: Heinz-Dietrich Fischer, ed., *Deutsche Zeitungen des 17. bis 20. Jahrhunderts* (Munich: Verlag Dokumentation, 1972).
40. Janet Ward, *Weimar Surfaces: Urban Visual Culture in 1920s Germany* (Berkeley: University of California Press, 2001).
41. At first, the vendors went to the publishers or the distribution points to collect the newspapers. During the 1920s, this method of distribution was abandoned and the publishing firms and large distributing companies began to employ the services of motorcyclists, bicyclists, and taxi drivers who brought the newspapers to agreed points where they met the vendors, thus making their cooperation more efficient.
42. Georg Simmel, "Die Großstädte und das Geistesleben," in: idem, *Das Individuum und die Freiheit* (Frankfurt a.M.: Fischer, 1993), 193.
43. Nahnsen, *Der Straßenhandel*, 48, gives only the numbers of those granted a license by the police to sell newspapers in the street. It is thus reasonable to suppose that the total number was much higher.
44. Kohut, *Zeitung und Zeitschriften*, 134.
45. Bücher, Der Zeitungsvertrieb, 227, in 1922 saw advertisements for sixteen different journals devoted to sport and horses alone in the journal the *Zeitungshändler*—the vendors newspapers in the streets. See also Geyer's interesting study of Munich: Martin H. Geyer, *Verkehrte Welt. Revolution, Inflation und Moderne. München 1914–1923* (Göttingen, Vandenhoeck & Ruprecht, 1998).
46. In the journal of the railway-station bookshops, which were in stiff competition with the street-vendors, there were many complaints of the tolerant attitude of the authorities to the phenomenon of trading in the street, and some claimed that political and commercial factors were behind this policy.

47. Groth, *Die Zeitung*, vol. 3, 146.
48. Bücher, Der Zeitungsvertrieb, 203.
49. Groth, Otto, *Die Zeitung*, vol. 1 (Mannheim: J. Bensheimer, 1928), 352–353; Hans Blinde, "Die Zeitung im Dienste der Reklame," Ph.D. diss., University of Erlangen, 1931, 73.
50. Walter Schubert, "Das Zeitungsplakat in Deutschland," *Archiv für Buchgewerbe und Gebrauchsgraphik* 65 (1928), 203–208.
51. Otto Ackva, "Die Abonnenten Versicherung der deutschen illustrierten Familienblätter," Ph.D. diss., University of Leipzig, 1923; Erwing Fink, "Die Abonnenten Versicherung in Deutschland," Ph.D. diss., University of Erlangen, 1917; Willy Blechschmidt, "Die Abonnentenversicherung," Ph.D. diss., University of Frankfurt a.M., 1931; Paul Niemczyk, *Die deutsche Abonnentenversicherung unter Reichsaufsicht* (Berlin: Curt Hamelsche, 1932); Eduard Rudolf, *Illustrierte Zeitschriften mit Abonnenten-Versicherung* (Berlin: published by the author, 1929); *Die Abonnentenversicherung* (Nürnberg: Nürnberger Lebensversicherungsbank, 1929).
52. M.J. Baldsiefen, "Abonnentenversicherung," in: Walther Heide, ed., *Handbuch der* Zeitungswissenschaft, vol. 1 (Leipzig: Verlag Karl W.H. Wesemann, 1940), 4.
53. Fink, Die Abonnenten Versicherung, 41.
54. "Das Reichsaufsichtsamt für Privatversicherung in der Denkschrift der Reichsregierung vom 11.1. 1913" From: Niemczyk, *Die deutsche Abonnentenversicherung*, 20–21.
55. Ludwig Arps, *Auf sicheren Pfeilern. Deutsche Versicherungswirtschaft vor 1914* (Göttingen: Vandenhoeck & Ruprecht, 1965); idem, *Durch unruhige Zeiten. Deutsche Versicherungswirtschaft seit 1914*, 2 vol. (Karlsruhe: Verlag Versicherungswirtschaft, 1976); Peter Borscheid, *Mit Sicherheit Leben* (Greven: Eggenkamp Verlag, 1989); Anette Drees, *Versicherungsstatistik Deutschlands 1750–1985* (St. Katharinen: Scripta Mercaturae Verlag, 1988).
56. Niemczyk, Die Abonnentenversicherung, 68.
57. Ernst Schmidt, ed., *Handbuch der Hauszeitschriften* (Cologne: Verlag Gebrüder Brocker, 1933).
58. Paul Ruben, ed., *Die Reklame ihre Kunst und Wissenschaft* (Berlin: Hermann Paetel, 1914); Hans-Heinz Meißner, "Das Inserat in den großen deutschen politischen Tageszeitungen von 1850 bis 1870," Ph.D. diss., University of Leipzig, 1931; Heinz Born, "Das Anzeigengeschäft der Tagespresse," Ph.D. diss., University of Freiburg i.Br, 1929; Albrecht Blau, *Inseratenmarkt der Deutschen Tageszeitung* (Berlin: Junker und Dünnhaupt, 1932); Fritz Scharf, "Umfang und Rhythmus der Werbung durch Anzeigen," Ph.D. diss., University of Heidelberg, 1937; Kurt Reumann, "Entwicklung der Vertriebs- und Anzeigenerlöse im Zeitungsgewerbe seit den 19. Jahrhundert," *Publizistik* 13 (1968), 226–271; Kurt Koszyk, "Geschichte des Anzeigenwesens," in: Eva Brand, Peter Brand, and Volker Schulze, eds., *Die Zeitungsanzeige* (Aachen: Hahner Verlag, 1990), 21–31; Fritz Redlich, *Reklame. Begriff—Geschichte—Theorie* (Stuttgart: Ferdinand Enke, 1935); Viktor Mataja, *Die Reklame. Eine Untersuchung über Ankündigungswesen und Werbetätigkeiten im Geschäftsleben* (Munich: Duncker & Humblot, 1926); Erwin Paneth, *Entwicklung der Reklame von Altertum bis zur Gegenwart* (Munich: R. Oldenbourg, 1926), 91–95; Johannes Schmiedchen, *Geschichte der deutschen Wirtschaftswerbung* (Tübingen: Werking-Verlag, 1953); Rudolf Seyffert, *Werbelehre* (Stuttgart: C.E. Poeschel, 1966); Dirk Reinhardt, *Von der Reklame zum Marketing. Geschichte der Wirtschaftswerbung in Deutschland* (Berlin: Akademie Verlag, 1993).
59. Werner Greiling, "Intelligenzblätter und gesellschaftlicher Wandel in Thüringen," Sonderdruck aus den Schriften des Historischen Kollegs, Vorträge 46, 1995; Gerhard Petrat, "Das Intelligenzblatt—eine Forschungslücke," in: Elgar Blühm and Hartwig Gebhardt, eds., *Presse und Geschichte*, vol. 2 (Munich: K.G. Saur, 1987), 207–231.
60. Peter Borscheid, "Am Anfang war das Wort. Die Wirtschaftswebung beginnt mit der Zeitungsannuce," in: idem, and Clemens Wischermann, eds., *Bilderwelt des Alltags. Werbung in der Konsumgesellschaft des 19. und 20. Jahrhunderts* (Stuttgart: Franz Steiner Verlag, 1995), 20–43.

61. Bücher also supported the idea of renationalizing the area of advertising, but he foresaw the parties foiling this idea. Karl Bücher, "Das Intelligenzwesen" in: idem, *Gesammelte Aufsätze zur Zeitungskunde* (Tübingen: Verlag der H. Lauppschen Buchhandlung, 1926), 106.
62. Josef Pantenburg, *Die Entwicklung des Anzeigenwesens der Berliner Presse von Aufhebung des Intelligenzzwanges bis zu den Generalanzeigen* (Berlin: Triltsch & Huther, 1938).
63. Figures about the advertisements published by the *Leipziger Tageblatt* indicate a similar trend. In 1819, 25 percent of the advertisements in the paper were for books, and they occupied 84 percent of its advertising space. By 1860 the corresponding figures had plummeted to 4 percent, or 5 percent of its advertising space: Peter Johan Bachem, *Das Eindringen der Reklame in die deutschen politischen Tageszeitungen* (Cologne: Verlag J.P. Bachem, 1929).
64. Ibid, 43.
65. Hellmut Rosenfeld, "Zur Geschichte von Nachdruck und Plagiat. Mit einer chronologischen Bibliographie zum Nachdruck von 1733 bis 1824," *Archiv für Geschichte des Buchwesens* 90 (1971), 337–372.
66. Horst Kliemann, *Die Werbung fürs Buch* (Stuttgart: C.E. Poeschel Verlag, 1923).
67. Stefan Haas, "Die neue Welt der Bilder. Werbung und visuelle Kultur der Moderne," in: Peter Borscheid, and Clemens Wischerman, eds., *Bilderwelt des Alltags* (Stuttgart: Franz Steiner Verlag, 1995), 78–90.
68. Wolfgang Huck, "Die kleine Anzeige, ihre Organisation und volkswirtschaftliche Bedeutung," Ph.D. diss., University of Heidelberg, 1914.
69. Viktor Mataja, *Heiratsvermittlung und Heiratsanzeige* (Munich: Dunker & Humbolt, 1920); Hans Zeuger, "Der Ehe Markt," *Der Bücherkreis. Sonderheft: Prostitution Liebe Ehe* 6 (1930), 24–26; Siegfried Kracuer, "Kampf gegen die Kuppelanzeige" (originally 1931), in: idem, *Berliner Nebeneinander. Ausgewählte Feuilletons 1930–33* (Zürich: Edition Epoche, 1996), 159–161.
70. Mataja, *Die Reklame,* 196.
71. Bachem, *Das Eindringen der Reklame.*
72. Groth, *Die Zeitung* vol. 3, 227.
73. Hans-Wolfgang Walter, *Generalanzeiger—Das Pragmatische Prinzip. Zur Entwicklungsgeschichte und Typologie des Pressewesens im späten 19. Jahrhundert* (Bochum: Studienverlag Dr. N. Brockmeyer, 1981); Emil Dovifat, "Die Anfänge der Generalanzeigerpresse," *Archiv für Buchgewerbe und Gebrauchsgraphik* 56 (1928), 163–184.
74. Karl Bömer, "Die allgemeinen Rentabilitätsgrundsätze der deutschen Zeitungswirtschaft," in: idem, and Friedrich Bertkau, *Der wirtschaftliche Aufbau des Deutschen Zeitungsgewerbes* (Berlin: Carl Duncker Verlag, 1932), 101–145.
75. Wilhelm J. Naumann, "Die Tageszeitung, wie sie ist," in: idem, ed., *Die Presse und der Katholik. Anklage und Rechtfertigung* (Augsburg: Haas & Grabherr, 1932), 118.
76. Otto Löffler, "Der Inseratenmarkt der illustrierten Zeitung," Ph.D. diss., University of Heidelberg, 1935; Wilmont Haacke, "Das Magazin, ein unentdeckter Zeitschriftentypus," *Archiv für Geschichte des Buchwesens* 90 (1971), 429–448.
77. *Ullstein Berichte* 1927–1933; Rudolg Seyffert, *Allgemeine Werblerher* (Stuttgart: C.E. Poeschel Verlg, 1929), 560; Ernst H. Lehmann, "Illustrierte Zeitschriften," in: Heide Walther, ed., *Handbuch der Zeitungswissenschaft,* vol. 2 (Leipzig: Verlag Karl W.H. Wasemann, 1940), 79–90.
78. Lehmann, modernen deutschen Modepresse, 36.
79. Quoted in Naumann, Die Tageszeitung, 226.
80. Brake Laurel, Bill Bell, and David Finkelstein (eds.), *Nineteenth-Century Media and the Construction of Identities* (Houndmills: Palgrave, 2000).
81. Menz, *Die Zeitschrift,* 57; Gerhard Muser, *Statistische Untersuchungen über die Zeitungen Deutschlands 1885–1914* (Leipzig: Verlag von Emanuel Reinicke, 1918); Ernst Umlauf, "Der deutsche Buchhandel bis 1930," *Europa Archiv* (1947), 168; Oskar Michael (ed.), *Handbuch Deutscher Zeitung 1917* (Berlin: Otto Elsner Verlagsgesellschaft, 1917), XXII;

Erhard Georgii, "Zur Statistik der deutschen Zeitung," in: *Handbuch der deutschen Tagespresse. 1932* (Berlin: Carl Duncker Verlag, 1932), 20; Richard Pape, *Handbuch der Fachpresse* (Berlin: Verlag des "Archiv für Gewerbepolitik und Volkswirtschaft," 1926), 12; Erich Lorenz, *Die Entwicklung des deutschen Zeitschriftwesens* (Berlin: Diss. Phill, 1936); Friedrich Bertkau, "Die stofflichen Grundlagen und methodischen Voraussetzung für eine Untersuchung der deutschen Zeitungswissenschaft," in: Friedrich Bertkau, and Karl Bömer, *Der wirtschaftliche Aufbau des Deutschen Zeitungsgewerbes* (Berlin: Carl Duncker Verlag, 1932), 48; Hans Kapfinger, "Der Werbfaktor der Deutschen Zeitungs-Industrie," *Die Reklame* (1930), 622–625.

82. Walter Williams, "Some Observations on the German Press," *The University of Missouri Bulletin* (1932), 1–19; Williams's research is based on data from the *Handbuch der Deutschen Tagespresse 1932* (Berlin: Carl Duncker Verlag, 1932).
83. Hans Kapfinger, "Die Struktur der katholischen Presse," in: Wilhelm J. Naumann (ed.), *Die Presse und der Katholik. Anklage und Rechtfertigung* (Augsburg: Haas & Grabherr, 1932), 226.
84. Hanns Kropff, and Bruno W. Randolph, *Marktanalyse. Untersuchung des Marktes und Vorbereitung der Reklame* (Munich: R. Oldenbourg, 1928); Hans Paul Roloff, "Experimentelle Untersuchung der Werbewirkung von Plakatenwürfen," *Schriften zur Psychologie der Berufseignung und des Wirtschaftsleben* (1927).
85. E.R. Uderstädt, "Die Stellung der Annoncen-Expeditionen im Deutschen Wirtschaftsleben," *Die Reklame* 22 (1929), 588–592; Gerd F. Heuer, *Entwicklung der Annoncen-Expeditionen in Deutschland* (Frankfurt a.M.: Diesterweg Verlag, 1937).
86. Karl d'Ester, *Das Studium der Zeitungswissenschaft in Deutschland* (Charlottenburg: Verlag Hochschule und Ausland, 1925); Karl Jaeger, *Von der Zeitungskunde zur publizitischen Wissenschaft* (Jena: G. Fischer, 1926); Hans Traub, "Zeitungswissenschaft und Berufsbildung," in: *Jahrbuch der Tagespresse 1930* (Berlin: Duncker Verlag, 1930), III–XIII.
87. Karl d'Ester, "Katholische Zeitschriften und ihre Leser," in: Wilhelm J. Nauman (ed.), *Die Presse und der Katholik. Anklage und Rechtfertigung* (Augsburg: Haas & Grabherr, 1932), 269.
88. Richard Pape, "Die Deutschen Zeitschriften in ihren Beziehungen zu Wirtschaft und Kultur," *Die Reklame* (1928), 41; Julius Hirsch, *Zur Preisbewegung des Inserates 1914 und 1927 bei den Tageszeitungen* (Berlin: Sondedruck, 1928), 12.
89. Lehmann, modernen deutschen Modepresse, 46.
90. Emil Dovifat, *Zeitungswissenschaft* (Leipzig: Walter de Gruyter, 1931), 116.
91. Kurt Loele, "Papierflut," *Der Bahnhofsbuchhandel* (26.3.1930).
92. Ward, *Weimar Surfaces,* 114.
93. Erich Glässer, "Die Rundfunkreklame in Deutschland," Ph.D. diss., University of Nürnberg, 1932; Hans Bausch, *Rundfunkpolitik in der Weimarer Republik* (Munich: dtv, 1980), 136–139; Felix Joachim Leonhard, ed., *Programgeschichte des Hörfunks in der Weimarer Republik* (Munich: dtv, 1998), 363–366.
94. Armin Kiehl, *Die Eigen-Werbung des Zeitungsverlag* (Eilenburg: C.W. Offenhauer, 1934).
95. Cf. for example Graf und Gräfin Baudissin, *Das goldene Buch der Sitte* (Stuttgart: Verlag von W. Spemann, 1913), no. 719.
96. Colin Campbell, *The Romantic Ethic and the Spirit of Modern Consumerism* (Oxford: Basil Blackwell, 1987); Friedrich Beckmann, "Lektüre als Konsumanreiz?" *Buchhandelsgeschichte* 10 (1991–1992), B49–B60.
97. Philomen Schönhagen, *Die Zeitung der Leser* (Munich: Publicom Medienverlag, 1993).
98. Mataja, *Die Reklame,* 222.
99. Anne Freidberg, *Window Shopping: Cinema and the Postmodern* (Berkeley, University of California Press, 1993).
100. Rudi Laermans, "Learning to Consume: Early Department Stores and the Shaping of the Modern Consumer Culture 1860–1914," *Theory, Culture & Society* 10 (1993), 92.
101. John Brewer, and Roy Porter, eds., *Consumption and the World of Goods* (London: Routledge, 1993); Ann Berminigham, and John Brewer, eds., *The Consumption of Culture*

1600–1800 (London: Routledge, 1995); John O. Jordan, and Robert L. Patten, eds., *Literature in the Marketplace. Nineteenth-Century British Publishing and Reading Practices* (Cambridge: Cambridge University Press, 1995).

102. "Bekämpfung unzüchtiger Inserate," Geheimes Staatsarchiv Preußischer Kulturbesitz. Rep 77 Tit 2772 No. 1, vol. 1 1920–1934.
103. Walter Benjamin, "Charles Baudelaire: ein Lyriker im Zeitalter des Hochkapitalismus Baudelaire," in: idem, *Gesammelte Schriften,* edited by Rolf Tiedemann & Hermann Schweppenhäuser, vol. 1, 2 (Frankfurt a.M.: Suhrkamp, 1974), 529.
104. Hans Traub, "Über die Kritik am Inseratenteil der Zeitung," *Die Reklame* 22 (1929), 903–908; Edgar Rubarth-Stern, "Der Konflikt Zwischen der Zeitung als moralischer Anstalt und als Wirtschaftsunternehmer," in: *Festschrift für Emil Dovifat* (Bermen: B.C. Heye, 1960); Wilhelm Scharrenbroich, *Irreführende und strafbare Werbeanzeigen* (Lübeck: Schmidt-Römhild, 1958).
105. Bücher, Der Zeitungsvertrieb, 220; see also Edlef Köppen, "The Magazine as Sign of the Times" (first published in 1925), in: Anton Kaes, Martin Jay, and Edward Dimendberg, eds., *The Weimar Sourcebook* (Berkeley: University of California Press, 1994), 644.
106. Hans Traub, *Zeitungswesen und Zeitungslesen* (Dessau: E. Dünnhaupt Verlag, 1928), 76.
107. Here quoted from Ward, *Weimar Surfaces,* 138.
108. Seyffert, *Allgemeine Werblerher,* 387.
109. Hanns Kropff, "Women as Shoppers" (first published in 1926), in: Anton Kaes, Martin Jay, and Edward Dimendberg, eds., *The Weimar Sourcebook,* 660–662.
110. Werner Sombart, *Liebe Luxus und Kapitalismus. Über die Entstehung der moderne Welt aus dem Welt dem Geist der Verschwendung* (Berlin: Wagenbach, 1996); Thorstein Veblen, *The Theory of Leisure Class: An Economic Study of Institutions* (New York: Mentor, 1899).
111. Mataja, *Die Reklame,* 255.
112. Josefin Trampler-Steiner, "Die Frau als Publizistin und Leserin," Ph.D. diss., University of Munich, 1938; On the politicization of women through consumption see: Margaret Finnegan, *Selling Suffrage: Consumer Culture and Votes for Women* (New York: Columbia University Press, 1999).
113. Helmuth Berking, *Masse und Geist. Studien zur Soziologie in der Weimarer Republik* (Berlin: WAV, 1984).
114. Karl Jaspers, *Die geistige Situation der Zeit* (Berlin: Walter de Gruyter, 1931), 110.
115. Naumann, *Die Presse und der Katholik,* 115.
116. Daniel Horowitz, *The Morality of Spending. Attitudes towards the Consumer Society in America, 1875–1940* (Chicago: Elephant Paperback, 1992); Don Slater, *Consumer Culture & Modernity* (Oxford: Polity Press, 1997); for the German context: Warren G. Breckmann, "Disciplining Consumption: The Debate about Luxury in Wilhelmine Germany 1890–1914," *Journal of Social History* 24 (1990–1991), 485–505.
117. On the distinction between book and newspaper reading see also Carl Briknkmann, "Presse und Öffentlichkeit," *Verhandlungen des Siebenten Deutschen Soziologentag von 28. September bis 1. Oktober 1930 in Berlin* (Berlin J.C.B. Mohr, 1931), 21.
118. On this see also John B. Thompson, *The Media and Modernity: A Social Theory of the Media* (Stanford: Stanford University Press, 1995).

Chapter IV

From Reading Books to Consumption of Books and Back Again

An examination of statistics about the book trade market in Germany between World War I and Hitler's assumption of power shows that despite the economic hardships, the social upheavals, and the political instability which followed the world war, the commercial reading-material market managed to recover amazingly quickly from the slump that overtook it during the world war, and even succeeded in showing signs of growth.[1] The downturn during the World War, marked by a drop in the total number of publications (books and magazines) produced in German-speaking areas—from 34,871 in 1913 to 14,910 in 1917—was followed by a spectacular recovery. As early as 1920, the number of publications had shot up to 32,345, in the following year swelling still further to 34,252.[2] Apart from the drop-off in the number of publications in 1923 and 1924, apparently in the wake of the galloping inflation in 1923 and changes in how data were collected in 1924,[3] the upward trend continued at least until 1927, when total publications reached an unprecedented figure of 37,866.

Given these figures, differences can be identified between the graph showing the publication of books—a figure which fluctuated throughout the 1920s, and magazines, where the number of publications rose steadily throughout the decade. However, despite the uneven performance of the book market, a comparison of data for book publishing in Germany and the equivalent in other countries (Table 4.1) shows that the number of titles published in the German-speaking world was significantly larger than elsewhere, including France, Italy, England, and the United States.[4]

The figures in Table 4.1 should be treated with extreme caution. It may reasonably be assumed that the source of the differences between the different columns is not the absolute number of titles published in each country, but rather differences in how the concept of a "book" is defined and the different methods used for data collection purposes.[5] Nevertheless, the Table data can provide some indication of how the book markets behaved in these countries. The data in the table suggest a certain similar-

Table 4.1
Book publication figures for Germany, France, Italy, England, and the USA[6]

Year	USA	England	Italy	France	Germany
1890	4,559 = 100	5,735 = 100	10,339 = 100	13,643 = 100	15,714 = 100
1900	6,356 = 139	7,149 = 125	9,975 = 96	13,362 = 98	24,792 = 158
1913	12,230 = 269	12,379 = 216	9,292 = 89	—	28,182 = 181
1922	8,638 = 189	10,842 = 189	5,561 = 53	9,432 = 69	30,804 = 196
1927	10,153 = 222	13,820 = 241	5,687 = 55	11,922 = 88	31,026 = 198
1930	10,026 = 210	15,393 = 269	9,426 = 91	9,176 = 65	26,961 = 172

ity between the German publications market and its American and English counterparts, at least in terms of the upward trend in number of publications. While the growth in the number of publications on the Anglo-American book market is far steeper than for its German counterpart, an analysis of the ratio between first editions and reprints shows that in England and the USA, there was a far greater tendency to produce reprints, while the German market was characterized by the tendency to produce new titles (Table 4.2). This figure is significant, since the investment in publishing a new title and the concomitant risk for a publisher who makes this investment is far greater than the corresponding investment and risk for a publisher producing a reprint of an existing title.

The question is therefore why German publishers tended to take this risk. Can this tendency be interpreted as an expression of the economic strength of the German book market, or perhaps of its cultural openness and innovation? Perhaps by the same token this economic pattern was the upshot of low sales volumes, unsuccessful commercial policy, and unsuitable structure on the part of the reading material market, which led to books failing to reach the reprint stage.

More accurate figures, particularly for the size of print runs and sales volumes of books, might help to provide us with answers to these questions. The absence of these data, as well as the partial information avail-

Table 4.2
First editions vs. reprints[7]

Year	Germany	England	USA
1920	2.90	3.85	7.09
1924	3.54	2.98	6.78
1925	3.32	3.09	5.41
1926	3.77	3.55	5.49
1927	4.03	2.97	6.01
1928	4.74	2.80	5.63
1929	4.58	2.77	4.52
1930	4.59	3.06	4.29

able to us concerning the methods used to collect and process data, and the underlying reasons for doing so, make these figures an unreliable historical source which cannot be depended upon to provide us with satisfactory answers to the questions posed above. Despite these limitations, the available statistical data can nevertheless give us an idea of the dynamism of the book trade market in postwar Germany. They can also provide some indication of the relationship between book-reading culture and the new consumer culture. This relationship is reflected not only in the increased printing of a particular product so it can be consumed—something which it may be assumed was one of the basic principles behind the effort to produce a statistical database for the book trade—but also in the methods of book distribution and the symbolic significance of book reading as an activity, as well as of books as objects in contemporary German society.

We will therefore now focus on how book-reading culture became part of consumer culture. The discussion will first examine the difference between reading borrowed books and reading bought books. The key question underlying this discussion is whether here we have two competing approaches, representing different views of book-reading culture, or whether they are simply different manifestations of one and the same book culture. In fact, we will see that these two ways of reading books are actually different expressions of the way that reading culture became part of the new consumer culture. This trend was particularly visible in the postwar period. It was at this time of economic hardships and increasing competition with the new media that the book trade market tried hardest to find new ways of encouraging reading and distributing books. These methods for the distribution and marketing of reading material show the complex nature of the book relationship at a time when consumer culture was becoming ever more dominant. The end of the chapter will discuss several of these manifestations of consumer culture as expressed in book-reading culture.

Reading: Borrowing vs. Buying

In the print age there are two main ways of reading books: borrowing or buying them. These two possibilities would appear to represent different ways of relating to book culture. The reading of books that have been purchased not only underscores the importance of reading a book several times as justification for its purchase, but also highlights book ownership as one of the basic values of book culture. In this case, a book becomes an object whose symbolic meaning goes far beyond the utilitarian value of reading it. The attention devoted to the form and appearance of books as well as the development of "reading furniture," designed specifically for reading and storing books, are manifest expressions of the symbolic significance of books as objects occupying a much prized place among the array of objects representing the "bourgeois" lifestyle.[8] The private ownership of books and the very possibility of buying books thus constitute an inseparable part of the enjoyment to which they give rise, as well as of their social and cultural significance. Books as collectors' items, and especially shops specializing in secondhand and antique books, which came about in Germany in the last third of the nineteenth century, are further expressions of the fetishistic nature of books as objects where the enjoyment derived from them involves acquiring and owning, not just reading them.[9]

In contrast, when reading takes place on the basis of borrowing, the focus of the activity is reading itself. In other words, loan-based reading negates the symbolic significance of book ownership, instead emphasizing reading per se as an activity with special value. In the case of loan-based reading, if we refer to book owning, this is collective ownership by the group that lends out books.[10] Emphasis on the importance of book reading at the expense of book ownership is also reflected in attitudes to the external form of books. For example, many lending institutions tended to rebind books in order to make them more durable, as well as to mark them as their property. This activity detracted considerably from books' aesthetic distinctiveness, as well as countering any fetishistic attitudes to them. The two manifestations of these different ways of approaching book reading are bookshops or the book trade on the one hand, and libraries on the other. The next section will describe these ways of book reading and their relationship with the new consumer culture.

The Book Trade

Gutenberg's perfection of printing technology in the 1440s marks the beginning of the printed book age. The invention of printing, allowing a written text to be mass produced and distributed to an unlimited public of potential readers, was undoubtedly of decisive importance for the development of the book trade.[11] However, despite the fact that the origins of the book trade lie in the pre-printing age, book trade historians identify the starting point of the modern book trade, as well as of the activity of reading as known to us today, as being located in the eighteenth century.[12] This was the time when book publishers began to replace patronage as bodies that supported and encouraged creative writing. The book trade began to change the principle underlying its operations from barter to money-based commerce, introducing a distinction between the production process and book distribution by separating printing works, publishing houses, and bookshops.[13] These developments resulted in the improvement and streamlining of book distribution methods, paving the way to the generation of new types of markets for books.[14]

A striking expression of the specialization of the book trade market was the steady increase in the number of German-language publications over this period. Between 1771 and 1800, the number of new publications registered in the Leipzig Book Fair's catalogue doubled from two thousand to four thousand. But the main change at this time was the expansion and diversification of areas in which books were published. Rolf Engelsing, who coined expressions to describe this change that still dominates reading research in Germany, described this development as a shift from intensive reading, characterized by the repeated reading of a restricted and defined canon of texts, to extensive reading, defined as the one-time reading of a broad range of texts. Today this shift is perceived as the essence of a "reading revolution" which took place in the West toward the end of the eighteenth century.[15] However, this revolution did not only take the form of the diversification of publishing areas in the course of the eighteenth century. Its main manifestation was the far greater numbers of belletristic works. The statistics available to researchers indicate that in 1740, the number of such publications barely constituted 6 percent of all published works, ranking sixth in the publishing lists. By 1770, the number of works in this field had climbed to 16 percent of all published works, making it the second most important area on the German-language book market. In 1800, when it made up 21 percent of all publications, belles lettres constituted the primary publishing area, outstripping theology. In the light of this development, historian Erich Schön has argued that the eighteenth century was not only the time when a new public of readers came into being, but also when the term "literature" as known to us today was coined.[16] This development also marks the shift in the nature of the reading activity itself, from a purposeful activity to an activity in its own right.[17] By analyzing pictures of readers and reading furniture, Erich Schön has shown how, from the eighteenth century onward, physical contact with books became ever more limited: reading became an activity of the eyes, with readers' bodies remaining motionless.[18] Reading became an intimate activity capable of being performed in practically any circumstances and any position. These developments, which did not escape the attention of contemporary observers, were commented on by the cultural critics of the time, who variously dubbed them "Lesesucht," "Lesefieber," or "Lesewut"—an "obsession or addiction," "fever," or "craze" for reading respectively—expressions which referred to the expansion of book readerships, and in particular to women's and adolescents' unbridled addiction to reading. These discussions focused attention on the harmful influence of reading, weakening the eyes, corroding moral values, and undermining proper social order. Novel reading in particular was perceived as a fad associated with the hedonistic lifestyle of the affluent social classes, or more precisely of the women belonging to these strata.[19]

The "reading revolution" that occurred in the eighteenth century is therefore an expression of the generation of a new need among society's affluent classes—a need that the book trade sought to nurture. This revolution in the field of reading did not emerge out of the blue. The eighteenth century, or what Reinhard Koselleck has dubbed the "Sattelzeit" ("saddle period")[20] between the early modern period and the modern period proper, is today also viewed by most historians of consumption as a milestone in the history of modern consumer culture. This link, whether genuine or ostensible, between reading and consumer culture has another historiographic expression. The two-stage model for viewing the history of consumption in the West, in which the eighteenth century as well as the transition period between the nineteenth and twentieth centuries constitute key reference points, also characterizes the historical description of the history of reading.[21] However, unlike the "reading revolution" of the end of the eighteenth century, which marks a qualitative shift in the nature of the reading activity, and relates to the reading habits of what is from our point of view a not particularly large group of literate people, beginning in the last third of the nineteenth century this process assumed an unmistakably quantitative nature.[22] The two key manifestations of the "second reading revolution" in the second half of the nineteenth century were the significant expansion of potential readerships and the mass publication of books. Rudolf Schenda has estimated that in 1770, the potential reading public was 15 percent of the total Central European population. Over the nineteenth century the percentage of literate people among the population shot up with dizzying rapidity, from 25 percent in 1800 to 90 percent in 1900.[23] In the light of this development, while a considerable proportion of the responsibility for the first reading revolution lies with affluent women becoming "novel readers" and joining the ranks of the reading public, the expansion of the reading public in the shape of male and female readers alike from the ranks of those of modest means from the second half of the nineteenth century on can clearly be considered the primary characteristic of the second reading revolution.

It is difficult to determine whether efforts to counter illiteracy, nineteenth-century improvements in the education system as well as its expansion, and above all the rise of the nation-state which made education an integral part of nation-building acted as factors that helped to expand the reading public, or whether rather these were intended to curb the spread of reading and try to make it conform to the needs of the state.[24] Regardless of whether one possibility is more valid than the other, or both are equally applicable, it can certainly be stated that the perfection of printing technology and paper production, which slashed the cost of book publishing and made its mass distribution possible from the last third of the nineteenth century onward, was a response to the growing demand for reading material. The book trade did not just meet demand for reading: it also invested major efforts in disseminating reading and fostering demand for reading material. In this sense, there is no doubting the book trade's contribution to the process of democratizing reading and the principle of production for the sake of consumption according to which it was run.

The process of commercialization and its complex influences on reading first became visible in the eighteenth century. It intensified in the course of the nineteenth century and received new impetus in the post-world war period. One of the most salient expressions of the acceleration of this process is the increase in the number of companies engaged in publishing. Thus for example, in 1802 some 473 companies were involved in the book trade, most of them in Saxony and a number of North German cities. Later in the nineteenth century, and in particular after the world war, as shown by the figures in Table 4.3, the numbers of these companies exploded.

Particularly noteworthy are the postwar figures, which reflect increased activity in the book trade market, at least up to the Great Depression at the end of the 1920s. In this connection, of interest also are figures about the founding of publishing houses and bookshops before and after the World War, as shown in Table 4.4. These data show that more companies involved in publishing and distributing reading material were founded after the world war than in the period immediately before it, from 1900 onward.

The number of locations with companies involved in the book trade also grew accordingly. From 1875 to 1910, the number of such locations practically doubled, increasing from 786 to 1,708. This tendency persisted after the world war, despite Germany's loss of territories. In 1919 companies involved in the book trade could be found in a total of 1,712 locations. In 1925 the equivalent figure was 1,681, and not until 1932 did this figure

Table 4.3

Number of bookshops and publishers, 1875–1939[25]

Year	Bookshops	Index	Publishers	Index	Total book dealers	Index
1875	2,670	100	803	100	4,654	100
1880	—	—	—	—	5,652	121.4
1885	3,884	145.4	1,340	166.8	—	—
1890	4,526	169.5	1,665	207.3	7,474	160.5
1900	5,405	202.4	2,192	272.9	9,360	201.1
1905	6,480	242.6	2,022	251.8	—	—
1910	7,408	277.4	2,424	301.8	12,650	271.8
1913	7,284	272.8	2,806	349.4	12,412	266.6
1920	—	—	—	—	12,475	268.0
1921	7,645	286.3	2,624	326.7	13,049	280.3
1925	9,023	337.9	3,380	420.9	13,706	294.4
1927	6,647	248.9	3,991	497.0	12,222	262.6
1930	6,394	239.4	3,771	469.6	11,763	252.7
1933	4,745	177.7	2,634	328.0	7,379	158.8
1939	6,066	227.1	3,252	404.9	9,318	200.2

Table 4.4
Establishment of bookshops and publishers 1901–1938[26]

	Founding of publishing houses		Founding of bookshops	
Period	No.	Annual average	No.	Annual average
1901–1913	101	7.8	374	28.8
1914–1918	15	3.0	62	12.4
1919–1923	102	20.2	269	53.8
1924–1928	96	19.2	288	57.6
1929–1932	79	13.2	208	52.0
1933–1938	79	13.2	231	38.5

fall to 1,595. It should be noted further that in 1919, more than half of the companies involved in the book trade were to be found in 47 urban areas, including 34 cities. But while the publishing houses were present solely in urban areas and above all in metropolises such as Leipzig, Berlin, Munich, and Stuttgart, which were home to over half of Germany's publishers, only a fifth or so of the country's bookshops were present in the large cities. Thus the bookshop, although an urban phenomenon, was not necessarily typically associated with metropolitan areas.

However, estimates of the book trade's turnover (Table 4.5) indicate that this market continued to grow, albeit at a moderate pace, after the world war. According to Gerhard Menz, who provided us with these figures, in 1926 bookshops' turnover represented 3 percent of Germany's total commercial turnover, although they constituted just 1.5 percent of the total number of retail outlets. Menz argues that these figures are indicative of the economic importance of the German book trade.

The 1920s, at least as indicated by the statistical data presented so far, especially the relatively stable period between 1924 and 1928, were peak years for the reading material market, at least in terms of the numbers of publications, as well as of publishers and bookshops.

Why, then, were so many bookshops and publishers established during this unlikely sounding period of economic hardships and growing com-

Table 4.5
Book trade turnover[27]

In 1865 around 25 million marks
In 1875 around 55 million marks
In 1913 around 500 million marks
In 1929 around 600 million marks

petition with the new media? Gerhard Menz identified a link between the factors responsible for this tendency and a view which saw the book trade market as an area with the potential for profits and an attractive professional field. Apparently, from 1907 to 1925 the number of people involved professionally in dealing in reading material grew by 27.5 percent, with the total numbers of those employed in the book trade sector growing by 59 percent in the same period. Others ascribed this tendency to the nature of books as a product which had dropped in cost as a result of reproduction, as well as to the process by which the book market became commercialized. It was claimed, for example, that modern market economics, based on mechanized mass production, could not allow production to grind to a halt because of its vested interest in ongoing production. This principle applied equally to the production of books. Hence in order to get over the crisis, whether real or imaginary, affecting the book market, the latter took steps which were specifically designed to increase rather than reduce book production.[28]

Arguments about the proliferation of book dealers, overproduction of books, and the commercialization of the book market did not originate in the 1920s. Similar arguments were advanced at the end of the eighteenth century and throughout the entire nineteenth century. Competition between diverse book-selling agents, and above all the repeated failure of the Book Sellers' Association to obtain exclusive rights in the area of publishing and selling books in Germany, were the main reasons that contributed to this feeling of overproduction and uncontrolled competition. The department stores, mail order book sales (*Versandbuchhandel*), or book clubs (*Buchgemeinschaften*), which made a decisive contribution to popularizing the book-reading culture, are just a few examples of attempts to undermine the monopoly of the German Book Sellers' Association on the German-speaking book market.

However, criticism of the process of commercializing the book market and making books into commodities which were traded in like any other consumer good was just one reaction to this process. It was the reverse of the commodification process, which promoted books' symbolic significance as objects and the value of private book ownership. Furthermore, this tendency reflected the emergence of a more optimistic approach to the relationship between book culture and consumer culture. The "cultural publishers," most of which were founded in the last decade of the nineteenth century, are one example of this optimistic approach to consumption, which sought to combine book culture with the new consumer culture. The cultural publishers not only aspired to encourage the consumption of books with the goal of inculcating culture: they also constituted a new type of publisher, who saw himself as organizing and actively promoting culture. The publisher as organizer (*Der Verleger als Organisator*), as Eugen Diederichs wrote in 1912, is no longer engaged in the random collecting and publishing of writings: rather, he consciously selects contemporary literature, guided by his own tastes and on the basis of criteria set by the publishing house. As a result, the book publisher has become a brand.[29]

This intensive addressing of the issue of the nature of books as a commodity reflected an attempt to create an appropriate conceptual system which could be used to relate to books as products combining culture and economic capital alike. True, unequivocal positions like those of Edmund Winterhoff, who saw books as products which operated like any other product on the basis of the free play of the market forces of supply and demand, or of Rudolf Borchardt, who stressed the intellectual aspects of books while ignoring their economic dimensions, were rejected by most people in the book trade, since they saw themselves as brokers between the intellectual and material worlds. For this reason, apparently, Gerhard Menz opted in the 1925 inaugural lecture at the Book Trade School, of which he was director, to address the issue of the nature, or more precisely the uniqueness, of books as a product.[30] Menz maintained that the perception of books as the materialization of intellectual life could not ignore the complex nature of books as a product combining both economic and cultural dimensions. Menz therefore drew attention to the fact that in the cultural sphere, and specifically where books were concerned, the business world of books (*Buchwirtschaft*) at the same time also constituted a cultural policy (*Kulturpolitik*). This special situation also provided the background to Menz's attempt to develop a unique view of the link between the worlds of business and culture—a view which he called "*Kulturwirtschaft*"—"cultural business." This view involved something of a pragmatic approach to the issue of the relationship between consumption and culture. It acknowledged that the book trade market operated according to the capitalist market's principles of supply and demand, and hence strove to channel this situation in order to bolster the position and level of culture generally, and book reading culture specifically. According to Menz's *Kulturwirtschaft* idea, boosting purchasing power and stepping up the consumption of books do not necessarily eliminate the "intellectual" uniqueness of books. Following this view, it is books' cultural capital which determines their status as consumer goods. Hence one of the book trade's main tasks is to create demand for books as cultural capital, thereby also increasing their economic capital.

It would appear that purchase-based reading turned the book culture, whether deliberately or otherwise, into a consumer biblioculture which was part of modern consumer culture. As explained earlier, this process decisively influenced the nature of the development of reading culture. However, before we go on to discuss the different forms and meanings of the link between consumer culture and purchase-based reading, we must first analyze the relationship between loan-based reading and consumer culture.

Libraries

As places where written material was collected, organized, preserved, and made available to readers, libraries go back to antiquity.[31] Libraries of yore, like their ecclesiastical, university, or private counterparts, particularly those belonging to the aristocracy, were intended to serve a select readership of scholars and academics. In a sense they were spaces designed to accumulate books rather than to read them. As a result, the eighteenth century enlightenment, one of whose primary goals was to disseminate culture among the uneducated classes, was a turning point in the history of libraries as well. However, it was not until the rise of the nation-state and the politicization of German society in the course of the nineteenth century, that the new approach to libraries, which saw reading as an activity with the potential to shape outlooks and contribute to nation-building, began to impact on the German library's character. During this period, not only did the library become a tool in the service of the ideal of spreading culture, but like magazines and newspapers, it also became an element in constructing the unique identity of various identity groups. Beginning in the second half of the nineteenth century, trade unions, the churches, industrial enterprises, and all kinds of associations began to set up libraries which competed for the expanding reading public. One of the major manifestations of this development were the public libraries, which the Germans called "people's libraries" (*Volksbüchereien*).[32]

In 1797, Heinrich Stephani (1761–1850) for the first time called for a network of libraries to be established in towns and villages, whose target audience would be drawn from the uneducated population. Although there was not much public response to Stephani's proposal, it was indicative of a change in attitudes to libraries. It was Karl Preuskers (1786–1871), considered the first important theoretician of public libraries, who succeeded in implementing this idea of the public library. Under his inspiration, the first libraries in Germany to deliberately target the uneducated classes were established in 1836 at Großenenhain and in 1839 at Plauen, near Dresden. In 1839, on Preuskers's initiative, in addition to the libraries intended for the urban populace, a number of mobile libraries were also founded with the goal of spreading culture in rural areas. Preuskers's approach was that the library's primary function was to bridge the divide between book culture and the broad strata of society for whom this was still an alien culture. In the course of the nineteenth century, and primarily with the founding of a variety of cultural associations on the initiative of socialist circles and their opponents, there was a strengthening of this view of the library as an instrument directed at society's weaker strata with the goal of improving their cultural level and enlisting them to serve diverse social and political goals.

In the 1890s this attitude to public libraries in Germany underwent a sea change. The model adopted for the new German approach to libraries was that of the American public library. In this model, the library was designed to eliminate the gap between libraries intended for educated circles and those serving the uneducated public. Instead, the library was supposed to become a place which would meet the reading needs of all social strata. This approach imparted new meaning to the concept of "people" (*Volk*). Instead of designating the lower orders, as in the past, it now referred to all strata which constituted society: or, as the slogan of the new public library put it, "public libraries must not renounce a single reader." This development is greatly reminiscent of the change in attitudes to the consumer public, whose most salient manifestation was the department stores which in Germany developed in the 1890s. Like the new public library, the department store was also an expression of the approach which saw all social classes as their potential target audience. Although a direct link between these two phenomena cannot be readily established, it is certainly possible to see these developments as different manifestations of an approach which views society as the most precious resource of the nation—or alternatively of consumption.

One of the most salient manifestations of this new awareness of libraries' target audience was the way that the new public library defined its social and educational vocations. As Konstantin Nörrenberg—the driving force behind the reform of Germany's public libraries in the 1890s—wrote in 1896, the new public library's educational mission is not education or culture for all, but the right education for each and every one, appropriate to individual status and abilities. This new approach to public libraries was not just an expression of the growing fear of an ever-widening gap between the educated classes and the rest of society: rather, against the background of the popularity of the gutter press and what was defined as trashy and pulp literature (*Schund- und Schmutzliteratur*), it also sought to tackle a new social reality in which all social classes had access to one of the manifestations of written culture. This tendency is most saliently expressed among those individuals who are considered the second generation of the public libraries movement in Germany, known as the "*Bücherhallenbewegung.*"

The controversial book on library policy by Paul Ladewig (1848–1940), *Politik der Bücherei,* which came out in 1912, is arguably the most systematic and original consideration of the challenges to the public library posed by the turn-of-the-century social realities. The approach espoused by Ladewig, who in 1898 was commissioned to set up Krupp Industries' public library (*Krupp'schen Bücherhalle*), was based on acknowledgment of the fact that from the nineteenth century onward, books had changed from a source of pleasure or a fundamental tool of scientific research to a utilitarian commodity. Ladewig argued that books were now tools for everybody ("Handwerkszeug für jedermann"), readily obtainable at low cost.[33] The upshot of this acknowledgment was that if the library wished to play a social role, it must adapt itself to this reality, in which books were consumer items. Or, as Ladewig himself put it in 1914 in his book *Katechismus der Bücherei:* "Das Buch ist—auch in der Bücherei—eine Ware und die Bücherei die Maklerstelle für diese Ware" (Books—in libraries too—are goods, and libraries are the places where these goods are traded).[34] What this meant for libraries was that if they were interested in readers, they could no longer afford to stock their shelves solely with quality books which made up the cultural canon that they wished to promote. Instead, it was imperative that they satisfy the demands and varied tastes of the general reading public. As Ladewig argued in the final chapter to his 1912 book:

> Libraries are not police stations with police measures and penalties for those who break the law (*Polizeimaßnahmen und Verordungsschikanen*). They are untrammelled places where the learned can enjoy themselves, just like those who wish to satisfy certain interests, generally educate themselves or merely seek entertainment.[35]

Like Nörrenberg, Ladewig saw public libraries, not as instruments designed to forcibly educate the masses, but rather as the counterparts of the Post Office or the railways—a service provider or industry. Consequently, for Ladewig the primary measure of a library's success was the number of its readers, reflecting its social mission. According to this approach, reading had a soothing influence on readers, and a library, with its heated reading rooms and the range of activities that it put on, was perceived as a refuge from everyday troubles, as well as a place which kept men in particular off the bottle and out of public houses and taverns. Thus the approach represented by Ladewig acknowledged the rise of the consumer society, of which it aspired to become an integral part by adopting a sales-based approach, which treated books as mass items and libraries as service-providing companies in constant competition with other service providers.

This pragmatic approach to libraries unleashed a storm of protest in the public libraries movement, splitting it into two camps.[36] The camp of Ladewig's supporters was called "the Old Line," with the conservative criticism of Ladewig being ironically dubbed "the New Line." The disagreement between these two lines (known in German as *Richtungsstreit*) focused on the issue of how to attract readers and by what means, as well as the library's role in guiding, not to say directing, reading.

Opposing the pragmatic approach of the "Old Line," the director of the Leipzig Public Libraries, Walter Hofmann, the most important representative of the "New Line," advocated an idealist and more conservative approach to libraries. True, Hofmann saw the public libraries, as representatives of the Old Line, as politically neutral bodies, but he contended that they were not ideologically neutral. Hofmann, who was close to Social Democrat circles, therefore rejected the view of libraries as nonideological bodies that simply provided reading services. Instead, he argued that libraries were required to have well-delineated profiles in the spheres of education and national values. In Hofmann's approach, as places of the German national literary memory, public libraries had a distinct educational goal: to kindle and strengthen national feelings among the different strata of society.[37] For this purpose, libraries had to select their book holdings with great care, assuming full responsibility for acting as "brokers" between readers and books. Hofmann's distinctive approach to the issue of book lending, which saw libraries as bodies whose role was to intervene in and guide every single reader's reading habits, also provided the backdrop to Hofmann's interest in studying the reading habits of different social groups.[38] In 1926, Hofmann founded the Institut für Leser- und Schriftumskunde as an institution which would undertake research into issues relating to the history and practice of reading and literature. This Leipzig-based body focused on studying readers' reading habits at the city's municipal libraries. The Institute's research activities, which dovetailed with Hofmann's personal philosophy, were designed to assist libraries in achieving their goals as bodies which were not only supposed to meet the reading needs of diverse social groups, but also to influence and shape their reading habits.

The most tangible expression of the difference between the two ideological "lines" was to be found in the actual structure and organization of the library itself. The "New Line" libraries were "*Schalterbibliotheken*"—literally, "window libraries"—with librarians acting as intermediaries between readers and books. Here, the librarian's role was to direct or guide the reader to suitable works. In contrast, "Old Line" libraries functioned as "*Thekenbibliotheken*"—"counter libraries," where readers were given greater freedom to come into contact with the library's books. Differences also existed on the level of the type of holdings in each type of library. The "old line" library had more novels and works of popular literature than nonfiction works. On the other hand, in the "new line" libraries, with their far more rigorous criteria for selection, the number of nonfiction works was on a par with works of belles lettres. Again, not only did the "old line" library allow readers far greater freedom of choice: they also had a more liberal approach to those books which were made available on loan. The controversy over this issue focused on the status of those works classified as falling into the somewhat vague category of "pulp and trashy literature." The "old line" libraries, which tried to adapt themselves to suit their clientele's tastes so as to attract as many readers as possible, were more tolerant of what was considered "inferior" literature. Erwin Ackerknecht (1880–1960), director of the Stettin public library and one of the most prominent representatives of the "old line," typically differentiated between works that were kitsch, and substandard literature considered pulp fiction. He argued that while libraries could not allow themselves to give shelf room to works that fell into the "pulp and trashy" category, kitsch writings—romantic novels, detective fiction, or all kinds of adventure tales—were not so harmful and could act as a convenient starting point for improving readers' tastes.[39]

In the immediate postwar period, the controversy between the two lines flared up again, not dying down until toward the end of the 1920s.[40] However, despite the fiery arguments that raged between the two approaches, the impression, at least with hindsight, is that what they had in common outweighed what divided them. Both sought to make libraries places that would serve the whole of society, eliminating social, economic, and cultural differences. In this sense, both trends were equally representative of a view that saw the people as the nation's most precious resource—a resource which had to be fashioned and nurtured for its sake. Neither the "New Line" nor the "Old Line" saw their purpose as simply encouraging reading: rather, they saw libraries as places where society could become acquainted with written culture, and one of whose primary roles in a world of print which featured increasing competition between the new media, was to critically process reading material and provide readers with guidance.[41] Following this approach, as early as the pre–World War period public libraries began to set up music and art libraries, as well as libraries specializing in children's and youth literature. There was also growing interest in libraries for the new media, such as film and radio.[42] Thus public libraries formed part of a state of affairs where reading was fast becoming a "mass product" and growing competition existed between the different media. They strove to present themselves as places that met varied cultural needs—an inseparable part of modern life.

Even though these developments occurred in the period before the world war, the 1920s are considered the "golden age" of public libraries in Germany. Both "new line" and "old line" libraries were amazingly popular during these years. In the 1920s, significant progress was achieved with the establishment of a network of libraries in rural areas, and at the end of the decade mobile libraries-on-wheels ("bookmobiles") were demonstrated for the first time in Germany. Also during the Twenties, the trend toward specialization at libraries gathered speed. Many libraries for music and art were established, and significant development began in the area of libraries for youth and children. Libraries specializing in new areas such as transport and technology were established. Special libraries for the blind were also set up within the public library framework. During this period librarianship also developed into a fully fledged profession, which was studied at special colleges with diplomas awarded by the State.[43]

In the postwar period, as economic hardships threatened to destroy libraries' economic foundations, many cities began to provide support for libraries, most of which had previously been financed by various private bodies. This development, which was associated with modifications in the way that libraries were organized and structured, reflects a change in the authorities' attitudes to public libraries. In contrast to the prewar period, when the local authorities were not particularly interested in the public libraries, after the war the public library became part of the array of educational and cultural services that the local authorities offered the population.[44] The main indicator of the libraries' success in the 1920s was the steady increase in their readerships. The world war, when reading was the main recreational activity, reductions in working hours, improvements in living conditions, and high book prices at the beginning of the 1920s were identified by contemporary observers as the main reasons for the flourishing of the libraries during this period. In addition, the public libraries at this time began to invest more effort in publicizing themselves. An example of this is the introduction of bookmobiles which used lorries to store and move their holdings about. These symbolized the fact that libraries had embraced technology and resolutely moved into the modern era. They also provided excellent publicity. Many libraries also began to advertise themselves in the local press and by means of billboards. In the wake of these initiatives, a wider range of people became more aware that libraries existed and were modern places. As a result, libraries' potential target audiences grew considerably.[45]

The late 1920s, a period of widespread unemployment and a recession which affected the entire country, are considered the high point in the flourishing of public libraries in Germany. During this period, a library became a refuge for the out-of-work from all social strata. In 1929 public libraries' holdings, having increased steadily throughout the decade, also reached an unprecedented level of close on 5.8 million books, with 15.4 million loans being handled that year.[46] These developments made the public libraries the book trade's most important customer. Hence unemployment and economic adversity helped to consolidate awareness of the economic importance that libraries and the principle of loans had for the very existence of the book trade market. These figures must be supplemented by equivalent data from competing libraries, such as those run by church organizations or political parties and trade unions. Such statistics indicate similar growth trends in readership figures and book holdings.[47] Practically all of Germany's libraries reported an increase of around 100 percent in their readerships. These reports also tell us that generally libraries had more male readers than female, and that the number of middle-class readers was generally the same as the number of readers from the working classes. By and large this finding rebuts the prevailing view of book reading as a sphere dominated by women and as one of the defining markers of bourgeois status. By the end of the 1920s, reading would appear no longer to be the province of a particular social class, having instead become an activity engaged in by all social echelons.

During the Depression, with unemployment widespread, libraries were therefore a cheap and convenient alternative way of meeting the growing demand for reading. In this sense, as places frequented by all social strata, they played an important role in preventing social unrest. The unemployed in particular, who either paid nothing for their loans or received a discount, were viewed as a public to be attracted to libraries. This is the reason why in 1931, Josef Wirth, Germany's Interior Minister, sent a memorandum to the country's various states (*Länder*) asserting that the public libraries "protect the out-of-work against cultural disintegration, despair and extremism."[48] He went on to warn the *Länder* against slashing resources allocated to the libraries, because such a move might have not only adverse cultural effects but also far-reaching political implications.

Loan-based reading thus removed the symbolic meaning of owning books as objects in reading culture, enabling anyone and everyone with an interest in reading books to do so in comfort and at the same cost to all. In this way, the library encouraged the demand for book reading as an activity in competition with other leisure activities. Generating demand for reading was a goal shared by libraries and the book trade alike, with both hoping it would benefit them. However, while public libraries were interested in encouraging the reading of a particular type of book, based on an outlook that viewed reading as an activity with the potential to improve society's cultural level and to contribute to social order, the book trade by the nature of things operated according to the free-market criteria of supply and demand. Another way of putting this would be to say that for the public libraries, reading was a means and readers were the end, while for the book trade reading was the end and readers a means. Given this state of affairs, the public library—as a nonprofit organization which allocated itself a social role, and as a place which sought to establish ties between written culture and society, whose task was to guide readers through a world abounding in reading material—appears to have offered an alternative to the book trade and to purchase-based reading.

These two approaches are not necessarily mutually exclusive alternatives. An examination of the history of loan-based reading as opposed to purchase-based reading shows that the gap between the two options is not as pronounced as might initially be thought. The most conspicuous examples of the blurring of the differences between these two routes to book reading are the commercial lending libraries (*Leihbibliotheken*) and the book clubs (*Buchgemeinschaften*), whose circulation of books using a subscription system circumventing the bookshops enabled them to also serve interest groups not operating solely according to commercial profit-and-loss considerations. These two approaches to book circulation were crowned by unprecedented success in the 1920s. Before moving on to a discussion of the commercial lending libraries and the book clubs, we will briefly discuss an attempt by one of pre–World War I Germany's major publishers, August Scherl (1849–1921), to set up a special library which aspired to combine commercial interests with cultural and national ideals. This initiative of Scherl's testifies to the problematic nature of the relationship between the two different approaches to reading, as described above.

August Scherl's Library

To date, not much has been written about August Scherl the man and his achievements. One of the main reasons for this state of affairs is Scherl's failure to leave behind him any form of orderly estate.[49] His contemporaries found him a withdrawn figure, a seasoned publisher who understood the common man's soul and somebody who had carved himself out an American-style career. Scherl acquired this reputation as a result of his diverse areas of activity, his business ambitions, and his original ideas, particularly in the area of the press. Together with Leopold Ullstein (1826–1899), Rudolf Mosse (1843–1920), and Leopold Sonnemann (1831–1909), Scherl was viewed as one of the press barons in pre–World War I Germany.

Until he turned to the press, Scherl was involved with the book-peddling trade known as colportage, as well as the entertainment business in the city of Cologne. His activities included organizing gambling. He also tried his luck with a skating rink, and in 1878 he even established a theater where his wife, singer and actress Flora Rosner, was supposed to star. In the wake of the theater's embarrassing failure, in 1880 an impoverished Scherl was forced to move to Berlin, where his father's failing book trade business awaited him. In the hope of escaping the economic adversity that had engulfed him, in 1883 Scherl founded the *Berliner Lokalanzeiger,* a newspaper whose audacity and innovative nature made him a trailblazer in the field of "*Generalanzeiger*" publications or "advertising papers" in Germany. The main goal that Scherl set for the new paper, at least according to Hans Erman in the only biography of Scherl to have been published to date, was to make money—lots of it.[50] The paper achieved this goal, fulfilling Scherl's expectations. In addition to publishing popular newspapers and magazines such as *Sport und Bild* (1904), *Die Woche* (1899), *Vom Fels zum Meer* (1901), and from 1904 onward also *Die Gartenlaube,* another publishing venture through which Scherl acquired his capital was that of city street and telephone directories. Scherl acquired an unassailable controlling position in this field, generating very respectable revenues.[51] Scherl's group, to a large extent like Ullstein's, was therefore perceived as having just one goal—to make money. Against this background, Scherl's 1908 initiative for the establishment of a library with the declared aim of disseminating cultural values and popularizing what was considered good literature received a stormy reception.[52]

The idea of "good literature for the people," Scherl's slogan for the library, was far from new. Nor was there anything innovative in the principle underlying the library's operations—"Go up in the world through reading" ("Lies sich empor")—which contended that by means of what were known as "dime novels" or "penny dreadfuls" (*Hintertreppenliteratur*), the library could reach a broad readership and gradually improve its reading "menu." What was new about Scherl's library was the way that it tried to put this principle into practice. In return for a 10 pfennig borrowing fee, any home could receive a book from his library for a week. Payment was made in cash when the book was received (COD). After a week, the book was supposed to be collected from the reader's home, in order to be rebound and then go on to a new reader. Unlike colportage, which brought unbound minibooks of just a few pages to readers' homes, Scherl offered his readers properly bound books, two hundred or more pages long, for the price of a slim volume. A unique feature of Scherl's library was also that it printed the books itself, enabling readers to choose between borrowing the books or buying them at an attractive price. With this system, readers enjoyed the convenience of having a freshly bound volume sent straight to their homes without making any commitment to a long-term association with a book or a library. They also had the option of buying the books if they were so inclined.

However, Scherl's library did not allow readers to choose the books. Instead, they had to accept those books which the distribution agents brought to their homes. In this case, the restriction on readers' freedom of choice was not the result of solely technical constraints as a result of the limitations of Scherl's publishing house or the number of books that a particular agent could carry in his bag: rather, this was a deliberate policy, part of Scherl's method. By restricting the books that were made available through the library, Scherl aimed to assume maximum control over the reading material entering readers' homes, and hence to try and improve the quality of such material. Restricting readers' freedom of choice therefore forced them to come into contact with a particular type of literature, the hope being that this encounter would popularize what Scherl's library called good literature.

Scherl invested around two million marks in setting up the library, using his newspapers' circulation network for distribution purposes. The fact that the initiative to set up this network of libraries was underwritten by a powerful combine was the main reason for the stormy debate stirred up by Scherl's library. The public libraries feared, for example, that the distribution principle espoused by Scherl's library would deprive them of readers, preventing many potential readers from finding their way to them. Walter Hofmann, the standard-bearer of the public libraries' struggle against Scherl's library, focused his criticism on the principle of "upwards reading" (*Auflesen*) on which Scherl's initiative was based. Like the debate which flared up a few years later over the book by Paul Ladewig, Hofmann argued that the "upwards reading" principle could not constitute a basis for improving the literary tastes of social strata who read cheap literature. He also attacked the arrogant view that underlay the "upwards reading" principle of Scherl's library, arguing that this approach—which looked on the society's less affluent groups as a mindless mass who were to be stuffed with good literature in order to improve their cultural level—entirely ignored the needs and desires of these social groups. According to Hofmann, the success of pulp literature should not be ascribed to the colportage system of distribution which brought reading material to readers' homes, or any other system of distribution used to circulate this form of literature: rather, it should be viewed as the symptom of a particular socioeconomic situation. Hofmann maintained that the key to improving the reading habits of the German people was to improve social conditions and raise the reading public's standard of living, instead of undertaking cultural activities, setting up libraries, or reducing book prices. As a result, he argued, if Scherl was interested in making a contribution to improving the German people's cultural level, he would do better to invest his capital in improving the living conditions of the poor instead of setting up a new library offering yet another—albeit cheap and convenient—way of reading books.[53]

Irrespective of these vigorous attacks on Scherl by Hofmann and others, the public libraries were so fearful of Scherl's library that some of them quickly adopted Scherl's circulation principle: for a modest fee of 10 pfennigs, they also began sending books to readers' homes.

It was primarily the colportage companies, whose elimination was one of Scherl's declared goals in establishing his library, who feared the competition with the distribution method used by Scherl's library. At the second annual conference of the colportage dealers' association (*Zentralverein Deutscher Buch- und Zeitschriftenhändler*), which took place on 16 June 1908 in Chemnitz, a discussion was held of possible ways to combat Scherl's initiative. At the end of the conference, the colportage dealers warned all book dealers about the destructive results for the entire book trade of eliminating colportage through Scherl's library.[54]

For their part, the book dealers had their own reasons for opposing Scherl's initiative. Bookshops in particular, which were engaged in tooth-and-nail competition with a variety of book distribution agents, were afraid that Scherl's library would adversely affect their business. At the convention of the local book dealers' associations (Verband der Kreis- und Ortsvereine im Deutschen Buchhandel) which took place on 16 May 1908 in Leipzig, a fiery argument erupted over the relationship between book loans and purchases. One approach saw borrowing as a preparatory phase for book buying, but this was countered by a claim that it was not possible to accustom readers to buying books if at any time they could read them at practically no cost in a library. The latter approach maintained that reading borrowed books, in whatever form, had an adverse effect on book buying, and the book dealers were called upon to demonstrate a united front in favor of buying and the value of owning books. However, irrespective of differences of opinion over the relationship between borrowing and buying books, the majority opinion among both bookshop owners and publishers was that Scherl's library was a threat to book dealers' interests.

Attacks on Scherl were not confined to the circles of the cognoscenti or to the pages of the specialist book trade press. They also appeared in the daily press. The political opponents of Scherl, the nationalist and anti-

Social Democrat, primarily attacked his motives in setting up the library. A constantly recurring claim was that the goal of the "upwards reading" principle of Scherl's library was not to lead readers to good literature, but to increase the circulation of Scherl's newspapers.

However, Scherl and his library did not have opponents only. The most prominent of those who supported the idea of Scherl's library was Ferdinand Avenarius, editor of the influential magazine *Der Kunstwart* ("Arts Sentinel"). Avenarius's attitude to Scherl's library not only fitted in with the cultural-political outlook of "culture for the people": it also presented a fairly pragmatic view of the relationship between cultural values and commercial interests. Avenarius argued that one should not expect that a library intended for the general public could be established and survive without a reliable economic base. In addition, he also argued that if Scherl was prepared to invest resources in a library which had as one of its goals the elimination of the colportage trade, this should be welcomed, even if there was disagreement over how this was to be done and the underlying motives.[55]

The storm aroused by Scherl's library was largely a storm in a teacup. Despite the resources that Scherl sank in setting up his library, it was nowhere near the success that its opponents feared so greatly. The reason for its failure was apparently to be found in Scherl's very system. Apparently, readers were not convinced that the price that they were required to pay for the convenience of receiving books in their homes was worthwhile. In addition, Scherl's lending system lacked flexibility and failed to satisfy the varied tastes and reading habits of the general reading public. For example, for fast readers the books came too slowly, while for slower readers the weekly exchange system was too fast. Scherl himself, who at this time preferred to devote most of his capital and energies to the idea of introducing a high-speed single-track railway in Germany, quickly lost interest in the library. In 1916, after Alfred Hugenberg (1865–1951) gained control over Scherl's combine, Scherl donated the books to the Berlin Municipal Library, marking the official end of Scherl's Library.

Despite the failure of Scherl's Library, it is undoubtedly an interesting illustration of the problematic relationship between loan-based and purchase-based reading, as well as of the difficulties of combining the aspiration to popularize what is considered good literature with an attempt to make the distribution of literature into a profitable business. An even more striking example of the blurring of lines between loan-based reading and purchase-based reading is provided by the commercial lending libraries, which were introduced in Germany in the course of the eighteenth century.

Commercial Lending Libraries

Historical research views the appearance of the commercial lending libraries in the course of the eighteenth century as an expression of the growing demand for reading during a period when most of the literate population could not afford to buy books.[56] As a result, the possibility of reading books in return for a lending fee was considered one of the main factors that helped to liberate books from the cultural-social fetters which had encumbered them until the eighteenth century as the exclusive province of the affluent/male/educated class. Initially, lending libraries were not bodies with specific class-related characteristics, but rather agents that distributed reading material and were intended for all literate individuals of all social strata. Thus in addition to the travelling lending libraries and the *Winkelbibliothek* or "corner library," which served literate people in rural areas and members of nonaffluent circles, the *Lesekabinette* (reading rooms) and *Lesemuseen* ("reading museums"), with their sumptuous reading facilities, extensive selection of books, and magazines, and a diverse range of cultural services at the turn of the eighteenth/nineteenth century replaced the *Lesegesellschaften,* the reading societies, as a meeting place for the educated strata of the upper middle class.[57] Many lending libraries also served a mixed public, and on their premises senior civil servants and demure ladies could rub shoulders with journeymen and maids. Around 1800, practically all German towns had commercial lending libraries. As the nineteenth century wore on, lending libraries came to small communities with scarcely more than a few thousand inhabitants.[58] In the course of the nineteenth century, the tendency for lending libraries to specialize strengthened. Special lending libraries for music and drama, lending libraries that specialized in professional literature, and libraries for youth and children, or lending libraries located in railway stations, hotels, and resorts which targeted holidaymakers, are just a few examples of this development. Despite the different types of lending libraries, all differing from each other in terms of reading material and target audiences, the rules of supply and demand on the free market were what dictated their nature. The lending libraries' success therefore depended primarily on demand and the intensity of reading activities. This situation promoted a form of reading and a very specific pattern of relating to books that the commercial lending libraries promoted. Consequently, since the lending libraries made their living from loan-based reading, they encouraged the one-time reading of a book as a fashionable product which lost all value after it had been read. Consequently, there was no point in buying it. Unlike the eighteenth century reading societies or *Lesegesellschaften,* which were a kind of literary club for group readings and discussions of literature conducted by a fairly restricted group of people, the commercial lending libraries focused on the individual borrowing of books and as a result operated across a far wider spectrum. In addition, it should be noted that since these libraries also operated according to the free-market principles of supply and demand, their success depended on their ability to be responsive to demand and to fluctuations in the literary tastes of as broad a readership as possible. Commercial book lending therefore helped to render contact with books anonymous and individualistic.

These characteristics constitute the background to the present study's major interest in the lending libraries as a barometer reflecting the literary tastes of their time, and in an alternative view as a factor which also decisively influenced approaches to the writing and publishing of books in the eighteenth and nineteenth centuries. Lending libraries were especially considered to be responsible for the increased publication of novels and the popularity of light fiction, since generally their holdings consisted largely of adventure stories, romantic novels, tales of chivalry, family novels, crime novels, and so on. The tendency to publish modest print runs of books at a high per-copy price was also associated with the popularity of loan-based reading at the commercial lending libraries. It reflected book production's ability to adapt itself to this book-circulation system. This state of affairs was also expressed in the actual writing of books. The commercial lending libraries played a not insignificant role in developing the publishing of novels in installment form, forcing readers each time to borrow a number of issues until they finished the story. This form of publication also influenced the form of writing. It required authors to end each episode on a note which made the reader want to continue reading the next installment of the serial tale. The increasing importance of book titles as a means of intriguing readers was also a result of the commercial lending libraries' activities, since their catalogues informed readers of new works. However, over and beyond the commercial lending libraries' influence on the way that books were received and, above all, produced, there was an additional dimension to their relationship with the book trade. Most of the lending libraries, at least up to the end of the nineteenth century, were owned by book dealers, for whom lending books on a commercial basis constituted a supplementary business activity in addition to book selling as such. Most bookshops were members of the German Book Dealers' Association, and when buying books they enjoyed the discount given to bookshops. This enabled them, as book-lending institutions, to offer a wide range of books on loan. This apparently schizophrenic situation, in which book dealers became embroiled as an institution which both lent and sold books, was able to exist as long as purchase-based reading was not sufficiently profitable for the bookshops to be asked to choose between selling and lending books.

The first half of the nineteenth century is considered the "golden age" of the lending libraries. However, their very success as an institution that met the reading needs of an expanding public of readers generated what was known as the "lending libraries problem" (*Leihbibliothekenfrage*). In turn, this contributed to the generation of conditions which brought about a change in the status of the lending libraries in the second half of the nineteenth century. The lending libraries were viewed as being primarily responsible for feeding the period's "reading fever," which spanned the late eighteenth and early nineteenth centuries. Later they were blamed for playing a central role in circulating pulp and trashy literature. However, "reading fever" was not merely an expression of the generation of demand for reading literature: it also marked a change in the relationship to creative writing itself. The discovery of a market of novel readers encouraged both the writing and the publication of novels. In tandem, the increasing supply and concomitantly the growing competition between authors as well as publishers brought about a conflict of interests between the production of books and their distribution through the commercial lending libraries. Viewed through the lens of how to increase book production, the lending libraries were, it is true, perceived as a factor that encouraged the consumption of reading as an activity. However, they were also viewed at the same time as a distribution system that prevented the expansion of the book-buying public, thereby eliminating potential profits which could be made from book sales were all book readers to become book buyers. Authors in particular, who began organizing in their own interest groups from the 1840s onward, saw themselves as the main group to suffer from the principle of commercial book lending, which prevented consumer book prices from being reduced and print runs from being increased.[59] In their view, this state of affairs adversely affected authors' earnings and the financial profits that they could make from their books. Authors accused the lending libraries of dealing in intellectual property which did not belong to them, and they called for the reading public to be educated to buy books instead of borrowing them.[60] In their efforts, authors even made use of health-based arguments, trying to convince readers that it was more hygienic to own books outright rather than running the risk of contracting infectious diseases through borrowed books.

Reducing book production costs and the tendency to publish enormous print runs consequently brought about a change in attitudes to the lending libraries. This trend enabled a wider readership to buy books. As a result, book publishing became a potentially profitable commercial domain. It was largely the decision of 9 November 1867 of the Bundesversammlung, the Federal Convention of German States, to remove the protection of copyright law from the works of all authors who had died prior to 9 November 1837, which had momentous ramifications for the status of the commercial lending libraries. At one stroke, this decision did away with the monopoly enjoyed by the Cotta publishing house (Cottaschen Verlagbuchhandlung) over publishing the writings of a number of German authors from the Goethe period. As a result, it became possible for all publishers to issue editions of these works. As soon as the Bundesversammlung decision was reached, a number of publishers wasted no time and began to issue enormous print runs of a number of works considered classics of German and world literature. Philip Reclam's Universal Library is perhaps the best known example of these publishing activities. On 15 November 1867, less than a week after the Bundesversammlung decision, the first volume in Reclam's new series came out—the first part of Goethe's *Faust* in a print run of five thousand copies and at a price of two *Silbergroschen* a copy. Within just a few months, the book's print run had shot up to two hundred thousand copies—an unprecedented success for the period. In the first fifty years of its existence, Reclam's library published some 18 million copies of German classical literature—Lessing, Wieland, Herder, Goethe, Schiller, and others; some 8.5 million copies of Greek and Latin literature, and 5 million volumes of philosophical literature, including 790,000 copies of the works of Immanuel Kant.[61] What were the factors behind the commercial success of Reclam's Universal Library? Was it the cheap price, the special format of Reclam's books, and the combination of light fiction with quality books from Germany and the world, or were there other factors, such as German national development, the educational ideal, or the development of an educational network that contributed to the Universal Library's success? Many interpretations can be advanced in response to this question. For our purposes, it should also be borne in mind that the releasing of what were viewed as literary classics from the protective fetters of the copyright law and their publication at the same price for all not only adversely affected the economic feasibility of book lending and the status of the lending library as the distribution agent of classical German literature, but also encouraged rival forms of distribution to the lending libraries.

One of the main beneficiaries of "classics year" (*Klassikerjahr*), the standard term for when classical German literature was removed from the protection of copyright law, was the colportage trade. Colportage became one of the main distribution agents for the new mass editions of classical German literature. The spectacular success of the colportage trade in the second half of the nineteenth century therefore marked a change in attitudes to the commercial lending libraries, and in particular to the principle of commercial lending operations. After all, colportage not only competed with the commercial lending libraries for the custom of the reading public: additionally, whether deliberately or not, its operations also reinforced purchase-based reading at the expense of loan-based reading. Furthermore, since large amounts of capital were no longer required in order to set up a lending library, reduced book prices led to increased competition between the lending libraries themselves. This also provided the background to the growing phenomenon of specialization by lending libraries, a strategy that they pursued in their efforts to survive. However, it was largely the flourishing of the press in the second half of the nineteenth century, and in particular of the novels that were published in various newspapers and magazines, which robbed the lending libraries of many of their readers. From the 1870s onward, the public libraries, as well as political, church, school, and various associations' libraries, began to put themselves forward as a cheap alternative to commercial book lending. The failure of the attempt to set up an organization to represent the disparate interests of the commercial lending libraries is perhaps the most salient expression of the crisis affecting commercial book lending at the end of the nineteenth century.

However, despite the difficulties affecting the commercial lending libraries, commercial book lending did not disappear from the landscape of reading-material distribution methods at the end of the nineteenth century. Indeed, in the second half of the nineteenth century the number of lending libraries shot up, from 779 in 1865 to 2,629 in 1890. Many bookshops continued offering lending services to their clientele, and in the 1890s the large department stores even began setting up lending libraries as part of the array of services that they offered the consumer public.[62] The commercial lending libraries continued operating in the second half of the nineteenth century, although during this period they lost the dominant position they had enjoyed at the beginning of the century as the main distribution agents of popular reading material. This change reflected the shift in the position of lending-based reading.

The second half of the nineteenth century, which contemporary research saw as the period in which the commercial lending libraries crumbled, was therefore a time when attitudes to book reading began to change. Essentially, this involved a shift from reading books taken out on loan to reading books that had been purchased. During this period, book ownership acquired enhanced value as an inseparable part of the purchase-based book-reading culture, becoming one of the characteristic features of what is normally considered the "bourgeois" lifestyle. Concomitantly, reading through the medium of borrowing became associated with economic hardships and the disadvantaged social strata, who lacked the means to buy books. For these social groups, reading was a need that they could satisfy for a modest sum by borrowing. The dominance of this view of loan-based reading being connected to economic adversity and the commercialization of reading can be gauged inter alia from the common explanation advanced for the popularity of the commercial and noncommercial lending libraries alike in the postwar period. This explanation attributes the popularity of loan-based reading to economic hardships, especially the reduced purchasing power of the bourgeoisie during that period. Around 1930 in particular, the lending libraries' popularity reached new heights, as according to contemporary reports they "sprang up overnight like mushrooms after the rain." Various estimates put the numbers of lending libraries at between 14,000 and 18,000, or alternately between 30,000 and 40,000. However, according to the Reich Statistics Office, in 1933 Germany had just 2,758 commercial lending libraries, with holdings of 20 million books, 10 million readers, and handling around 720 million loans a year. The reason for the wildly differing estimates is that many businesses did not declare themselves to be lending libraries. At the time, book lending was a field at which any business with the space for a bookshelf tried its luck. Grocery shops, greengrocers, hairdressers, chemists, laundries, haberdashers, and tobacco and cigar shops were just some of the locations where books could be borrowed. But the most salient indication of the flood of commercial lending libraries at that time was the introduction of a new type of lending library. Unlike the commercial lending libraries which charged a deposit for borrowing operations in addition to the borrowing fee, at the end of the 1920s lending libraries opened which did not charge a deposit. Anyone could borrow books from this second type of lending library in return for ten to twenty pfennigs a week, or one pfennig a day per book, without paying a deposit. This new type of lending library came into being in the working-class boroughs of Berlin. However, in no time at all most lending libraries in the bourgeois parts of Berlin as well as other cities throughout Germany became "deposit-free."

Some attributed the new lending libraries' popularity to speculation on the part of book wholesalers, trying in this way to make a profit from the book stocks which by definition were in their possession but for which they could not find buyers. Many doubted the profitability of the new lending libraries, considering them distribution agents which would not be able to survive for long. However, it soon became clear that the new lending libraries were not a fleeting phenomenon, but rather a genuine answer to the "hunger for reading" (*Lesehunger*), particularly that of the large numbers of unemployed people at the time. The German Book Dealers' Association was called upon to adopt a more energetic attitude to the new lending libraries. The bookshops in particular wanted to combat the phenomenon of lending libraries situated in businesses utterly unrelated to the book trade. In parallel, the numbers of bookshops involved with lending books went up from 464 in 1925 to around 800 in 1933. This trend was also the backdrop to the call issued to recognize the commercial lending libraries as stepsons of the book trade and to organize them as part of the Book Dealers' Association. The publishers also recognized the importance of the new phenomenon and its economic potential. Especially in the wake of the Great Depression at the end of the 1920s, the lending libraries became an important customer of the publishers. At the beginning of the 1930s, for example, the publisher of popular writer Edgar Wallace sold five thousand copies of the total print run of six thousand to the lending libraries. On the initiative of a number of publishers, a number of associations such as the Vereinigung der Leihbibliothekswesen interessierten Verleger or the Verein der schönwissenschaftlichen Verleger, were set up in 1932 with the goal of cooperating with the lending libraries. For their part, in the same years authors were more supportive of the lending libraries. They were also interested in benefiting from "the return to book reading" through the commercial lending libraries. At the beginning of 1933 the biggest authors' interest body, the Schutzverband deutscher Schriftsteller, signed an agreement governing royalties with one of the commercial lending libraries' organizations (Reichsverband Deutscher Leihbüchereien), which was established in 1932. The public libraries had less tolerant attitudes to the commercial lending libraries, since the former were interested in having a monopoly over loan-based reading.

The commercial lending libraries, which historically predated the public libraries, were to a large extent the initial model for those public libraries which were set up in the course of the nineteenth century. However, the negative image of commercial book lending led to a situation where the public libraries did not wish to be identified with the commercial lending libraries. As a result, one of the first tasks for the public libraries was to improve the image of reading through the medium of borrowing. This desire constituted the background to the generation of a cognitive distinction between commercial and educational book lending, as two competing forms of lending representing different attitudes to book reading. The reinvigorated popularity of the commercial lending libraries around 1930 threw into higher relief the problematic nature of the relationship between these two forms of lending. During this period, public library circles called for State intervention in order to eliminate the phenomenon of the lending libraries. Commercial book lending was perceived as being at the mercy of the reading public's taste in reading, because in order for lending libraries to make a profit, they had to satisfy the masses' hunger for sensationalism and their "addiction to things new."

Unlike commercial lending libraries, which saw themselves as neutral mediators between books and readers, the public libraries aspired to the status of guides through the world of print, directing readers and book dealers to good literature. According to this approach, the main difference

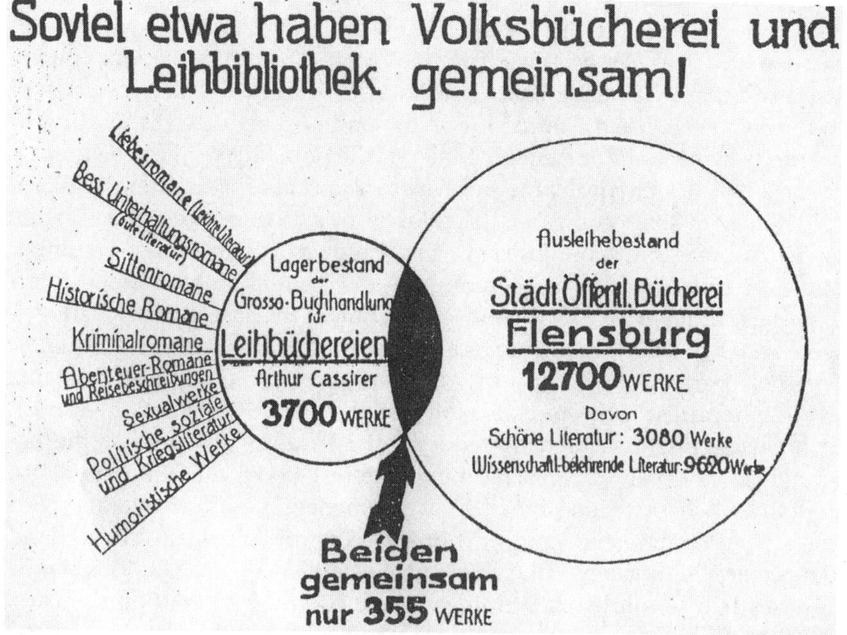

Picture 7: The difference between commercial lending libraries and public libraries

between a public and a commercial lending library was not just their book holdings (see picture 7), but the fact that public libraries encouraged book buying while the commercial lending libraries made books into fashionable commodities which were no longer worth buying after they had been read. As we have shown, these arguments contain little that is new, but rather testify to the importance attached to owning books as part of the book culture, and to the link between loan-based and purchase-based reading in consumer culture.

The commercial lending libraries therefore sold the activity of reading as such. Loan-based reading only became a competitor of purchase-based reading as demand for reading grew. In other words, loan-based reading is only a substitute to purchase-based reading insofar as loan-based reading attaches greater importance to the act of reading as such than to book ownership. However, since the value of book ownership was so dominant, loan-based reading was not perceived as a genuine alternative to purchase-based reading, but as an introduction to book buying and practically the only possible way of reading books during economically difficult times which impacted on the reading public's purchasing power. Loan-based and purchase-based reading were therefore two different expressions of the way that book-reading culture combined with the new consumer culture from the end of the eighteenth century onward.

The postwar period was characterized not only by the flourishing of loan-based reading, through both the commercial lending libraries and the public libraries, but also by the strengthening of the value of book ownership through "reading through buying." One of the conspicuous manifestations of this trend took the form of the book clubs (*Buchgemeinschaften*) that were introduced in Germany in the 1920s.

Book Clubs (*Buchgemeinschaften*)

According to Helmut Hiller's "Book Dictionary," book clubs (*Buchgemeinschaften* or *Buchklubs*) brought together a variable number of members or subscribers who, in return for a fixed amount, received a book issued by the book club at set intervals.[63] The organizing of reading by subscribers, whether on the initiative of readers or different interest-based organizations, was not an innovation on the part of the post–World War I book clubs.[64] The reading societies (*Lesegesellschaften*) of the second half of the eighteenth century are perhaps the most prominent example of the "organization of reading" by readers becoming organized on a voluntary basis.[65] In the course of the nineteenth century, different groups—normally of students, scholars, and bibliophiles—also came together in order to act as a counterweight to the book dealers and protect readers' interests as book lovers and consumers. The special requirements of different readers' groups and the importance attached to reading as a cultural-educational activity that helped to construct personal and group identity also constituted the backdrop to the publishing and marketing of books for specific groups of readers. The possibility of distributing books to reading subscribers was therefore a means that helped define the group's boundaries. The association bookshops (*Vereinsbuchhandel*), most of which were founded at the end of the nineteenth century by interest groups and a variety of trade unions or professional associations such as chemists, doctors, engineers, pharmacists, and so on, were just one example of this trend. In 1910 the number of these publishers reached 234.[66] For associations with manifestly educational-ideological goals such as the Evangelical Gustav Adolf Association (*Verein der Gustav Adolf Stiftung*), 1832, or the Catholic St. Karl Borromäus Association (*Verein vom Heiligen Karl Borromäus*), 1844, this individual book-marketing method formed an inseparable part of their working methods and a key element in their efforts to promote a special group awareness on the part of their target audience.

The interests of book-loving readers and book consumers, as well as educational-ideological motives were one reason behind this trend toward organizing readers and distributing books to a defined group of readers. The advantages of this method of distribution, which organized a group of readers and sent books directly to their homes, did not escape the attention of various entrepreneurs. The sending of books direct to readers' homes by commercial entrepreneurs specializing in this distribution method—the mail order book business (*Versandbuchhandlungen*)—is the best example of a method of distribution in competition with the direct selling of books in the bookshops. Alongside the latter, which operated according to the "take-away" principle (*Holprinzip*), the "send-me" principle (*Bringprinzip*) of the mail order book business became one of the most profitable ways of distributing reading material from the last third of the nineteenth century onward. But the mail order book business was generally speaking an intermediate body between publishers and readers. The mail order book business used catalogues to offer an anonymous reading public a range of books. In contrast, the principle of subscription-based distribution was introduced in 1876 by Hermann Schönlein, a publisher, when he founded the "Recreational and Knowledge Library" (*Bibliothek der Unterhaltung und des Wissens*) in Stuttgart. Within a short time, the series's subscribers reached almost thirty thousand readers. Although Schönlein marketed his library through the colportage trade, his initiative was considered the cornerstone of the modern idea of book clubs in Germany.

In the name of ideals of culture and education for the people, which concealed manifestly commercial interests, in the last decade of the nineteenth century a range of cultural associations began to distribute books by means of the subscription method. The "Book Lovers' Association" (*Verein der Bücherfreunde*), for example, which was founded in 1891 and by 1894 had twelve thousand subscribers, declared that one of its main aims was to save the German reading public from the lending libraries and accustom them to having their own bookshelf. But since the "Book Lovers' Association" (which obliged its members to acquire at least eight books a year) did not publish the books itself and acted as a broker between readers and publishers, it was not considered a book club as we would define it in the postwar period. August Scherl's library, with its "upwards reading" principle, was also considered one of the forerunners of the postwar book clubs. After the elimination of Scherl's library, in 1912 Heinrich Konrad (otherwise known as Dr. Hugo Sturm), who had drawn up the book list for Scherl's library, tried to sell the idea of the library for twelve thousand marks to George Müller's neoconservative publishing house. Although the parties reached the stage of signing a contract, the library in the form envisaged by Konrad never materialized.

Thus the system of marketing books to a defined readership using a subscription method offered numerous advantages to publishers and readers alike. This method reduced the risk of book publishing for an unknown audience. It tied a specific group of readers for a set time to publishers, thereby guaranteeing an income for the latter and also enabling them to promote a particular kind of literature according to the type of public that they wished to address. Since readers undertook in advance to acquire a number of books, this method of distribution also saved the cost of advertising every single book. Because a direct link was created between publisher and readers, there was no need for the wholesaler, thereby making it possible to further reduce book prices and improving service to readers, who enjoyed the convenience of receiving the books in their homes. However, despite this distribution method's series of advantages, and unlike newspaper publishers, who generally preferred the subscription-based method of distribution, the book trade remained faithful to the direct sales method in which books were sold in bookshops. Against this background, the proliferation of book clubs after the world war is a new phenomenon on the reading material distribution scene in Germany. The postwar book clubs were set up by entrepreneurs who were not members of the book dealers' associations. In most instances they were limited liability companies (GmbH), combining a commercially based organization which itself published and distributed books with promoting goals which had a patently educational-cultural and politico-ideological agenda.

Founded in 1916 by Germany's largest trade union of salaried employees, the *Deutschnationale Handlungsgehilfe Verband* (DHV), the *Deutschnationale Hausbücherei* (which in 1924 changed its name to the *Deutsche Hausbücherei*) was considered the first book club of this kind. The DHV, one of the bastions of the German new right wing and the standard-bearer of anti-semites in postwar Germany, did not limit subscriptions to its book club to its own members, instead seeking to promote German national thinking (*deutschnationale Gedanken*) by distributing quality books among all social strata. For this purpose, in 1914 the DHV set up a publishing house, the Hanseatische Verlagsanstalt. In the 1920s this published, among other authors, Ernst Junger, Wilhelm Stapel, Alfred Bartels, Friedrich Grimm, and many others who belonged to the ranks of the new right of the time. The DHV's book club was not the hoped-for success. Up to 1919, the Deutschnationale Hausbücherei had no more than six hundred members. It was only during the 1920s, in part after it allowed women to join, that its membership grew, reaching forty thousand in 1930. The *Volksverband der Bücherfreunde GmbH* (People's Association of Book Friends Ltd.), established in 1919, was more successful. One of its key aims was to "combat the danger of books becoming luxuries, in particular for the middle classes who have their backs against the wall" (*schwer kämpfender Mittelstand*).[67] Two years after its establishment, the *Volksverband der Bücherfreunde* had hundred thousand members, and despite the political upheavals and economic hardships of the early 1920s, membership of the book club grew steadily, topping three hundred thousand in 1933. Some six book clubs were set up in 1924, and the success of the book club as a method of distributing books became an established fact.

The best-known of the book clubs founded in 1924 was the *Buch-Gemeinschaft*, whose name became synonymous with this method of distributing books. The Buch-Gemeinschaft offered itself as a "cooperative venture" (*Gemeinschaft*) set above all political, religious, or social divisions, with the goal of enabling private libraries to be set up for all social classes, and not as a commercial business interested only in deriving pecuniary gain from selling books. There was nothing new in this, of course. What was unique about the Buch-Gemeinschaft was its innovatory approach to marketing and promoting the idea of the book club. Unlike the other book clubs, which required their subscribers to purchase at least four books over the year, normally without any great choice, the Buch-Gemeinschaft aspired to broaden its subscribers' options under the slogan "completely free choice" (*völlig freie Wahl*). To do so, the Buch-Gemeinschaft offered different kinds of subscriptions, so that every three months readers could choose how many books they wanted to buy. In addition, the Buch-Gemeinschaft expanded the range of books on offer to its readers. For example, in 1925 readers could choose from 72 titles; by mid-1933 the number of titles had shot up to 450. Apart from German and world classics, the club offered its members the works of a whole range of contemporary authors, such as the Mann brothers (Heinrich and Thomas), Jacob Wasserman, Hermann Hesse, Frank Thiss, Hans Fallada, Gerhard Hauptmann, and others. Even in its publications the Buch-Gemeinschaft made a point of not using terms such as "commitment" (*Verpflichtung*) or "obligation" (*Zwang*), instead referring to freedom of choice and reducing the cost of books. These semantics, as shown by the data about the Buch-Gemeinschaft's membership, fell on interested ears among readers and above all among the civil servants whom the Buch-Gemeinschaft saw as its preferred target audience. The Buch-Gemeinschaft's membership enjoyed linear growth in the 1920s, swelling from 11,000 in 1924 to 400,000 readers in 1929, including 75,000 outside Germany's borders, and marketing over a million books annually.[68]

The model for liberalizing relations with readers that was introduced by the Buch-Gemeinschaft became a veritable how-to guide for all book clubs. This new approach to readers did not stop at expanding the selection available to readers: it also meant striving to involve readers in picking the book clubs' range of publications. An example is the conservative Volksverband der Bücherfreunde, which in 1926 began to ask its members which of the club's books they had liked and why. In order to encourage readers to reply to the survey, the club offered 200 monetary prizes, worth between RM 5 and RM 200, for a total value of RM 3,500, for which a draw was arranged among those answering the questions.

The book clubs were so successful that the Book Dealers Association, in addition to fighting the new phenomenon tooth and nail, in 1926 went so far as to set up its own book club, the *Buch-Einkaufs-Gemeinschaft*. This initiative was designed to curb the popularity of the new book clubs, while at the same time also aspiring to benefit from the new situation. However, after the call to boycott the book clubs had fallen as flat as its attempt to set up a book club, the Book Dealers' Association resigned itself to the book clubs' existence and toward the end of the 1920s it even began to cooperate. A striking example of this cooperation was the distribution in 1930 of Thomas Mann's novel *Buddenbrooks* through the Buch-Gemeinschaft. Until November 1929, the price set by the S. Fischer publishing house, which issued the book, was RM 17, but when Mann was awarded the Nobel Prize for Literature in 1929 and *Buddenbrooks* was distributed in 1930 by the Buch-Gemeinschaft, Mann's novel, now selling at RM 2.85, became a best seller, with a total of over 1,165,000 copies being bought.[69] In return for granting permission to distribute his novel through the Buch-Gemeinschaft, Mann received RM 60,000 from the book club, while Fischer Publishers paid him just RM 40,000.[70] This is a telling example of how even authors benefited from the introduction of the new book clubs. But the latter did not just act as brokers between publishers and readers: they also published books themselves, either acquiring rights or commissioning books directly from writers. The upshot of this state of affairs was that the book clubs generated a new source of income for authors and increased competition for their services. In this sense the book clubs were book distribution agents who encouraged literary output in the 1920s.

By 1933, over thirty different book clubs had been set up. At the end of 1925, the book clubs had a total membership of around seven hundred thousand readers, a figure which had swollen to a million and a half by 1933. Despite the fact that the book clubs' success can be seen as something of an expression of the longing for togetherness or community (*Gemeinschaft*), a tendency which undoubtedly helped to promote the book club idea in the 1920s, the book clubs equally reflect the social and political fragmentation characteristic of their time: the trade unions' Büchereigilde Gutenberg; the Social Democrats' Bücherkreise, the Communists' Universum Bücherei für Alle, the Brauner Buch-Ring of the Nazis, the Buch-Gemeinschaft, and the Volksverband der Büchereifreunde with their national-conservative leanings, targeting mainly the middle class; the Protestants' Evangelische Buchgemeinde, the Catholics' Bonner Buchgemeinde, and the Jews' Heinebund were just some of the great variety of book clubs during this period which tailored their offerings to a particular audience. Although we lack figures on male/female ratios in the book clubs, it may reasonably be assumed that women made up a considerable proportion of the book clubs' target audiences. This is primarily borne out by the book clubs' own advertisements, which very noticeably targeted women. Despite this tendency, no women-only book club was ever founded in Germany. The book clubs were therefore a means by which various groups, which primarily defined themselves by political, religious, and class criteria, tried to promote their interests and became an element in constructing their collective identities. In this sense, the book clubs reflect the social divisions of their time, and above all the dominance of political, religious, and class categories of thought in determining their character. In addition, the book clubs reflect the way that technology—by improving methods for producing and distributing reading material, and bringing down its cost to the consumer—contributed to this tendency toward social fragmentation. Competition between the book clubs was an unmistakable expression of this tendency. Every book club professed to offer something that no other book club offered, in part through the "introduce a friend" scheme which also sought to reinforce book club members' feeling of "us"; publishing their own magazines; and distinctive features such as logos and special designs for the club's books.

However, apart from differences between the various book clubs, there are also a number of common features which show how the book clubs at the same time reflected the tendency toward programming society while also being an expression of the tendency toward its standardization. This was helped not only by the book clubs' common structural features, but above all by the similar values of book-reading culture which the various book clubs promoted. Reducing book prices and making graphically high-caliber books accessible to readers were the two principles shared by all book clubs. For instance, the Buch-Gemeinschaft and the Volksverband der Büchereifreunde both offered their members books with luxury bindings, sometimes of leather, with tooled gilt decorations. The book clubs of the workers' movement also paid great attention to book design: some of them even purported to promote a new book design that would make it possible to reduce printing costs, but result in a book which could be read in comfort and was attractive to look at. In the magazine of the Büchereigilde Gutenberg's book club, articles appeared lauding the virtues of book owning and advancing the following arguments against borrowing books:

> At times of infectious diseases such as tuberculosis (with sputum contaminated with bacilli), measles, scarlet fever, diphtheria, typhoid fever, dysentery, etc., books must not be taken out of lending libraries. […] A book may make a basically clean impression but still convey a health hazard. […] People who enjoy reading will be able to enjoy the aesthetic pleasure of holding a clean book and be able to devote themselves to enjoying it without a second thought. This is naturally only completely possible in the case of those works which one owns and looks after oneself.[71]

The book clubs, therefore, helped not only to increase awareness of books and the popularization of reading through buying, but also to strengthen the value of owning books as objects of symbolic value that should be present in every self-respecting home. As a result, book buying became a declarative act of consumption in which the reader-cum-consumer acquired the attributes associated with the lifestyle represented by book ownership. Book buying thus became part of the aspiration to upward social mobility. In this sense the book clubs express the increasing importance of consumption in contemporary German society, in which in principle it was possible to buy a desired lifestyle if one had enough money. The book clubs apparently met this demand, selling books as culturally valuable commodities which conferred social prestige—all at a relatively affordable price. As a result, the success of the book clubs, particularly in Berlin and Germany's other metropolises, was not solely a result of the economic hardships of the 1920s, but was also an outcome of the rise of the new salaried class and its aspiration, despite low salary levels, to adopt a lifestyle which would distance it from the proletariat and bring it closer to the bourgeoisie.[72] In this context it is also noteworthy that despite the differences between the different book clubs in terms of content and forms of publishing, most of the clubs, including those associated with the labor movement, continued to publish works categorized as part of the traditional canon of classical German and world literature. Furthermore, the various book clubs did not just sell books: they also circulated a range of printed and illustrative matter—calendars, pictures, and prints—as well as records and tickets for plays and concerts. Thus the book clubs sold the entire ideal of bourgeois education, and not just part of it. This tendency was an expression of the hegemony of the bourgeois lifestyle in contemporary Germany society, and of the way that this lifestyle reproduced itself.

In the 1920s, as publication numbers grew steadily, the book clubs became a kind of tool which helped readers to navigate a world of ever more publications and increasing competition between a variety of media. The book clubs' publications speak volumes on this point. Unlike the book trade's traditional publicity, which focused on books as such, the book clubs' promotional material emphasized the unique relationship between the book clubs and the world of books, with the titles of the books themselves coming second. The book clubs would therefore appear to be part of this tendency of seeking ways to steer a course through the world of print. They were a means whose services helped to inculcate differential consumption patterns of books and in this way rendered possible the mass circulation of books among broad sectors of readers.

The book clubs are therefore an example of the complexity of the act of consumption, which as Arjun Appadurai has aptly noted, must be seen in terms of sending a social message and its receiving status also.[73] Contemporary observers were also aware of this link between the book clubs and the new consumer culture, which lay at the center of the criticism directed at the clubs. As a number of passages in earlier chapters have shown, even the critical attitudes to the book clubs revealed ambivalent attitudes to the new consumer culture and its links with book reading culture. On the one hand, it was claimed that the book clubs operated according to purely commercial considerations and tried, by reducing book prices through larger print runs, solely to derive financial profits out of selling books. A common argument was that while reducing book prices encouraged the petty bourgeois consumption of books as objects intended to decorate the walls of the home, the insistence on increasing print runs forced the book clubs to address the widest common denominator of readers—in other words resulting in a policy that adversely affected the quality of publications and encouraged the uniformization of literary taste. According to this approach, the book clubs made price the main component in decisions as to whether or not to buy a book, with its literary qualities coming second.

On the other hand, it was argued that the book clubs reduced readers' freedom to choose and prevented competition between publishers. Such competition was considered one of the primary conditions for creative literary output and innovativeness. The argument can be summed up as follows: even though the book clubs remained true to the pattern of production for the sake of consumption, reducing the risks associated with book publishing for an unknown readership by organizing consumers engendered the fear that this system of distribution, with production equal to consumption, would homogenize demand, smother the publishing market, and stifle literary creativity. Unlike the bookshops, which met disparate reading needs, and where readers were basically asked to demonstrate at least a minimum degree of understanding and literary knowledge so that they could choose from the selection of books for sale, it was argued that the book clubs "force-fed" their readers with books, in the process encouraging passive attitudes and literary ignorance.

Irrespective of whether the new consumer culture was viewed in an optimistic or a pessimistic light, the book clubs were perceived as book distribution agents which were jeopardizing publishing quality and threatening to establish a dictatorship over literary taste. To a large extent, such arguments echo the negative views of the idea of socializing the book trade at the beginning of the 1920s, as discussed in Chapter I. It was no wonder, therefore, that these arguments originated among book dealers with whom the book clubs competed for the reading public's purse. However, book dealers' reactions were not confined to engaging in polemics against the book clubs, calling for a boycott, or trying to set up a rival book club. They even went so far as to try to expand book consumption through the traditional publishers and bookshops.

From Advertisements for Books to Books as Advertising

As a body that acts as a broker between authors and readers, the book trade reflects the generation of demand for books. In order to guarantee its own existence, this area of business endeavor therefore had to promote such demand. Mismatch between book-production possibilities—books being one of the first products to lend themselves to mass reproduction and distribution to an unlimited public of consumers—and demand was one of the main reasons why the book dealers adopted advertising as a means of increasing demand for their stock-in-trade.[74] Book advertising was one of the harbingers of modern commercial advertising as we know it today. In the late eighteenth and early nineteenth centuries, the period of the first reading revolution when the reading public was still fairly small, most newspaper advertising was for books. In contrast, beginning in the last third of the nineteenth century, when the second reading revolution took place, book advertising was banished to the sidelines of the advertising pages of the daily papers and popular magazines. The reasons behind this change may entail shifts in the composition of the newspaper reading public, which given the increasing importance of other consumer goods made newspapers an unsuitable medium for advertising books. It is also possible that this situation reflected the fact that books no longer needed to be advertised in the press. Whatever the reasons underlying this change, the fact that from the end of the nineteenth century onward commercial advertising was no longer associated with books does not mean that commercial advertising of books simply disappeared.

The expansion of the reading public, increased book production, and fiercer competition with the new media as well as between the various book distribution agents combined to increase the need for publicity for books. At the same time the range of means available for advertising increased. This situation gave rise to numerous questions about the nature of books. Are books cultural items intended for a select class of readers with refined tastes, or commercial goods looking for mass distribution and seeking to make economic capital? Many book people could not make up their minds whether the "process of trivialization" should be encouraged in the case of books, making them a commonplace or standard part of day-to-day existence, or whether they should be promoted as luxury goods not falling within the purview of humdrum mass culture. What kind of demand for books should be considered desirable? These were the key issues on the agenda of intellectual discourse all the way from the end of the eighteenth century well into the twentieth. A commonly assumed position concerning the nature of books as commodities argued that unlike other mass-produced items, which were based on repeated consumption, what made books unique as products was that although they were mass-produced, they were only consumed once. The "reading fever" of the early nineteenth century, or the fight against pulp and trashy literature at its end, were really discussions about unwelcome demand for books. At a time when most of the population was literate, books therefore became objects which, as Arjun Appadurai has noted in discussing luxury goods generally, should be seen: "Not so much in contrast to necessity, but as goods whose principal use is rhetorical and social, goods that simply incarnated signs."[75] However, books as goods of symbolic value and reading as a culturally important activity not only became part of the new consumer culture, but also helped to promote it. The rest of this chapter will examine some of the manifestations of these complex interactions between reading and consumption.

Book Advertising

In 1887 the German booksellers' umbrella organization revised its book price policy. The Kröner Reform, named after the organization's then chairman, stipulated that consumer book prices would be set in advance by the publishers, and would be binding on all bookshops. Under this system, a bookshop's profit would be guaranteed by a discount on every copy of a book that it sold.[76] Introducing a system of fixed prices on the German book market not only reflected fears of uncontrolled competition between book dealers, but was also designed to encourage the establishment of bookshops and to guarantee their survival. To put it another way, the intention was to increase publicity for books.

The bookshop, as a place where books and readers met, was perceived as the main sales promotion agent for books. Shop windows were in particular considered far and away *the* means of promoting books. This approach helped stress the importance of book jacket design, whether using a unique design for each individual book, or a distinctive design for a particular series of books. The color of the cover, its form, or the publisher's logo became distinctive elements which were intended to speak to the contents and quality of a book. Even the book's title and shop window designs were utilized to attract the gazes of passersby. Personal contact between booksellers and readers was considered invaluable in influencing book consumption habits. In 1926, for example, a bookshop owner reported that 80 percent of his customers who enjoyed plot-driven literature did not ask for a particular book when they came to his shop, instead expecting the salesman to recommend a suitable book for them. It was for this reason that in the 1920s, bookshop owners would periodically visit their customers' homes in order to update them about the latest publications and encourage them to visit their shop and buy books.[77]

Bookshops thus acted as collective book sales promoters. As a result, publishers focused most of their advertising efforts on the book dealer community. An unavoidable result of this tendency was that many bookshops began to add the letter "W" to their addresses in the book dealers' directory. The W stood for "*wählen*" (to choose), meaning that they preferred to make their own choice of books rather than receive promotional material from the publishers. The cost of advertising also contributed to this distinction between advertising directed at book trade professionals and that intended for the reading public, as did doubts about the effectiveness of book advertisements in the press, at the time still the main form of advertising. Advertisements in the daily papers or popular magazines were appropriate for books of potential interest to the general reading public. However, even in this case there was a danger that an advertisement for a book would go unnoticed among the abundance of advertisements. As a result, the book trade manuals advised publishers to direct their promotional material at a specific readership, normally by advertising in a variety of specialist journals or by approaching potential readers directly, and to make less use of the general press and popular magazines that addressed an anonymous reading public with disparate areas of interest.[78] This distinction between advertising for the general public on the one hand and for specialists on the other illustrated the differences in the promotional interests of authors, bookshops, and publishers: the latter were trying to promote certain books, while the bookshops were trying to sell as many books as possible irrespective of author or publisher.

The difficulty of advertising a particular book was one of the factors that persuaded many publishers to publish series of books. The "Blue Book" series (Blaue Bücher) from Karl Robert Langewiesche's publishing house, Ullstein's Yellow Series, S. Fischer's Library of Contemporary Novels (Bibliothek zeitgenössicher Romane), the Insel Library (Inselbücherei), and Knaur Publishers' "World Novel" (Roman der Welt) series are just a few examples of this tendency. Promoting a number of titles under a single brand name was a cheaper and more efficient way of advertising individual titles. Publicity in catalogues or promotional material where publishers presented a selection of their publications was also part of this tendency toward "collective advertising."[79] However, this trend toward collectively advertising a number of titles did not solve the conflict of interests between publishers and bookshops, whose owners were afraid that the publishers would find alternative ways of marketing books. Furthermore, this trend toward collective book advertising quite often ran into feelings of frustration among authors (normally of less successful books), who claimed that their books were not being promoted sufficiently.

The need to reconcile the conflicting interests of publishers and bookshops, as well as the necessity to increase the demand for book reading, were the main factors in the November 1923 establishment of the book trade's central advertising body (*Zentrale für das gesamte buchhändlerische*

EINIGE FÜLLINSERATE IN SCHRIFT UND BILD, DIE DIE WERBESTELLE DES BÖRSENVEREINS DER DEUTSCHEN BUCHHÄNDLER ZUR BUCHWERBUNG FÜR DIE TAGES- UND ZEITSCHRIFTENPRESSE HERAUSBRACHTE

Picture 8: Examples of advertisements by the center for book advertisement

Werbewesen), the initiative for which came from the book dealers' organization. The advertising center (*Werbestelle*) was intended to provide assistance to book dealers so as to make their advertisements more effective and also promote them, as well as to act as a body for the collective promotion of books. In this sense, the advertising center was a pioneer in joint advertising for a particular business sector—a practice more common at the time in the USA than in Germany. The center issued manuals, offered courses on advertising, organized exhibitions which presented different types of publicity devices, and undertook its own book advertising campaign. To this end, the advertising center issued posters and advertising stamps (*Briefverschlussmarken*) which became sought-after objects for collectors of all ages, organized lectures, put on book exhibitions in a variety of locations, and provided support for the production of advertising and instructional films about the book trade as well as radio programs which discussed book-related matters. Since collective publicity for books was not allowed to relate to individual books, it was forced to concentrate on book marketing as such.

The book advertisements (see examples in picture 8) referred to book reading as a leisure activity which could be engaged in at any time—before, on the way to, and after work, and in any situation at home or on the move. These advertisements stressed the mobility and flexibility of book reading, which met the needs of modern man. They highlighted the cultural value of book reading as helping to promote the intellect, and as the perfect complement to physical activities. One advertisement read: "German style means being strong and smart" (*Deutsche Art heisst: stark und klug sein*), showing an athlete, and a book reader as perfection incarnate. Advertisements also showed book reading as a suitable activity for both men and women of all ages, addressing them as individuals. In other words, reading was presented as an activity suitable for the private sphere. In the 1920s the process of individualizing reading, which started as far back as the eighteenth century, would thus appear to have come to an end. In this sense, group reading, which was still accepted in the late nineteenth century, was replaced by the cinema, competitive sports events, and group listening to records and the radio. Advertisers therefore made the effort to present reading as an activity which belonged to the modern world rather than being a leftover from the old one.

Another conspicuous element in advertising books was their special significance as objects. One advertisement pointed out that borrowing books meant "eating out of the same pan as lots of others!" (*Bücher leihen heißt, mit vielen aus einer Pfanne essen!*)

Special attention was devoted to the symbolic value of books as gifts. Particularly in the pre-Christian period, advertisements focused on giving books as presents. Special catalogues were issued for Christmas books, with publishers and bookshops running a special joint Yuletide advertising campaign. The advertisements asked, "What books shall I give as

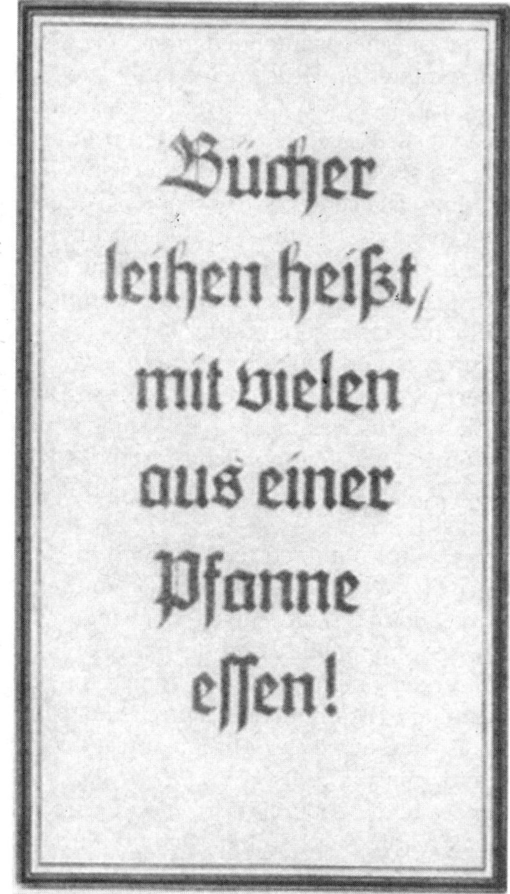

Picture 9: borrowing books means eating out of the same pan as lots of others!

Picture 10: Books as presents

presents at Christmas?", or urged people to think about giving books as presents (*Beim Schenken an Bücher denken*). Books were presented as ideal gifts, combining attractive appearance with substance, at a reasonable price.

This advertising campaign focused on young readers. The advertising center issued "wish lists" (*Wunschzettel*), with one side showing a photo and the other the youngster's "wishes" in the following form: "Folgende Bücher wünsche ich mir" (I'd like the following books), with a number of blank lines to write down the names of the desired books. These lists were distributed by the thousands at bookshops and to school pupils.

In the 1920s, it was not standard practice to target a juvenile readership. A programmatic article by a book dealer called Hans Semm, specifying some of the basic principles governing bookshop sales, made the point that booksellers should draw particular attention to children. Semm

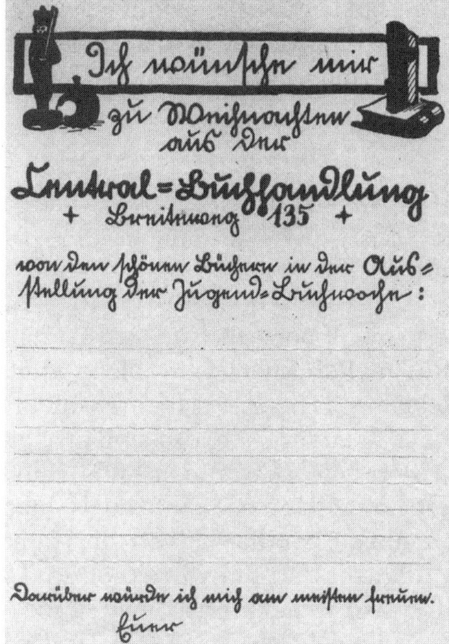
Ich wünsche mir
zu Weihnachten
aus der
Zentral-Buchhandlung
von den schönen Büchern in der Ausstellung der Jugend-Buchwoche:

Darüber würde ich mich am meisten freuen.

Bestellzettel für Weihnachtsbücher.
Entwurf: Ahrlé-Photo, Leipzig

Picture 11 and 12: A wish list

not only explained this statement by arguing that children are potential future book buyers, but also drew attention to this public's influence on parental consumption habits.[80] In the 1920s, an awareness would appear to have been emerging of the fact that children and adolescents constitute a public of consumers in the proper sense of the term. This development did not escape the sharp eyes of Walter Benjamin, who even recalls that his introduction to civic life at the end of the nineteenth century had been as a consumer.[81]

The joint book advertising campaign was a new pillar which expanded traditional publicity by the book publishers. It fitted in with the general tendency toward increasing publicity for books in the 1920s. The world war and its consequences were perceived as the main factors influencing the increase in publicity for books and the demand for professionalization. Horst Kliemann, who in the 1920s designed the theoretical campaign for undertaking book publicity, saw the economic circumstances affecting postwar Germany as the main reason why increased advertising was needed. The impoverishment of the traditional book-reading public forced the book dealers to expand their target audience so as to protect themselves against bankruptcy, and advertising was supposed to help them achieve this goal. What is interesting about this widespread attitude is that it shows that specifically during times of penury, when money lost much of its value, efforts were made to boost consumption. In the case of book consumption, this goal was of special significance, since demand for books could be met in a variety of ways—not necessarily by buying them. This fact was apparently the reason why emphasis was placed on the value of book ownership and on strengthening purchase-based reading after the world war. As Semm put it:

> One of the few good consequences of the war is indeed the desire to read, which is present among a far broader spectrum of the people than previously. And we must use advertising to increase this desire, until the desire becomes first a question and then a purchase.[82]

Following the world war, the advertising of books became such an intensive and self-evident activity that Reclam Publishers were able to adopt the slogan, "Reclam braucht keine Reklame." The use of the new media such as film, radio, and records in order to advertise books similarly attested to this trend. A film version of a literary work would be highlighted in book advertising. Sometimes, advertising made a book into the written version of a film. There were even attempts to produce advertising films for books. The Berlin-based Heinrich Tillgner publishing firm produced a short animated movie for its classic German writers series, while Brockhaus and the Bibliographic Institute in Leipzig also made advertising films for their encyclopedias and lexicons.[83] Some publishers placed advertising signs in cinemas, and a group of book dealers were even interested in setting up an association of booksellers in cinemas. The radio, especially during book discussion programs, became the place to promote book sales. It is noteworthy that more and more use began to be made of "hidden" advertising for books. Courts and libel cases in particular provided publishers with a means of advertising that they used in order to penetrate public awareness and thereby promote their sales.

However, advertisements, catalogues, personal contacts with clients, and above all turning to what were called "duplicators," generally book reviewers, were the primary means available in the 1920s for publicizing books. As in other fields, the problem facing publishers was to find suitable means of promoting the sales of every single one of their books. Works of nonfiction in particular, having only limited target audiences with an interest in a specific subject, tried to come up with new approaches to expanding their circle of potential consumers. An example is a report about the publicity campaign for a salesman's concise reference work (*Handwörterbuch des Kaufmanns*) by the right-wing Hanseatische Verlagsanstalt publishing house. The report, which appeared in the *Advertising* magazine (*Die Reklame*), relates how the publishers' first step was to change the book's title, which was over-long and complicated.[84] The new title was *Der Grosse Bott*, which hinted at a link with the major reference works by the Brockhaus and Mayer publishing houses (*Der Grosse Brockhaus* and *Der Grosse Mayer*). Changing the title of the dictionary formed part of the marketing strategy for the book, and was designed to expand its advertising possibilities. Apart from the standard advertising resources, such as advertising in magazines or catalogues, during a major commercial fair in Leipzig, renowned for its trade shows, the publishers erected a giant bill-

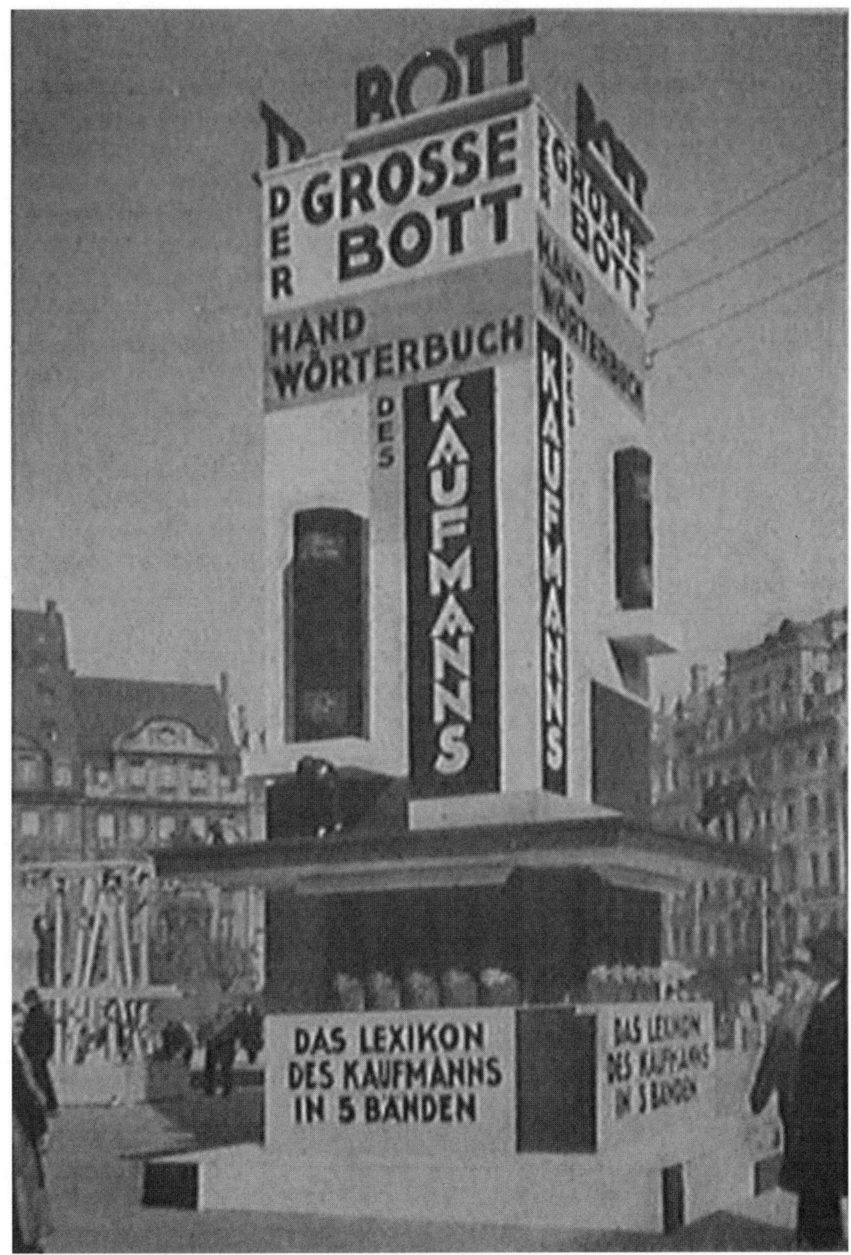

Picture 13: The Great Bott

board on the city's Market Square (see picture 13) bearing the title *Der Grosse Bott*. Their idea was to make the dictionary's title into a brand name which would be etched in the minds of passersby.

Advertising strategies varied from one book to the next, depending on the publisher's nature and means, the kind of book, and its potential target audience. Advertisements for detective stories, romantic novels, or adventure stories used bold lettering, illustrations, and color photographs in promising readers thrilling experiences. These advertisements primarily stressed the experiential value of book reading. The same tendency was also expressed in these books' designs, which were normally of low graphic quality. With their garish covers, they sold at low prices. In contrast, in advertisements for nonfiction works or what was considered quality plot-driven literature, the text took greater precedence. These advertisements laid greater stress on the benefit that could be derived from the book, its cultural and aesthetic merits, and the value of books as objects whose purchase was a worthwhile long-term investment.

Notwithstanding the differences between the various types of book advertisements, a number of common attributes can be identified. The author's and publisher's names, details about the book's contents and quotations from favorable reviews, plus the number of copies printed and the cost of the book were the main details given in most book advertisements. Success was also a central theme which recurred in many advertisements. Success meant honor and recognition: its most conspicuous expression was large sales turnovers. Hence the author's reputation and enthusiastic reviews and articles about him and his book would be highlighted in advertisements. Less well-known authors were treated as hitherto undiscovered versions of successful authors. Indicating the number of copies printed and sold in Germany or abroad was also part of this trend toward creating a successful image for a book and its author. Emphasizing the size of a book's print run was intended to draw bookshop owners' attention to the profit-making potential that the book could secure for them, while its message to readers was that if they bought this book, they would not be buying a pig in a poke. Advertisements also referred to aspects of the book's design, and even its cost. A book's price was a key element in attempts to convince readers that it was worthwhile to buy it. An example of this was F.A. Brockhaus's slogan for its series of travel books: "Brockhaus führt Dich durch die Welt mit viel Genuß und wenig Geld!" (Brockhaus will guide you round the world with much pleasure and at low cost!). Similarly, Mayer's advertisement for the 1930 edition of its twelve-volume encyclopedia at the price of RM 363 argued that, given the number of books for which its reference work was a substitute, it was cheap at the price and buying it made economic sense (see picture 14).

Other details which many advertisements made a point of stressing included special paper; printing techniques; numbers of illustrations, pictures, maps, and tables as well as the number of pages. Books were thus marketed as objects possessing aesthetic qualities, and combining technological progress, enjoyment, and culture. Undoubtedly the popularity of the new media decisively influenced the growing importance of stressing books' technical and visual aspects in advertisements.

Another striking feature characteristic of the majority of book advertisements was their authoritative nature. In contrast to book sales in shops, where thrusting books at customers and ordering them to buy was not recommended, advertisements for books quite often used the imperative. The *Nimm und Lies!* (*Take and Read!*) magazine is a perfect example of this propensity.[85] Advertisements also tended to quote from authoritative figures who extolled the book. Relying on the recommendations of "good judges" who knew what they were talking about was not limited to advertisements. Articles in the culture pages of newspapers, and book reviews in particular were considered of decisive importance in determining the success of book sales.[86] Directly approaching individuals of status and repute was considered an acceptable way of promoting book sales. This is illustrated in the report of an advertising executive called Sebastian Watzal on a publicity campaign for a book about the history of an anonymous spa town in Germany, whose name he refrained from giving. The book's entire print run was deposited with no return

Picture 14: Mayer's advertisement

option in the storerooms of the publisher's printing house.[87] The erudite nature of the book, and the fact that it concentrated on a particular area, were the main factors that made it difficult to market it. Watzal therefore suggested an advertising campaign targeting people in a variety of positions, including headmasters, senior civil servants, army officers, and so on, both in and outside the area where the spa was located. The idea was that these people would become "duplicators" for the book. A copy of the book was sent to them, with an accompanying personal letter asking them for their opinion of it. In this case, the advertisers did not limit themselves to approaching only men in positions of authority. They also sent out letters specifically addressing ladies living in the vicinity of the spa, presenting the book as a cultural article which every self-respecting home should have.

Women were perceived as the primary group comprising the book-reading public and the success of a book, particularly a novel, was related to the extent to which it was of interest to a female readership. This marketing approach fitted in with the standard outlook which saw consumption as the province of women. There are a number of possible interpretations of the extent to which this approach was responsible for the authoritative nature of book advertising—a domain under male control. A number of surveys which tried to identify the factors that influenced book buying referred to recommendations of books as the central factor in the array of considerations that led to a decision to buy a book among men and women alike.[88] However, as shown by the data collected by Diederichs Publishers in 1914, while women's decisions to buy books were more influenced by the recommendations of people they knew, men were more influenced by "objective" advertising for books in book reviews, advertisements, and shop windows. What is interesting is that this finding was not viewed as an expression of women's consumer skills, but rather as an indication of the problematic nature of women as a public of consumers whose book-consuming habits were determined by a cautious, not to say parsimonious approach and an all-consuming desire to be entertained.[89]

Authors constituted a group which needed no convincing of the importance of book advertising. The 1920s show more and more involvement by authors in promoting their works' sales. Radio and press interviews, evenings of readings, and writing radio scripts were the main means through which authors tried to promote their works and expand their readerships. In his doctoral thesis about bookshops located in department stores, Rudy Klotzbach reports on a series of afternoon encounters under the title "Literarisch-musikalische Nachmittage" which took place in 1930 at Rudolf Karstadt's department store located on Berlin's Hermannplatz. Guests at these *conversaziones* included Heinrich Mann, Felix Mendelssohn, and others.[90]

From 1927 onward, the literary journal *Die Literarische Welt* published lists of best sellers. Instead of using the German term "Schlager," it adopted the English term. What is the secret of a best seller? How do you write a best seller? Is there a formula for writing a best seller? Can one predict who (or what) is going to become a best seller? These were questions which during this period serious magazines and well-known authors had to address for the first time. Siegfried Kraucauer has explained the best seller's growing importance as a sociological phenomenon which attests to the standardization of German society in the wake of the world war, in the course of which more people than previously shared common experiences and similar lifestyles.[91]

The State also began to intervene in the area of book reading. In 1929 the Reichstag declared 22 March, Goethe's birthday, "German Book Day." Unlike Spain and Italy, on whose "book days" special markets were held where books were sold, Germany's book day was marked by special information and PR activities, articles, lectures, and encounters between

Picture 15: The German Book Day

readers and authors.[92] Although in the 1920s publishers and bookshops, as well as the department stores, organized book exhibitions and special promotions where books were presented and could be bought, supporters of the so-called German "book day" model argued that the book markets in Italy and Spain did not suit the German character.[93] Book Day, it was argued, had to be devoted to the intellectual meaning of books, not to selling books at special markets. This approach was heavily criticized by large numbers of people in the book trade, who doubted the extent to which "Book Day" could effectively increase awareness of books and promote sales. Willy Haas, editor of the journal *Die Literarische Welt*, called for book dealers to adopt the Italian book day model and demonstrate more boldness and innovativeness in distributing books.[94] Many complaints from the owners of publishing houses and bookshops also appeared in the German book dealers' paper, the *Börsenblatt*, about the over-academic nature of Book Day, arguing that it failed to influence book sales. Disagreements about the nature and goals of Book Day reflected disparate approaches to the nature of books as objects and how they should be marketed. One of the most conspicuous expressions of this issue was the area of book prices.

Cheap Books vs. Expensive Books

A whole complex of factors led to the process by which books steadily became cheaper from the end of the eighteenth century all the way into the twentieth. Mounting demand for book reading and an expanding reading public; the development of the book trade and literary output; the insistence on disseminating cultural values among broad sectors of society; and a whole series of technological improvements which enabled considerable savings to be made in book production and distribution costs were the main factors that paved the way to reduced book prices. Which of these is more important than the others is a moot point. The introduction to the first volume of the reduced-price edition of a number of the most important classical German authors produced by Göschen Publishers in 1817 makes the following statement:

> These are to be editions which will make the thrifty German who has the means to acquire them wish to do so. German forbearance, but nothing fancy, simple and straightforward, good lettering on attractive paper: this is what I wish to provide.[95]

In contrast, Karl Josef Mayer, who in 1826 founded the Bibliographical Institute in Leipzig, under the motto "Education liberates!" (*Bildung macht frei!*) published paperback books priced at two pennies (*Groschen*), which he intended for distribution among all social strata.

The economic justification for publishing Göschen's reduced-price editions as opposed to the ideal of disseminating "culture to the people" which resulted in Mayer's publishing a series of paperbacks, reflect different attitudes to book-reading culture and the reasons for reducing book prices. However, at a time when the reading public was not particularly large, reductions in book prices primarily attracted readers from affluent bourgeois circles.

Hence cheaper book prices helped save a large numbers of readers from bourgeois backgrounds from having to patronize the commercial lending libraries and hence made them part of a book-consuming public. This tendency undoubtedly played a decisive role in the process of generating the late-nineteenth century ideal of the educated bourgeoisie, with special value accruing to book ownership. The cost of books thus became a key factor in their popularity. The success of Reclam's Universal Library was perhaps the most striking expression of this trend. To a large extent the cheap books published by Reclam and other companies brought book buying back to its zero level: i.e., buying in order to read. When Reclam installed book-vending machines in railway stations throughout Germany before World War I, this was perhaps the most salient expression of the commodification of book reading. Reclam's books were cheap and easy to carry around. As a result, they were particularly suitable for travelling, and like the newspaper or magazine, if readers forgot them in a train or a tram, they were not too upset.

The publication of cheap editions of what was considered classical literature was based on the commercially successful formula of light fiction, which was published in large, low-priced editions. In the late eighteenth and early nineteenth centuries, the bourgeoisie constituted the primary target audience of this form of literature. The popularity of the colportage trade from the second half of the nineteenth century onward helped to diversify its target audience. As indicated in Chapter III, the success of the various kinds of light fiction could not be attributed to certain strata of contemporary German society rather than others. Given this situation, rectification is required of the argument advanced by Ronald Fullerton concerning the emergence in the wake of the development of the colportage trade of two mutually exclusive book markets—one for the lower orders, and one for educated circles.[96] This statement must be amended to the effect that, despite the differences between the literature intended for the educated bourgeoisie and that intended for the general reading public, the disparity between these markets was not as great as originally appeared to be the case. There are two main reasons for this state of affairs: first, as book consumers, bourgeois circles helped to popularize "cheap literature"; and second, it would appear that the same publishing houses which brought out and distributed the German literary canon were also involved in distributing popular works. Examples of this state of affairs are both Brockhaus and Mayer, which in addition to their dictionaries and encyclopedias—the bedrock of educated bourgeois culture—also published popular literature which they distributed at railway stations and through the colportage trade.

It should be remembered that publishers were far from passive conduits constituting a neutral passageway between writers' desks and readers' bookshelves. Rather, they encouraged creative writing, promoted authors and different areas of publishing, and even took the initiative in respect of large-scale literary enterprises such as the writing of dictionaries and encyclopedias, which decisively influenced the accumulation and development of human knowledge. Just as publishers promoted what was considered "high" culture, so these selfsame publishers made just as major a contribution to the production of the popular culture viewed as "inferior" by some.

All this meant that many publishing houses had a kind of Jekyll-and-Hyde existence. One of the clearest expressions of this "duplicity" was the distinction drawn at the time between expensive, good books, which were enjoyed by a restricted circle of readers with refined tastes, and cheap, bad books which were widely distributed. This hierarchical distinction was responsible for the demand to combat "cheap literature" by means of quality literature distributed at cheap prices. The end of the nineteenth century and the beginning of the twentieth saw the founding of organizations such as the Deutsche Dichter-Gedächtnis-Stiftung and the Dürerbund, which saw their role as fulfilling this mission.[97] At the same time the commercial publishing houses, in particular "cultural publishers" such as Fischer, Diederichs, Insel, Langwiesche, and others, began to issue low-price series of quality books in an attempt to acquire new classes of readers. One of the interesting aspects of these developments is that they saw the reduction of book prices as the key to popularizing them. Given this state of affairs, it comes as no surprise that after the world war, during a period of economic hardship, ever more vociferous demands were made to make books cheaper.

Discussions as to whether German books were too expensive clearly reflected this situation. A widespread view, particularly among authors, was that German books were indeed too expensive and the publishers were blocking the reduction in book prices. Bookshop owners were prepared to defend book price policies: they tried to show that compared with the increased cost of other products, book prices were actually cheap, even relative to their prewar prices. One of the manuals issued for bookshops even recommended booksellers to show buyers the price catalogue from the prewar period in order to prove to them that book prices had not gone up significantly following the world war. Another question frequently discussed at this time was: should German books be cheap? Particularly in public library circles, views were expressed against "cheap books." The argument was that the inferior graphic quality of low-priced books, combined with their tendency to fall to pieces very quickly, would do more harm than good in terms of promoting the reading of quality books. After the war, at a time when the public libraries were booming, a crisis engulfed "cheap books" as an instrument of disseminating cultural values. The reduction in the cost of books, which became a means of light entertainment (*Unterhaltungsmittel*), was considered to adversely affect the status of books as cultural objects.[98] As Lother Brieger wrote, "Since we are inclined on the basis of our entire development to evaluate things according to what they cost, in Germany only expensive books can engender a genuine appreciation for books and hence a really intellectual form of culture."[99]

Discussions over the question of book prices therefore reflected the fear of the ever-growing importance of consumption as a factor capable of widening social gaps and at the same time helping to blur differences between social classes and bring about a mass society.[100] One of the ways of tackling this two-way fear was the insistence on separate categories, with a distinction being made between cheap books and expensive books. In 1929, Willy Haas argued in an article entitled "Books that nobody is going to marry" that the problem of publishers in Germany was that they did not distinguish between books with fancy bindings and softback books with less impressive graphic qualities. Unlike the situation in France, where these were acknowledged to be two different types of publications differing both in form and in price, Haas argued that in Germany publishers professed to publish books which would occupy pride of place on their owners' bookshelves for the next fifty years, while in fact the quality of these publications was so poor that they fell to pieces after just a few years, even though they cost the same as more elegant and better-produced books. Haas concluded that the book trade had to undergo a kind of "sexual reform," with a clear-cut distinction being made between two types of books: paperbacks of low printing quality selling for a similarly low price, intended for a "one-night stand"; and books of high graphic quality, leather bindings, and gilt ornamentation selling for a high price, with which the reader enters a matrimonial relationship.[101]

Similar arguments were advanced by book dealers' circles also. The success of the book clubs, emphasizing what contemporary critics called "the dictatorship of the bookshelf," was what spurred the traditional book trade into finding new ways of increasing book sales. One result of this process was the emergence of a new type of book publishing, selling at the magic price of RM 2.85. Knaur, followed by S. Fischer Publishers, were the first publishing houses to start issuing this new type of book in 1928. Unlike the cheap editions of the nineteenth century, which were condensed and edited versions of well-known texts, generally printed on low-quality paper, the 2.85 books were unedited versions of well-known texts, and the printing was of high graphic quality. The graphic quality and unabridged texts of the 2.85 books, combined with their easy-to-read typefaces, simple and solid design, and affordable prices, made them a completely new type of book, situated somewhere between the luxury, high-price book and "cheap books" with poor design and textual quality. In this sense the Everyman's or "popular editions" (*Volksausgabe*) of the late 1920s were the forerunners of the paperbacks familiar to today's readers. However, unlike their modern counterparts, which are reduced-price versions of more expensive editions, the 2.85 books were intended primarily for books whose success was a foregone conclusion. The upshot was a situation where the price of a book by anonymous author X could be far higher than that of a book by famous author Y.

These 2.85 books made it possible for a broader readership than previously to buy books. They enhanced the value of purchase-based reading, and helped disseminate the canon of classical German and world literature. In 1929 the Knaur publishing house, which advertised itself as "the Publishers' Ford" (*Ein Ford der Verleger*), offered three different versions of books: a patent leather binding with gilt tooling at 4.80 marks a book; a half-bound luxury edition with gilt tooling at 3.75 marks; and a cloth-bound paperback with illustrated cover at 2.85 marks. Knaur's range of 2.85 books, each of which was printed in minimum print runs of one hundred thousand copies, was of impressive breadth: it included novels by Zola, Dostoyevsky, Strum, and Fontane, as well as Bismarck's memoirs. In addition, Knaur also published an atlas, an encyclopedia, and Büchmann's *Dictionary of Quotations*, which was considered one of the essential works for the educated bourgeoisie in Germany.[102]

What the 2.85 books did was to eliminate the distinction between cheap books with their low textual and graphic quality and expensive, high-quality books. In this way they managed to meet the demand for books on the part of a broader range of readers during a period of economic hardship. According to contemporary reports, the popular editions were particularly successful with that public which had already acquired the habit of reading—the bourgeois classes. In contrast, sporadic book readers—workers and farmers—were only prepared to spend money on books with luxury leather bindings, a large number of pages, and prestigious appearance.[103] This predominant consumption pattern shows that for these social strata, the symbolic significance of books as objects was far more important than actually reading them. As a result, it would appear that at the same time that readers from a bourgeois background were beginning to relinquish adherence to the value of owning every book as a precious object with unique aesthetic qualities in favor of an approach which treated the text and reading itself as the primary components which determined a book's symbolic value, expensive books continued to attract consumers from classes unaccustomed to book buying. In this sense these disparate book consumption habits are a fascinating example of how aesthetic tastes dictate social stratification.[104]

From Good Form to New Design

The transition period between the nineteenth and twentieth centuries is considered a turning point in the history of book design. Basically, this change involved a shift from designing books as objets d'art to the industrial design of books as consumer articles.[105] Graphic artist Jan Tschichold has explained that the difference in reading techniques in the modern era—i.e., the shift from slow reading out loud to rapid, silent reading, the application of technology to practically all walks of life, and the flourishing of the new media in the modern age all compelled book designers also to find new ways of designing books which would make it easier to read them, reduce book prices, and enable them to be mass-distributed.[106]

The publishing of series in the early twentieth century pioneered the industrial design of books as products. For this design trend, aesthetics, as an inspirational domain which did not fall within the pragmatic realm of humdrum daily existence, was no longer a self-contained aim. Books as products which were reproduced by a piece of machinery, as articles intended to be used on a daily basis, were key items which dictated the new aesthetics in designing books as commodities or staples. The new approach to book design did not come into being out of a vacuum. It was part of a general development in the realm of industrial design in Germany which was known as *Neue Sachlichkeit* (New Objectivity), which sought in particular to aestheticize function. Many new book designers belonged to this movement. Both the schools of design which were founded at the beginning of the twentieth century and the Werkbund, which was set up in 1907 as an organization to bring together craftsmen and designers, are representatives of the organizations which played a leading role in the design revolution that took place during these years. Terms such as commercial art (*Gebrauchsgraphik*) or books as commodities (*Gebrauchsbuch*) also date from this period. Books thus joined a range of objects which were designed for everyday use and at this time became products intended for mass consumption.[107] This development received impetus from publishers, artists, and the German printing industry, at the time one of the most highly developed in the western world. Statistics about the number of printers' works in Germany indicate that practically every single German town and city had at least one printing works. The amount of paper manufactured in Germany also increased at a dizzying speed, from 20,000 metric tons in 1800 to 1,140,000 metric tons in 1900.[108] Books, newspapers, and advertising material were not solely responsible for this growth: increasing use was also made of printed matter in a range of everyday spheres. Forms, invoices, stamps, visiting cards, playing cards, and so on were just some of the areas that also increased awareness of the need for graphic design of printed items which could facilitate their use and render it more efficient. These developments in the field of design, as Walter Benjamin observed, turned graphic artists, industrial designers, photographers, and also engineers and architects to the originators of the modern "collective" imagination.[109]

Following World War I, the trend toward designing books as mass-consumption products was reinforced by such factors as competition with the new media, the fear that the prevailing economically harsh conditions would destroy the book market, and views about the social role of book design. In this way books joined what Janet Ward has defined as "Germany's New Objectivist (*neue Sachlichkeit*) surface style."[110] What is interesting in this attitude to books is that it established a nexus between using and reading books. In the prewar period, greater stress was still being laid on the external form of books, and above all on jackets and bindings, whereas by the 1920s the emphasis had moved to typography and the insistence on designing books from the inside out, becoming the focus of diverse attempts to redesign books. Type was viewed as the bedrock of this new architecture of books.[111] In this context, the vacillation over the type of letter—what was known in German as *Fraktur* or "black letter," commonly and not quite rightly called "Gothic" by the English, or roman, in Germany still called by its historical name of *Antiqua*—which engaged postwar book designers is of particular interest.

Fraktur or Antiqua—Black Letters or Roman

The history of this indecision over the right type to use for books is largely rooted in the history of the German printing trade itself.[112] It is therefore hardly surprising that in the transition period round the turn of the nineteenth/twentieth centuries, the struggle between "fractured typefaces" (*gebrochenen Schriften*: Fraktur) and rounded typefaces (*runden Schriften:* Antiqua) should have become more acute. During this period, Art Nouveau (known in Germany as *Jugendstil*), with its predilection for Fraktur fonts, was extremely popular in Germany, while the new schools of design, which wanted to discard old forms of expression and create new forms of representation, preferred Antiqua. The question of which form was more legible was one of the key issues debated at the time. The various camps used research-based support by doctors and psychologists to identify the advantages or disadvantages of each type of lettering.[113] Each camp appealed to national sentiment, presenting itself as the German national lettering (*Nationalschrift*) and its rivals as the non-German version. Before World War I the dispute came before the Reichstag, which refrained from taking a decision about these two types of letter.

Just as in the "old/new line" dispute in the public libraries, so the world war—which many saw as offering a window of opportunity for changing the face of German society—brought about a flare-up in the "typeface dispute." At this time the disagreement centered on the question of the extent to which Fraktur lettering suited the spirit of the times and the modern form of book reading. The opponents of Fraktur, such as Jan Tschichold and Paul Renner, who were closely associated with the Bauhaus School, saw Fraktur as a printed version of handwriting, and insisted on a complete separation between printed and handwritten lettering. Renner asserted that the purpose of writing was to be read, not written ("Der Gebrauchszweck, dem die Schrift ihr Dasein verdankt, ist nicht geschrieben, sondern gelesen zu werden").[114] So as to adapt writing to the modern age, Renner even proposed reforming German spelling. This involved such things as spelling words which are pronounced the same way (e.g., *das* and *daß*, or *viel* and *fiel*) in the same way, dropping the letter c from the combination "sch," changing "ph" to "f," and dropping initial capitalization of nouns.[115]

The influential Russian graphic artist El Lissitzky drew attention to the centrality of the eye in book design. In his programmatic essay "Typographical Facts," which appeared in the *Festschrift* or commemorative publication marking the twenty fifth anniversary of the founding of the Gutenberg Museum in Mainz, he wrote:

> Sie sollen von dem Schriftsteller fordern, daß er seine Schrift wirklich stellt. Denn seine Gedanken kommen zu ihnen durch das Auge und nicht durch das Ohr. Darum soll die typographische Plastik durch ihre Optik das tun, was die Stimme und die Geste des Redners für seine Gedanken schafft.
>
> (You should insist that the author really typeset his own writing. Because his thoughts come to you through the eye, not through the ear. This is why typographical plastic art should accomplish through its optical impact what the speaker's voice and gestures do for his thoughts.)[116]

In contrast to Fraktur with its stylized, ornate forms, the simple and economical Antiqua was considered more suitable for the modern era in which books were mass commodities. Clarity, austerity, and precision were the three basic principles of the design school which opposed Fraktur and wanted to reduce typography to its most basic and simplest elements.[117] Consequently, the designers of "new" or "elementary typography," as they were variously known, even rejected the use of ornaments, embellishments, illustrations, or woodcuts, which were still popular at the time. Instead, they allowed the use of photographs as a modern medium suitable for the mechanical production of books to accompany the printed letter.[118] The combination of photography and typography, known as "Typofoto" or "Fototypographie" (photo typography), was considered the new representative form of books suitable for modern times. "What is a typophoto?" asked László Moholy-Nagy, a designer and photographer, in 1925. He replied: "Typography is communication in printed form. Photography is the visual representation of that which can be perceived optically. The typophoto is communication represented in visually exact terms."[119]

The combination of photography and the simple, symmetrical form of the printed letter was intended to enhance the representational possibilities of text and to accelerate reading speeds in order to bring them up to the same level as watching films and listening to the radio. This combination was also perceived as the cut-off point between old and new typography. The essence of the typographical revolution, as Tschichold explained in 1928, was to be found in the shift from flat to three-dimensional typography.

> "all-flat typography belongs to the past. as a result of the photoplate we have got hold of space and its dynamics. it is the contrast between the apparently three-dimensional construction (gebilden) of photos and the flat forms of writing which provides the basis for the striking effect of present-day typography.[120] (All lowercase in original)

Adapting books to the modern surface required making reading into a form of gaze. In this sense books joined the department stores, tour packages, and films which, as Anne Friedberg has shown, transformed the gaze into a product which was sold to the consumer-spectator.[121]

The call to modernize book reading was the main, but not the sole cause of the criticism of using Fraktur. Another reason for rejecting Fraktur was political in nature. As a German national typeface, Fraktur could not be one of the basic elements in typography.[122] Moreover, Renner, Tschichold, and others argued that in an era of international standardization, at a time when Germany should be striving to join the family of nations, it was inappropriate for there to be a national typeface which would increase tendencies towards nationalism and isolate Germany in the world.

In the postwar period, the call to abandon Fraktur generated major opposition among large numbers of book designers. Fraktur was perceived as the original German type, whose aesthetic distinctiveness and suitability to the German language had led to the average German reader finding it easier to read in Fraktur than in any other type of font. Even moderate criticism of the new typography warned that the aspiration to simplicity and elementary forms would make reading far too easy, and hence superficial and mechanical.

Statistics about the ratio between the number of publications in Fraktur and Antiqua respectively reflect the complex relationship between these two typefaces. Figures from 1928 indicate that 57 percent of books published in German were in Fraktur, with only 43 percent in Antiqua. For magazines, Fraktur occupied an even more sizable slice of the market: 60 percent compared with 40 percent for Antiqua. In contrast, a study of one thousand advertising billboards carried out by Rudolf Seyffert in the mid-1920s revealed that Antiqua enjoyed an indisputable lead in the advertising stakes: 87 percent of the billboards used Antiqua, with just 13 percent in Fraktur.[123]

Despite the politicization of the "typeface dispute," publishers' political identities could not always be deduced from the typefaces that they used. For example, Erich Remarque's pacifist book *All Quiet on the Western Front* came out in Fraktur, while a nationalist book such as Hans Grimm's *Nation without Room* (*Volk ohne Roum*) was also printed in Antiqua. Some of the SPD (Social Democrat Party) Book Club (*Bücherkreis*) publications were also in Fraktur. A nationalist and antisemitic publisher like the Hanseatische Verlagsanstalt published in Antiqua, while Paul Renner, a modernist, to give one more example, worked for ten years at the neoconservative publishing house of George Müller. This situation resulted not only from the disagreement over which of the two typefaces was the real German one, but also from the view that this uncertainty was not a matter of principle. The midway approach to the Fraktur-or-Antiqua issue advocated keeping both typefaces as forms of expression which served different purposes. Antiqua was perceived as more suitable for nonfiction and scientific works, and in particular for commercial publications, while Fraktur, with its personal style, was more typically attributed to belles lettres and works of poetry. The purpose of typography therefore, according to graphic artist Fritz Schröder, was not solely to create possibilities for reading (*Lesemöglichkeiten*): "typography must arouse the desire to read [and ultimately] influence the reader in accordance with the atmosphere."[124] As a result, it was considered vital that both typefaces be cultivated in order to maintain the expressive and affective possibilities of designing books as products intended for mass consumption. They were viewed as a manifest expression of the process by which reading was commodified.

The struggle between Fraktur and Antiqua illustrates the complex nature of German modernism during these years. Primarily, it embodies the difficulty of reaching an agreement which would provide a base for standardization, which so characterized German society at least up to 1933. One of the manifest expressions of this "German" state of affairs in the 1920s was the inflation that took place in typefaces of both the Fraktur and Antiqua families. According to the *Handbuch für Schriftarten*, published in 1926, at this time there were 2,468 different fonts in Germany, 64 percent of them Antiqua and 36 percent Fraktur. Not without cause did Hans Bockwitz—in 1929 appointed director of the German Book Museum in Leipzig—declare that the struggle between the typefaces had led to a profusion of fonts and an unprecedented flourishing in the field of book design.[125] The 1920s are still considered the golden age of typography in Germany. The structure of the German book market at the time and the growing competition for the reading audience discussed in the first part of this chapter were some of the main reasons for this proliferation. It was in particular the book clubs and the 2.85 books, operating on the basis of the principle of mass book production, which provided designers of all schools with an opportunity to try out new design ideas so as to expand the book-consuming public as far as possible. Thus books became a consumer product par excellence, with great attention being devoted to their design as an eye-catching medium.

In 1933 the struggle between Fraktur and Antiqua officially came to an end. With the assumption of power by the Nazis, who until then had made a point of using only Fraktur in their publications, it was decided that typefaces in Germany must be standardized. Fraktur became the German national typeface and all official publications, newspapers, and textbooks were required to use it. This decision did not eradicate rounded typefaces. In the 1930s we find abundant use of Antiqua fonts in books, magazines, and advertisements. Whether National Socialism was unwilling or unable to eradicate Antiqua is an interesting question, whose methodical investigation could add an additional dimension to descriptions of the complex nature of this regime. It may be reasonably assumed that economic vested interests, combined with political and propaganda needs, constituted the backdrop to the decision published by Hitler's Chancellery on 3 January 1941, when Germany was still at the pinnacle of its power, stipulating that Fraktur was in reality a version of Jewish characters (*Judenlettern*) which had invaded the German language via the Jewish proprietors of newspapers and printing works and that Antiqua was the true German type. This decision, which Fritz Helmut Ehmcke—one of the most important book designers in the first third of the twentieth century (at the time still using Fraktur)—described in 1947 as the assassination of the German type, in practice marked the end of "fractured typefaces." Following the end of World War II, Fraktur was used more and more infrequently.

The process by which reading was commercialized was not only a result of the effort to increase the consumption of books or of books combined with the new visual culture of the "spectacle." Not only did consumer culture, we would argue, serve book culture: books also operated in such a way as to in turn promote and strengthen the values of consumer culture. The following discussion examines a number of manifestations of this process.

The Book as Advertisement

In his 1929 book on commercial advertising, Rudolf Seyffert drew attention to the advertising character of literary works:

> It is the intention of numerous literary products to bring influence to bear so that their contents will be voluntarily absorbed, implemented and passed on. In that sense they are written with a promotional intent and hence can be considered as promotional material.[126]

Literature, he asserted, had proven itself a particularly effective publishing device for promoting religio-political interests. We have examples in abundance of how books are used as a means of propaganda in these areas. For example, even a politician such as Adolf Hitler, who cautioned against reading and argued that only the spoken, not the written word could bring about momentous changes, made a point of issuing an authorized version of his view of the world in the form of a weighty tome.[127] However, books not only constituted the arena for religious and political struggles: they were also a medium that enabled a wide spectrum of those with vested interests to promote matters of concern to them. Nor did books' promotional powers go unnoticed by the commercial sector. Given the realities of the time the effectiveness of written texts, and in particular of books, as a promotional medium took a number of forms, as will be shown below.

Books were places where commercial publicity could be displayed. Many publishing houses included in every book a number of pages where they presented some of their other publications.[128] In manuals, theoretical works, and popular science books, we also find a fair number of advertisements by companies related to the field addressed by the book. Even colportage books and the different "penny dreadful" series (*Groschenhefte*), such as detective stories or westerns, would be accompanied by commercial advertising. This helped reduce the cost to the consumer of a single copy.

However, to use Henri Lefebvre's terms, books were not just a "space of representation": they were also, by the same token, representational space, advertising various goods and services.[129] Thus books on which a film was based or which were themselves based on films became advertising for films or vice versa. Some film producers even published promotional brochures giving an overview of the plot in words and pictures.[130] Many commercial companies distributed printed matter to be used as promotional calendars and postcards. Of particular interest are the albums for collecting photos which were generally distributed by companies that produced such products as margarine, cigarettes, chocolate, and coffee. The photos, which were normally packaged together with the products, were collected mainly by children and stuck into special albums supplied by the product distributors. They soon became a popular collectors' item for adult collectors too.[131] History and the army, sport and religion, nature and science, fashion and family life, technology and transport, geography and economics were just some of the areas covered by these albums, which had enormous distribution figures. Generally the pictures were accompanied by explanations, either on the back or in the album itself. In contrast to the prewar period, in the 1920s when this form of publicity was all the rage, albums were bound together as books, becoming a kind of encyclopedia which could occupy a rightful place on a bookshelf. It therefore comes as no surprise that in his autobiography *From Labourer to Astronomer,* Bruno Bürgel admitted that the different kinds of advertising booklets had been responsible for guiding his steps toward the world of science.[132] The photo albums of the 1920s thus provide a fascinating example of how the dissemination of bourgeois educational values was combined with manifestly commercial interests. They show extremely clearly how commercial advertising penetrated the very fabric of day-to-day existence, targeting children in particular.

Even historical writing was enlisted to serve sales promotion. The publication of a book describing the history of a company, for example, was considered a solid means of advertising testifying to tradition and reputation.[133] There were commercial companies which would even publish nonfiction works or plot-driven tales which did not necessarily have a direct link with the specific products of the company itself. An example of such a publication is the "tobacco book" (*Buch vom Tabak*) which was published by the Neuerberg publishing house (Verlag Haus Neuerberg). The publishing house was the initiative of the Cologne cigarette company known as the Haus Neuerburg Zigarettenfabrik. In the book's epilogue, which provides a matter-of-fact description of the history of tobacco and smoking, the cigarette company stated that its reasons for publishing the book were the love of tobacco and the desire to share this passion with other tobacco devotees. Only in a separate appendix, under the title *From Tobacco Leaf to Cigarette,* did it among other things recommend a number of its cigarettes, produced in accordance with the high manufacturing standards described in the book. According to the book's author, Robert Cudell, the separation of direct advertising from the text as such led the bookshops to distribute the book like any other book, paying no attention to the fact that in this case this was no normal publishing house, but rather a commercial company which was interested in promoting the sales of its cigarettes.[134]

The Stuttgart-based Waldorf-Astoria cigarette company adopted a different advertising strategy. In 1926 it began to enclose in one out of every twenty five packs of cigarettes a sixteen-page minibook on a range of topics. The German Library catalogue in Leipzig lists two special series on unspecified topics, and twenty nine series on topics such as: anecdotes; wonders of the world; short stories, including by authors such as Theodor Strum, Gottfried Keller, and Ludwig Thomas; businessmen's tales; successful men, such as Henry Ford, Alfred Krupp, Zeppelin, Karl Benz, and Rudolf Mosse; Beautiful Germany; children's stories; and so on. Since each series consisted of eight minibooks, the cigarette company published no fewer than 248 different minibooks—a very respectable performance for a company supposedly engaged in producing cigarettes.

In a special booklet presenting the goals and motives for advertising the Waldorf Library, the publishers explained that without interaction between producers and consumers there could be no base for creative economics, and that only economics was capable of promoting culture. The Waldorf Library, as its slogan proclaimed, wanted to be an advertisement which would serve the consumer (*Eine Werbung, die dem Verbraucher dient!*).

Reklameholzschnitt

für die Waldorf-Astoria Zigarettenfabrik A.-G., Stuttgart

Zeichnung von Kunstmaler Gumbart, Stuttgart

Picture 16: Waldof-Astoria woodcut advertisement

The combination of books and cigarettes, in the view of Waldorf-Astoria, was designed to do no more and no less than to contribute to German economic and cultural life. At the end of the booklet, there were even quotations from well-known authors such as Thomas Mann, Hermann Hesse, Alfred Döblin (the doctor), and Walter von Molo, applauding and praising the new advertising initiative. Even a well-known opponent of advertising such as the sociologist Werner Sombart wrote to the cigarette factory: "The form of your most recent advertisement—if advertisements there must be!—seems to me to be highly praiseworthy."

American author Herbert Casson's book on the influence of advertising was translated into German in 1927. Casson explained that literature's power lay in the fact that it addressed the affective sphere, as well as in its ability to arouse sentiment, one of the most effective ways of promoting sales.[135] This principle was apparently responsible for the popularity of advertising poems, which were very popular at the time. However, some also tried to use prose as an advertising stratagem. An example of this use of books was the series of adventure stories published by the Hans Stosch-Sarrasani circus.[136] Under the title *Travels and Adventures* (*Fahrten und Abenteuer*), eighty adventure stories were published in 1923, starring circus manager Hans Stosch-Sarrasani, the only character who appeared in every single story. In the introduction to all the minibooks, which were initially published by Mignon in Dresden and then by Stosch himself, readers were invited to visit the circus and see Hans Stosch-Sarrasani in person with their own eyes. A 1927 estimate put the number of copies of these minibooks distributed by the circus to date at around a million and a half. According to another estimate, in February 1927 alone a total of six hundred and thirty thousand copies of the series were distributed at Berlin schools.[137] In 1929, Stosch published a second edition of the series, adding another twenty new tales. At the end of each booklet, children were urged to beg their parents and teachers to allow them to go to the circus for a unique experience which would remain engraved in their memories for the rest of their lives. These booklets were distributed through the medium of the local press or placed in mailboxes and schools in all the places visited by the circus. Stosch did more than just present his exciting adventures: he took delight in presenting himself to every child as a model along the lines of the "American Dream," as somebody who had achieved success solely on the basis of his own powers, as a result of hard work, resourcefulness, thrift, and self-control: "The person who has youth has the future. Somebody that young people view as a model is a really important man."[138] This declaration by Stosch was apparently a reaction to an attempt to ban the publishing of his series under the Law for the Protection of Young People against Trash and Filth of December 1926. Stosch took up the cudgels in defense of the series, which had proven itself a rather effective means of publicity. He argued that the stories could not have a harmful effect on young people since their guiding principle was that good always prevails over evil. Despite Stosch's protests, and although the series was not found to constitute an immediate moral danger, the Ministry of Youth in Düsseldorf issued an opinion recommending that the series be banned on the grounds that such inferior writings (*untergeistiges Schrifttum*) were trash that kept children from reading literature of genuine value.

The Law for the Protection of Young People against Trash and Filth, like censorship generally, therefore assumed that reading had the power to change patterns of behavior, to instill values and shape ways of thinking. The Frank Allen series type of detective novels, many of which reached Germany from England and the United States, were also perceived as a medium which promoted the values of materialism and as a salient example of the industrialization of literary writing.[139] The "hunters" of pulp writings in the 1920s estimated that between thirty and fifty thousand "Frank Allen" books were sold every week, with some fifty authors involved in writing them.[140] Similar charges were also levelled against writers such as Karl May, whose readership in the 1920s consisted of around 50 percent adults, Richard Voss, Hedwig Courths-Mahler, and many others whose books were distributed on an enormous scale. This popular writing was not perceived as an independently valuable body of artistic literature with distinctive aesthetic qualities, but as a product which came into being as a result of the consumption of such material, thereby boosting materialism and consumer culture. This approach is a perfect reflection of an ambivalent relationship to consumer culture, in which readers were perceived both as a mass without a mind of its own, subject to manipulation by the manufacturers of cheap novels, and at the same time as a public with independent desires which dictated the nature of publications. In this sense the Law for the Protection of Young People against Trash and Filth was in fact an attempt to regulate supply-and-demand relationships, particularly by limiting the distribution of this literature, not only to young people but also to adults. This issue is explored in greater depth in Chapter V.

What influence did this popular body of literature have on readers? Was it just harmless "fairy tales," as claimed by Courths-Mahler, for example,[141] or as the "hunters" of pulp literature asserted, was this a dangerous form of literature that severed its readers from reality, nurturing false hopes and promoting the values of materialism and consumer culture? Against this background, it may even be asked whether the figure of the detective as an athletic man with a fondness for luxury and modern technology, whose exceptional physical and intellectual prowess guaranteed him a worldwide reputation as someone able to solve all mysteries; the detective who was ready to defend the oppressed and help the authorities when they were helpless in the face of the forces of evil; whether this figure of the detective—whose feelings of justice and duty unfailingly took precedence over sweeping the girl off her feet—was indeed a longed-for figure and a model to be imitated in the eyes of the readers of these works.[142]

When tackling this issue of interpretation, one cannot confine oneself to the aspect of the meaning that the authors attached to their texts or the way in which the critics interpreted them. Rather, it is necessary to turn to readers themselves and investigate how they read the texts, and what factors influenced their interpretation.[143] Such an analysis will inter alia provide clues about the various factors that influence the interpretation of reading material. A survey carried out by the *Social Democrat German Civil Servants' Journal*, for example, shows that marriage, marking the beginning of the process of women's politicization, was the key factor that influenced the reading habits of many civil servants' wives. Until they got married, these women mainly read light fiction or the advertising pages in the daily press; following this auspicious event, their reading "menus" acquired more social and political dimensions.[144] In contrast, a study of the attitudes of adolescent boys and girls in 1930 Berlin to Courth-Mahler's books and the Frank Allen series of detective novels indicates that the readers of this form of literature were far more sophisticated than had been supposed, and that this body of literature reinforced rather than weakened its readers' bourgeois world of values.[145]

Examining the issue of nonprofessional readers' interpretations is a challenge that poses numerous theoretical and methodological difficulties. A separate research study would be needed in order to deal systematically with this area. Despite this research void, the link between the modern form of reading as an intimate activity which takes place in the private domain and consumer culture can be readily identified. In this sense there is no significant difference between reading newspapers and reading books. Reading and consumption were closely intertwined, showing that the process of commercialization and the rise of consumer culture contributed to the dissemination of reading, and that conversely reading encouraged consumption and helped to shape and disseminate its values. One of the most conspicuous manifestations of this complex relationship between reading and consumption, and of the difficulty in coming up with an appropriate conceptual framework for addressing relationships between these areas, is to be found in attempts to control reading as reflected in contemporary studies of reading and the struggle against trashy and pulp literature. These issues will be discussed in the last chapter of the book.

Notes

1. Ernst Umlauff, *Beiträge zur Statistik des Deutschen Buchhandels* (Leipzig: Verlag des Börsenvereins der deutschen Buchhändler, 1934); idem, "Zur Struktur der europäische Kulturwirtschaft. Der deutsche Buchhandel bis 1930," *Kultur Archiv des Europa Archivs* 2 (1947), 889–902; Ludwig Schönrock, "Die buchhändlerische Produktions-Statistik," in: Friedrich Burgdörfer, ed., *Die Statistik in Deutschland nach ihrem heutigen Stand* (Berlin: Verlag Paul Schmidt, 1940); Erwin Stemmle, *Das deutsche Buchgewerbe in Konjuktur und Krise* (Zürich: Polzgraphischer Verlag, 1958); Johannes Müller, *Deutsche Kulturstatistik* (Jena: Verlag von Gustav Fischer, 1928); Gerhard Menz, *Kulturwirtschaft* (Leipzig: Linder Verlag, 1933); Hans Ferdinand Schulz, *Das Schicksal der Bücher und Buchhandel* (Berlin: Walter de Gruyter & Co., 1960).

2. Umlauf, *Beiträge zur Statistik,* 62.
3. Thorsten Grieser, "Buchhandel und Verlag in der Inflation. Studien zu wirtschaftlichen Entwicklungstendenzen des deutschen Buchhandels in der Inflation nach dem Ersten Weltkrieg," *Archiv für Geschichte des Buchwesens* 51 (1999), 1–188.
4. Alfred Druckenmüller, *Der Buchhandel der Welt* (Stuttgart: C.E. Poeschel Verlag, 1935).
5. Robert Escaprit, *Das Buch und der Leser. Kunst und Kommunikation* (Cologne: Westdeutscherverlag, 1961).
6. Umlauf, Zur Struktur der europäische Kulturwirtschaft, 892.
7. Umlauf, Zur Struktur der europäische Kulturwirtschaft, 894.
8. Eva-Maria Hanebutt-Benz, *Die Kunst des Lesens. Lesemöbel und Leseverhalten vom Mittelalter bis zur Gegenwart* (Frankfurt a.M.: Museum für Kunsthandwerk Frankfurt a.M., 1987); Reinhard Wittmann, "Was there a Reading Revolution at the End of the Eighteenth Century?" in: Guglielmo Cavallo, and Roger Chartier, eds., *A History of Reading in the West* (Amherst: University of Massachusetts Press, 1999), 284–312.
9. Gerhard Menz, *Was weisst Du vom Buch?* (Priern: Anthropos Verlag, 1924); Rudolf Schenda, *Volk ohne Buch. Studien zur Sozialgeschichte der populären Lesestoffe 1770–1910* (Frankfurt a.M., Vittorio, 1970), 461; Ludwig Hamann, *Der Umgang mit Büchern und die Selbstkultur* (Leipzig: Verlag von Ludwig Hamann, 1898).
10. James Raven, "From Promotion to Proscription: Arraignments for Reading and Eighteenth Century Libraries," in: idem, Hellen Small, and Naomi Tadmor, eds., *The Practice and Representation of Reading in England* (Cambridge: Cambridge University Press, 1996), 175–202; Roger Chartier, *The Order of Books* (Stanford: Stanford University Press, 1994).
11. Marshall McLuhan, *The Gutenberg Galaxy* (Toronto: University of Toronto Press, 1962).
12. Paul Raabe, *Bücherlust und Leserfreuden. Beiträge zur Geschichte des Buchwesens im 18. und frühen 19. Jahrhundert* (Stuttgart: J.B. Metzlersche Verlagbuchhandlung, 1984); Reinhard Wittmann, *Geschichte des deutschen Buchhandels. Ein Überblick* (Munich: C.H. Beck, 1991).
13. Paul Loewenstein, *Der deutsche Sortimentsbuchhandel. Seine wirtschaftliche Entwicklungsgeschichte* (Innsbruck: Wagner, 1921); Reinhard Wittmann, "Das literarische Leben 1848 bis 1880," in: Max Bucher, ed., *Realismus und* Gründerzeit, vol. 1 (Stuttgart: J.B. Metzlersche Verlagbuchhandlung, 1976), 163–258; Ilsedore Rarisch, *Industrialisierung und Literatur* (Berlin: Colloquim Verlag, 1976).
14. Alexandra Günert, "Die Professionalisierung des Buchhandels im Kaiserreich," *Archiv für Geschichte des Buchwesens* 47 (1997), 267–350.
15. Rolf Engelsing, "Die Perioden der Lesergeschichte in der Neuzeit," in: idem, *Zur Sozialgeschichte deutscher Mittel und Unterschichten* (Göttingen: Vandenhoeck & Ruprecht, 1973); on the same development in American context: David Hall, "The Use of Literacy in New England 1600–1850," in: idem, Richard Brown, and John Hench, eds., *Printing and Society in Early America* (Worcester: American Antiquarit Society, 1981), 1–47.
16. Erich Schön, *Der Verlust der Sinnlichkeit oder die Verwandlungen des Lesers* (Stuttgart: Klett-Cotta, 1987), 41.
17. Reinhard Wittmann, Was there a Reading Revolution, 284–312.
18. Erich Schön, "Mentalitätsgeschichte des Leseglücks," in: Alfred Bellebaum, and Ludwig Muth, eds., *Leseglück. Eine vergessene Erfahrung?* (Opladen: Westdeutsche Verlag, 1996), 151–176; Fritz Nies, *Bahn und Bett und Blütenduft* (Darmstadt: Wissenschaftliche Buchgesellschaft, 1991); Rudolf Schenda, "Bilder vom Lesen—Lesen von Bildern," *Internationales Archiv für Sozialgeschichte der deutschen Literatur* 12 (1987), 82–106.
19. Rolf Engelsing, *Der Bürger als Leser* (Stuttgart: J.B. Metzlersche Verlagsbuchhandlung, 1974); Helmut Kreuzer, "Gefährliche Lesesucht? Bemerkungen zu politischer Lektürekritik im ausgehende 18. Jahrhundert," in: *Leser und Lesen im 18. Jahrhundert* (Heidelberg: Carl Winter Universitätsverlag, 1977), 62–75; Jean Marie Goulemont, *Gefährliche Bücher* (Hamburg: Rowohlts, 1993).
20. Reinhart Koselleck, *Futures Past: On the Semantics of Historical Time,* translated by Keith Tribe (Cambridge, Mass.: MIT Press, 1985).

21. Reinhard Wittmann, "Was there a Reading Revolution"; Peter N. Stearns, "Stages of Consumerism: Recent Work on the Issues of Periodization," *Journal of Modern History* 69 (1997), 102–117.
22. Martyn Lyons, "New Readers in the Nineteenth Century: Women, Children, Workers," in: Guglielmo Cavallo, and Roger Chartier, eds., *A History of Reading in the West* (Amherst: University of Massachusetts Press, 1999), 313–344; Wolfgang Langenbucher, "Die Demokratisierung des Lesens in der zweiten Leserevolotion," in: Hurbert G. Göpfter, ed., *Lesen und Leben* (Frankfurt a.M.: Buchhändler-Vereinigung, 1975), 12–35.
23. Schenda, *Volk ohne Buch*, 444; for a more general overview see David Vincent, *The Rise of Mass Literacy* (Malden: Polity Press, 2000).
24. On the ideological use of literacy: Jenny Cook-Gumperz, *The Social Construction of Literacy* (Cambridge: Cambridge University Press, 1986); Brian Street, "Introduction: The New Literacy Studies," in: idem, ed., *Cross-Cultural Approaches to Literacy* (Cambridge: Cambridge University Press, 1993), 2–19.
25. Stemmle, *Das deutsche Buchgewerbe*, 181.
26. Stemmle, *Das deutsche Buchgewerbe*, 147, 152.
27. Menz, *Kulturwirtschaft*, 106–107.
28. Max Wieser, "Die geistige Krisis des Buches und die Volksbibliotheken," *Preußische Jahrbücher* 191 (1923), 182–201, here 190–191.
29. Eugen Diederichs, "Der Verlag als Organisator," in: idem, *Eugen Diederichs. Selbstzeugnisse und Briefe von Zeitgenossen* (Cologne: Eugen Diederichs, 1967), 37.
30. From: Friedrich Uhlig, "Zehn Jahre Seminar für Buchhandelsbetriebslehre an der Handels-Hochschule zu Leipzig," *Börsenblatt für den deutschen Buchhandel* 102 (1935), 1053–1057; idem, "Das Seminar für Buchhandelsbetriebslehre an der Handels-Hochschule zu Leipzig," in: idem, ed., *Buchhandel und Wissenschaft* (Gütersloh: Bertelsmann Verlag, 1965), 31–73.
31. Georg Leyh, ed., *Handbuch der Bibliothekswissenschaft* (Wiesbaden: Otto Harrassowitz, 1957); Guglielmo Cavallo, and Roger Chartier, eds., *A History of Reading in the West*, translated by Lydia G. Cochrane (Amherst: University of Massachusetts Press, 1999).
32. There is an extensive literature on the history of public libraries in Germany. See for example: Johannes Langfeldt, ed., *Handbuch des Büchereiwesens* (Wiesbaden: Harrassowitz, 1973); Wolfgang Thauer, and Peter Vodosek, *Geschichte der öffentlichen Bücherei in Deutschland* (Wiesbaden: Otto Harrassowitz, 1978); Karl-Wolfgang Mirbt, *Pioniere des öffentlichen Bibliothekswesens* (Wiesbaden: Harrassowitz, 1969); Peter Vodosek, *Vorformen der öffentlichen Bibliothek* (Wiesbaden: Harrassowitz, 1978); Christel Aubach, *Die Volksbücherei als Bildungsbücherei in der Theorie der deutschen Bücherhallenbewegung* (Cologne: Greven Verlag, 1962); Paul Röhrig, "Volksbildung," in: Karl-Ernst Jeismann, and Peter Lundgreen, eds., *Handbuch der deutschen Bildungsgeschichte 1800–1870* (Munich: C.H. Beck, 1987), 334–362.
33. Paul Ladewig, *Politik der Bücherei* (Leipzig: Wiegandt Verlagbuchhandlung, 1912), 4.
34. Paul Ladewig, *Katechismus der Bücherei* (Leipzig: Wiegandt Verlagbuchhandlung, 1914), 7.
35. Ladewig, *Politik der Bücherei*, 397.
36. On the so-called *Richtungsstreit* (the direction fight): Hans Joachim Kuhlmann, *Anfänge des Richtungsstreites* (Reutlingen: Bücherei & Bildung, 1961); Otto-Rodulf Rothbart, *Bibliothekarische Buchkritik. Bestandsaufnahme und Standortbestimmung* (Wiesbaden, Harrassowitz, 1992); Süle Tibor, *Bücherei und Ideologie. Politische Aspekte im Richtungsstreit deutscher Volksbibliothekare* (Cologne: Greven Verlag, 1972); Wolfgang Thauer, *Politik der Bücherei. Paul Ladewig und die jüngere Bücherhallenbewegung* (Wiesbaden: Otto Harrassowitz, 1975).
37. Walter Hofmann, *Buch und Volk und die volkstümliche Bücherei* (Leipzig: Schriften d. Zentralstelle f. Deutsche Volktüml. Büchereiwesen, 1916); idem, *Der Weg zum Schrifttum. Gedanke und Verwirklichung der deutschen volkstümlichen Bücherei* (Berlin: Verlg d. Arbeitsgemeinschaft, 1922); idem, *Volksbücherei und Volkswerdung* (Leipzig: Quelle und Meyer,

1925); idem, *Das Gedächtnis der Nation. Ein Wort zur Schrifttumspflege in Deutschland* (Jena: Diederchs, 1932).

38. Cf. for example: Walter Hofmann, "Die Organisation des Ausleihdienstes in der modernen Bildungsbibliothek," *Volksbildungsarchiv* 1 (1910), 55–72, 227–344; 2 (1911), 29–131; 3 (1913), 319–374.
39. Erwing Ackerknecht, *Der Kitsch als kultureller übergangswert* (Bremen: Verein Deutscher Volksbibliothekar, 1950, org. 1934).
40. Jürgen Eyssen, "Bildung durch Bücher? Volksbücherei während der Weimarer Republik," in: Paul Raabe, ed., *Das Buch in den zwanziger Jahren* (Hamburg: Hauswedell & Co. Verlag, 1977), 75–89.
41. Willhelm Schuster, "Die Soziologie der literarischen Geschmacksbildung und die Volksbücherei," *Bücherei und Bildungspflege* 11 (1931), 1–8; Max Wieser, "Soziologie des Buches," in: *Buch und Gesellschaft* (Berlin: Hillger Verlag, 1927), 23–25.
42. Erwin Ackerknecht, *Das Lichtspiel im Dienste der Bildungspflege* (Berlin: Weidmann, 1918); idem, *Lichtspielfragen* (Berlin: Weidmann, 1927); *Rundfunk und Volksbildung* (Berlin: Tagung des Berliner Ausschusses zur Bekämpfung der Schund- und Schmutzliteratur, 1926); Max Wieser, "Buch und Rundfunk," *Die Tat* 17 (1927), 737–757.
43. Adolf v. Morze, "Beruf und Ausbildung 1893–1933," in: Johannes Langfeldt, ed., *Handbuch des Büchereiwesens* (Wiesbaden: Harrassowitz, 1973), 861–938. Alexandra Habermann, "Der Stadtbibliothekar—Die Stadtbibliothekarin. Der Beginn der Professionalisierung bibliothekarischer Tätigkeit im Kaiserreich," in: Jörgen Fligge, and Alois Klotzbücher, eds., *Stadt und Bibliothek. Literaturversorgung als kommunale Aufgabe im Kaiserreich und in der Weimarer Republik* (Wiesbaden: Harrassowitz, 1997), 379–401.
44. On this see Friedrich List, *Grundriß eines Bibliothekrechts* (Gießen: Verlag von Emil Roth, 1928) and the volume edited by Fligge, and Klotzbücher, *Stadt und Bibliothek.*
45. Erwin Acherknecht, "Büchereiplakate," *Bücherei und Bildungspflege* 32 (1931), 257–262; Hildur Lundeberg, "Einige neuere Methoden der Buchpropaganda in der Jugendabteilung der Büchereien," *Bücherei und Bildungspflege* 13 (1933), 28–32.
46. The data are from the reports: *Jahrbuch der deutschen Volksbücherei* (Leipzig: Harrassowitz, 1909ff.).
47. Dieter Langewiesche, "Freizeit und Massenbildung. Zur Ideologie und Praxis der Volksbildung in der Weimarer Republik," in: Gerhard Huck, ed., *Sozialgeschichte der Freizeit* (Wuppertal: Peter Hammer Verlag, 1980), 235.
48. Quoted in: Johannes Langfeldt, "Zur Geschichte des Büchereiwesens," in: idem, ed., Handbuch des Büchereiwesens (Wiesbaden: Harrasowitz, 1975), 778.
49. In the only biography to have been written to date about Scherl, it is claimed that he deliberately destroyed a great amount of documentation: Hans Erman, *August Scherl. Dämonie und Erfolg in Wilhelminischer Zeit* (Berlin: Universitas Verlag, 1954).
50. Ibid., 88.
51. Joachim Schanz, *Die Entstehung eines deutschen Presse-Grossverlages* (Berlin: Scherl. 1932).
52. Walter Hofmann, Archiv (Privatnachlass Stuttgart). Bibliothek Scherl, Kasten 21 Mappe 3.
53. Walter Hofmann, "In Sache Scherl," *Der Kunstwart* 21 (1908), 129–138.
54. *Börsenblatt für den deutschen Buchhandel* 75 (1908), 6762.
55. Ferdinand Avenarius, "Scherl Leihbibliothek," *Kunstwart* 21 (1908), 219–222.
56. Georg Jäger, and Jörgen Schönert, eds., *Die Leihbibliothek als Institution des literarieschen Lebens im 18. und 19. Jahrhundert* (Hamburg: Ernst Hauswendell, 1980); Albert Martino, *Die Deutsche Leihbibliothek* (Wiesbaden: Harrassowitz, 1990); Raimund Kast, "Der deutsche Leihbuchhandel und seine Organisationen im 20. Jahrhundert," *Archiv für Geschichte des Buchwesens* 36 (1991), 165–349.
57. John Ormrod, "Bürgerliche Organisation und Lektüre in literarischgeselligen Vereinen der Restaurationsepoche," in: Günther Höntschel, ed., *Zur Sozialgeschichte der deutschen Literatur von der Aufklärung bis zur Jahrhundertwende* (Tübingen: Niemever Verlag, 1985), 123–150.

58. Bernd v. Armin, and Friedeich Knilli, *Gewerbliche Leihbüchereien* (Gütersloh: Bertelsmann Verlag, 1966); Georg Jäger, "Die deutsche Leihbibliothek im 19. Jahrhundert. Verbreitung—Organisation—Verfall," *Internationales Archiv für Sozialgeschichte der deutschen Literatur* 1 (1977), 96–100.
59. Britta Scheideler, "Zwischen Beruf und Berufung. Zur Sozialgeschichte der deutschen Schriftsteller 1880–1933," *Archiv für Geschichte des Buchwesens* 46 (1997), 1–336.
60. Joseph Kürschner, ed., *Deutscher Literaturkalender* (Berlin: Spemann, 1884), 53.
61. Gerd Schulz, "Das Klassikerjahr 1867," in: Dietrich Bode, ed., *125 Jahre Reclams Universal-Bibliothek 1867–1992* (Stuttgart: Reclam, 1992), 9–11.
62. Käthe Lux, *Studie über die Entwicklung der Warenhäuser in Deutschland* (Jena: Gustav Fischer Verlag, 1910); Rudi Klotzbach, "Deutsche Warenhäuser als Buchhändler," Ph.D. diss., University of Leipzig, 1932.
63. Helmut Hiller, *Wörterbuch des Buches* (Frankfurt a.M.: Vittorio Klostermann, 1954), 62.
64. Kurt Zickfeldt, "Die Umgestaltung des Buchmarktes durch Buchgemeinschaften und Fachvereinsverlage," Ph.D. diss., University of Freiburg i.Br., 1927; Walter Neckel, "Die Kartellformen im Buchhandel," Ph.D. diss., University of Munich, 1934; Brigitte Scholl, "Buchgemeinschaften in Deutschland," Ph.D. diss., University of Göttingen, 1990; Peter Rudolf Meindelder, "Die Entwicklung der Arbeiterbuchgemeinschaften in der Weimarer Republik," Ph.D. diss., University of Jena, 1991; Otto Oeltze, "Die Buchgemeinschaften," in: Friedrich Wilhelm Schaper, ed., *Handbuch des Buchhandels,* vol. 4 (Wiesbaden: Verlag für Buchforschung, 1977), 406–454; Urban van Melis, *Die Buchgemeinschaften in der Weimarer Republik* (Stuttgart: Hiersemann, 2002).
65. Otto Dann, ed., *Lesegesellschaften und bürgerliche Emanzipation* (Munich: C.H. Beck, 1981); John Ormord, "Lesegesellschaften und das Sozialsystem Literatur," in: Monika Dimpfel and Georg Jäger, *Zur Sozialgeschichte der deutschen Literatur im 19. Jahrhundert* (Tübingen: Niemeyer Verlag, 1990), 1–17.
66. Wilhelm Volkmann, *Grundfragen des Vereinsbuchhandels* (Leipzig: Breitkopf & Härtel, 1921).
67. *Das Werk des Volksverbandes der Bücherfreunde* (Berlin: Volksverband der Bücherfreunde, 1924), 7–9.
68. *50 Jahre Deutsche Buch-Gemeinschaft 1924–1974* (Darmstadt: Buch-Gemeinschaft, 1974).
69. Sächsisches Staatsarchiv Leipzig. Börsenverein der deutschen Buchhändler zu Leipzig. Buchgemeinschaften No. 12.4, 344–361.
70. Peter de Mendelssohn, *S. Fischer und sein Verlag* (Frankfurt a.M.: Fischer Verlag, 1970), 1189.
71. Max Grünewald, "Umgang mit Büchern," *Die Büchergilde* 4 (1928), 153.
72. To this thesis Joseph Antz, "Von der Krise des deutschen Buches und den Möglichkeiten zu ihrer Überwindung," in: idem, *Der Lehrer im Volksdienst* (Saarlouis: Hausen Verlag, 1932), 176–178; Erich From, *Arbeiter und Angestellte am Vorabend des Dritten Reiches* (Munich: dtv, 1983), 152; Siegfried Kracauer, *Die Angestellten* (Frankfurt a.M.: Suhrkamp, 1971).
73. Arjun Appadurai, "Commodities and the Politics of Value," in: idem, ed., *The Social Life of Things* (Cambridge: Cambridge University Press, 1986), 31.
74. Fritz Schnabel, "Die Werbung fürs Buch," *Die Reklame* 17 (1924), 346–348; Horst Kliemann, *Die Werbung fürs Buch* (Stuttgart: Poeschel, 1925); idem, *Die Werbung fürs Buch* (Stuttgart: Poeschel, 1937); Gisela Welsche, "Studien zur Werbung für die Dichtung in neuerer Zeit," Ph.D. diss., University of Cologne, 1947; Cornelia Schultze-Giseviua, "Buchwerbung in der Weimarer Republik," M.A. Thesis, University of Mainz, 1995; Hermann Staub, "Buchhändlerische Reklamemarken," *Buchhandelsgeschichte* 10 (1996), 84–90.
75. Appadurai, Commodities and the Politics of Value, 38.
76. Reinhard Wittmann, "Streifzüge zur Geschichte des festen Ladenpreises für Bücher," *Buchhandelsgeschichte* 13 (1976), 385–392.

77. Heinz Friedrich, "Wie verkaufe ich Romane und Novellen?" *Buchhändlergilde-Blatt* 10 (1926), 129; Otto Quitzow, *Verkaufsgespräche im Sortiment* (Leipzig: Verlag des Börsenverein der Deutschen Buchhändler, 1925).
78. Christian Bry, *Buchreihen. Fortschritt oder Gefahr für den Buchhandel?* (Gotha: Verlag Friedrich Andreas Pertheas, 1917); Fritz Schröder, "Grundfragen der Verlagreklame," *Die Reklame* 17 (1924), 343–345.
79. Horst Kliemann, "Der Börsenverein und seine Werbestelle," *Die Reklame* 17 (1924), 364–366; Erhard Wittek, "Korporative Buchwerbung im gegenwärtigen Augenblick," *Offset-Buch-Werbekunst* 3 (1926), 180–182; August v. Lowis, "Moderne Deutsche Buchwerbung," *Die Reklame* 21 (1928), 499–504; Gerd Schulz, "Die Gründung der Werbestelle des Börsenvereins," *Börsenblatt für den Deutschen Buchhandel* 20 (1964), 1869–1871.
80. He proposed, for instance, to approach children with the polite form 'Sie' and not as accustomed as 'Du': Hans Semm, "Vom Verkaufen im Sortiment," *Buchhändlergilde-Blatt* 11 (1927), 39.
81. On this in: Susan Buck-Morss, *The Dialectics of Seeing: Walter Benjamin and the Arcades Project* (Cambridge, Mass.: The MIT Press, 1989), 284.
82. Hans Semm, "Wie werde ich meinem Kunden gerecht?" *Buchhändlergilde-Blatt* 10 (1926), 33.
83. Horst Kliemann, "Der Buchreklamefilm," *Börsenblatt für den Deutschen Buchhandel* 90 (1923), 7176–7177; Friedrich Pollin, "Das Buch im Lichtbild und Film," *Börsenblatt für den Deutschen Buchhandel* 93 (1926), 1014–1017; Richard Brodführer, "'Geist und Maschine.' Der erste buchgewerbliche Großfilm. Deutschland und die Buchwerbung durch den Film," *Börsenblatt für den Deutschen Buchhandel* 93 (1926), 1017; Günther Kreuzhag, "Buch—Film—Propaganda," *Die Reklame* 17 (1924), 355–359.
84. Karl Bott, ed., *Handwörterbuch des Kaufmanns. Lexikon für Handel und Industrie* (Hamburg: Hanseatische Verlagsanstalt, 1927).
85. The journal was free. Until 1929 it reached a circulation of three million copies.
86. Frirz Eckardt, *Das Besprechungswesen* (Leipzig: Verlag des Börsenvereins der Deutschen Buchhändler, 1927).
87. Sebastian Watzal, "Wie wir ein Buch verkaufen," *Die Reklame* 21 (1928), 173–174.
88. Horst Kliemann, "Hilfstabellen für Buchwerbung," in: idem, *Die Werbung fürs Buch* (Stuttgart: C.E. Poeschel, 1937), 391–395.
89. Margarete Giese-Hueser, "Zur Psychologie des Bücherkäufers," *Deutsche Psychologie* 3 (1921); Horst Kleimann, "Neuere Motivstatistiken im Buchhandel," *Die Reklame* 20 (1927), 745–749; idem, "Die neue Einstellung zum Bücherkäufer," *Die Reklame* 21 (1928), 505–508.
90. Klotzbach, Deutsche Warenhäuser als Buchhändler, 111.
91. Siegfried Kraucauer, "Über Erfolgsbücher und ihr Publikum," in: idem, *Der verbotene Blick* (Leipzig: Reclam, 1992), 236–246; see also Werner Faulstich, *Bestandsaufnahme Bestseller-Forschung. Ansätze—Methoden—Erträge* (Wiesbaden: Otto Harrassowitz, 1983); Donald Ray Richards, *The German Bestseller in the Twentieth Century. A Complete Biography and Analysis 1915–1940* (Bern: Lang, 1967); Curt Riess, *Bestseller. Bücher, die Milionen lesen* (Hamburg: Wagner Verlag, 1960); Helmut Popp, *Der Bestseller* (Munich: R. Oldenbourg, 1975).
92. "Veranstaltung Tag des Buches," in: Geheimes Staatsarchiv Preußischer Kulturbesitz. Rep 77 Tit 2772 No. 4 vol. 1 1928–1931.
93. Friz Schnabel, *Büchertage und Bücherwochen* (Leipzig: Verlag des Börsenvereins der Deutschen Buchhändler, 1924).
94. Willy Haas, "Ein 'Tag des Buches'?" *Literarische Welt* 5 (1929), 25.
95. From: Günther Jeremais, "Das billige Buch. Entwicklung und Erscheinungsform," Ph.D. diss., Humboldt University of Berlin, 1938, 6.
96. Roland Fullerton, "Creating a Mass Book Market in Germany: The Story of the Colporteur Novel 1870–1890," *Journal of Social History* 11 (1977), 265–284; idem, "Toward a

Commercial Popular Culture in Germany: The Development of Pamphlet Fiction, 1871–1914," *Journal of Social History* 13 (1979), 489–513.

97. Gerhard Kratzsch, *Kunstwart und Dürerbund. Ein Beitrag zur Geschichte der Gebildeten im Zeitalter des Imperialismus* (Göttingen: Vandenhoeck u. Ruprecht, 1969); Rüdiger v. Bruch, "Kunstwart und Dürerbund," in: Diethart Kerbs, and Jürgen Reulecke, eds., *Handbuch der Deutschen Reformbewegung 1880–1933* (Wuppertal: Peter Hammer Verlag, 1998), 429–438; Marcel Müller, "Die >>Deutsche Dichter Gedächtnis Stiftung<<," *Archiv für Geschichte des Buchwesens* 31 (1986), 131–275.
98. Walter Hofmann, "Von billigen Bucheinbänden und ähnlichem," *Hefte für* Büchereiwesen 10 (1925–1926), 108–110.
99. Lothar Brieger, "Billiges oder Teures Buch?" *Das Heftland* (1922–1924), 89.
100. Warren G. Breckmann, "Disciplining Consumption: The Debate about Luxury in Wilhelmine Germany, 1890–1914," *Journal of Social History* 24 (1990–1991), 485–505.
101. Willy Haas, "Bücher, die man nicht heiratet. Zum Niedergang des broschierten Buches," *Literarische Welt* 5 (1929), 49–50; idem, "... aber manche Bücher heiratet man doch! Ein Paar Betrachtungen zum gebundenen Buch," *Literarische Welt* 5 (1929), 65–66.
102. Wolfgang Frühwald, "Büchmann und die Folgen. Zur sozialen Funktion des Bildungszitaten in der deutschen Literatur des 19. Jahrhundert," in: Reinhard Koselleck, ed., *Bildungsbürgertum im 19. Jahrhundert*, vol. 2 (Stuttgart: Klett-Cotta, 1990), 197–219.
103. Horst Kliemann, "Die neue Einstellung zum Büchverkäufer," *Die Reklame* 21 (1928), 505; Kurt Klaber, "Der proletarische Massenroman," *Linkskurve.* 5 (1930), 23.
104. On this notion that aesthetic tastes dictate social stratification: Pierr Bourdieu, *Distinction. A Social Critique of the Judgement of Taste* (Cambridge: Harvard University Press, 1984).
105. Georg Kurt Schauer, *Deutsche Buchkunst 1890 bis 1960* (Hamburg: Maximilian Gesellschaft, 1963); Hans Peter Willberg, "Zur Situation der Buch und Schriftkunst in den zwanziger Jahren," and Gerhardt W. Claus, "Typographie im Deutschland der zwanziger Jahre. Ein Überblick," both in: Paul Raabe, ed., *Das Buch in den zwanziger Jahren* (Hamburg: Hauswedell, 1978), 47–73; Wilhelm Haefs, "Ästhetische Aspekte des Gebrauchsbuchs in der Weimarer Republik," *Leipziger Jahrbuch zur Buchgeschichte* 6 (1996), 353–382; for a general account in the English of the emergence of German graphic design between 189 to 1945: Jeremy Aynsley, *Graphic Design in Germany 1890–1945* (Berkeley: University of California Press, 2000).
106. Jan Tschichold, "zeitgemäße Buchgestaltung" (org. 1927), in: idem, *Schriften 1925–1974* (Berlin: Brinkmann & Bose, 1975), 17–26; idem, *Die neue Typographie* (Berlin: Verlag des Bildungsverbands der deutschen Buchdrucker, 1928), 223–233; see also: Rudolf Emil, "Das Buch als Gegenstand" (org. 1911), in: Friedrich Pfäffing, ed., *100 Jahre S. Fischer Verlag 1886–1986. über Bücher und ihre äußere Gestalt* (Frankfurt a.M.: S. Fischer, 1986), 89–99.
107. Fritz Helmuth Ehmcke, "Das Maschinenbuch," in: idem, *Persönliches und Sachliches* (Berlin: Verlag Hermann Reckendorf, 1928), 129.
108. Hans-Jürgen Wolf, *Geschichte der Druckverfahren* (Elchingen: Historia-Verlag, 1992); Reinald Schräder, *Die Industrialisierung des Buchdruckgewerbes in Deutschland im 19. Jahrhundert und ihre Folgen* (Stuttgart: Verlag Clemens Koechert, 1993); Max v. Wussow, *Die deutsche Papierindustrie in Zahlen und Bildern* (Berlin: Kraus & Baumann, 1927); Ernst Krichner, "Statistik der Papier und Pappeerzeugung in Sachsen und in Deutschland 1800–1900," *Wochenblatt für Papierfabrikation* (27.02.1904), 622.
109. On this in: Susan Buck-Morss, *The Dialectics of Seeing*, 255.
110. Janet Ward, *Weimar Surfaces: Urban Visual Culture in 1920s Germany* (Los Angeles: University of California Press, 2001).
111. Julius Zeitler, "Gebrauchsgraphiker und Buchkünstler," *Die Reklame* 17 (1924), 373–375; Georg A. Mathey, "'Architektur des Buches' Führer der deutschen Buchkunst," *Archiv für Buchgewerbe und Gebrauchsgraphik* 61 (1924), 41–46; Frirz Helmuth Ehmcke, "Bucharchitektur" (org. 1911) in: idem, *Persönliches und Sachliches* (Berlin: Verlag Hermann Reckendorf, 1928), 27–34.

112. Siegfrid H. Steinberg, *Die Schwarze Kunst* (Munich: Prestel, 1958); Donald A. Shelley, *The Fraktur Writing* (Pennsylvania: the Pennsylvania German Folklore Society, 1961); Albert Kapr, *Fraktur. Form und Geschichte der gebrochenen Schriften* (Mainz: Hermann Schmidt, 1993); Horst Heiderhoff, *Antiqua oder Fraktur?* (Wiesbaden: Burgverein e.V Eltville am Rein, 1971); Christiana Killius, *Die Antiqua Fraktur Debatte um 1800 und ihre historische Herleitung* (Wiesbaden: Harrassowitz, 1998); Silvia Hartmann, *Fraktur oder Antiqua: Der Schriftstreit von 1881 bis 1941* (Frankfurt a.M.: Peter Lang, 1998).
113. August Kirschmann, *Antiqua oder Fraktur?* (Leipzig: Verlag des Deutschen Buchgewerbevereins, 1912); Rudolf Schwegmann, "Experimentelle Untersuchung zur Lesbarkeit von Fraktur und Antiqua und von Groß und Kleinschreiben," Ph.D. diss., University of Göttingen, 1935.
114. Paul Renner, "Type und Typographie," *Archiv für Buchgewerbe und Gebrauchsgraphik* 65 (1928), 456.
115. Paul Renner, *mechanisierte grafik* (Berlin: Hermann Verlag, 1931), 58–80.
116. El Lissitzky, "Typographische Tatsachen," in: Aloys Leonhard Ruppel, ed., *Gutenberg Festschrift* (Mainz: Verlag der Gutenberg Gesellschaft, 1925), 153.
117. Ladislau Moholy-Nagy, "Zeitgemässe Typographie—Ziele, Praxis, Kritik," in: Aloys Leonhard Ruppel, ed., *Gutenberg Festschrift,* 308.
118. By emphasizing the special place of photography in modernity, especially by suggesting that photography brought about a revelation in how we see, this approach anticipated the major topics of photography analysis since the 1970s. See for example the works of: Susan Sontag, *On Photography* (Harmondsworth: Penguin, 1979); and Ronald Barthes, *Image, Music, Text,* translated by Stephen Heath (London: Fontana, 1977).
119. László Moholy-Nagy, "Typo-Foto," *Typographische Mitteilungen. Sonderheft: Elementare Typographie* 23 (1925), 202; idem, *Mahlerei. Fotographie. Film* (Munich: Albert Langen Verlag, 1927).
120. Jan Tschichold, "fotographie und typographie" (org. 1928), in: idem, *Schriften 1925–1974* (Berlin: Brinkmann & Bose, 1991), 47.
121. Anne Friedberg, *Window Shopping: Cinema and the Postmodern* (Berkeley: University of California Press, 1993), 4.
122. Jan Tschichold, "Elementare Typographie," *Typographische Mitteilungen. Sonderheft: Elementare Typographie* 23 (1925), 198.
123. Kapr, *Fraktur*, 78; Rudolf Seyffert, *Allgemeine Werbelehre* (Stuttgart: C.E. Poeschel, 1929), 282–284.
124. Fritz Schröder, "Von Grundlagen der Typographie," *Archiv für Buchgewerbe und Gebrauchsgraphik* 68 (1931), 464.
125. Hans H. Bockwitz, "Deutsche Buchgestaltung," *Archiv für Buchgewerbe und Gebrauchsgraphik* 65 (1928), 599.
126. Seyffert, *Allgemeine Werbelehre,* 387.
127. Adolf Hitler, *Mein Kampf* (Munich: Eher, 1926), 36–38, 522–535.
128. Erhard Wittek, *Das Buch als Werbemittel* (Leipzig: Verlag des Börsenvereins der Deutschen Buchhändler, 1926).
129. Henri Lefebvre, *The Production of Space* (Cambridge; Basil Blackwell, 1991).
130. Reinhard W. Noack, *Filmbroschüren. Leitfaden für Film-Reklame* (Berlin: Verlag bei Werkkunst Fr. K. Koetschau, 1925).
131. Erich Wasem, *Sammeln von Serienbildchen: Entwicklung und Bedeutung eines beliebten Mediums der Reklame und der Alltagskultur* (Landshut: Trausnitz Verlag, 1981); idem, *Das Serienbild. Medium der Werbung und Alltagskultur* (Dortmund: Harenberg, 1987).
132. Bruno H. Bürgel, *Vom Arbeiter zum Astronomen* (Berlin: Ullstein, 1919), 74.
133. Rolf Schörken, *Geschichte in der Alltagswelt. Wie uns Geschichte begegnet und was wir mit ihr machen* (Stuttgart: Klett-Cotta, 1981); Mike Seidensticker, *Werbung mit Geschichte* (Cologne: Böhlau, 1995).
134. Robert Cudell, *Das Buch vom Tabak* (Cologne: Neuerburg Verlag, 1927); idem, "Das Buch als Industrie-Werbemittel," *Monatsblätter für Bucheinbände und Handbindekunst* 4 (1928), 7.

135. Herbert N. Casson, *Wirksame Werbung* (Better Advertisement) (Berlin: Josef Singer Verlag, 1927), 113.
136. On this circus: Hans Stosch-Sarrasani, *Durch die Welt im Zirkuszelt* (Berlin: Volksverband der Bücherfreunde, 1940); Marline Otte, "Sarrasani's Theatre of the World: Monumental Circus Entertainment in Dresden, from Kaiserreich to Third Reich," *German History* 17 (1999), 527–542.
137. "Zirkus Stosch-Sarrasani und die Schundliteratur," *Der Schundkampf* 17 (1927), 14.
138. "Herr Stosch-Sarrasani gegen die Schundtäter," *Der Zeitungshandel* 17 (1927), 10.
139. Hans Epstein, *Der Detektivroman der Unterschicht. Die Frank Allan-Serie* (Frankfurt a.M.: Neuer Frankfurt Verlag, 1930)
140. Heinrich Benfer, *Schundkampf und literarische Jugendpflege* (Berlin: Verlag von Julius Belz, 1932), 26.
141. On this see: Walter Krieger, *Unser Weg ging hinaus. Hedwig Courths-Mahler und ihre Töchter als literarisches Phänomen* (Wien: Herbert Stubenrauch Verlagsbuchhandlung, 1954), 19.
142. Mathilde Kelchner, and Ernst Lau, *Die Berliner Jugend und die Kriminalliteratur. Eine Untersuchung auf Grund von Aufsätzen Jugendlicher* (Leipzig: Verlag von Johann Ambrosius Barth, 1928); Gottlieb Fritz, "Kriminalromane," *Bücherei und Bildungspflege* 12 (1931), 81–88; Siegfried Kracauer, *Der Detektiv-Roman. Ein philosophischer Traktat* (Frankfurt a.M.: Suhrkamp, 1979, orig. 1925); Heinrich Mann, "Detektiv-Romane," *Die literarische Welt* 5 (1929), 1–2.
143. On theoretical research to reader response: Wolfgang Iser, *Der implitzite Leser* (Munich: Fink, 1994); Robert Hans Jauss, *Ästhetische Erfahrung und literarische Hermeneutik* (Frankfurt a.M.: Suhrkamp, 1982); Peter Uwe Hohendahl, *Sozialgeschichte und Wirkungsästhetik* (Frankfurt a.M.: Athenäu Verlag, 1974); Susan R. Suleiman, and Inge Crosman, eds., *The Reader in the Text: Essays on Audience and Interpretation* (Princeton: Princeton University Press, 1980); Jane P. Tompkins, ed., *Reader-Response Criticism: From Formalism to Post-Structuralism* (Baltimore: John Hopkins University Press, 1980). On historical work in this field: Robert Darton, "Readers Respond to Rousseau: The Fabrication of Romantic Sensitivity," in: idem, *The Great Cat Massacre and other Episodes in French Cultural History* (London: Penguin, 1984); Jonathan Rose, "Rereading the English Common Reader: A Preface to a History of Audiences," *Journal of the History of Ideas* 53 (1992), 46–70; idem, "How Historians Study Reader Response: Or, What did Jo Think of Bleak House?" in: John O. Jordan, and Robert L. Patten, eds., *Literature in the Marketplace. Nineteenth-Century British Publishing and Reading Practices* (Cambridge: Cambridge University Press, 1995), 47–70.
144. From: "Was lese ich?" *Allgemeine Deutsche Beamtenzeitung* 10 (1930).
145. Robert Dinse, *Das Freizeitleben der Großstadtjugend* (Berlin: R. Müller, 1932); Ilse Weickert, *Die Lese-Interessen der werktätigen Mädchen zwischen 14 und 18* (Bonn: Ludwig Röhrscheid, 1933).

Chapter V

THE STRUGGLE OVER READING: STUDIES OF READING AND THE FIGHT AGAINST SCHUND- UND SCHMUTZSCHRIFTEN

The activity of reading has attracted the attention of a number of disciplines. At the end of the nineteenth century, for example, the evolving science of psychology began to show increasing interest in the phenomenon of reading, particularly in the framework of both experimental and cognitive psychology.[1] However, most of the research into reading was primarily promoted by bodies with commercial interests and people with vested interests, purporting to act in the name of cultural and educational values. Beginning well before World War I, librarians, educators, literary figures, economists, journalists, and people in the book trade sought to systematically investigate a variety of aspects related to the phenomenon of reading.[2] Yet it was not until after the World War that this interest was expressed on an institutional level. The twelve research institutes working in the area of the press which were established in Germany during the 1920s saliently reflected the process by which diverse aspects of reading came to be studied as a specialized field. The 1885–1938 years saw the publication of a total of 1,260 doctoral theses on the press, 614 (48.7 percent) of these appearing between 1918 and 1933.[3] This flourishing of research in the area of the press, and the fact that it became an academic discipline in the postwar period, comprised part of efforts to improve Germany's propaganda machinery and increase its sophistication in the wake of World War I. The war may therefore be seen as a watershed event that changed attitudes toward reading.

The growing dependence on reading as a means of conveying information on the one hand, and the propaganda war on the other, were indicative of the importance of reading as an activity mediating between people and their surroundings. Accordingly, it became necessary to come to grips with this activity more systematically than in the past. Furthermore, competition with the new media also increased interest in the fate of reading and its position as an activity which both reflected and shaped perceptions of the reality in which people were situated. It was on the basis of this realization that in the 1920s a number of individuals with a variety of interests in the area conducted surveys to determine whether the public was still reading books, or had switched over entirely to going to the cinema and listening to the radio. These developments also provided the backdrop to the establishment of two research institutes focusing on studies of book reading and the book trade in Germany in the 1920s.

Thus 1925 saw the founding of the School for Book Trade Studies at the Leipzig Commercial College (Seminar für Buchhandelsbetriebslehre an der Handelshochschule Leipzig). Its director was Gerhard Menz, who at the time was the editor-in-chief of the official journal of the German book trade organization, the *Börsenblatt für den deutschen Buchhandel.* The School's goal was twofold: to train personnel for the book trade, and above all to encourage and develop research in this domain.[4] The German Book Dealers' Association was responsible both for the initiative behind the establishment of the School and for its finances. The fact that a body representing blatantly commercial interests was financing an academic research institution was not per se a new phenomenon in the 1920s. In particular, the link between academic research and industry and commerce was strengthened following the setting up in 1920 of the Notgemeinschaft der deutschen Wissenschaft (German Science Aid Association), whose self-declared goal was to enroll the support of industry and commerce for the benefit of scientific research.[5]

Coming to academic research from the world of the book trade, Gerhard Menz sought to marry theoretical research with practical experience, or as he expressed it: "Forschung aus der Praxis für die Praxis" (research based on practical experience in order to better serve practice). One of the school's primary tasks was consequently to lay the applied and theoretical foundations for market research in the book market. In addition to general issues relating to the structure of the book market, the school also encouraged research into such areas as book consumption habits and the psychology of book consumers. The School for Book Trade Studies therefore related to reading primarily as the consumption of reading material. Its activities were designed to reinforce the tendency to rationalize the book trade market as an economic undertaking operating in accordance with the principle of production for the sake of consumption. Another institute, founded in Leipzig almost a year after Menz's own organization, examined the phenomenon of reading from a different angle.[6]

In 1926 Walter Hofmann (1879–1952), at the time director of the Leipzig Public Library (Volksbibliothek) and one of the most important figures in the history of the public libraries in Germany, founded the Institute of Reading Studies (Institut für Leser- und Schriftumskunde) in Leipzig. With the establishment of this institute, which studied the history of reading and literature, Hofmann reached the pinnacle of his research career, having begun by investigating the reading habits of library users when he was still in charge of the Dresden public library before the World War.[7] In Hofmann's outlook, research into the reading patterns of library users was intended to provide tools for implementing the public library's national-educational purpose.[8] This objective was to be achieved through the three departments which made up the Institute: 1. The Research Department, which collected and processed data from the public libraries in Leipzig. These data provided the basis for the studies carried out under the Institute's auspices. 2. The German Bibliography Department which, on the basis of the results of the reading studies, drew up catalogues and lists of recommended books. These catalogues were intended to provide librarians and readers with tools to help guide readers to locate books suitable for them. 3. The Librarian Training Department.

Thus the approach which constituted the basis of most of the period's research attitudes toward reading saw reading not just as a phenomenon reflecting a given social reality, but also as an activity through which it was possible to influence patterns of behavior and shape the conceptual system through which people perceive the reality in which they are situated. Consequently, the primary motive behind the interest in the phenomenon of reading was the attempt to influence and control it, whether for commercial reasons or on social and cultural-educational grounds.

It would appear, therefore, that the more the process of the democratization of reading speeded up, together with the individualization of reading as an activity belonging to the private domain, the greater the interest in reading as a social activity of demonstrable significance. Factors which contributed to this process undoubtedly included watching films and listening to the radio together, which from the turn of the century onward replaced the shared experience of reading out loud and in company, previously common practice. Thus the new visual media helped to bolster the autonomous and intimate nature of reading as an activity which gave the reader more or less full control over what material to read, in what form, and above all how to react to it. In this sense a parallel may be drawn between consumption and reading. Both made it possible, especially for weak or underprivileged social groups, to create an area which they could influence, and in which they could move practically unhindered. Given this state of affairs, it is no coincidence that the main research studies conducted in the area of reading focused on investigations into the reading habits of those social groups which were perceived as being, on the one hand, most easily influenced and, on the other, as constituting a threat to the social order headed by the self-appointed male educated middle classes. There were three such groups: women, workers, and young people.[9] Research into these groups and the structure of relationships between the object of investigation and the investigating subject embodied a system of social power relations which conferred on the stratum of educated males the ability to define the status and nature of the objects being investigated. Like peoples which have undergone a process of colonization, as Edward Said has so aptly put it in his many publications, the status of the social groups which constituted the subject of reading studies "has been fixed in zones of dependency and peripherality, stigmatized in the designation of underdeveloped, less-developed, developing states."[10]

We will now give some representative examples of these research studies. We shall see how research into reading reflected efforts to integrate in the controlling culture those social groups which were perceived as weak links in the social order. In this sense, reading studies had a twofold role: Identifying and defining the otherness of certain social groups firmly established the otherness of these groups, while at the same time constituting the background to their acceptance on the basis of this otherness. This activity helped also to define the unique identity of "The Gazers," i.e., that narrow stratum of predominantly educated middle-class men who aspired to achieve hegemony in German society. This tendency will become even clearer in the discussion of the struggle against pulp fiction which forms the last part of this book. The purpose of this discussion will be to present the complex nature of this struggle which, against the background of a flourishing popular commercialized culture, became one of the most conspicuous markers of a lifestyle which defined itself as middle class. Reading studies and the struggle against pulp fiction were therefore both patterns of action which helped to construct the domain of a hegemonic culture. This was primarily done by strengthening the feeling and attitude of bourgeois subjects in contemporary Germany society.

Women

From the eighteenth century onward, women became a significant part of the book-reading public, and in particular a target audience for plot-driven literature. Hence Rolf Engelsing argues that women's joining of the book-reading public exercised decisive influence on the nature of publications, and above all the shift from intensive to extensive reading, in which the reading of novels played a key role. According to Engelsing, reading, and in particular novel reading, provided women with a form of escape from the world controlled by men, enabling them to enter a universe whose nature was dictated by women's abilities and their special needs.[11] According to this approach, as an activity taking place in the private sphere, reading, with its ability to disconnect individuals from their immediate surroundings, constituted a declarative act for a woman, through which she could demonstrate her independence and uniqueness.[12]

A salient example of how this identification of the special nature of women's reading habits was manifested in the first third of the twentieth century comes from research into women's reading habits carried out by Walter Hofmann under the auspices of the Leipzig Institute of Reading Studies.[13] Hofmann's research was based on data collected from the public libraries in the city of Leipzig over the 1922–1926 period. During those turbulent years, the number of active male readers at Leipzig's libraries totalled 25,035 (65 percent of total readers), and they were responsible for 532,145 (68 percent) of the total book loans made by the libraries. In contrast, the number of female readers was 13,550 (35 percent), with just 248,647 (32 percent) of loans.[14] Some explained this discrepancy between the number of male and female readers by the high caliber of books at public libraries. A widespread argument maintained that women tended to meet their reading needs mainly through so-called colporteur (peddled) books and commercial lending libraries which circulated material more suitable for their tastes in reading.[15] Hofmann rejected this possibility, which implied that it was the dearth of this alternative literature (*Surrogatliteratur*), as he defined it, in Leipzig's public libraries which kept women readers away from libraries. For him, the consumption by large numbers of men of such literature at railway station bookshops constituted proof that this form of literature could not be seen as the exclusive province of women, and hence its absence from the public libraries could not in his view be the reason for women not going to libraries.

Data from other studies also show that women, in particular working women, did not devote a great deal of time to reading as a leisure activity. For example, in two surveys conducted among women employees at the end of the 1920s, most women claimed that their heavy workloads and insufficient resources prevented them from devoting time to reading.[16] A similar conclusion was reached in a study which examined leisure time patterns of more than two thousand female textile workers in the Westphalia area. This research shows that 41 percent of the women did not read at all, 40 percent read on Sundays only, while just 19 percent of the respondents reported that they read every day, generally for between a quarter and half an hour, but rarely for as long as an hour.[17] Given these findings, it may be assumed that workloads, particularly for women whose work outside the home did not release them from their numerous domestic duties, were one of the contributory factors in women borrowing fewer books than men, as well as the reason why more housewives than working women and more middle-class women than women from the working classes used Leipzig's public libraries.

However, in addition to differences between the numbers of female and male readers, the book-loan data from the Leipzig libraries also indicate different borrowing patterns for men and women. They show that differences between men's and women's reading habits are far more significant than differences between different socioeconomic strata, between generations, or by the criterion of readers' educational levels.

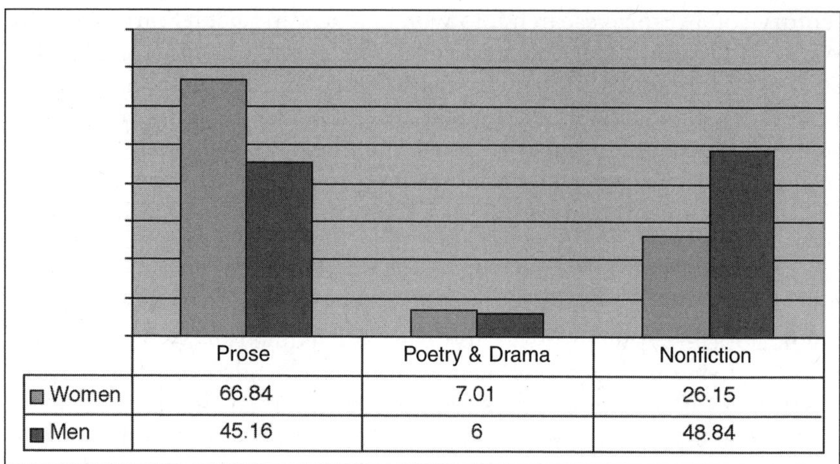

	Prose	Poetry & Drama	Nonfiction
Women	66.84	7.01	26.15
Men	45.16	6	48.84

Figure 1: Type of books borrowed by male/female readers

Hofmann made a distinction between educated women, or as he defined them, "intellectualized women," whose borrowing patterns were closer to those of men, and the group of so-called "undifferentiated women" (UF), which included women of all ages and social strata, who mainly read novels and whose reading patterns were fairly chaotic. Notwithstanding these differences, however, Hofmann considered women a homogeneous group, whose reading habits were largely dictated by fantasy and emotional needs. Furthermore, according to Hofmann the difference between women's and men's reading habits proves that women constitute an exclusive group which is markedly differentiated from male readers, with what he called sexual solidarity outweighing class solidarity. Hofmann based this conclusion on an analysis of book-borrowing data for women in various categories of loans. He showed that not only did women read more novels than nonfiction (see Figure 1), but that in each category of loans there were also differences between women and men in respect of areas of interest (as shown in Figure 2).[18]

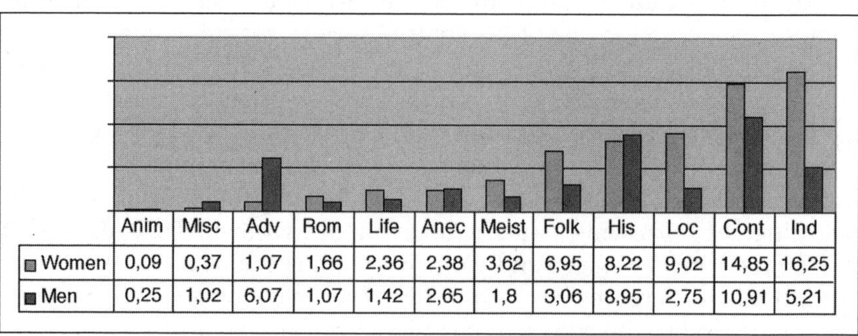

	Anim	Misc	Adv	Rom	Life	Anec	Meist	Folk	His	Loc	Cont	Ind
Women	0,09	0,37	1,07	1,66	2,36	2,38	3,62	6,95	8,22	9,02	14,85	16,25
Men	0,25	1,02	6,07	1,07	1,42	2,65	1,8	3,06	8,95	2,75	10,91	5,21

Figure 2: Borrowing patterns of various types of fiction classified by gender

These figures show that women read more novels of a local and national nature (*Heimaterzählungen, Dorfgeschichten, Bauernromane,* etc.) than men did. In contrast, men read more historical novels and travel books. In the nonfiction area, women had a slight preference for fields such as education, art, and biographies than all other areas, particularly science and technology, which were practically entirely dominated by men. Moreover, the loans figures collected in Leipzig show that even in the same areas of interest, men and women borrowed different books. For example, the list of "top loans" for books about music gives the following picture:[19]

List of top loans—music: Women (* for Books that appear in both lists)

		No. of loans
1.	Litzmann: Clara Schumann, ein Künstlerleben. Nach Tagebüchern und Briefen	269
2.	Beethoven: Briefe	58
3.	Wagner: Mein Leben	52
4.	Krebs: Haydn, Mozart, Beethoven*	52
5.	Schering: Musikalische Bildung und Erziehung zum musikalischen Hören*	50
6.	v.d. Pfordten: Beethoven*	38
7.	Storck: Der Tanz	36
8.	Rietsch: Die Grundlage der Tonkunst*	35
9.	Frimmel: Ludwig van Beethoven	33
10.	Reinecke: Meister der Tonkunst. Mozart, Beethoven, Haydn, Weber, Schumann, Mendelssohn	31

List of top loans—music: Men

1.	Wasielewskie: Die Violine und ihre Meister	171
2.	Schering: Musikalische Bildung und Erziehung zum musikalischen Hören*	137
3.	Krebs: Haydn, Mozart, Beethoven*	87
4.	Rietsch: Die Grundlage der Tonkunst*	84
5.	Bussler: Praktische Harmonielehre in Aufgaben mit Beispielen für den Unterricht	84
6.	Neitzel: Klassiker und Romantiker der deutschen Oper	81
7.	Volbach: Die Instrumente des Orchesters. Ihr Wesen und ihre Entwicklung	67
8.	Richter: Die Elementarkenntnisse der Musik.	67
9.	v.d. Pfordten: Beethoven*	64
10.	Bie: Das Klavier und seine Meister	63

Only four books appear in both lists, and the three first places in the list of women's top loans do not appear at all in the men's list. In another area of common interest such as art, the difference between women and men is even more marked. In this case, only two books appear in both men's and women's top loans lists.[20] Even in an area such as fiction, which is dominated by women borrowers, a similar picture emerges:

List of top loans—fiction[21]

	Undifferentiated women		Male laborers	
1.	Francois: Die letzte Reckenburgerin`	1076	Polenz: Der Büttenerbauer	1123
2.	Anzengruber: Der Schandfleck*	1018	Anzengruber: Der Schandfleck*	1016
3.	Polenz: Der Grabenhänger*	929	Freytag: Soll und Haben	976
4.	Anzengruber: Der Sternsteihof*	829	Polentz: Der Grabenhänger*	965
5.	Viebig: Das tägliche Brot	790	Franzos: Ein Kampf ums Recht	786
6.	Ebner-Eschenbach: Unsühnbar	725	Anzengruber: Der Sternsteihof*	773
7.	Ebner-Eschenbach: Das Gemeindekind	714	Andersen-Nex: Pelle der Eroberer	759
8.	Polenz: Thekla Lübekind	699	Dahn: Ein Kampf um Rom	700
9.	Ebner-Eschenbach: Lotti die Uhrmacherin	628	Zola: Germinal	697
10.	Wolf: Hanneken	626	Rosegger: Jakob der Letzte	686

These differences in borrowing patterns show that not only do women's areas of interest differ from those of men, but the differences in reading tastes between men and women actually result in two different groups of books, i.e., "women's books" as opposed to "men's books." In other words, even if the same books appear in the lists of top-ranking loans, this does not mean that therefore each group has the same interest in a particular book or that the book is read in the same way. According to Hofmann's analysis, women tended to borrow books written by women, above all describing the stories of women's lives. Or as he put it in his conclusion to the study:

> Living in the imagination, living in what is experienced by the senses, which can be reproduced in the imagination. But within this sphere, a pronounced tendency towards the human element, or what can be humanized, as dictated by personal interests. The concrete world, at the same time replete with the human element, as the epitome of what attracts. But within this circle, interest in oneself, in women's lives and women's fate, and based on this also a modest interest in books about women's fate and women's duties.[22]

For Hofmann, the special nature of women's reading habits constituted the backdrop to drawing up a special catalogue for women. The purpose of this catalogue was to provide a link between a paper-based world and a woman's special needs.[23] The women's catalogue was intended to act as an alternative catalogue for women, who allegedly found it difficult to use the library's objective academic men's catalogue. The former professed not only to present a list of "women's books" in various areas, but also to reinforce women's social awareness, or to use Hofmann's terms, to provide a link between a woman's world and her surroundings. This tendency is expressed above all in the last part of the catalogue. Under the title of "Frau und Öffentlichkeit. Ein Blick in die Zeit und ihre Aufgaben" (Women and the public sphere: Insights into the times and their role), the catalogue tried to present books designed to help women in coping with the challenges and new tasks confronting women in modern society.

What was special about the women's catalogue, therefore, was that it was intended for a specific social group.[24] Other catalogues were drawn up specifically for young people and for workers who, as we will see below, were also considered to have special requirements and to need pointing toward suitable literature with the goal of strengthening awareness and their sense of social and national responsibility. From this point of view, these catalogues reflected the way that the educated male bourgeoisie related to these social groups. In other words, this male stratum tried to integrate these groups in the dominant culture by defining their otherness and acknowledging an autonomous area unique to them. The production of a women's catalogue and the defining of a special body of literature for women is a perfect example of this tendency.

Workers

In a 1932 article, the sociologist Theodor Geiger summed up his impressions of the many research studies of the working classes. He argued that the gap between blue-collar workers and middle-class intellectuals was so great that even intellectuals sympathetic to the working classes thought, like missionaries or ethnologists, that they had to penetrate an utterly foreign mental world in order to grasp the nature of the working-class man.[25]

A salient example of this form of "othering" of workers is provided by a research project carried out by Erich Thier under the auspices of Walter Hofmann's Leipzig-based Institute of Reading Studies.[26] It examined workers' reading habits at Leipzig public libraries. The original version of the research was completed at the beginning of 1932, entitled "Workers and the historical world. A contribution to reading studies and the sociological study of the present." Following the Nazis' rise to power, the manuscript was first shelved and then, after being brought into line with Nazi ideology, published in a revised 1939 version.[27] The following observations will relate mainly to the first, unedited version of Thier's manuscript from 1932. While this version focuses on workers' reading habits in the field of history books, it also contains far more statistical information, providing a fairly accurate picture of the borrowing habits of both the working and the middle classes in various fields at the Leipzig libraries.[28]

The main criterion for attributing middle- or working-class status was the husband's job or profession.[29] Walter Hofmann, who determined how the data from the Leipzig libraries were collected and organized, included in the group of blue-collar workers those readers who owned no means of production whatsoever, performed manual labor, and did not have generous means of support. Based on these characteristics, in the 1922–1926 period the Leipzig public libraries had 7,187 readers who were blue-collar workers (above the age of 18), or 19 percent of the total, accounting for 162,717 loans or 21 percent of the total. A total of 9,295 readers (24 percent) were defined as middle class and accounted for 200,015 loans (26 percent of total loans). As these figures show, the gap between middle-class and working-class readers at Leipzig's libraries was not as great as that between male and female readers, for example.[30]

The similarity between these two social groups is also reflected in lending patterns themselves. The first feature is the predominance of loans in the nonfiction area over all other fields. Furthermore, analysis of the borrowing figures shows that working-class readers tended to borrow more books in the realm of nonfiction than did their middle-class counterparts. Thus 81,847 (50 percent) of workers' loans (over the age of 18) fall into the class of nonfiction works, compared with 94,037 (47 percent) of books borrowed by middle-class readers. This tendency may be ascribed to the special policy pursued by Leipzig's *Schalterbibliotheken* ("window libraries") which promoted theoretical works, as well as the special nature of the workers in the city of Leipzig. As the German book capital, Leipzig employed large numbers of blue-collar workers in the fields of printing and graphics. These workers were considered the aristocrats of the working classes.[31] However, this fact did not prevent Thier from adopting an approach which stressed that laborers had different tastes in reading from middle-class readers. In his opinion, a distribution analysis of the various

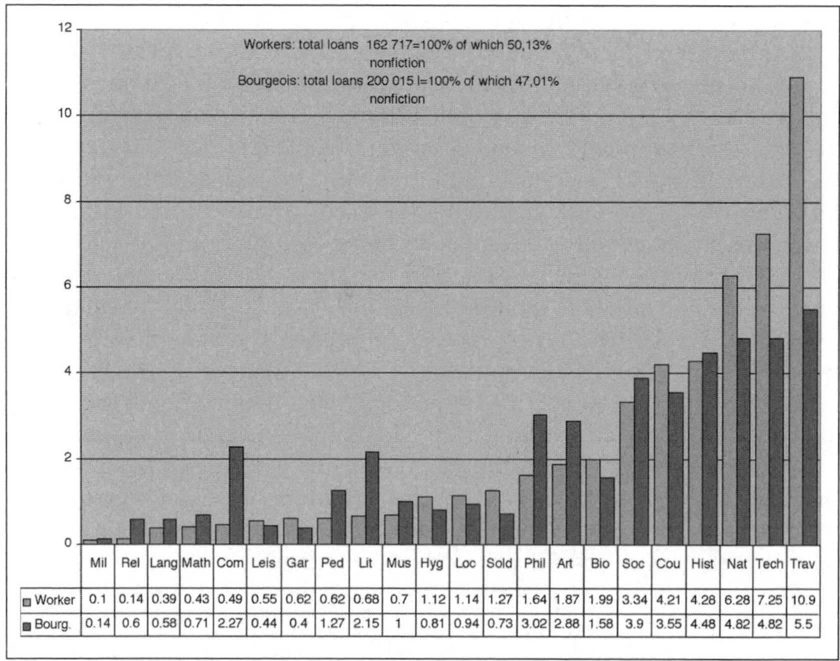

	Mil	Rel	Lang	Math	Com	Leis	Gar	Ped	Lit	Mus	Hyg	Loc	Sold	Phil	Art	Bio	Soc	Cou	Hist	Nat	Tech	Trav
Worker	0.1	0.14	0.39	0.43	0.49	0.55	0.62	0.62	0.68	0.7	1.12	1.14	1.27	1.64	1.87	1.99	3.34	4.21	4.28	6.28	7.25	10.9
Bourg.	0.14	0.6	0.58	0.71	2.27	0.44	0.4	1.27	2.15	1	0.81	0.94	0.73	3.02	2.88	1.58	3.9	3.55	4.48	4.82	4.82	5.5

Figure 3: Distribution of loans: Workers vs. Bourgeois[32]

areas of the nonfiction works borrowed from libraries provided proof of the special nature of this group's reading.

For Thier, the intensive nature of workers' book borrowing behavior, as opposed to the extensive nature of loans by middle-class readers, was just one dimension of the gap between workers and the bourgeoisie.[33] In his view, the dominance of travel books provided evidence of the special nature of laborers' taste in reading, determined by imagination and experience alike. In order to bolster this conclusion, Thier turned his attention to a possible link between the number of marriages solemnized, job-seekers, and travel books borrowed. These figures indicate that as the number of marriages declined and jobless figures soared, more travelogues were borrowed. This borrowing pattern indicates, according to Thier, a tendency to escape from the reality affecting this social group.

Borrowing patterns in the narrow area of history books, which in Thier's view played a key role in constructing the national consciousness of the various social groups, also indicate a similar tendency to escapism, primarily among the working classes. An examination of the way that loans of history books fit into the overall borrowing patterns of different groups of readers yields the following picture: working-class girls—0.90 percent; working-class women—1.05 percent; middle-class girls—1.95 percent; middle-class women—1.99 percent; working-class boys—2.38 percent; middle-class boys—3.90 percent; working-class men—4.28 percent; middle-class men—4.83 percent. These figures show that adults read more history books than youngsters, men are more interested in history than women, and middle-class readers show more interest in historical literature than workers. Another interesting fact is that the difference between middle-class male adults and boys is far smaller than that present in the working classes between young people and their elders. The data cited here constitute additional evidence to the effect that class-related differences are less pronounced than gender or generation differences. However, despite the fact that the gap between the middle and working classes on the level of the adult population is not particularly significant, according to Thier an analysis of the actual books borrowed does indicate differences between the different social groups. The list of the top-ranking loans to males aged over 18 in the 1922–1926 period was supposed to corroborate this finding:

Table 5.1

Most popular books borrowed—history[34]

Workers	Middle class	Academics
1. Maspero, Das alte Ägypten (41) 0.75	Die Tragödie Deutschland (27) 0.57	Carlyle, Geschichte der französischen Revolution (11) 0.64
2. Freytag, Bilder aus der Reformationszeit (42) 0.77	Cortez, Eroberung von Mexiko (28) 0.60	Cortez, Eroberung von Mexiko (11) 0.64

continued

Workers	Middle class	Academics
3. Schwab, Sagen des klassischen Altertums (46) 0.84	Grube, Charakterbilder aus der vorchristlichen Zeit (28) 0.60	Einhart, Deutsche Geschichte (11) 0.64
4. Freytag, Aus dem Jahrhundert des grossen Krieges (47) 0.86	Hansen, Inquisition und Zauberwahn (28) 0.60	Hellmann, Frühes Mittelalter (11) 0.64
5. Inglis, Memoiren aus dem indischen Aufstand (48) 0.88	Reisen des Marco Polo (28) 0.60	Laukhardt Magister, Leben und Schicksale (11) 0.64
6. Spengler, Untergang des Abendlandes I (51) 0.93	Kropotkin, Geschichte der Französischen Revolution (29) 0.62	Meineke, Weltbürgertum und Nationalstaat (11) 0.64
7. Häussers, Geschichte der französischen Revolution (56) 1.02	Friedrich, Aus der französischen Revolution (31) 0.66	Schurtz, Lebenserinnerungen (11) 0.64
8. Cortez, Eroberung von Mexiko (57) 1.04	Bismarck, Gedanken und Erinnerungen (32) 0.68	Taine, Ursprung des modernen Frankreich (11) 0.64
9. Wägner, Hellas (58) 1.06	La Bruyere, Charaktere aus dem Zeitalter Ludwig XIV (33) 0.70	Birt, Zur Kulturgeschichte Rom (12) 0.69
10. Zimmermann, Grosser deutscher Bauernkrieg (62) 1.13	Freytag, Vom Mittelalter zur Neuzeit (42) 0.89	Burckhard, Weltgeschichtliche Betrachtungen (12) 0.69
11. Jäger, Geschichte des Altertums (64) 1.17	Hinderburg, Aus meinem Leben (43) 0.91	Katharina II, in ihren Memorien (12) 0.69
12. Schurtz, Lebenserinnerungen (66) 1.20	Ludendorff, Kriegserinnerungen (47) 1.00	Birt, Aus dem Leben der Antike (13) 0.75
13. Freytag, Vom Mittelalter zur Neuzeit (67) 1.22	Freytag, Bilder aus der Reformationszeit (50) 1.06	Egelhaaf, Geschichte der neuesten Zeit (14) 0.81
14. Kropotkin, Memorien (70) 1.78	Schurtz, Lebenserinnerungen (59) 1.25	Wägner, Hellas (14) 0.81
15. Friedrich, Aus der französischen Revolution (77) 1.41	Freytag, Aus dem Jahrhundert des grossen Krieges (60) 1.28	Freytag, Aus dem Jahrhundert des grossen Krieges (15) 0.87
16. Grube, Charakterbilder aus der vorchristlichen Zeit (79) 1.44	Kielland, Napoleon (71) 1.51	Dieter Schäfer, Weltgeschichte (15) 0.87
17. Kropotkin, Geschichte der französischen Revolution (79) 1.44	Freytag, Vom Mittelalter zur Neuzeit (75) 1.59	Bismarck, Gedanken und Erinnerungen (16) 0.93
18. Kielland, Napoleon (84) 1.53	Katharina II, in ihren Memorien (83) 1.76	Carlyle, Helden und Heldenverehrung (18) 1.04
19. Katharina II, in ihren Memorien (99) 1.83	Spengler, Untergang des Abendlandes I (90) 1.91	Freytag, Bilder aus dem Mittelalter (19) 1.10
20. Freytag, Bilder aus dem Mittelalter (120) 2.19	Freytag, Bilder aus dem Mittelalter (92) 1.96	Spengler, Untergang des Abendlandes II (21) 1.21
21. Laukhardt Magister, Leben und Schicksale (144) 2.63	Laukhardt Magister, Leben und Schicksale (110) 2.34	Spengler, Untergang des Abendlandes I (30) 1.74

This listing of the most popular books borrowed by the different groups appears to shed more light on the variety of periods and subjects which interested readers than on particular borrowing patterns characteristic of each group. Just seven works appear in all three lists: *Laukhardt Magister,* Cortez, Schurtz, Katharina *II,* and two books by Freytag: *Bilder aus dem Mittelalter, Aus dem Jahrhundert des grossen Krieges* and the first volume of Spengler's famous book *Untergag des Abendlandes.* A more precise analysis of the lists shows a more significant difference (ignoring the differences in the number of loans taken out by each group) between the group of academics and the two other categories.[35] Twelve books appear only in the academics' top-ranking loans list, compared with six in the middle-class readers' list and seven in the workers' list. In contrast, eight books appear on the top loans list of the academics' group as well as their middle-class counterparts, while just six books appear on both the academics' list and that of the working classes. Furthermore, in the top loans list of the group which is defined as academic, in contrast to the other lists where narrative history dominates, it is historians with a theoretical and academic bent who predominate, such as Meinecke, Burckhardt, Carlyle, and of course Spengler.

The differences between the middle-class and working-class lists are less significant. Thirteen books out of twenty-one appear on both these lists, and of the four books which head the top loans table, three are the same for both groups. It is especially interesting to note the popularity of the national-liberal writer Gustav Freytag (1816–1895), who appears four times on the working-class top loans list, five times on the middle-class list, and twice on the academics' top loans list. No other book on German history was as successful in Leipzig's libraries as Freytag's five-volume *Bilder aus der deutschen Vergangenheit* ("Pictures of German Past"), which first appeared in the years 1859–1867. This series of books, which conservative historian Georg von Below acclaimed as the best history of German culture, therefore constituted the main historical reading material of Leipzig library readers.[36] Apart from Freytag's popularity, also to be noted is the autobiography of Friedrich Christian Laukhardt (1757–1822), which was published in six volumes between 1792 and 1802 and primarily focused on the years when Laukhardt served in the Prussian army in the war against France, which he presents in all its horror. Why these specific books were so popular, and what can be learned from this state of affairs about contemporary Germans' historical awareness, may be variously interpreted. It must be remembered that the Leipzig lending libraries were not a neutral domain situated midway between readers and books. To a large extent these libraries' book holdings reflected a bourgeois-national world of values. They deliberately tried to influence their readers' reading habits and increase their national awareness.

Thier's analysis indicates that the workers' top loans list is characterized by the predominance of books about revolutionary history (occupying places 7, 10, 14, 15, 17, and perhaps 5 and 12 as well), and the history of ancient peoples (rankings 3, 9, 11, and 16). Thier interprets interest in these two areas as part of workers' escaping reality by taking refuge in bygone cultures, tales of adventure, and periods when far-reaching changes seemed to be occurring in the everyday realities of life. In contrast, the list of top loans by the middle-class group reflects special interest in the category of German history (places 1, 8, 9, 10, 11, 12, 13, 15, 17, 20). Thier interprets this interest as the outcome of this group's highly developed national consciousness, and in particular as part of coping with the harsh realities of life in Germany in the wake of the world war. What is particularly interesting is the absence from the middle-class list of books on the classical period. This category reappears in the academics' list, but with nuances, as Thier hastens to emphasize, which differ from those characteristic of the workers' top loans list. In Thier's opinion, the academic group's interest in the classical period is not a sign of escapism or an apolitical stance, but is rather part of a striving for culture which characterizes the borrowing patterns of this group. Another feature common to the academics' and workers' top loans lists is the absence of books dealing with contemporary history. Apart from Spengler's book, which was extremely popular during the first half of the 1920s, and Kropotkin's memoirs in the workers' list, no other works fall into this category.

The categories that Thier used for the various lists of loans therefore indicate a tendency by the academics' group to borrow theoretical works. National and political awareness characterizes the loans taken out by the group defined as middle class and is manifest in the experience-based type of books typical of loans by the working class. Basing himself on these differences, Thier infers the different relationship and role of reading generally, and of the reading of historical literature specifically, in each group. His analysis shows that while workers' borrowing patterns indicate that for them reading was primarily a way of escaping from the realities of day-to-day existence, for the middle classes it formed part of coping with the social and political situation that engulfed Germany following the war. In contrast, the list of top loans taken out by the academic group did not contain this political element: rather, it had a strong theoretical slant, which highlighted not only the role played by reading historical literature as a means of unraveling historical processes and developments, but also the aesthetic and cultural value of reading generally, and in particular of historical literature.

Despite these differences, the 1930 loan-structure figures show that the borrowing patterns of workers and the middle classes were tending to converge, as can be seen both from how the loans graph behaves in the field of history, as well as the different numbers of history books borrowed by each group.

Furthermore, the 1930 figures for books about the war period show that workers were more interested in this subject than middle-class readers:

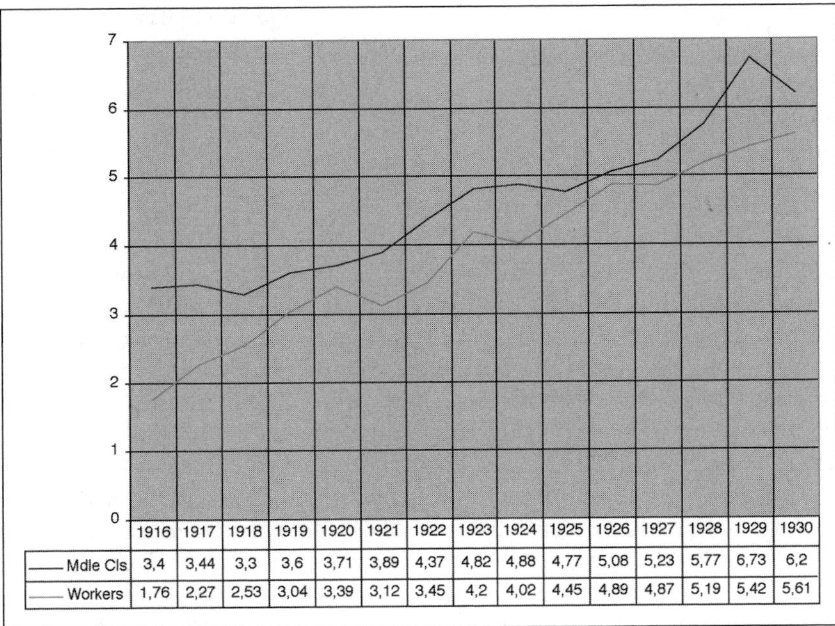

	1916	1917	1918	1919	1920	1921	1922	1923	1924	1925	1926	1927	1928	1929	1930
Mdle Cls	3,4	3,44	3,3	3,6	3,71	3,89	4,37	4,82	4,88	4,77	5,08	5,23	5,77	6,73	6,2
Workers	1,76	2,27	2,53	3,04	3,39	3,12	3,45	4,2	4,02	4,45	4,89	4,87	5,19	5,42	5,61

Figure 4: Borrowing distribution

	Middle class	Workers
Fischer, *Die kritischen 39 Tage*	5	8
Seelhoff, *Der Weg in den Krieg*	11	17
Persius, *Menschen und Schiffe in der kaiserlichen Flotte*	10	1
Stumpff, *Warum die Flotte zerbrach*	34	15
Alboldt, *Die Tragödie der alten deutschen Marine*	27	15
Scheibe, *Die Seeschlacht vor dem Skagerrak*	5	1
Schuwecker, *So war der Krieg*	44	20
Das König Sächs. 7. Infanterieregiment No. 106	8	6
Das König. Sächs. 7. Infanterieregiment No. 107	12	5
Beumelburg, *Loretto*	5	3
Nicolai, *Nachrichtendienst, Presse und Volksstimung im Weltkrieg*	7	13
Wrigt, *Wie es Wirklich war*	7	10
Aufzeichungen des Generalmajors Max Hoffmann	18	25

In all, workers borrowed 193 works in this category, constituting around 3 percent of total loans by this group, compared with 139 books taken out by middle-class readers, or just 2.66 percent of this group's borrowings in the domain of history. In this connection it is perhaps worth adding the loans of novels about the world war, which were extremely popular at the end of the 1920s. This results in the following picture:

	Middle Class	Workers
Remarque, *Im Westen nichts Neues*	585	234
Renn, *Der Krieg*	420	305
E. Jünger, *In Stahlgewitten*	157	152
Grote, *Die Höhle von Beauregard*	110	113

These figures show that the workers were not remote from the political and social realities of their time as Thier's interpretation indicated. An examination of the reader's cards of people classified in the working-class group shows how complex and varied their reading world was. For example, the reader's card of a twenty-one-year-old carpenter reveals that over a two-year period, he borrowed volume after volume of Schiller's and Goethe's letters. The reading diary of a thirty-three-year-old waiter shows that for three years, he borrowed only books about philosophy and religion, and from 1922 to 1926 a twenty-six-year-old laborer systematically borrowed books about history and geography. Works on his reading list included nine volumes of Sybel's *Geschichte der Revolutionszeit* (*History of the Revolutionary Period*), ten volumes of Schlosser's *Weltgeschichte* (*History of the World*), and much more. These figures are a valuable source for exploring the autodidact phenomenon among these social strata, whose areas of interest and tastes in reading to a large extent developed outside the formal frameworks of the educational establishment.[37]

Thier's manuscript is supplemented by working-class readers' reading reports, which provide a one-off glimpse of how nonprofessional readers read and interpreted different texts.[38] As an example of these reports, below are the impressions in 1930 of H.S., a thirty-year-old textile worker, of World War literature:

H.S. Discussion and criticism of the war literature

The following is neither perfect nor complete. However, it is done with good intentions and can be judged by anyone who was himself in the war. First the question must be looked at as to whether war literature, which has grown into such an enormous body, has any purpose?! Many say it does not, but I say it does, and I'll say that a hundred times and more. The World War is horror, destruction, chaos on a gigantic scale. It is the most awful crime ever perpetrated against people (with such a highly praised culture??). To record and recognize this and prevent it for future generations—this is already a reason which provides justification a thousandfold for the works which have appeared. People should read Schauweckr's "Aufbruch der Nationen" (Emergence of the Nations). This infernal, demonic raging of technology, this machine-like murdering of mankind. A convincing book that cries out in condemnation. Baron Grote describes the same thing in his "Flanders 17". Or Koeppen in "Army Report". Particularly the artillery battles in the latter. But I think the best war book was written by Beumelburg in his "Bosemüeller Group". He sings the praises of comradeship. All the pleasures and problems of corporals. Every figure is shown true to life. This lyrical work casts its spell over everybody. It tries to limit genocide, that dreadful monster, in the love of comradeship. The same idea is presented by the great Frenchman, H. Barbusse, in "The Fire", and the less good Frenchman Dorgeles in "The Wooden Crosses". It is the leitmotif of Remarque's much-criticized "All Quiet on the Western Front". It is also to be found in the American J. Dos Passos' "Three Soldiers", as well as Michael's "Infantryman Perhobstler". Who knows of the suffering of POWs? Let him read Wilke—"Prisoner Halm", and A. Zweig—"Sergeant Grischa". This lyrical, moving work that cries out in condemnation, about the suffering of a poor Russian who is done to death. And he understands and loathes war. All these authors are champions of an eternal peace. These also include L. Renn ("The Warrior"), G. v. Vring ("Soldier Suhren"), who knows the life of civilians in occupied areas? The struggle by the English? Let him read Mottram's "The Spanish Smallholding". On both sides, precious, red, live blood has been spilt in vain?! And is this to be forgotten? Read the story of the orderlies (Frez—"The Box of Plasters"), the experiences of the conscripts (Beradt—"Ships at the Front"), study Carossa—"Romanian Diary". Who writes about the silent experiences of suffering humanity? Who thinks of the suffering of the civilian population? (Gläser "Class of 1902"). Of our boys in blue? (Plivier "Der Kaiser Kuli") and (Admiral Scheer "Germany's Fleet in the World War"). Of the battles of our lost colonial forces? (Lettow-Vorbeck "Memories of East Africa"). Everywhere destruction, devastation. All of this speaks an all too clear language. And one needs to keep looking at images of the world war, as well as the distressing book by Friedrich: "War on War!" And much, much more in the same vein. Also noteworthy is the still highly controversial book by E. Jünger, "In Storms of Steel". Here there's an individual who, unconcerned by all the suffering and death, still approves of war. But the exception simply confirms the rule. Lachmann's novel of the cavalry, "Four Years a Cavalryman", is written in a bad, flat style. Beumelburg's "Barrage at Germany" is an amazing compilation of everything, from start to finish, providing a brief general survey. My personal opinion is that apart from Barbusse and Plivier, the authors are not yet sufficiently reckless in condemning war. Where is the reckless unmasking of those who dragged the war out, the shirkers, the incapable diplomats, the scholars, who scientifically made ersatz products tasty to the people? (thereby prostituting science). Who kept the warmongering machine going? The hoarders, the bon vivants, the incapable party leaders? Where's the unmasking of the wretched lying press and the Church which had no conscience, which saw its true vocation as treating the masses as fools? Where were Germany's intelligent minds? Where were the noble poets and thinkers? These are the people who need to come to maturity in the countries of the world. Every single person should read this war literature over and over again and should realize how low mankind could sink once. Why?? The next man should do it better.

To work! H.S.

Thier defined H.S. as an energetic man who delighted in every opportunity to argue with librarians and other readers about the books that he read. H.S.'s list of loans is of impressive length: between May 1930 and June 1931, this man borrowed over 120 books. According to Thier, H.S.'s decided views and stubborn nature prevented him from joining the ranks of the German Communist Party, the KPD, to which he was closest in terms of his views. As a result, his "victims" were his family members, to whom he would read out the daily newspaper every day, making them discuss current affairs. Although H.S. only took part in the final stages of the world war, it was an extremely significant event for him. How did this experience influence his personal world view? Was the war an experience which strengthened national awareness, or did it rather reinforce class-based patterns of thinking? Unfortunately, H.S.'s list provides no clues which might help in answering these questions. According to Thier's input, at least, the impressions of the world war as a collective experience of the German people were so strong that they even overshadowed H.S.'s interest in society. Nevertheless, H.S.'s list shows that while he relates to the war and the postwar situation in national terms, he also highlights the importance of the literature of the world war as a warning sign to all, not just the German people. In this context it is particularly interesting to see how he relates to Ernst Jünger, whom he considered the exception to the rule, extolling as he did the experience of war rather than distancing himself from it as the great majority did. Nevertheless, in another list H.S. turned his attention to the contradictions in the antimilitarist positions, as presented for example in Ludwig Tureck's autobiography, *A Worker's Tale*.[39] Apart from his criticism of Tureck's antimilitarist positions, H.S. criticized the room which Tureck devoted to his sexual experiences in the book, declaring:

> I energetically reject this book. I don't like the fact that the author recounts his sexual and erotic experiences in it.[40]

A different reaction to Tureck's book was provided by R.K., a fifty-two-year-old blue-collar worker (iron planer). In 1930 he summarized his impressions of Tureck's book as follows:

> A book of masterly power and force, worthy to stand side by side with Zola. Let me start by saying: if there were ten thousand Turecks, Germany would look very different today. There are many descriptions of youth, such as *From the Country of Semper's Youth,* which also describe great suffering. But the suffering there and here—what a difference. Then the time of the soldiers. He was only briefly at the front, but with what verve, what mastery war is described here, by far eclipsing *All Quiet on the Western Front.* The chapter on prisoners in a fortress is written with such elemental force. Here the mask of human bestiality and cruelty is exposed without mercy. Even where he touches upon the erotic, he never lifts the last veil or wallows in the mire. He describes the episode with the black girl from Africa with such a gentle touch. He wins us over with all the fighting and labor in the Ruhr

area. The fact that the SPD comes off so badly in his book is its own fault. The descriptions in Lithuania are written in just as compelling a style. All in all, a book which every thinking person should be given. There are three books which I read thirty years ago—Dante's *Divine Comedy,* Bälsche's *Nature's Love Life,* A. Dodel, *From Love and Science*—and now a fourth one, Tureck, *A Worker's Tale,* which are books which one does not forget for however long one lives.

It is a moot point to what extent the lists of these two men, H.S. and R.K., are representative of how far this literature was accepted, intended as it was for workers in the social group to which they belonged or at least in their immediate surroundings. Nevertheless, it would appear that these lists suffice to indicate the complexity and diversity of the reading world of members of the working classes. Despite this fact, Thier did not waver in his basic approach to the role that reading played for the working classes. True, he argued that analysis of developments in borrowing patterns over time indicated a tendency toward the nationalizing of the workers, and he also differentiated between different types of working-class readers.[41] Nevertheless, he insisted on interpreting the various statistics as an expression of differences between the different social groups. What is interesting in this interpretation is that Thier did not see reading as an activity which instituted or established forms of identity for workers. Instead, he preferred to adopt a manifestly psychological and sociological approach according to which workers possessed a passive status, simply reacting without reflection to a given situation. A paradigmatic expression of this prevailing approach to workers was provided by writer Joseph Roth after a visit to the Ruhr area, which he summed up as follows: "A worker wishes above all to be instructed. He is constantly told, 'knowledge is power.' He takes this literally and wants to know."[42]

As for women, this attitude, which viewed workers as a passive mass devoid of independent opinions, constituted the backdrop to drawing up special catalogues designed to guide workers to literature suitable for their needs and nature. However, unlike the case of the women's catalogue, which was primarily intended to reinforce women's social awareness, one of the salient characteristics of the catalogues designed for workers was their national nature. Thus for example, the Social Democrat libraries recommended as being of value to workers the catalogues of an organization which had pronounced nationalist leanings such as the Dürerbund.[43] Cultural conservatism was reflected not only by the kind of books which were intended to improve workers' cultural level and strengthen their national awareness, but as shown at the end of Chapter IV, also in the requirement that they be given suitable form.

The third element which made up this strange and special group examined by bourgeois intellectuals like ethnologists on a missionary quest was youth.

Youth

The vast amount of data collected in the 1920s about young people's reading habits could be used for a separate research study in its own right.[44] What makes these databases unique is that they not only present a broad and varied picture of young people's reading habits, but also contain a great deal of material in which boys and girls reported on the books they had read. For example, in 1928 the German Book Dealers' Association announced an essay competition in which boys and girls aged seven to twenty were invited to recommend books and give the reasons for their choice. Competition entries comprised some 717 essays by boys and 871 by girls, and prizes totaling 3,000 Reichsmarks were awarded in the form of book tokens. In all, 580 authors and 940 titles were put forward. The ten most popular authors referred to in the essays were as follows:[45]

		Girls	Boys
Else Ury	68 times (with 9 stories)	68	—
Gustav Freytag	58 times (including *Soll und Haben* 30 times)	22 (11)	29 (19)
Hermann Löns	38 times (including *Werwolf* 30 times)	12 (2)	26 (9)
Waldemar Bonsel	34 times (including *Biene Maya* 26 times)	30 (24)	4 (2)
Johana Spyri	32 (including *Heidi* 24 times)	32	—
Felix Dahn	31 times (*Kampf um Rom*)	10	21
Theodor Strom	30 times (including *Schimmelreiter* 9 times)	22 (6)	8 (3)
Agnes Sapper	28 times (including *Familie Pfüffing* 19 times)	25	3
Lewis Wallace	24 times (*Ben Hur*)	13	11
Sophie Wörishöffer	24 times (with 19 stories)	5	19

An examination of the ten most popular authors shows that more books were read by girls only than books read only by boys. The more extensive list, containing over eighty authors, shows that in contrast to seventeenth "girls' books," just three books were read by boys only: Conscience H., *The Lion of Flanders* (Der Löwe von Flanden); Walter von Molo, *How They Forced Life* (Wie sie das Leben zwangen); and Fritz Witschetzky, *The Black Boat* (Das schwarze Schiff).

Perhaps this situation was the upshot of the fact that boys steered clear of reading works which were considered girls' books. An inevitable result of this tendency was the creation of a female sphere which did not include boys. In contrast, girls were not limited in the same way, and were free to read books with a far more varied nature. Contemporary thinking interpreted this tendency as an educational problem, of course, affecting girls and not boys.[46]

Educator Wilhelm Fronemann, who analyzed the German Book Dealers' Association survey results, argued that the creation of a special domain of reading for girls, and in particular the intensity of reading in that domain, reflected the fundamental disparity between the sexes. In his opinion, the source of this disparity was to be found in the tradition which limited the areas in which girls were supposed to be interested and prevented them from getting a rounded education (*Vollbildung*), something which boys did receive.[47] As a result, girls mainly preferred books written by women and addressing the lives of women, and their narcissistic taste in reading lacked the social and political dimension. In contrast, boys, whose interest in books was less one-dimensional, read more adventure books and works with a national character, such as the books of Hermann Löns.[48] For Fronemann, therefore, the German Book Dealers' Association survey provided additional proof of the importance of books to young people. As he put it: "Books often become the dominant focal point of thought and emotion, they reveal enormous power of experience and are recognized as spiritual and moral guides."[49] It was this recognition of the central role of books in young people's lives that gave rise to the great interest in youngsters' reading patterns, as well as the fear of the dangers looming as a result of irresponsible reading.

The German Book Dealers' Association interest in essay-writing competitions was not only cultural and educational in nature: it also served manifestly commercial purposes, and hence such contests acted as market survey tools.[50] It was for this reason that in 1930 the Book Dealers' Association announced a similar competition for girls aged fifteen to twenty, where 443 prizes were offered for a total of three thousand Reichsmarks. The results of this event were published on the occasion of 1931 Book Day, which was devoted to the topic of books and women. Under the title "What we expect from books!" the German Book Dealers' Association distributed, in bookshops and schools throughout Germany, 125,000 copies of a circular in which girls were asked to answer the following questions:

—Which book or books have been of special importance to me?
—What kind of books can hold me spellbound?
—Do you have an idea about books which you could use today but you don't come across? e.g., books which would give you advice for your day-to-day life? Or have you been disappointed by books when you think you have found them? Do you think that you should be offered books other than those for boys?[51]

The Book Dealers' Association received some 1,900 essays, of which 1,756 were considered suitable. This rich source, which is still awaiting systematic examination and analysis, provides a unique glimpse into the reading world of fifteen- to twenty-year-old girls throughout Germany at the end of the 1920s. One of the things these essays show is that the prevalent argument about girls being apolitical should not be accepted uncritically. A nineteen-year-old student of philosophy whose father was an office worker typically relates to book reading as a liberating activity which should help shape both the reader's personality and a philosophy of life. An extract from her essay reads as follows:

> In my eyes, the writer is a person who sees and makes us aware of things which we could only imagine previously or even if we know them, cannot express properly. This is why a book always makes a particularly great impression on me if it somehow touches on problems which are of concern to me and helps me in trying to solve them. This is why about four years ago Zola's "Paris", Hauptmann's "Weber" and Tolstoy's "Resurrection" had the greatest influence on me. This was right at the time that I began to detach myself from my parents' petit bourgeois views and came to Socialism.... Later my unconditional belief in the path to Socialism gradually dissipated, I no longer saw everything in such nice simple terms, doubts overtook me. I then read in quick succession Heinrich Mann's "Die Armen" and Leonhard Frank's "Bürger." These confirmed my doubts, but unfortunately did not show me a new path.... I long for a book which will manage to restore my unmitigated belief in socialism (in the broadest sense) and make me once again able to develop an inner enthusiasm and willingness to sacrifice myself, without having to constantly doubt ... perhaps I need a book which can show us "today's" girl, with all her hopes, conflicts and difficulties.

Why did this girl, who wrote the above in December 1930, not refer to National Socialism? What did National Socialism symbolize for her? Might 30 January 1933 have been the change for which she had hoped? These are questions to which the available sources cannot provide unambiguous answers.

Despite the centrality of reading in these essays, the prevailing attitude to young people's reading habits was largely pessimistic. Contemporary analyses of the survey's findings highlighted the special motivation of the girls who took part in the competition, arguing that it did not necessarily reflect the general picture for this age group. Second, it was feared that such surveys did not reflect youngsters' real attitudes to book reading, but rather the expectations that young people ascribe to the world of their elders. And third, other studies—on the whole carried out by psychologists, librarians, and educators—presented a far more complex and pessimistic picture of young people's reading habits.[52]

However, despite the dominance of the pessimistic attitude to youth reading culture, one of the key characteristics which recurs throughout most of these studies indicates that it is not any lack of interest in reading which is perceived as young people's main problem, but the reading material itself. Thus for example, statistics collected at the end of the 1920s at a school in the working-class district of a large city showed that adults read less than their younger counterparts—a tendency which might well relate to the popularity of the cinema in a metropolis. Nevertheless, this study deduced that fears about films, radio, and sport undermining the role of reading had proved unfounded.[53] Another study, which looked at young people's recreational activities in Berlin in 1930, found that reading was the most common recreational activity for youngsters, with boys tending to read more than girls.[54] And yet another survey, this time carried out at a girls' vocational school in Düsseldorf, indicated that of 260 pupils, 80 percent were particularly fond of reading; 13 percent read only newspapers and magazines; and just 7 percent admitted that they did not read anything.[55] Furthermore, the various studies made the point that there were no significant differences between young people's reading habits in the large cities and the rural areas, or between Protestant and Catholic regions.[56] Thus the reading list of a fourteen-year-old boy from a small town in Thuringia shows that he mainly read detective series of the Frank Allen, Nick Carter, and Harald Hart variety. Another boy from a small town in Pomerania reported:

> I love reading light books (Schmöker). Frank Allen, "The Avengers of the Dispossessed" (Der Rächer der Enterbten). They're exciting tales. I also like reading war stories. Won't have a thing to do with mysteries. Love stories are smashing. There's all that kissing and hugging. Great fun to read. Only cost 50 pfennigs. The Review (Revue), True Stories (Wahre Geschichten), Uhu, Magazine, and educational issues. "Marriage" (Die Ehe) is smashing too; it's got lovely pictures.[57]

We have an abundance of similar reports from rural and urban areas. In the large cities these works were so widely circulated that special lending libraries were set up, together with secondhand shops, detective series fan clubs, and clubs for swapping these publications. Youngsters organized themselves in groups, reading the stories together, adopting the world of the expressions used in the books, and imitating their characters.[58]

Different surveys also showed that reports about disasters and accidents, descriptions of crimes, serialized novels, and above all the sports section were the main parts in the daily paper which attracted youngsters' attention.[59] In this connection, a survey carried out by the Vocational Guidance Centre in the city of Kassel in 1930 is particularly interesting. Pupils aged fourteen and fifteen were asked to indicate what they knew about the following list of well-known figures:[60]

1. Max Schmeling (boxer)	90%	Known
2. Heinrich Stuhlfauth (goalkeeper for the Nuremberg football team)	85%	Known
3. Gustav Stresemann (German Foreign Minister 1923–1929)	80%	Known
4. Dr. Eckner (builder of Zeppelins)	77%	Known
5. Harry Piel (German cinema star)	71%	Known
6. Hermann Löns (writer)	66%	Known
7. Karl May (writer)	54%	Known
8. Henry Ford (American industrialist)	49%	Known

Such reports from Germany's small towns and rural areas aroused apprehension among contemporary educators and moralists, and provided evidence for an approach which said that the hunger for experience and sensationalism constituted the primary factor in determining the areas of interest to young people and what they read.

The various studies also considered differences in reading habits, particularly between girls and boys from different social strata. For example, the popularity of detective books with girls was attributed to their interest in the special characters described in the story and the psychological dimension of plot development. In contrast, violence, solving the "whodunnit" riddle, and the descriptions of catching the criminal were considered the main components in boys' attraction to detective stories. Or alternatively, boys' interest in love stories was perceived as part of their sexual awakening and curiosity, while girls' attraction to these tales was attributed to their addiction to the world of romanticism and kitsch.[61]

A more complex picture is provided by the Book Dealers' Association survey of girls, in which the respondents were asked to give their views about the distinction between girls' and boys' books. Some of the girls argued that the differences between the sexes and the different roles ascribed to men and women made it necessary to read different forms of literature. In contrast, others argued that this distinction was not particularly significant, and that in any case boys and girls read the same books, even if not always at the same time. Or, as expressed by a fifteen-year-old girl from Frankfurt am Main whose father was a shipping clerk: "Today, since women have the same rights and hence the same interests as men, it seems quite natural to me that they read the same books." And another girl the same age, whose father was a grammar school headmaster in Berlin, wrote:

> We girls don't need different books than boys because there is only one truth and only one life. Of course we would like to have books which can give us advice for life too, if only there were people who are capable of providing the advice and don't just imagine that they are capable of doing so.... That's really how we are, but only as long as it is absolutely necessary in order to be able to protect us against the horrors of the struggle for existence. But we have a far richer emotional life than our enslaved mothers and grandmothers had in their youth. We do not simulate any false feelings, nor do we deny any genuine ones.

However, what bothered those who carried out the survey more than the actual difference between boys' and girls' reading habits was the popularity of what was described as pulp literature. Working-class boys and above all girls were perceived as easy marks for such works. For example, a study which compared the fantasy world of adolescent boys from working-class families with that of boys from middle-class backgrounds argued that the fantasy world of the former was not as rich as that of their middle-class peers. The imaginations of working-class youngsters were more down-to-earth and bound up with the reality of their lives. In contrast, the fantasy world of boys from middle-class homes testified to richer imaginations and more autonomy. According to these findings, the aesthetic ideal of these fantasies on the part of the middle-class boys, compared with the practical ideal of the fantasies of the working classes, made pulp fiction more damaging for boys from a working-class background than for their middle-class contemporaries.[62]

A survey carried out at the Cologne Technical College for Women's Careers identified a similar picture of the reading habits of girls aged seventeen to twenty from different social strata. The girls from middle-class homes, whose fathers were civil servants or in the liberal professions, demonstrated a fairly refined reading pattern. Their reports mention authors such as Thomas Mann (*Buddenbrooks*), Stefan Zweig (*The Eyes of the Eternal Brother*), Tolstoy, Knut Hamsun (*Hunger*), and Remarque (*All Quiet on the Western Front*). Particularly noteworthy is the popularity of Hermann Hesse with *Siddartha*, which was apparently a best seller at the college that year. One of the (Protestant) girls who took part in the poll summarized her impressions of Hesse's book as follows:

> Hesse's language is adapted to the material through its sentence structure and expressions: it is impressive and profound. There is much in Buddhism which is beautiful, a great deal which is worthwhile for us too. But Buddha's teachings are only something for the select, his ideals cannot be implemented for the masses. For me, Buddhism is attractive. It has ideas which one can admire and about which one can be enthusiastic. However, in general we are somewhat alienated from it, because this mystical asceticism does not correspond to the European's philosophy of life.[63]

In their reading reports the girls made a point of emphasizing how important reading was for them, in particular as part of their process of growing up, which was described as a form of becoming wiser.[64] According to the women who administered the survey, no such process took place among girls from working-class circles, who remained enamored of girls' books, romantic novels, and detective stories.

Else Weickert ascribed this gap between middle-class and working-class girls to workers' living conditions. In a study she carried out in Düsseldorf in the late 1920s she showed that girls from working-class families generally read in the tram on the way to and from work or school. Even if the girls did manage to find time to read at home, overcrowding and difficult living conditions made the reading of quality literature, with the concomitant need for concentration and intellectual effort, a practically impossible task. In her opinion, this situation determined the girls' expectations of books, as expressed for example in the response to the question, "When do I like a book?"[65]

If	Number of answers
— it is exciting, thrilling	81
— it is instructive (i.e., if you can learn something from it which makes it easier to get on in life)	43
— it is funny	27
— it is varied, entertaining, about fate and characters	14
— it is sad	10
— it depicts reality, if you can "turn it into facts"	7
— it is short (little free time!)	7
— it is mysterious, supernatural	4
— it describes nature	3
— it has been on at the theater or cinema	3
— it is about real love and fidelity	3
— it has children in it	2
— it has a happy ending	1
— it makes you think of other things	1
— it varies the level of excitement	1
— it has a good style	1

A conventional interpretation of these figures saw them as conclusive proof of the relationship between living conditions and reading patterns. In other words, difficulties on a day-to-day basis encourage escapism from reality, something which is perceived as being responsible for the popularity of trashy literature among the underprivileged social classes.

Another element which undoubtedly influenced youngsters' reading patterns was curiosity with a simultaneous recoiling from the adult world. This tendency explains such things as the popularity of adolescent girls' books (*Backfischbücher*), and in particular of romantic novels, which gave many girls a glimpse into the adult world. Apparently reading this type of literature enabled girls to shake off the control of the adult world and their dependency on it for information. It provided them with a refuge which enabled them to surmount the adult world, and at the same time acted as a source of information about the world awaiting them. It is a moot point to what extent declarative reading was an expression of the creation of a special world for adolescent girls which differed categorically from the adult world's system of values and expectations. In her 1931 study, Elisebeth Lippert argued that girls developed a special language of their own, whose vocabulary and images were taken from this literature. In addition, she also highlighted the way that these writers adapted themselves to the reality of postwar life. For example, before the world war "girls' books" presented the trainee and nurse as the main activities for women, but during the postwar era different female figures began to appear as heroines in these novels, including grammar school pupils, students, journalists, and office workers.[66] However, the researcher studying these works and girls' reactions to them has the impression that the way that they relate to such things as the position of the family, the image of women, role allocation, and relationships between the sexes, or political and social matters is not so revolutionary, to a large extent reflecting contemporary limits on expectations and the bourgeois world of values, with all its complexity and contradictions.[67] Despite this state of affairs, in the eyes of contemporary educators, men and women alike, who viewed with concern girls' special reading patterns, "the beautiful world and the happy ending" which were constantly recurring motifs in many of these novels threatened to distort the girls' picture of the world and their attitudes to the realities of life awaiting them. In many ways the Frankfurt School, especially through the treatment of what the Critical Theory calls "affirmative cultural," provided the most comprehensive account of this notion of the gap between reality and the "dream world" of popular culture. For Herbert Marcuse, for instance, the most decisive feature of the "affirmative cultural" is the assertion of a better and more valuable world that must be affirmed: "a world essentially different from the factual world of the daily struggle for existence, yet realizable by every individual for himself 'from within,' without any transformation of the state of facts."[68]

Yet, Wickert's study also showed that a disparity existed between what the girls read and what they wished was available for them to read, had they been free to choose. This is the conclusion of a comparison between the reading list of 357 pupils at a Düsseldorf vocational school and the list of books which they were interested in reading, based on the following four main categories:[69]

	Actually read	Want to read
1. Pulp	5%	2%
2. Kitsch	24%	12%
3. Specific	10%	18%
4. Good books	40%	44%

According to these figures, it appears that had the girls been more flexible in their reading-related wishes, the amount of trashy literature (items 1 to 3) would have dropped by half. It must be assumed that this difference relates to ambitions to improve the girls' living conditions and transform their social milieu, as well as the girls' awareness of what the adult world expected of them. Such findings confirmed the position of especially Marxist oriented intellectuals, like Walter Benjamin, who saw the mass marketing of dreams within a class system that prevented their realization as an obvious result of the growth of industry.[70] However, these figures also show that despite fears about the proportion of the girls' reading menu constituted by trashy writing, their reading list shows that books defined as "good" (category 4) still have the edge over books classified as dubious (categories 1 to 3).

At this point, it is necessary to discuss the different criteria used to examine the various reading lists and reading reports. How, for example, did Weickert define the various categories that she used to examine the girls' reading lists? Weickert proposed the following index-based definition for the different categories:[71]

1. Pulp (Tarzan, detective stories, etc.)
2. Kitsch ("True Stories" (*Wahre Geschichte*), "True Romances" (*Wahre Romane*), Courts-Mahler, Wothe, Lene, Marlitt, etc.)
3. Specific (girls' books such as Koch, Ury, as well as Karl May)
4. Literature of questionable value (Dumas, some of Herzog's and Ganghofer's works, Voss and Biesenbach)
5. Good books

The first question that a modern reader will undoubtedly ask in light of this list is, which books fall into the category of good literature? In this instance at least it is clear that everyone is supposed to be aware of what constitutes this category of books. It would appear, however, that this rule also applied to the other categories, for here too Weickert does not offer any clear-cut criteria for defining the "trashy" literature which apparently everyone was supposed to be able to identify. There is no need to point out that had the same figures been processed on the basis of different categories, the result would have been an utterly different picture of the reading habits of the group being investigated. On the other hand, an examination of how many of the boys and girls related to the reading material shows that they were perfectly capable of distinguishing between good literature and what was considered trashy literature—a state of affairs which did not prevent many of them from continuing to read the latter.

What, then, led readers to this type of literature? The fact that they were banned from reading certain works undoubtedly acted as a significant factor in heightening their attractiveness to young people. However, a standard attitude of the time considered the popularity of these trashy works to be a reaction to contemporary social changes, i.e., the processes of accelerating industrialization and urbanization, the modern division of labor, and the tendency toward rationalizing every area of life, as well as part of the reaction to the world war. Another way of putting it is that these works were read in order to escape from the political chaos and economic hardships which continued to afflict Germany throughout the 1920s. These were viewed as processes which resulted in the dispossession of individuals' specific value, their alienation, and attempts to escape this grinding reality for good. Reading, therefore, was seen as an intimate activity which took place within the individual and was not only a way of escaping to an alternative reality and meeting the needs and desires of each individual, but also an expression of social resistance and protest in the face of contemporary realities.[72] According to contemporary studies, young people's reading habits manifestly reflected this tendency. An example of this approach is provided by the finding of a wide-ranging study carried out in 1930 at the initiative of the Prussian Welfare Ministry (*Volkswohlfahrt*), to the effect that:

> Our times, whipped up to a veritable frenzy by war, inflation and political confusion, allow the individual person no possibility whatsoever of having a major impact. An uncontrollable urge to self-realization, already present in nature, is tremendously increased by these circumstances. It is only natural to think: how does this affect young people? But young people are in the midst of life, they are not living an experience which is separate from that of adults: rather, all the forces which exert a formative influence in their lives impact on them to a greater extent. The adult seeks to drown the craving for life by becoming intoxicated—the children imitate him. For the adolescent, reading is a suitable means of doing this, because he can evade all supervision in doing so. He fills his life, which is lacking in eventfulness, with intoxicating experiences by reading about events which come fast and furious, without restraint. And anyone observing such eager readers will note unmistakable signs of a certain degree of inebriation.[73]

These studies suggested that fantasy, emotional impulses, passiveness, escaping from reality, and the absence of the political dimension were the primary characteristics of young people's reading habits, as well as those of women and workers. These groups were perceived as the three main elements which made up the primitive type of the Other, i.e., a member of the anonymous masses. These were the characteristics which constituted the background to the special interest in these groups' reading habits. However, this interest was not just an expression of intellectual curiosity or some feeling of a missionary vocation which sought to "civilize" these groups so as to integrate them in the social order: it also indicated how greatly they were feared—or to put it differently, the fear of the "dictatorship of the consumers." One of the salient expressions of this fear was the struggle against pulp fiction, as discussed above.

The Struggle against Pulp Writings (*Schund- und Schmutzschriften*)

An amazing volume of works which fall under the heading of "the struggle against pulp writings" came out in Germany between 1870 and the Nazi takeover of power. Articles in the press, pamphlets, books, lectures, exhibitions, and special journals designed to combat this form of literature, as well as calls to boycott the shops where it was sold and to burn the books in question were just some of the efforts to wage war on works which were considered to be "trash" and "pulp." The list of institutions and organizations which participated in this struggle is also impressively long. The government and local authorities, the churches, the educational system, the political parties, the different kinds of libraries, a variety of

Picture 17: The pulp reader

Picture 18: The trash fighter

cultural and moral associations, organizations set up in more than 33 cities specifically in order to wage war on pulp literature, and the Book Dealers' Association were the main bodies which set themselves the goal of combating pulp fiction and promoting good literature.[74] Practically all of Germany's state and city archives have holdings documenting this struggle. In contrast to the intensive involvement at the time with pulp literature, historical research into this phenomenon is still in its initial stages.[75] Even this present chapter will be unable to fill this enormous void. The purpose of discussing a number of aspects of the war on pulp writings will therefore be to focus attention on the importance of filling this research gap, which will undoubtedly contribute a further additional layer in the historical understanding of German society during the transitional period comprising the end of the nineteenth and the early years of the twentieth century.

Contemporaries viewed pulp literature as a social problem of the first order. The vast amount of material available to today's researcher is perhaps the best proof of fears about the destructive influence of these works, which were referred to by such terms as pulp (*Schmutz*), trash (*Schund*), smut (*Unzucht*), inferior (*untergeistige*) writings, and kitsch.

The main damage ascribed to reading these writings included corruption of values, encouraging violence, undermining the authority of religious and state authorities, offending against good taste and proper social order, distorting reality, and encouraging hedonism and speculation. Those who actively engaged in combating trash (*Schundkämpfer*), most of them educated men, saw these writings as a manifestation of a rival culture which was threatening to undermine the social order at whose head the educated male bourgeoisie had set itself. As shown earlier, it was this approach which was responsible for the interest in the reading patterns of women, workers, and youth. These groups were perceived as the weak links in the bourgeois social order, the main target audience for pulp literature and particularly vulnerable to the destructive influence of this culture.

Pulp writings therefore became the scapegoat for all of society's social ills—or to put it another way, the stratum of educated bourgeois men found it difficult to deal with them.[76] In particular pornography, homosexuality, internationalism, and capitalism were viewed as diseases of society which they blamed on the popularity of pulp literature. At the same time, these phenomena were generally associated with Judaism and the Jews. However, despite the prominence of Jews in the publishing world, an examination of the history of the war on pulp literature shows that it was not particularly marked by antisemitism. That is to say, those who in any case blamed the Jews for all of society's woes would also hold them responsible for the flourishing of pulp literature. However, this approach did not constitute a focus of the struggle against "trash," in which it was only a marginal factor. Even a magazine designed to wage war on trash such as *Hochwach,* with its manifestly nationalist leanings, did not voice antisemitic positions in its struggle against pulp literature.[77] On the contrary, during the period prior to the world war we find articles in the context of the anti-trash struggle praising the cultural virtues of the Jews and their superior taste in reading. It goes without saying that whether as individuals or organizations, Jews played an active role in this struggle both before and after the war.[78]

In the post–World War I period, when the first official lists of pulp publications were drawn up, they also contained a number of works with a manifestly national and antisemitic character. These works, which fell into the category of patriotic trashy literature (*patriotische Schundliteratur*), were banned from distribution following the coming into force of the Law for the Protection of Young People against Trash and Filth of December 1926 (referred to below as "the Law").

Despite the positive image enjoyed by the Jews in the context of the struggle against pulp writings, as well as efforts to repress works with a manifestly antisemitic character, it would be going too far to conclude that the struggle against pulp literature generally, and specifically the Law, were used as tools for combating antisemitism. Thus for example, at the end of 1928 the Rhine-Westphalia Youth Welfare Department in Düsseldorf tried to ban an issue of the Nazi Party newspaper the *Westdeutscher Beobachter,* because of an article entitled "Sex Crime in the House of Tietz." The article described in great detail indecent sexual acts allegedly perpetrated by a Jew against a German girl at the department store owned by Hermann Tietz, a Jew, in Cologne. The Düsseldorf Youth Welfare Department considered this article to be pornographic and harmful to young people, and demanded that distribution of the relevant issue of the newspaper be banned. After the application was rejected by the Berlin Examining Bureau for Trash and Filth on the grounds that banning the paper would constitute political censorship, the Chief Examining Bureau for Trash and Filth, based in the German Library in Leipzig, ruled that the need to protect young persons against corruption of moral values outweighed the defense of the freedom of political expression. However, since the article was published in a daily newspaper the Bureau ruled that the risk of corrupting youth had passed and it no longer saw fit to ban the newspaper.[79]

Antisemitism was therefore viewed as a political outlook, not a social problem. Why, given this state of affairs, did antisemitism, as an ideology which provided a response to the "social question," not play a key role in the framework of the struggle against pulp writings?[80] Undoubtedly an entire complex of factors was responsible for this situation. I would argue that a key factor was the special nature of the struggle against pulp works as what may be called "consumer discourse" rather than "producer discourse." In other words, the Jews were not viewed as one of the groups comprising the masses which were the target audience of this poor-quality literature, but rather as part of that group of producers whose power was weakened in direct proportion to the growing power of the consumer masses.[81] Examination of additional elements of the anti-pulp writing discourse will strengthen this conclusion about the fear of a dictatorship of the consumers: in other words, fear of a situation in which consumers' taste and demand would determine literary output and supply.

As the middle class grew more powerful, it also became increasingly fearful of the emancipation of the masses and loss of its own status in society. At the same time the struggle against pulp is a further expression of the view that the masses were the nation's most precious resource, which must be nurtured and shaped for its sake. However, an examination of the history of the war on pulp literature also shows that, despite the substantial efforts and resources invested in this struggle against these "inferior" writings, culminating in the Law for the Protection of Young People against Trash and Filth of December 1926, these works retained their popularity. How can this failure be explained?

It is quite possible that the very ban on reading these writings actually contributed to their popularity. From this point of view, the struggle against pulp literature found itself in a paradoxical position: on the one hand it tried to penetrate the public consciousness in order to increase awareness of the dangers inherent in reading publications of a particular kind. On the other hand, this very action constituted a vital factor in promoting sales of these publications. Publishers and distribution agents were sophisticated enough to use this anti-trash campaign as publicity material. An example is the *Gross-Berliner Neueste Nachrichten* weekly, which was defined as pornographic and in one of its issues published the following mocking exchange:

A. Is it true, Emil, that you're going to publish a new joke journal?
B. As you can see, yes. The red fliers are already ready—"Banned at railway stations."[82]

Given this state of affairs, during the period following the world war when the Prussian Interior Ministry was working on drawing up lists of banned works, there were doubts as to the status of this catalogue. Was it itself a pulp work? Should its circulation be restricted, or should it be publicized among the general public despite the risk of thereby contributing

Picture 19: In the cellar: Patience, children, there'll soon be a law against pulp writings—and you'll feel better!

to the circulation of those very works which it wished to ban? These were some of the questions which troubled those involved in drawing up the list of these proscribed works at that time.[83]

Germany's economic and social situation was also perceived as a key factor which contributed to the popularity of pulp works. At the time people considered reading an activity which reflected a given social situation and was perceived as a reaction to the hardship and distress of people's lives. This approach argued that the phenomenon of pulp works could

Picture 20: The law for the protection of young people against trash and filth: Build apartments instead of paragraphs!

only be eliminated by improving the living conditions of as many sectors of society as possible. For those who held this view, the widespread economic adversity and political instability condemned the struggle against pulp works to failure from the outset.

Another possible explanation for the failure of the struggle against pulp works is to be found in the sources on which this conclusion is based. In other words, the struggle against pulp literature assumes a priori that it is on the defensive in the face of a rampant rival culture. This viewpoint not only tends to exaggerate the scope of the danger, but sometimes also uses the extent of the threat as a justification for the struggle and the means brought into play against it. A striking expression of this tendency is to be found in estimates about the circulation of trashy publications. In 1909, for example, Ernst Schultze estimated that the Germans were spending fifty million marks a year on pulp writings.[84] Following the world war, the struggle against this form of literature received new impetus, with estimated circulation figures spiralling accordingly. The collapse of the old political order, the establishment of the Republic, the easing of censorship, as well as the prevailing economic hardships and the wave of Americanization were perceived as the primary factors which contributed to increased circulation of pulp publications. The result was that in 1920, the Dürerbund estimated that 70 percent of Germany's paper-based output was earmarked for the publication of pulp works. In 1926, Judge Hermann Popert did some calculations, and found that some two billion works which fell into the category of pulp were published in Germany every year.[85] In 1930, the Munich Examining Bureau for Trash and Filth estimated that Germans were spending around two billion marks annually on these writings.[86] These exaggerated estimates were the outcome not only of the dynamics of self-justification of the anti-trash struggle, but also of the difficulties of reaching some sort of consensus on the criteria for defining these "dangerous" writings.

In the period prior to, during, and after the world war, no categorical definition was ever issued of these works. Even the Law to Protect Young People against Trash and Filth, which followed a tortuous path until it was finally passed by a majority comprising the centrist and bourgeois right-wing parties, with opposition by the SPD and KPD, refrained from defining these writings. Instead, it left it up to the three Examining Bureaus for Trash and Filth in Berlin, Munich, and Leipzig to determine what constituted trash and filth.[87] This situation not only aroused fears about restrictions on freedom of expression and creative work, but was also responsible for the disappointment of the large numbers of people engaged in the struggle against trash who had hoped for a far more draconian law.[88] The Law was therefore seen as a compromise which the various sides found difficult to accept. However, responsibility for this situation also lay with the Weimar Republic's Constitution, which did not relate unequivocally to the issue of censorship. Section 118 of the Constitution stated that there was to be no censorship. However, apparently this referred to the abolition of precensorship only. At the same time the Constitution recommended establishing censorship for the cinema, as well as special legislation for the anti-pulp struggle, not necessarily as part of protection for young people. In other words, for those who demanded legislation, limiting the law to protecting young people only was a compromise.[89]

This ambiguous attitude to the issue of censorship is also expressed in other laws which limited the freedom of expression. Thus during the period of the Weimar Republic, blasphemy was an offense for which a number of writers were prosecuted. Karl Einstein—*Die schlimme Botschaft* (*The Sad Tidings*), Ernst Gläser—*Seele über Bord* (*Soul Overboard*), Walter Hasenclever—*Ehen werden im Himmel geschlossen* (*Marriages are Made in Heaven*), and Kurt Tucholsky—*Gesang der englischen Chorknabern* (*English Choirboys Poems*) are just a few of the writers who appeared in the dock on charges of blasphemy.[90] Both Section 184, and in particular Section 184a which was known as the Lex Heinze Code of 1900 and prohibited the dissemination of obscene writings, were adopted by the Weimar Republic's statute book. For example, in 1921 author Kurt Corrinth was found guilty of the offense of having produced an obscene work for the purpose of disseminating it.[91] He was sentenced to a fine of three hundred marks or thirty days in prison. The book's publisher, Albert A. Rossen, was ordered to pay a fine of five hundred marks or spend fifty days in prison. The court gave the following grounds for its decision:

> It may well be that an art critic or a professional writer does not feel his moral sensibilities to be offended by reading the novel *Bordell* ("Brothel") … [but] the task of the judge, who on the basis of his own expert knowledge must give his opinion on the question of *obscenity* independently goes further. He must consider whether the work is likely to transgress the views *generally* prevailing among the *people* in respect of that which is morally offensive in sexual matters. Thus the court's judgement is not based on the sensibilities of a few literary connoisseurs, but rather on the moral sensibilities which under normal, average circumstances prevail among those sectors of the population to whom the work has been made accessible.[92] (Emphasis in original)

This ruling makes it quite clear that had the novel not been disseminated to the general public, but to a limited audience of connoisseurs only, it would not have been considered obscene.[93] As we will see below, the court's distinction between a defined audience of cognoscenti on whom these writings have no influence whatsoever, and a general audience on whom these works may have a harmful effect, was just one dimension of the fear of the popularizing of those writings defined as trash and filth.

We have conflicting statistics about the total number of convictions in the 1920s under this section. According to figures published in 1926 by Reverend Reinhard Mumm, a Reichstag representative of the right-wing DNVP (Deutschnationale Volkspartei) and one of the most active figures in the anti-pulp struggle of the 1920s, it would appear that in 1921 there were ten convictions for offenses under Section 184a, and just six in 1923.[94] However, the German crime statistics for those years show far higher figures: 1,100 convictions in 1921, compared with 431 in 1923.[95] It should be noted that in order to enforce the Lex Heinze Code of 1900, from 1910 onward Germany had a Police Bureau for Combating Obscene Pictures, Writings, and Advertisements, and later a similar bureau was set up in Munich. Despite these means, those combating obscenity did not consider the law to be sufficient to curb the expansion of the phenomenon of pulp and trashy literature. As a result, they continued to demand the application of the Constitution's recommendation that special legislation be enacted in this area. In this respect the Law constitutes a further example of the Weimar Republic's tendency to interfere in as many areas of life as possible.

What is *Schund*?

Despite the absence of a definition of pulp and trashy literature, and notwithstanding the fears about the results of this situation, there was fairly broad-based agreement about the existence of these works and the need to combat them. What, then, were the writings which were commonly meant when the terms "pulp" and "trash" were used?

The difficulty in coming up with an agreed definition for these writings was generally the result of an inability to achieve consensus about the dividing line between works of art and trashy works. What was particularly problematic was the status of ethical and aesthetic characteristics as criteria for defining the dividing line between these two areas. Thus, for example, disagreement frequently arose over the status of erotic motifs, sexual preferences, or outlooks and political positions as characteristics of trash. Not so when it came to viewing trash as a product whose sole goal was obvious: profit-oriented publication. Right and left alike viewed materialism and commercialization as the key characteristics of pulp and trashy works. The "culture industry," to use here the well-known term coined by Theodor W. Adorno and Max Horkheimer, was conceived as administrating a non-spontaneous, reified, phony culture rather than a real one. As acknowledged also by Judge Hermann Popert, for example, in his book on the struggle against pulp works in Hamburg:

> I believe that it cannot honestly be denied that the memorable events recounted by Casanova inflame the sexual urges. The same applies to practically all of Balzac's "Contes Drolatiques"; it applies to Boccaccio's "Decameron," and it further applies to many of the most important manifestations of

> world literature. But I would consider a hypocrite and a fool anyone who wanted to treat a normal edition of one of these works as "trash." Because first of all every one of these works is of artistic value, and secondly the normal book edition is not intended for mass distribution. But if a resourceful publishing company with a lot of capital were to select a story by Boccaccio or Balzac—or if it were to take all of Casanova's tales—and to commission a brightly coloured, alluring cover—which would specifically tempt young people—which would excite the sexual urges, in other words, if by means of such a cover it were to utterly drown the artistic character in an appeal to sensuality—if it were to distribute this sorry effort to the masses, possibly as a "series"—then this sorry work of smutty capital should be viewed as pure unalloyed "trash" and combatted as such.[96]

According to this approach, therefore, the difference between the creation of art and pulp works lay not only in external characteristics such as distribution, form, and target audience, but also in source. To put this idea somewhat differently, the dichotomy presented here is not necessarily between "light" and "serious" culture, but rather between culture that was market-oriented and culture that was not. Thus the creation of art is perceived as something which emerges from the author's fevered brain, in isolation from his readership, in contrast to pulp and trashy works whose nature and content are determined by demand emanating from readers. Interesting this notion of the autonomy of art became a central element in the Frankfurt School of Critical Theory, which ascribed to it a significant political and social role. "Art," wrote for example Theodor W. Adorno, "and [the] so-called classical art no less than its more anarchical expressions, always was, and is, a force of protest of the humane against the pressure of domineering institutions, religious and otherwise, no less than reflects their objective substance."[97]

Especially during times of economic hardship there was a growing fear that many authors would be tempted to work for the "trash industry," whose practice was to entice writers by means of advertisements such as:

> Wanted, authors for short moral novels around 64 printed pages long. Only interested in manuscripts which will pass the censor and yet must have "that certain something".[98]

Such advertisements attracted many responses.[99] These works were viewed as a product churned out on an industrial scale in order to make profits, not as literature. Capitalism was thus perceived as a force which commodified writing, turning it to a product to be consumed by a passive audience. As a result, books were not considered as having been written at all, but rather as mechanically manufactured.[100] From this point of view the struggle against pulp works reflected a fear of the dictatorship of the consumers, i.e., fear that demand would determine supply and dictate the literary taste of the period.

The War on Supply as Opposed to the War on Demand

The most conspicuous expression of this fear of the dictatorship of the consumers is to be found in the Law itself. This laid down a prison term of up to a year and/or a fine of up to RM 10,000 only for an individual who distributed those writings which appeared on a list of pulp and trashy works. In other words, the Law refrained from punishing the producers or consumers of these works. However, the significance of focusing on their distribution was that the Law not only "protected" young people under the age of eighteen against trash works, but also prevented adults from coming into contact with such writings. In this context the ban on distributing magazines to the homosexual public is particularly noteworthy. As of the end of 1929, seven different editions of homosexual papers were included in the list of works whose distribution was proscribed, even though they were intended for an adult audience and distributed to subscribers.[101] Nevertheless, those who primarily suffered as a result of this method, which tried to combat obscene publications by limiting their distribution, were the various intermediaries who handled the distribution of reading material. It is hardly surprising that these agents, comprising bookshops (particularly those at railway stations), bookstalls, and street sellers, warned against focusing the struggle against obscene publications on the material distributed by them.[102] The argument raised time and time again in their journals was that publishers and distributors were simply the victims of the demand for this form of literature, and that in order to eradicate the phenomenon of pulp and trashy works, the struggle must focus on educating readers and changing their reading habits, instead of limiting the supply of these works. Viewing demand as the main cause determining supply, this approach sought to become the starting point of the struggle against pulp and trashy works. Furthermore, it was conventionally accepted that a link existed between limiting the supply of literary works and restricting the freedom of literary output. Thus the *Aktionsgemeinschaft für geistige Freiheit,* an organization set up in order to defend freedom of expression and artistic creation which also enjoyed the support of various intellectuals, argued, "It is only when there is free competition that a people's culture can develop. This free competition can only be envisaged in the absence of censorship."[103]

As shown in earlier chapters, the link between freedom of artistic creation, free competition, and economic liberalism was particularly cherished by people in the book trade. This nexus was generally referred to in the framework of their struggle against various attempts at reform involving the collectivization of the book trade. Examples of this included the debate over socialization at the beginning of the 1920s, or the opposition to book clubs in the mid-1920s. Even educators, who insisted that publishers and distributors alike must assume greater responsibility for the works handled by them, some even trying to increase controls over such writings, acknowledged the limits of the proscriptive struggle against trash. For them, limiting the supply of these works was just one means in the struggle to increase the demand for what was considered good literature.

Fears that the Law would adversely affect free competition in the world of print soon proved to be unjustified. The main reason for this state of affairs was to be found in the very system set up to ban the distribution of various writings by means of a list of prohibited titles.[104] When the Law came into force on 1 January 1927, this list contained 202 titles. By the end of 1932, a further 164 titles whose distribution was prohibited had been added to the list of works by the examination boards by virtue of their status as authorities with the power to rule on works of trash and filth.

However, the Law did not require publishers to submit their publications to the authorities for prior approval: instead, it banned the distribution of works subsequent to their publication. It was the responsibility of the various regional youth welfare departments to monitor what was published and to send the Examining Bureaus those works which they considered harmful to young people. In practice this process, which on average took nine months, excluded the daily press from the purview of the Law. Even when a magazine was involved, the method meant that by the time a particular title was added to the list of pulp works, an entire number of the title in question might have been sold or no longer be current. Given this situation, some even argued that in this form, the Law was actually encouraging the distribution of pulp writings.[105] At the same time, it would appear that most of the youth welfare departments made no special efforts to enforce the Law. Up to the end of 1932, no more than seven youth welfare departments had seen fit to apply to the examining bureaus for a ban on various works.[106] There was also sharp criticism about the efficiency of the various examining bureaus and the relationship between the cost of the anti-trash struggle and its results. For example, of 276 titles examined by the various bureaus up to April 1929, only 75 were added to the list of pulp and trashy works. For those combating trash, this was output on the lean side. Others drew attention to the high costs of this struggle, which exceeded one hundred thousand marks a year.[107] A Dresden daily newspaper asked in 1929 whether, in a period of such great economic hardships, the State could afford to finance such a struggle simply to limit the distribution of a number of dubious writings.[108]

Inspecting the various distribution points was also a more or less impossible task. Figures show that in 1928, 99 people were convicted of the offense of distributing works on the list of banned writings. In 1929 the number of convictions rose to 270; in 1930, it was just 80; in 1931, 93; and in 1932, only 43 convictions were obtained.[109] Available sources provide limited information about the identity and sentences of those who were found guilty. According to a report published in the Prussian Ministry for Social Welfare newsletter for the struggle against pulp and trashy works, in 1929 there was just one conviction of a bookshop owner for distributing works from the list of banned writings.[110] It is also unclear whether these figures relate solely to convictions for an offense against the Law only, or whether they also involved Section 184a, which remained in force in parallel. Thus in 1932 over thirty convictions were filed in the archives of the German National Library in Leipzig under the heading of "court rulings on pulp and trashy literature"—all of them for offenses under Section 184a,[111] i.e., the distribution of "pornography," which was just one element of the aggregate known as pulp and trashy works.

"Smut Capital" and the Bourgeoisie's Double Moral

Another factor which undoubtedly made a decisive contribution to the failure of supervising the various distribution points relates to the identity and status of the actual distributors of these works. Behind some of the distribution agents for pulp and trashy works were highly respectable book publishing houses and powerful economic interests. From this point of view, what was sometimes called "smut capital" (*Schundkapital*) even helped to finance what was considered decent culture. A publishing house such as that of George Stilke is the perfect embodiment of this situation. On the one hand, it owned a considerable proportion of the bookshops at railway stations and bookstalls in Northern Germany, locations which were considered the main distribution points for those works classified as trash. On the other hand, Stilke Publishing put out the respected liberal-national periodical called the *Preussische Jahrbücher*, and it specialized in publishing books of law and jurisprudence. Furthermore, in its jurisprudence series, a well-known jurist, Albert Hellwig, published a book containing interpretations and explanatory material on the Law. Hellwig, who had the reputation of an uncompromising opponent of pulp writings, was the most prominent representative of an approach which claimed that an unequivocal causal relationship existed between the reading of pulp works and crime. It would appear, however, that his unbending views on pulp fiction did not prevent him from having his books issued by a publishing house which derived a considerable portion of its income from the distribution of those selfsame works which he was combating; and conversely, Hellwig's extreme positions did not prevent Stilke Publishers from issuing his book.

Such double standards on the part of the male, educated, bourgeois social class, which on the one hand waged war on pulp and trashy works, and on the other enjoyed the commercial success of these works, undoubtedly constituted another factor which weakened the struggle against pulp and trashy works. However, this approach, which differentiated between the bourgeoisie's economic and cultural interests, viewing them as separate and mutually antagonistic areas, also constituted the background to a desire to reconcile the ideal of promoting good culture with the princi-

Picture 21: I fight against pulp writings—and my maid pinched my Casanova!

ple of production for the sake of consumption: or to put it another way, to bridge the gap between the bourgeoisie's economic and cultural capital through a popular culture which the stratum of educated bourgeois males tried to prescribe. In other words, a form of culture, as the anti-trash campaign periodical of a Protestant young men's association put it, which would defeat the three Ms—*Mammon, Macht, Masse* (money, might, and masses) by means of the three Gs—*Geist, Gewissen, Gesinnung* (mind, conscience, and attitude).[112] From this point of view the struggle against pulp and trashy works was not only an expression of the struggle between two competing cultures, but also a struggle over the very nature of bourgeois culture itself. This diagnosis is bolstered by an examination of the readership of those works which were defined as pulp and trash.

Who reads *Schund*?

A standard approach in studies of the struggle against pulp and trashy works to a large extent adopted the viewpoint of the anti-pulp struggle itself. In this approach, pulp and trashy works are seen as an expression of alternative culture which was dictated primarily by the needs of women, blue-collar workers, and young people. For example, Detlev Peukert argued that the protracted efforts of middle-class educators and the labor movement to combat pulp and raise the working classes' cultural level had actually resulted in a widening of the gap between the workers' day-to-day experiences and the culture which they sought to instill. Inevitably, the upshot of this situation was that working-class culture as the culture of the labor movement was remote from the popular culture of the workers.[113]

Kaspar Maase proposes a different approach to examining the phenomenon of works of pulp and trash among young people. Maase analyzes these writings as an expression of autonomous youth culture. Their popularity, and above all the way that readers organized themselves in fan clubs, developing a variety of methods for swapping these publications between readers, were perceived by Maase as an expression of how this commercialized/popular culture made possible the creation of a unique cultural space for young people which was managed without adult intervention. The extent to which this secondary youth culture differed from the official culture which the adult world wished to instill in the younger generation is open to various interpretations. According to Maase, at the very least the struggle against pulp and trashy works was an expression of the bourgeois world's fear of the democratization of culture and the deforming of society by young people and their special culture.[114] However, if Maase's assertion is correct, it should not be considered to be the outcome solely of relationships between the adult world and young people, or between men and women, or the middle classes and the working classes. In other words, any future analysis of the various manifestations of commercialized culture cannot ignore the contribution that the middle-class strata themselves made to its development.

The conclusion that the middle classes were not lacking in connections with the written commercialized culture is not based solely on these social strata's contribution, as producers of culture, to the formation of this culture: it also takes account of their active participation in this process as consumers. Wherever trashy writings were distributed—railway stations, kiosks, department stores, groceries, tobacconists' shops, commercial lending libraries, barbers' shops, street traders—the paths of all kinds of people from every imaginable social background crossed. This being the case, it was not reasonable to assume that responsibility for the popularity of those writings which were defined as pulp and trash lay solely with certain social strata in isolation from all other strata. This conclusion is underpinned by a great deal of contemporary evidence. Elisabeth Lippert, for example, describes the different ways that adolescent girls managed to get hold of the much-vilified teenage girls' books ("Backfischbücher"). Apparently many girls received these books as "hand-me-downs" from aunts and big sisters, or as birthday and Christmas presents. Heinrich Benfer, an educator, to quote another example, criticized the double standards of many parents who themselves read "inferior" literature, while at the same time forbidding their children to read the same.[115] Others cautioned against the popularity of mystical literature after the world war, particularly among middle-class women. Examination of the journals of bookshop owners at railway stations and street newspaper sellers also reveals a far more varied picture of the consumers of works defined as pulp and trash. Apparently when preparing for a train trip, even educated middle-class men whose bookshelves at home held only quality books bought publications which fell into the category of pulp and trashy works. It would therefore appear that even these population strata were also interested in such "inferior" works.[116]

These reports also indicate that during the 1920s, the public's reading tastes varied and so concomitantly did their reading menu. Thus for example, in the immediate post–World War period, pornography was especially popular; in the early 1920s detective novels and reports of trials attracted the attention of the reading public[117]; while later in the decade sports became increasingly popular. This evidence, however, does not allow us to make distinctions in respect of different social groups' tastes in reading. We can, however, state for example that books hawked by peddlers ("colporteur novels") were particularly popular in small towns and among suburban shop owners and the lower-middle classes; books about Indians were read especially by adolescent boys; romantic novels were read overwhelmingly by women from the urban middle classes; and detective stories were popular with the middle classes, intellectuals, and the higher strata of the working class.[118]

Although we will find it difficult at this stage to determine how the middle classes, and in particular the stratum of educated males, adopted those writings which have been defined as pulp and trash, there is no reason whatsoever to exclude them from the general public which contributed to the success of this commercialized culture.[119] What this means is that this popular culture created a space which enabled members of different social strata and groups, including the male educated bourgeoisie, to throw off the shackles of social conventions and give expression to desires which did not necessarily fit in with the social reality surrounding them. Inter alia this tendency, which as has been pointed out did not escape the scrutiny of contemporary observers, was responsible for a twofold fear: that a process of fragmentation would occur with a subsequent further widening of gaps in an already divided German society; and at the same time that the differences between different social strata would be blurred with the resultant formation of a mass society in which the male educated bourgeois elite would lose its influence.[120]

Disintegrating Bourgeoisie and the Transition to a Middle-Class Lifestyle

This antagonistic process of homogenization vs. heterogenization therefore provided the background to the constant feeling that existed from the end of the nineteenth century and continued into the twentieth century that the bourgeoisie was disintegrating. Hence the struggle against pulp and trash was not just an expression of a fear of losing cultural hegemony in the wake of the dictatorship of the consumers, or part of the struggle for the nature of bourgeois culture: rather, it became a factor in the construction of bourgeois identity itself. In other words, those social strata which were largely credited with the process of commercializing culture in particular, and the rise of the consumer society in general, made the struggle against this process one of the characteristics of their lifestyle. In this sense, the struggle against pulp and trash can be seen as a version of the Foucaultian spiral of power which views sexual pleasure and its repression as two processes which complement and encourage each other.[121]

The importance of the struggle against pulp and trash therefore lies in the struggle itself. The anti-pulp struggle was not merely a form of cultural action embodying only fears and anxieties about diverse social processes, or a mechanism intended to curb the popularization of works defined as harmful. The true importance of the struggle against pulp and trashy works is to be found in the instilling of a system of concepts which provided a hierarchical perception of the social reality. In this sense, the struggle against pulp and trashy works was a mechanism which helped strengthen the feeling of bourgeois subjectiveness. As such, the success of the struggle lay substantially in the very existence of the struggle itself. Notably, the system of concepts which it coined to a large extent determined German society's relationship with commercialized popular culture until the 1960s, if not later.

We can therefore conclude that the above discussion of reading studies and the struggle against pulp and trashy works has revealed a social reality which is far more complex than might have originally been expected. In addition, the analysis has shown that, in contrast to the argument that recurred throughout the chapter on the "book crisis" concerning the crumbling of book-reading culture, reading was not a dying phenomenon. In other words, it was not the shrinking of demand for reading, but rather the type of demand which constituted the problem that concerned those groups which assumed responsibility for education and the dissemination of culture in society. In particular following the world war, a period when contemporary critics identified the phenomenon of a "thirst for reading," interest in reading actually intensified. Reading was perceived as a private-domain activity, which not only reflected a given social reality but also, by virtue of its intervention in that reality, had the power to change it. Studies of reading and the struggle against pulp and trashy works therefore tried to shape reading habits in a period when reading was no longer an activity identified with a particular social class, but had instead become part of the reality of life of all social strata. Interest in the reading habits of specific groups in German society was therefore part of the attempt to shape and disseminate a lifestyle among these classes, and it reflected the social power relationships of the period: i.e., the dominance of the educated male stratum.

Notes

1. See for example: Julius Wagner, "Experimentelle Beiträge zur Psychologie des Lesens," Ph.D. diss., University of Leipzig, 1918; Otto Heigl, "Untersuchungen Über das Lesen und die Zahlauffassung sowie deren Beeinflussung durch Tee," *Archiv für die gesamte Psychologie* 69 (1928), 257–299; Hans Thorner, "Experimentelle Untersuchungen zur Psychologie des Lesens," *Archiv für die gesamte Psychologie* 70 (1929), 127–184.
2. On this literature cf. Johan Goldfried, *Geschichte des Deutschen Buchhandels* (Leipzig: Verlag des Börsenvereins der Deutschen Buchhändler, 1913); Karl Bömer, *Bibliographisches Handbuch der Zeitungswissenschaft* (Leipzig: Otto Harrassowitz, 1929); *Wolfenbütteler Bibliographie zur Geschichte des Buchwesens in deutschen Sprachgebieten 1840–1980* (Munich: Saur, 1990ff).
3. The data are from: Wakther Heide, ed., *Presse-Dissertationen an deutschen Hochschulen 1885–1938* (Leipzig: Verlag des Börsenvereins, 1940).
4. On the history of this Institute: Friedrich Uhlig, "Der erste Hochschul-Lehrstuhl für Buchhandelsbetrielehre," and "Das Seminar für Buchhandelsbetriebslehre an der Handels-Hochschule Leipzig," both in: idem, ed., *Buchhandel und Wissenschaft* (Gütersloh: Bertelsmann Verlag, 1965), 31–73; Ewa Tomicka-Krumrey, "Gerhard Menz—Buchhandelsbetriebslehre und Wirtschaftsjournalismus an der Handelshochschule Leipzig," *Wissenschaftliche Zeitschrift* 19 (1992), 104–110.

5. *Bericht der Notgemeinschaft der Deutschen Wissenschaft über ihre Tätigkeit bis zum 31. März 1922* (Wittenberg: Herrofe & Ziemsen, 1922), 5; Gerald Feldman, "The Politics of Wissenschaftspolitik in Weimar Germany: A Prelude to the Dilemmas of Twentieth-Century Science Policy," in: Charles Maier, ed., *Changing Boundaries of the Political. Essays on the Evolving Balance Between the State and Society, Public and Private in Europe* (Cambridge: Cambridge University Press, 1987), 255–285; idem, *The Great Disorder: Politics, Economics and Society in the German Inflation 1914–1924* (Oxford: Oxford University Press, 1997), 542.
6. On the close working relationship of the two institutes: *Buch und Gesellschaft* (Berlin: Hilger Verlag, 1927), 24.
7. His most important research work from this period is Walter Hofmann, "Die Organisation des Ausleihdienstes in der modernen Bildungsbibliothek," *Volksbildungsarchiv* 1 (1910), 55–72, 227–344; 2 (1911), 29–131; 3 (1913), 319–374.
8. Walter Hofmann, *Der Weg zum Schrifttum. Gedanke und Verwirklichung der deutschen volkstümlichen Bücherei* (Berlin: Verlag d. Arbeitsgemeinschaft, 1922); Wolfgang Thauer, ed., *Die Öffentliche Bücherei der Weimarer Zeit* (Wiesbaden: Harassowitz, 1984), Ch. II.
9. On this see also: Martyn Lyons, "New Readers in the Nineteenth Century: Women, Children, Workers," in: Guglielmo Cavallo and Roger Chartier, eds., *A History of Reading in the West* (Amherst: University of Massachusetts Press, 1999), 313–344.
10. Edward Said, "Representing the Colonized: Anthropology's Interlocutors," *Critical Inquiry* 15 (1989), 207.
11. Rolf Engelsing, *Der Bürger als Leser* (Stuttgart: J.B. Metzlersche Verlagsbuchhandlung, 1974), 299.
12. Ian Watt, *The Rise of the Novel* (London: Penguin, 1957); Janice A. Radway, *Reading the Romance* (Chapel Hill: University of North Carolina Press, 1984); idem, "Interpretive Communities and Variable Literacies," in: Chandra Mukerji, and Michael Schudson, ed., *Rethink Popular Culture* (Berkeley: University of California Press, 1991), 465–486; Heidi Beutin, *"Als eine Frau lesen lernte, trat die Frauenfrage in die Welt"* (Hamburg: Bockel Verlag, 1995).
13. Walter Hofmann, *Die Lektüre der Frau* (Leipzig: Quellen & Meyer, 1931).
14. Ibid, 9–14. This picture repeats itself in public libraries in other areas in Germany. For example, reports from the public library of the city of Mülheim on the Ruhr show that more than 50 percent of the readers of the library were men while only 30 percent were women. From: *Berichte der Stadtbücherei Mülheim a.d. Ruhr.*
15. On this: Walter Hallbauer, "Die Frau und die volkstümliche Bücherei," *Hefte für Büchereiwesen* 10 (1925–1926), 190–198; Heinrich Benfer, *Schundkampf und literarische Jugendpflege* (Angensalza:Verlag von Julius Beltz, 1932), 32.
16. Susanne Suhr, *Die weiblichen Angestellten* (Berlin: Zentralverlag des Angestelltenbund, 1930), 46; Rudolf Braun, "Was sie lesen: Drei Stenotypistinnen," *Frankfurter Zeitung* (21.4.1929).
17. Lydia Lueb, "Die Freizeit der Textilarbeiterinnen. Eine Untersuchung über die Verwendung der Freizeit der Arbeiterinnen des christlichen Textilarbeiterverbandes Bezirk Westfalen," Ph.D. diss., University of Münster, 1929, 30; cf. also Alf Lüdtke, ed., *Mein Arbeitstag—Mein Wochenende. Arbeiterinnen berichten von ihrem Alltag 1928* (Hamburg: Ergebnisse Verlag, 1991).
18. Explanations of the abbreviations: *Adv*—Voyages, tales of colonial adventures, etc.; *Anim*—Animal tales; *Count*—Contemporary, social novels and novels of manners; *Folk*—Tales of village life, novels of the soil, folk tales; *His*—Historical novels and tales; *Hum*—Anecdotes, comical tales, amusing short stories; *Ind*—About individuals and destiny (the psychological pedagogical novel); *Life*—Lifestyles and folkways of foreign peoples; *Loc*—Modern regional tales of general significance; *Meist*—The essence of things German in tales of the German Meister; *Misc*—Miscellaneous; *Rom*—Classical heritage and Romanticism.
19. Hofmann, *Die Lektüre der Frau*, 35.

20. Hofmann, *Die Lektüre der Frau,* 36.
21. Hofmann, *Die Lektüre der Frau,* 177. The figures for male readers come from the Walter Hofmann archive file named *'Schöne Literatur. Autorenliste'* II KS.
22. Hofmann, *Die Lektüre der Frau,* 193.
23. Klara Geppert, *Frauenbücher.* Eine Auswahl unterhaltender, praktischer und belehrender Bücher aus dem Erlebens- und Arbeitsgebiet der Frau (Leipzig: Deutsche Zentralstelle für volkstümliches Büchereiwesen, 1930)..
24. On library catalogues as means of controlling and shaping of knowledge: Armando Petrucci, "Reading to Read: A Future for Reading," in: Guglielmo Cavallo and Roger Chartier, eds., *A History of Reading in the West* (Amherst: University of Massachusetts Press, 1999), 348–352.
25. Theodor Geiger, "Zur Kritik der arbeiterpsychologischen Forschung," *Die Gesellschaft* 8 (1932), 239. On the problem of representation in modern anthropology: Johannes Fabian, *Time and The Other* (New York: Colombia University Press, 1983); idem, "Presence and Representation: The Other and Anthropological Writing," *Critical Inquiry* 16 (1990), 753–772.
26. Erich Thier (1902–1968) was a student of the famous sociologists Theodor Litt and Hans Freyer at the University of Leipzig. He wrote his dissertation on *Rodbertus, Lassalle und Adolf Wagner.* During his studies, he started working as a librarian and a researcher at Hofmann's Institute. After the Second World War he decided to become an Evangelical minister. More on Thier can be found in his denazification documents in: Heidelberg Universitätsarchiv, Erich Thier, Pa 6073.
27. Erich Thier, *Gestaltwandel des Arbeiters im Spiegel seiner Lektüre. Ein Beitrag zu Volkskunde und Leserführung* (Leipzig: Otto Harrassowitz, 1939).
28. For a similar research study on the historical consciousness of schoolchildren, Kurt Sontag, *Das geschichtliche Bewußtsein des Schülers* (Erfurt: Verlag Kurt Stenger, 1932). Important work on the subject of working-class reading habits has been done mainly in England: Richard Hoggart, *The Uses of Literacy* (Boston: Beacon Press, 1966); David Vincent, *Bread Knowledge & Freedom* (London: Methuen, 1981); idem, *Literacy and Popular Culture* (Cambridge: Cambridge University Press, 1989); Jonathan Rose, *Intellectual Life of the British Working Classes* (New Haven: Yale University Press, 2001).
29. Other definitions can be found under the terms Arbeiter and Proletariat in: Otto Brunner, Werner Conze and Reinhard Koselleck, eds., *Geschichtliche Grundbegriffe* (Stuttgart: klett-Cotta, 1972).
30. This state of affairs is worthy of further consideration, because Leipzig had a fairly well-developed network of workers' libraries which provided an alternative for these population strata. On workers' libraries in Germany: Reinhard Buchwald, *Die Bildungsinteressen der deutschen Arbeiter* (Tübingen: J.C.B. Mohr, 1934); Dietrich Langewiesche and Klaus Schoenhoven, "Arbeiterbibliotheken und Arbeiterlektüre im Wilhelminischen Deutschland," *Archiv für Sozialgeschichte* 16 (1976), 132–204; Peter Vodesk, *Arbeiterbibliotheken und Öffentliche Bibliotheken* (Berlin: Deutscher Bibliothekverband, 1975); Felicitas Marwinski, *Sozialdemokratie und Volksbildung. Leben und Wirkung Gustav Hennigs als Bibliothekar* (Munich: K.G. Saur, 1994).
31. On the special character of the working class in Leipzig: Thomas Adam, *Arbeitermilieu und Arbeiterbewegung in Leipzig 1880 bis 1933* (Cologne: Bölau, 1999).
32. Abbreviations: *Art*—Visual arts; *Bio*—Biographies; *Com*—Commerce; *Coun*—Countries and ethnology; *Gar*—Home and garden; *Hist*—History; *Hyg*—Hygiene; *Lang*—Writing and Language; *Leis*—Handicrafts, sports, games; *Lit*—Literature and drama; *Loc*—Local history; *Math*—Mathematics; *Mil*—Military science; *Mus*—Music; *Nat*—Natural sciences; *Ped*—Education and teaching; *Phil*—Philosophy; *Rel*—Religion; *Soc*—Social sciences; *Sold*—War memoirs; *Tech*—Technology; *Trav*—Travel.
33. On the intensive character of the worker reading habits see also Martyn Lyons, "New Readers in the Nineteenth Century," 331–342.
34. The absolute number of loans appears in brackets.

35. According to Hofmann, *Die Lektüre der Frau,* the number of academic readers in these years was 2,210 or 6 percent of the readership with 43,087 loans or 5 percent of the total number of loans.
36. Georg v. Below, *Die deutsche Geschichtsschreibung von den Befreiungskriegen bis zu unseren Tagen* (Munich: Verlag R. Oldenbourg, 1924), 69.
37. On this issue see Rose, *Intellectual Life.*
38. Despite the intensive theoretical work on reader responses, the empirical research into this question is still at its beginnings. For an attempt in this direction by Jonathan Rose, *Intellectual Life,* and also Jonathan Rose, "Rereading the English Common Reader: A Preface to the History of Audiences," *Journal of the History of Ideas* 53 (1992), 47–70.
39. Ludwig Tureck, *Ein Prolet erzählt* (Berlin: Malik-Verlag, 1929).
40. All quotations are from Thier's manuscript.
41. On different types of working-class readers: Walter Hofmann, *Lesetypen innerhalb der erwachsenen männlichen Arbeiterschaft* (Leipzig: Deutsche Zentralstelle für volkstümliches Büchereiwesen, 1928); Karl Kossow, "Was liest der deutsche Arbeiter?" *Die Literatur* 29 (1926–1927), 503–505.
42. Joseph Roth, "Privatleben des Arbeiters," *Frankfurter Zeitung* (10.4.1926).
43. Alfred Kleinberg, *Ratschläger für Arbeiterbuchwarte* (Karlsbad: Graphia, 1924); Wilhelm Scheffen, ed., *Buch und Arbeiter* (Gotha: Verlag Friedrich Andreas Perthes, 1924).
44. Scattered analysis of this data can be found in: Gisela Wilkending, *Literaturpädagogik in Kaiserzeit* (Paderborn: Schöning, 1982); Detlev Peukert, *Jugend zwischen Krieg und Krise* (Cologne: Bund-Verlag, 1987); idem, *Grenze der Sozialdisiplinierung* (Cologne: Bund Verlag, 1986); Jürgen Reulecke, "Jugend und 'Junge Generation' in der Gesellschaft der Zwischenkriegszeit," in: Dieter Langewische and Heinz-Elmar Tenorth, eds., *Handbuch der deutschen Bildungsgeschichte,* vol. 5 (Munich: C.H. Beck, 1989), 86–110.
45. *Kannst Du ein Buch empfehlen?* Zum Schülerpreisausschreiben des Börsenvereins der Deutschen Buchhändler Leipzig (Leipzig: Verlag des Börsenvereins der Deutschen Buchhändler, 1928), 6. On this survey: Willhelm Fronemann, "Das Buch im Urteil des Kindes und Jugendlichen," *Börsenblatt für den Deutschen Buchhandel* 95 (1928), 1396–1398, and 96 (1929), 9–16.
46. Cf. for example: Albert Rumpf, *Kind und Buch. Das Lieblingsbuch der deutschen Jugend zwischen 9 und 16 Jahren* (Berlin: Dömmels Verla, 1928), 60–82, 118–122.
47. Fronemann, Das Buch. For a different approach: Erich Sielaff, "Was lesen unsere Jungmädchen, und was sollen sie lesen?" *Bücherei und Bildungspflege* 10 (1933), 1–23.
48. On Löns: Marianne Weil, "Der Wehrwolf von Hermann Löns," in: idem, ed., *Wehrwolf und Biene Maja. Der deutsche Bücherschrank zwischen den Kriegen* (Berlin: Edition Mythos, 1986), 203–227.
49. *Kannst Du ein Buch empfehlen?* 7.
50. For example, in 1927 a similar competition was held with an unspecified public of readers being asked, "Which twelve books written during the last three generations should be in every educated German's home library?" in: *Nimm und Lies!,* 5 (1927), 8. In all, 708 replies (507 by men and 201 by women) provide a rather interesting picture of the literary canon, which does not for example include Goethe and Schiller. The list is headed by Gottfried Keller, followed by Gustav Freytag, Bismarck, Nietzsche, Wilhelm Raabe, and Theodor Strum.
51. *Was wir vom Buch erwarten!* Antworten der 15- bis 20jähr. Mädchen (Leipzig: Börsenverein der Deutschen Buchhändler, 1931).
52. On this research cf. Wilhelm Fronemann, *Das Erbe Wolgas. Ein Querschnitt durch die heutige Jugendschriftenfrage* (Langensalza: Verlag von Julius Beltz, 1927); Sevrin Rüttgers, *Literarische Erziehung. Ein Versuch über die Jugendschriftenfrage auf soziologischer Grundlage* (Langensalza: Verlag von Julius Beltz, 1931).
53. Willhelm Gensche, "Was liest unsere Jugend?" in: idem, Herta Siemering and Erna Barschak, *Was liest unsere Jugend?* (Berlin: Decker's Verlag, 1930), 44.
54. Robert Dinse, *Das Freizeitleben der Großstadtjugend* (Berlin: R. Müller, 1932), 45.

55. Ilse Weickert, *Das Lese-Interesse der werktätigen Mädchen zwichen 14 und 18* (Bonn: Ludwig Röhrscheid, 1933), 23.
56. On the reading habits of youth in Catholic areas see Gensche, *Was liest unsere Jugend.*
57. Gensche, *Was liest unsere Jugend,* 62, 76.
58. Heinrich Benfer, *Kampf dem schlechten durch das gute Buch* (Dortmund: Ruhfus Verlag, 1926), 46; Elsa Maß and Ernst Seeger, *Gesetz zur Bewahrung der Jugend vor Schund- und Schmutzschriften* (Berlin: Carl Heymanns Verlag, 1927), 12; Georg Jäger, "Der Kampf gegen Schund- und Schmutz," *Archiv für Geschichte des Buchwesens* 33 (1988), 165; Dieter Richter, "Die Verfolgten Abenteurer. Lese- und Detektivbände von Jugendlichen in der Zeit vor dem Ersten Weltkrieg. Ein Fallstudie," in: Rainer Notleinus, ed., *Alltag, Traum und Utopie* (Essen: Klartext, 1988), 101–110; Kasper Maase, "Kinder als Fremde—Kinder als Feinde. Halbwächsige, Massenkultur und erwachsene im Wilhelminischen Kaiserreich," *Historische Anthropologie* 4 (1996), 93–126.
59. On the popularity of sports: Hans Wingender, *Bekämpfung von Schmutz- und Schundliteratur, Bewahrung der Jugend vor Schund- und Schmutzschriften* (Düsseldorf: Verlag des Landesjugendamts, 1928).
60. Philipp Künkele, "Vom Sporterleben unserer Vierzehnjährigen," 6 *Die Leibesübungen* (1930), 339.
61. Mathilde Kelchner and Ernst Lau, *Die Berliner Jugend und die Kriminalliteratur* (Leipzig: Verlag von Johan Ambrosius Barth, 1928), 78; Hans Bosse, *Das literarische Verständis der werktätigen Jugend zwischen 14 und 18* (Leipzig: Verlag von Johan Ambrosius Barth, 1923), Ch. II; Elisabeth Lippert, *Der Lesestoff der Mädchen in der Vorpubertät* (Erfurt: Verlag Kurt Stenger, 1931), 100.
62. Hubert Jung, *Das Phantasieleben der männlichen werktätigen Jugend* (Münster: Helios-Verlag, 1930), 106.
63. From: "Bücher, die mich fesselten," *Westdeutsche Blätter für Büchereiberatung* 2 (1930), 60.
64. Ibid.
65. Weickert, *Das Lese-Interesse,* 30.
66. Malte Dahrendorf, *Das Mädchenbuch und seine Leserin* (Weinheim: Beltz, 1978); Diana Voigt-Firon, *Das Mädchenbuch im Dritten Reich* (Cologne: Pahl-Rugenstein Verlag, 1989); Carmen Wulf, *Mädchenliteratur und weibliche Sozialisation* (Frankfurt a.M., Peter Lang, 1996).
67. Bettina Hurrelmann, *Jugendliteratur und Bürgerlichkeit* (Paderborn: Ferdinand Schöningh, 1974); idem, "Stand und Aussichten der historischen Kinder und Jugendliteraturforschung," *Internationaesl Archiv für Sozialgeschichte der deutschen Literatur* 16 (1992), 105–142; Helga Brandes, *Politische Mythen und Symbole im Mädchenbuch der Gründerzeit* (Oldenbourg: Bibliotheksgesellschaft Oldenbourg, 1993); Dagmar Grenz, *Mädchenliteratur* (Stuttgart: Metzler, 1981); idem and Gisela Wilkending, eds., *Geschichte der Mädchenlektüre* (Weinheim: Juveta Verlag, 1997); Otto Kreiner, *Das Triviale Abendteuer* (Wien: Jung und Volk, 1980); Inge Marßolek, "Internationalität und kulturelle Klischees am Beispiel der John-Kling-Heftromane der 1920er und 1930er Jahren," in: idem, Alf Lüdtke, and Adelheid v. Saldern, eds., *Amerikanisierung. Traum und Alptraum im Deutschland des 20. Jahrhundert* (Stuttgart: Steiner Verlag, 1996), 144–160.
68. Quoted in: Martin Jay, *The Dialectical Imagination: A History of the Frankfurt School and the Institute of Social Research, 1923–1950* (Boston: Little, Brown and Company, 1973), 180.
69. Weickert, *Das Lese-Interesse,* 29.
70. Susan Buck-Morss, *The Dialectics of Seeing: Walter Benjamin and the Arcades Project* (Cambridge, Mass.: The MIT Press, 1989), 284.
71. Weickert, *Das Lese-Interesse,* 25.
72. For a modern formulation of this thesis see Maase, Kinder als Fremde, and Morg Shiach, *Discourse on Popular Culture* (Cambridge: Polity Press, 1989).
73. Gensche, Was liest unsere Jugend, p. 56.
74. "Organisationen, Vereine etc. zur Bekaempfung der Schund- und Schmutzschriften," in: Geheimes Staatsarchiv Preußischer Kulturbesitz. Berlin, Rep 77 Tit 2772 No. 12.

75. Many articles have been written on this subject, yet we still have no comprehensive analysis of this complex phenomenon. Rudolf Schenda, "Schundliteratur und Kriegsliteratur," in: idem, *Die Lesestoffe der Kleinen Leute* (Munich: C.H. Beck, 1976), 78–104; Robin J.V. Leman, "Art, Society, and the Law in Wilhelmine Germany: the Lex Heinze," *Oxford German Studies* 7 (1973), 86–113; Gary Stark, "Pornography, Society, and the Law in Imperial Germany," *Central European History* 14 (1981), 200–229; Kaspar Maase and Wolfgang Kaschuba, eds., *Schund und Schönheit. Populär Kultur um 1900* (Cologne: Böhlau, 2001); Kaspar Maase, "Die soziale Konstruktion der Massenkünste: Der Kampf gegen Schmutz- und Schund 1907–1918," in: Martina Papenbrock, ed., *Kunst und Sozialgeschichte* (Pfaffenweiler: Centarus-Verlag, 1995), 262–278. For the post–World War I period: Klaus Petersen, *Zensur in der Weimarer Republik* (Stuttgart: Verlag Metzler, 1995); Detlev Peukert, "Der Schund- und Schmutzkampf als 'Sozialpolitik der Seele'," in: Hermann Haarmann, Walter Huder, Klaus Siebenhaar, eds., *"Das war ein Vorspiel nur…" Bücher Verbrenung in Deutschland 1933* (Berlin: Akademie Verlag der Künste, 1983), 51–63; Stephan Füssel, "Vom Schaufenstergesetz zur Bücherverbrennung," *Buchhandelsgeschichte* 10 (1992–1993), 55–64; Margaret F. Stieg, "The 1926 German Law to Protect Youth against Trash and Filth: Moral Protectionism in a Democracy," *Central European History* 23 (1990), 22–56; Kaspar Maase, "Der Schundkampf Ritus," in: Rolf W. Berdnich and Walter Hartinger, eds., *Gewalt in der Kultur* (Passau: Pasauer Studien zur Volkskunde, 1994), 511–524; Horst Heidtmann, "Von der 'Schmutz- und Schund' Bekämpfung zur 'Ausmerzung von Büchern'," in: Manfred Komorowski and Peter Vodosek, eds., *Bibliotheken während des Nationalsozialismus* (Wiesbaden: Harrassowitz, 1989), 389–397; Robin Lenman, "Mass Culture and the State in Germany 1900–1926," in: Roger J. Bullen, Hartmut Pogge v. Strandmann Pogge, and A.B. Polonsky, eds., *Ideas into Politics. Aspects of European History 1880–1950* (New Jersey: 1984), 51–59; Winfried Speitkampf, "Jugendschutz und Kommerzielle Interessen. Schunddebatte und Zensur in der Weimarer Republik," in: Hartmut Berghoff, ed., *Konsumpolitik.* Die Regulierung des privaten Verbrauchs im 20. Jahrhundert (Göttingen: Vandenhoevk & Ruprecht, 1999), 47–75; Sarah L. Leonard, "The Literary Dangers of the City: Policing 'Immoral Books' in Berlin, 1850–1880," in: Malcolm Gee and Tim Kirk, eds., *Printed Matters. Printing, Publishing and Urban Culture in Europe in the Modern Period* (Aldershot: Ashgate, 2002). Further references are to be found in: http://www.schmutzundschund.de/Explorer/Einleitung/literatur.pdf
76. Schenda, Schundliteratur und Kriegsliteratur, 95.
77. On this magazine and its publisher Karl Brunner, who became famous after the war as the Weimar Republic film censor, cf. Paul Samuleit, "Aus der Geschichte des Kampfes gegen den Schund," in: idem and Hans Brunckhorst, eds., *Geschichte und Wege der Schundbekämpfung* (Berlin: Carl Heymanns Verlag, 1922), 3–22.
78. Schenda, Schundliteratur und Kriegsliteratur, 172; Gabriele v. Glasenapp and Michael Nagel, *Das jüdische Jugendbuch* (Stuttgart: Verlag Metzler, 1996), 103.
79. Archiv der Deutschen Bücherei Leipzig, 351/4/1, Protokolle der Oberprüfstelle für Schund- und Schmutzliteratur 1929, 13. Cf. also Hans Wingender, *Erfahrungen im Kampf gegen Schund- und Schmutzschriften* (Düsseldorf: self-published by the author, 1929), 50–54.
80. On the "Social Question" and antisemitism: Shulamit Volkov, "Antisemitism as a Cultural Code: Reflection on the History and Historiography of Antisemitism in Imperial Germany," *Leo Baeck Year Book* 23 (1978), 25–46; Moshe Zimmermann, "Die 'Judenfrage' als 'die soziale Frage.' Zu Kontinuität und Stellenwert des Antisemitismus vor und nach dem Nationalsozialismus," in: Christoph Dipper, Rainer Hudemann and Jens Petersen, eds., *Faschismus und Faschism im Vergleich* (Cologne: HS-Verlag, 1998), 149–163.
81. I elaborate on this in: Gideon Reuveni, "'Productivist' and 'Consumerist' Narratives Regarding Jews in German History," in: Neil Gregor, Nils Roemer, and Mark Roseman, eds., *German History from the Margins* (forthcoming in Indiana University Press).
82. Geheimes Staatsarchiv Preußischer Kulturbesitz, Berlin, Rep 77 Tit 2772 Vol. 1 No. 5, 134.
83. Geheimes Staatsarchiv Preußischer Kulturbesitz, Berlin, Rep 77 Tit 2772 Vol. 1 No. 7.

84. Quoted by Schenda, Schundliteratur und Kriegsliteratur, 87. At the time Schultze's book was considered the standard work on the subject. By 1925 three editions had appeared. Ernst Schultze, *Die Schundliteratur. Ihr Wesen. Ihr Folgen. Ihre Bekämpfung* (Halle: Verlag Buchhandlung des Waisenhauses, 1909).
85. Hermann Popert, *Hamburg und der Schundkampf* (Hamburg: Deutsche Gedächtnisstiftung, 1926), 5.
86. These inflated evaluations were also criticized by contemporary commentators. For example, one bookshop owner did some calculations and found that in order to reach this figure, each adult German—whose numbers he estimated at fourty million out of a total of sixty million Germans—would have to spend fifty marks a year on purchases of such works. As we have seen in the chapter on reading budgets, this figure is far higher than the amount which any well-off family in Germany spent on reading material during this period. From: Norbert Lutz, "Welche Menge Schund- und Schmutzliteratur gibt es in Deutschland?" *Börsenblatt für den Deutschen Buchhandel* 97 (1930), 468.
87. The Bureau in Leipzig served as a higher instance. Many famous writers and intellectuals like Thomas und Heinrich Mann, Ernst Toller, Lion Feuchtwanger, Walter von Molo, Theodor Lessing, Hugo v. Hofmannstahl, Eduard Spranger, and many others took part in the proceedings of these Bureaus.
88. Kurt Richter, *Der Kampf gegen Schund- und Schmutzschriften in Preußen* (Berlin: Decker Verlag, 1931); Albert Hellwig, *Jugendschutz gegen Schundliteratur* (Berlin: Georg Stilke Verlag, 1927); Herbert Meißner, "Das Schund- und Schmutzgesetzt in seiner strafrechtlichen Bedeutung," Ph.D. diss., Humboldt University Berlin, 1929; Christian Rau, "Der strafrechtliche Begriff der unzüchtigen Schrift," Ph.D. diss., University of Leipzig, 1931; Erich Kormann, "Die Verbreitung unzüchtiger Schriften," Ph.D. diss., University of Erlangen, 1931; Lothar Reisner, "Die unzüchtige Schrift," Ph.D. diss., University of Würzburg, 1936; Hubert Tönies, "Die rechtlichen Grundlagen zur Bekämpfung von Schund- und Schmutz im Schrifttum, Film, Theater und Revuen," Ph.D. diss., University of Hamburg, 1943; Friedrich Weber, "Schundlitertur und jugendliche Verbrecher," University of Munich, 1942.
89. Cf. Petersen, *Zensur in der Weimarer Republik*, 64; Reinhard Mumm, "Kampf gegen Schund- und Schmutzliteratur," *Deutsche Arbeit* 11 (1926), 281.
90. Jürgen Dieter Koegel, ed., *Schriftsteller vor Gericht* (Frankfurt am Main: Suhrkamp, 1996).
91. Kurt Corrinth, *Bordell* (Berlin: Jatho-Vrlag, 1920).
92. Geheimes Staatsarchiv Preußischer Kulturbesitz. Rep 77, Tit 2772 Vol. 1. No. 5, 114–119.
93. According to the publisher of this book he had already sold five thousand copies of the book at the very high price of 12 to 15 RM.
94. Mumm, Kampf gegen Schund, 283.
95. Albert Amend, *Die Kriminalität Deutschlands 1919–1932* (Leipzig: Ernst Wiegandt, 1937), 55.
96. Popert, *Hamburg und der Schundkampf*, 7.
97. Quoted in Martin Jay, *The Dialectical Imagination*, 179.
98. This announcement was originally published in a journal called *Literarische Rundschau der Schriftsteller-Zeitung*. The quotation here is from Benfer, *Schundkampf und literarische Jugendpflege*, 73.
99. Russell A. Berman, "Writing for the Book Industry: The Writer under Organized Capitalism," *New German Critique* 19 (1983), 39–56.
100. On this see Guglielmo Cavallo and Roger Chartier, eds., *A History of Reading in the West*, translated by Lydia G. Cochrane (Amherst: University of Massachusetts Press, 1999), 5. A notable discussion on the effects of this process of commercialization on the place and role of the author in society is Walter Benjamin, "Der Autor als Produzent," in: ibid, *Lesezeichen* (Leipzig: Reclam, 1970), 351–372. In this context it is important also to mention Roland Barthes, "The Death of the Author (first published in 1968)," in: ibid, *Image, Music, Text*, edited and translated by Stephen Heath (New York: Hill, 1977),

142–149. In this provocative essay Barthes claims that the birth of the reader must be at the cost of the death of the Author. Most famous is Michel Foucault's reaction to Berthes's challenge in which he claimed that in the modern world the author has become a function: Michel Foucault, "What is an Author?" *Language, Counter-Memory, Practice,* translated by Donald F. Bouchard (New York: Cornell University Press, 1977), 124–127.

101. Wilhelm Fronemann, "Die Wirkung des Reichsgesetzes zur Bekämpfung von Schund- und Schmutzschriften," in: idem, *Lesende Jugend* (Berlin, Belz Verlag, 1930), 261.
102. Niederschrift über die Besprechung von 26. März. 1925 über Schund- und Schmutzschriften auf den Bahnhöfen," in: Geheimes Staatsarchiv Preußischer Kulturbesitz, Berlin. Rep. 77, Tizt 2772 Vol. 1 No. 8, 123.
103. Writers like Alfred Doblin, Carl v. Ossietzky, Theodor Lessing, Willi Haas, and others supported this organization. Cf. the organization's official journal *Die Stimme der Freiheit. Monatsschrift gegen geistige und wirtschaftliche Reaktion* 1 (1929), 157.
104. "Polumbi Katalog," in: Geheimes Staatsarchiv Preußischer Kulturbesitz, Berlin, Rep 77 Tit 2772 No. 7 Vol. 1 1922–1937.
105. Hans Wingender, "Das Schundliteraturgesetz eine Kräftigung des Schundkapital?" *Die Wohlfahrtspflege in der Rheinprovinz* 4 (1928), 135–138; Wilhelm Fronemann, "Der heilige Bürokratismus und der Schutz der Jugend," in: idem, *Lesende Jugend* (Berlin: Belz Verlag, 1930), 267–269.
106. The cities are Berlin, Breslau, Hamburg, Düsseldorf, Lippe, and Wiesbaden.
107. According to the journal *Die Stimme der Freiheit,* 1 (1929), 174, every new title that was added to this list cost around 4,000 RM. Cf. also Archiv der Deutschen Bücherei Leipzig. Finanzverwaltung Grundstücksverwaltung überlassungen von Räumen an die Oberprüfstelle für Schund- und Schmutzliteratur, 315/4.
108. From: Dresdener Neuesten Nachrichten 4.8.1929. Reprinted in: Wolfgang Bertholz, "Das Schund- und Schmutzgesetz in der Praxis," *Die Stimme der Freiheit* 1 (1929), 173.
109. Amend, *Die Kriminalität Deutschlands,* 56.
110. *Nachrichtendienst zur Bekämpfung von Schund- und Schmutzschriften* 1 (1929), 43.
111. Archiv der Deutschen Bücherei Leipzig, "Gerichtsurteile im Sache Schund- und Schmutzliteratur," 315/4/2, 1932, 1933.
112. H. Baede, "Notzeit des Buches," *Der Schundkampf. Blatt der Reichsschundkampfstelle der evangelichen Jungmännerbünde Deutschlands* 9 (1929), 7.
113. Peukert, *Der Schund- und Schmutzkampf,* 59.
114. Maase, Kinder als Fremde, 126. For a similar approach see Speitkampf, Jugendschutz.
115. Wilhelm Fronemann, "Die Volksliteratur, das Gesetz und die Volksbildung," in: idem, *Lesende Jugend* (Berlin: Belz Verlag, 1930), 276–284.
116. This point is also made in: Hans Epstein, *Der Detektivroman der Unterschicht. Die Frank Allan-Serie* (Frankfurt a.M.: Neuer Frankfurt Verlag, 1930), 4.
117. Maria Tatar, *Lustmord. Sexual Murder in Weimar Germany* (Princeton: Princeton University Press, 1995).
118. Paul Honigsheim, "Zur Soziologie und Sozialpsychologie der Schundliteratur und Kinodrama," *Volksbildungsarchiv* 10 (1923), 134.
119. On the American case: Michael Denning, *Dime Novels and Working Class Culture in America* (London: Verso, 1987); idem, "Cheap Stories: Notes on Popular Fiction and Working-class Culture in Nineteenth Century America," *History Workshop* 21 (1986), 1–18.
120. On the fear of mass culture in Weimar Germany: Adelheid v. Saldern, "Massenfreizeitkultur im Visier. Ein Beitrag zu den Deutungs- und Einwirkungsversuchen während der Weimarer Republik," *Archiv für Sozialgeschichte* 33 (1993), 21–51.
121. Michel Foucault, *The History of Sexuality* Vol. 1 (New York: Vintage Books, 1980).

CONCLUSION

Western culture is still dominated by an approach which distinguishes between reading culture, representing intellectualism, and consumer culture, associated with materialism.[1] In Germany in particular we can identify the pervasiveness of this approach, which views mind and matter as separate and mutually antagonistic areas. The present study has sought to evaluate the validity of this stance. Its goal was to investigate the way in which these two ostensibly distinct areas are related, and to explore the significance of this hierarchical separation between intellectual culture and material culture as expressed in the nexus between reading culture and consumer culture in pre-1933 Germany. There were two main ways of approaching these undertakings. One approach, with which we opened and concluded this study, had as its focus an examination of discourse about reading after World War I. The second focused on a description and analysis of various (mainly structural) aspects of reading culture and how it dovetailed with the new consumer culture.

The discourse analysis of book reading following World War I has shown how this discourse was dominated by a sense of crisis. The essence of this book crisis was the awareness that books were no longer selling as they had in the past. For contemporary figures, this state of affairs was an expression of the disappearance of book-reading culture, for which various explanations were advanced. Some ascribed the critical situation of books to the flawed economic structure of the book trade market. Others saw the crisis as an expression of a cultural decline resulting from the process of Americanization, as well as the popularity of the new media and recreational amenities in the wake of the World War. However, the most prevalent attitude during these years blamed the book crisis on the postwar disintegration of the bourgeoisie, which was viewed as the main target audience for the book market specifically, and for German culture in general.

The chapter with which this study concludes discusses various aspects of the discourse about reading. Here the analysis focuses on studies of reading carried out during the 1920s and the early 1930s, and the struggle against those publications which were defined as pulp and trashy works. This chapter has shown that reading studies focused on investigating the reading habits of those groups which were viewed as the weak links in the bourgeois social order, at whose apex the stratum of educated males had placed itself: in other words, women, workers, and youth. These groups were perceived as being easy to sway and hence particularly vulnerable to the harmful influence of the consumer culture. An analysis of research into reading has identified a pattern of action which sought, on the one hand, to include these social groups in the framework of bourgeois society by reinforcing their sense of social and national responsibility, and, on the other, to maintain their cultural individuality as groups with their own distinctive identities. In this respect research into reading was part of high-modernist schemes to shape and standardize society. It reflected efforts to integrate in the controlling culture those social groups that were perceived as weak links in the social order and by doing so it helped to construct and preserve the domain of a hegemonic culture.[2] However, this pattern has also shown that despite the awareness of the "book crisis," the problem troubling this group of mainly educated males fearful of the disintegration of the bourgeois social order was not whether a particular group did any reading or not, but what these groups were reading. In other words, it reflected reservations as to what extent the printed word could serve as a vehicle of bourgeois culture. A manifest expression of this tendency was the struggle against pulp and trashy works. We have seen how these writings were viewed as part of the development process of commercialized culture, which was extremely popular with broad swaths of society, and how the struggle against it reflected the fear of the dictatorship of the consumers: in other words, a situation in which demand dictated literary supply and the aesthetic tastes of the period.

Discourse about the position of reading therefore reflected the changes which had affected reading culture, and in particular constituted an expression of fears about the process of the rise of the new consumer culture, which threatened both to blur the differences between social groups and to engender the homogenization of society. Discourse about commercialization and consumers therefore comprised discussions about the book crisis, reading studies, and the struggle against pulp and trashy literature. One of the most striking characteristics of this kind of discourse was the schizophrenic attitude toward the reading public. This was viewed as a mass or multitude without a mind of its own, prey to all forms of manipulation, and at the same time as a force capable of controlling the publications market. Discussions about the book crisis typified the first approach, while the chapter on reading studies and in particular the discussion of the struggle against pulp and trashy literature embodied the second attitude.

This conclusion regarding the special nature of the discourse about reading as consumer discourse is not based solely on a discourse analysis of reading, but relates also to what we would have expected to be addressed in this discourse, such as attitudes to the "Jewish issue." Although the number of Jews in the publishing world was out of all proportion to their representation in the German population at the time, the examination of reading discourse did not identify any special references to them. True, those who blamed the Jews for all the woes of German society viewed them as also being responsible for the deterioration, whether real or imaginary, of reading culture in Germany. However, this approach was to a large extent tangential to the discourse about reading, and failed to constitute the nub of reading discourse or to influence the form and subjects with which it dealt. In other words, despite Jews' prominence in the publishing world, they were not a "topic" of reading discourse. Perhaps this situation related to the numbers and importance of the Jews in the group of publishers undertaking this discourse. Yet, a more logical explanation for this state of affairs involves the nature of reading discourse itself as a discourse about consumers. Rather than being perceived as one of the groups which made up the mass of consumers, Jews were viewed as belonging to the public of producers whose power had been weakened in direct proportion to the strengthening of consumer power. For this reason this discourse refrained from relating to the Jews—or for that matter to any other group affiliated with the producers of reading matter—as a special group with the power to influence the demand and literary taste of the general public. Furthermore, reading discourse tended to relate to publishers as a more or less homogeneous group perceived as a victim of the demand for reading matter.

The approach which viewed consumers and producers as two separate groups with exclusive interests perpetuated the separation between the economic and cultural capital of the world of print. To a large extent it also helped to strike a balance between them, because making capital out of the distribution of popular reading matter was viewed as a necessary evil which permitted the existence of refined literature destined for a select public of readers. By taking the material dimension out of intellectual culture and setting them up as two separate, competing cultures, it therefore became possible for the publishing world to alternate between the two categories and to come to terms with promoting the ideal of enriching the intellectual world in one field, while commercializing the world of print and making economic capital out of the other. The most striking example of this dualism was the Georg Stilke publishing house. While part of Stilke published law and jurisprudence books including the important National Liberal periodical *Preußische Jahrbücher*, another of the firm's divisions owned most of the bookshops at railway stations in Northern Germany and the kiosks in the city of Berlin, which were the main distribution agents for the selfsame commercialized popular culture.

The analysis of the discourse on reading has, therefore, disclosed the highly complex nature of the reading phenomenon. It has revealed the context within whose framework reading must be evaluated as part of the process of the emergence of the new consumer culture and the bourgeois classes' complex relationship to it. The study's other chapters have discussed a range of aspects of reading culture and its concrete link with consumer culture. This discussion has highlighted the close interaction between reading and commercialization and shown how commercialization encouraged reading culture, and conversely how reading contributed to promote the new consumer culture.

We first investigated the reading budgets of various social groups, finding that in fact the impoverished classes allocated relatively more resources to the consumption of reading matter than did their affluent counterparts, and that the gap between urban and rural areas in terms of outlay on reading was not particularly significant. Reading budgets also showed that the First World War and the immediate postwar years were periods which increased the consumption of reading matter. In this sense, World War I was an event in the history of reading. The relevant factors were primarily the demand for up-to-date information from the front lines and the home front, and the fact that when times were hard, reading was a cheap and efficient way of transmitting information, easing tensions during leisure time. Household account books also showed that it was not simply that, following the war, reading became an inseparable part of the basket of basic necessities for families of all social classes: at this time all social strata were earmarking greater resources for reading needs than for other media and recreational amenities such as films, radio, music, or sports. During this period, then, reading as a time-saving and time-using activity constituted an inseparable part of the daily routines of all social classes. This state of affairs documented that the fear that competition with the new media was having a negative impact on the consumption of reading matter was unfounded in terms of facts on the ground. Indeed, the opposite is true: a meticulous examination of reading budgets has shown that competition with the new media, far from being a negative factor, actually increased the consumption of reading matter.

In the other chapters of the work we have examined the process of commercialization of newspapers and books and the way that this process permeated readers' daily routines. This discussion focuses on such topics as distribution methods for reading matter, publicity for and in reading matter, developments in the area of reading matter design, and the process of the commodification of reading. Here a variety of components, some of them not previously the subject of historical research, have been identified in relation to the distribution and publicity methods of newspapers and books. Analysis of bookshops in railway stations and department stores, kiosks, the *Lesezirkel,* book clubs, and the deposit-free commercial lending libraries illustrated very clearly the process of commercialization of reading culture, the ways in which this process became part of daily routines, and how reading adapted itself to the realities of the time. For example, the deposit-free commercial lending libraries, on the one hand, and the book clubs, on the other, were striking manifestations of how both "reading through borrowing" and "reading through buying" adapted themselves to the realities of the economic hardships and mounting competition between the various media during the period following the World War. These distribution methods diversified the possibilities of accessing reading matter, expanded the reading public, and showed that even in a period of economic hardship and political crisis, there were ways of distributing reading matter which met the diversified demand for reading.

An examination of the various distribution methods for reading matter has also revealed the ambivalence of attitudes toward consumption itself. Together with the pessimistic attitude toward consumption, which interpreted the process of commercialization and industrialization of the world of print as an expression of the disappearance of reading culture, a more optimistic approach to consumption has been identified. According to this approach, the process of commercialization and the constant attempt to increase the consumption of reading matter, among other things by using new marketing and distribution technologies, would sooner or later pave the way to making the reading public more discerning. In their own way, the "cultural publishers" (*Kulturverlage*) which were founded from the 1890s onward, as well as the "upwards reading" principle of August Scherl's library, both embodied this optimistic approach toward consumption.

The description of the various distribution methods for reading matter therefore helps to highlight the nature of reading as a consumed activity which stands in competition with other leisure activities. It becomes clear that three main factors contributed to the success of reading in the special circumstances of economic hardship and tough competition with the new media following World War I. First, reading, as an intimate activity which takes place in the private domain, made it possible to "escape" from a reality in which the reader was a passive object, to a world controlled entirely by the reader. Thus precisely at a time when the group readings which had been standard practice up to the end of the nineteenth century were being replaced by the communal watching of films and group listening to the radio, the process by which reading was individualized became an aspect that heightened its attraction as an activity suitable for the modern world. Second, reading was a skill which did not require many resources and was a flexible activity which both helped pass the time and saved time, and which could be carried out in a variety of locations and situations: at work, at home, and on the move from one place to another. The third element, which made no less important a contribution to shaping the attraction of reading, relates to its symbolic meaning as an activity emblematic of high culture and a key to upward social mobility.

By examining a number of aspects related to the area of reading matter design, we have been able to identify the forms in which the three factors responsible for the success of reading were expressed. We have seen that in the 1920s, there was an ever more marked tendency to design books as a mass commodity. The aim of this design approach was to reduce the cost of producing books and make them easier to read, ensuring that as mass commodities they would be in tune with the nature and pace of modern living. Nevertheless, even this design-oriented approach did not rush to abandon the aesthetic distinctiveness of books, and the value which it attached to owning them was no less than that of reading them. Furthermore, much contemporary evidence, which stressed the aesthetic importance of books and their symbolic value as objects with emblematic value, indicates that members of the impoverished classes preferred to buy "respectable looking" books rather than publications with inferior graphic and aesthetic qualities. The attention paid to the solid appearance of the 2.85 RM books and the success of the book clubs, which marketed an impressive-looking bookcase to members of various social classes, were both results of this tendency.

Another interesting example of this amalgam of the pragmatic dimension with the ideal of reading during the postwar period were the "insurance newspapers" (*Versicherungszeitschriften*). These were not just advertising devices intended to encourage newspaper reading, but also helped to reinforce the worth of saving and insurance—typical bourgeois values—among classes of the population for whom insurance had previously been unattainable and was sometimes an alien concept. The insurance newspapers were not just an example of a combination of economic interests and bourgeois cultural values such as insurance and reading: in a period of crisis and economic hardship they became a mechanism which helped many social strata to adapt to the new realities and enabled them to achieve an orderly lifestyle which benefited from economic security and the ability to plan for the future.

Our discussion has sought not only to trace the process of the commercialization of reading and its attendant implications, but also to bear out the contention of close interaction between reading and consumption, in the framework of which the world of print became an area in which the world of symbols and images of the new consumer culture developed. Two key processes have helped us to provide a basis for this argument:

1. The process by which reading changed from a skill mastered by a narrow social stratum to an activity considered one of the basic needs common to all social classes.
2. The process of commercialization of the world of print and the commodification of reading.

The separation between these processes was an analytical one only, since it is impossible to determine whether the process of commercialization of the world of print was a result of the increased demand for reading or vice versa. Nevertheless, what can certainly be stated is that reading culture played a key role in the antagonistic process by which society was simultaneously homogenized and heterogenized. In the era of technical reproduction, reading as an activity that deciphers printed symbols represented a significant contribution to the process of standardization and homogenization of society. The constant striving to expand the reading public and to develop new publicity and distribution methods directed at this aggregate as an anonymous public while implementing the principle of production for consumption's sake were developments which undoubtedly contributed to the process of homogenizing German society. This trend emerged principally in the 1920s, which experienced the phenomenon of best sellers and enormous print runs by newspapers and magazines. At the same time, reading as an activity which took place in the private domain, where individual readers had practically complete control over the form of their own reading, choice of reading matter, and way of reacting to what was read, turned reading into an activity through which anyone could make his or her hearts' desires come true. To put it another way, of all times it was when the new media were heightening the collective nature of reception through viewing and listening, that the demonstrative nature of the act of reading was revealed as a socially significant individual activity.

But reading did not just underscore the process by which society became individualized: it also became a key component in the construction of various groups' social identities within it. The great diversity of the publications market in Germany is perhaps the most striking expression of this state of affairs. Every single interest group and every single issue was able to have its very own platform in the world of print. Especially from the 1890s onward, we witness a veritable flourishing of publishing houses, libraries, newspapers, and magazines intended for a particular public, with the goal of promoting its distinctive identity. Against this background, reading became an integral component in the construction of the individual's identity in society, and an activity that expressed the simultaneous occurrence of the processes by which the modern era underwent both homogenization and heterogenization. Nor did this process escape the keen eyes of contemporary observers. One of the striking reactions to it was the distinction between intellectual culture and material culture, or to put it another way:

1. The separation between material culture and intellectual culture came into sharper focus as the process of commercialization and integration of reading culture in consumer culture became stronger. Identifying something as belonging to one or the other culture was a mechanism that helped to draw the boundaries between different "cultures." This process can be interpreted as part of an overall trend in which consumer culture enabled different social groups to establish a range of meanings for objects and activities, thereby expressing their own distinctive worlds.
2. The separation between material culture and intellectual culture was an expression of an attempt to control the new consumer cul-

ture by establishing a hierarchical relationship between various elements within it.[3] Intellectual culture was perceived as something homogeneous with a specifically unique nature, whose existence went beyond the set of daily needs. On the other hand, material culture was perceived as fragmentary, an immediate response to fleeting impulses.

The separation between intellectual culture and material culture did not, therefore, seek to dismiss the new consumer culture as a material culture. However, it did try to channel the influence of consumer culture, and became part of the struggle to attain a position from which it would be possible to dictate its nature. This struggle was almost entirely waged in the narrow framework of the male, educated bourgeois class, between disparate groups within it with a variety of economic, political, and cultural interests. These groups—of authors, publishers, politicians, educators, industrialists, and so on—were in fact the people who drove forward the process by which the new consumer culture was created. They were also those who reaped most of the fruits of its success. However, it was also among these same social groups that there was voiced most of the criticism of the process leading to the emergence of the consumer culture as well as of its concomitant dangers for society generally, and especially for the bourgeoisie as the stratum representing economic interests.

From this point of view, it is obvious that the struggle against pulp and trashy literature was not only an expression of the fear of the "dictatorship of the consumers," but a mechanism designed to regulate relationships between the cultural and economic capital of the world of print. As we saw in the chapter which discussed this struggle, beyond the criterion of commercialization there were never any shared characteristics which could be used as a basis for defining these writings. In other words, the struggle against pulp and trashy literature never could and in fact had no need to define "pulp and trash." The importance of the struggle against these (ostensibly) inferior works was the struggle itself, which became an integral part of the construction of "bourgeoisness" and "good culture," a kind of mechanism which strengthened the feeling of bourgeois subjectivity. In this respect it reflected what Bourdieu calls the "hierarchy of hierarchies," that is to say whether economic capital or cultural capital should have the upper hand defining structures of legitimate taste.[4] From this conclusion we learn that the sense of crisis and the relentless disintegration of the bourgeoisie were in fact part of a long-term process in which the bourgeoisie changed from a social group which enjoyed status attributes into a lifestyle which sought to achieve a hegemonic status in society. The bourgeoisie's success in turning its lifestyle into a social ideal which transcended class, or more accurately the shift from bourgeoisie to bourgeoisness, therefore forms the nucleus of the dialectic process of the disintegration of the bourgeoisie. This process also marks the beginning of the new consumer culture which, as Don Slater has put it, "appears to emerge from a series of struggles to organize and tame, yet at the same time to exploit commercially, the social space and time in which modernity is acted out."[5] A description of a number of developments in the world of print beginning at the end of the nineteenth century and continuing during the first third of the twentieth century, together with how they were dealt with, has therefore underscored the similarities in the development of consumer culture in Germany.

German society in the pre-1933 period was not, then, a "consumer society" as we would identify it from the second half of the twentieth century onward. In the first third of the twentieth century, most Germans still lived in small towns and rural areas, still dominated by tradition, well-established primary groups, and powerful social organizations such as the extended family, the church, and trade unions, which had the power to block the spread of the new consumer culture and to offer an alternative to it. This was a time when the new consumer culture was still coming into being: a period in which it was fighting for cultural hegemony, and its contradictions and weaknesses were beginning to be exposed. The First World War and the situation which followed it speeded up this trend. In this period, the gap between the consumer-culture paradise, as manifested in the world of print, and the realities of daily existence was at its most extreme. On the one hand, the social changes and economic hardships in the wake of the world war strengthened the ethos of the consumer culture and the aspiration to put its values into practice. One of the most striking manifestations of this trend was the unprecedented popularity of reading culture in these years. On the other hand, this selfsame period, with its chronic hardship and sense of crisis, prevented large parts of the population from achieving their hearts' desires and realizing the lifestyle to which they aspired. Hence the gap between daily existence after the war and the paradise of consumer culture as expressed in the world of print grew ever wider. This process increased feelings of frustration and discrimination among broad swaths of the populace, and intensified fears of the potential results. Given this state of affairs, it is small wonder that the criticism of the new consumer culture and the difficulty of finding an appropriate conceptual system which could be used to address the rapid changes and many contradictions inherent in consumer culture led to heightened competition after the war between different parts of the "producer stratum," an increase in the demand for a radical change in the realities of contemporary life, and the popularization of cure-all solutions to its problems. Such solutions centered on blanket notions such as *Volk,* race, or class. In this sense, the politicization of German society after 1918 and the increase in the state's involvement in regularizing many aspects of its existence can be interpreted as reactions to the blocking of the development of the consumer society and fears of the exacerbation of the gap that existed between people's day-to-day existence and the horizon of expectations and desires harbored by a good part of the German population in those years.

This conclusion is still at odds with the widespread view which sees the process of the commercialization and rise of consumer culture in Germany generally, and in the 1920s in particular, as following an escapist pattern. This approach—which views consumption, and in particular the consumption of culture, as an apolitical sphere which acted as a kind of refuge in which to shelter from the realities of economic hardship and a quickening process of politicization and radicalization in the postwar period—to a large extent takes on board the contemporary criticism of consumer culture, ignoring the diverse manifestations and autonomous nature of the act of consumption. Furthermore, this approach uncritically adopts the view of politics as a narrow sphere in which dialogue is undertaken between parties in the organized structural parliamentary framework, attaching secondary importance to all activities which ostensibly take place outside this domain, or more accurately outside its direct influence. However, the social and political realities are far more complex and they cannot be addressed, especially in the first third of the twentieth century in Germany, solely in terms of the struggle between political parties and such issues as the question of support for or opposition to the German republic alone. As this work has shown, Weimar's fourteen years were not just a time of surviving political instability and economic hardship, but rather a period when consumer culture began to occupy an increasingly central position in the construction of personal and collective identity in Germany determining in many ways the course of its history in the twentieth century.

Notes

1. On this approach, Paul Du Gay, ed., *Production of Culture/Cultures of Production* (London: Sage, 1997); Morg Shiach, *Discourse on Popular Culture* (Cambridge: Polity Press, 1989).
2. On this see especially: James C. Scott, *Seeing Like a State: How Certain Schemes to Improve the Human Condition have Failed* (New Haven: Yale Uiniversity Press, 1998).
3. On this notion cf. especially Pierre Bourdieu, *The Field of Cultural Production* (Oxford: Polity Press, 1993).
4. Ibid., on this see also Daniel Miller, *Material Culture and Mass Consumption* (Oxford: Basil Blackwell, 1987), 152.
5. Don Slater, *Consumer Culture & Modernity* (Oxford: Polity Press, 1997), 15.

BIBLIOGRAPHY

Archives and special libraries

Bundesarchiv, Abt. III Deutsches Reich, Berlin.

Geheimes Staatsarchiv Preußischer Kulturbesitz, Berlin.

Sächsisches Staatsarchiv, Leipzig. (Bestand des Börsenvereins der deutschen Buchhändler zu Leipzig)

Börsenverein des Deutschen Buchhandels Archiv und Bibliothek, Frankfurt a.M.

Die Deutsche Bibliothek Deutsche Bücherei, Leipzig.

Die Deutsche Bibliothek Deutsche Bücherei-Hausarchiv, Leipzig.

Deutsches Buch und Schriftmuseum, Leipzig.

Hochschule für Bibliotheks- und Informationswesen—Walter Hofmann-Archiv (Privatnachlass), Stuttgart.

Leipziger Städtische Bibliothek Abt. Fachbibliothek—Dienstnachlass von Walter Hofmann, Leipzig.

Schiller-Nationalmuseum und Deutsches Literaturarchiv, Marbach.

Primary Literature

Die Abonnentenversicherung (Nürnberg: Nürnberg Lebensversicherungsbank, 1929).

Abb, Gustav, ed. *Bücher und Bibliotheken in Berlin* (Berlin: Struppe & Winkler, 1928).

Ackava, Otto, "Die Abonnenten Versicherung der deutschen illustrierten Familienblätter," Ph.D. diss., University of Leipzig, 1923.

Ackerknecht, Erwing, *Büchereifrage* (Berlin: Weidmann, 1926).

———, *Das Lichtspiel im Dienst der Bildungspflege* (Berlin: Weidemann, 1918).

———, *Lichtspielfragen* (Berlin: Weidmann, 1927).

———, "Büchereiplakate," *Bücherei und Bildungspflege*, 11 (1931), 257–262.

Ackermann, Eduard, "Zur Sozialisierung des Buchwesens," *Börsenblatt für den Deutschen Buchhandel*, 86 (1919) 837–837.

Adam, Willi, "Buch und Buchwerbung," *Monatsblätter für Bucheinbände und Handbindekunst*, 1 (1925), 13–16.

Albrecht, Gerhard, "Breslauer Haushaltsrechnungen," *Concordia. Zeitschrift der Zentralle für Volkswohlfahrt* 12 (1912), 417–419.

Amend, Albert, *Die Kriminalität Deutschlands 1919–1932* (Leipzig: Ernst Wiegand, 1937).

Amonn, Alfred, *Die Hauptprobleme der Sozialisierung* (Leipzig: Quelle & Meyer, 1920).

Antz, Josef, *Die Lehrer im Volksdienst* (Saarlois: Hausen Verlag, 1932).

Aster, Ernst v. "Die Krise der bürgerlichen Ideologie," *Die neue Rundschau*, 42 (1931), 1–13.

Avenarius, Ferdinand, "Scherl Leihbibliothek," *Kunstwart*, 21 (1908), 219–222.

Bachem, Johann Peter, *Das Eindringen der Reklame in die deutschen politischen Tageszeitungen* (Cologne: Verlag J.P. Bachem, 1929).

Baede, H. "Notzeit des Buches," *Der Schundkampf*, 6 (1929), 7.

Baudissing, Graf, and Gräfing, *Das goldene Buch der Sitte* (Stuttgart: Verlag von W. Spemann, 1913).

Beitrag zur Frage der internationalen Gegenüberstellung der Lebenshaltungskosten (Genf: Internationales Arbeitsamt, 1933).

Benfer, Heinrich, *Kampf dem schlechten durch das gute Buch* (Dortmund: Fr. Wilhelm Ruhfus, 1923).

———, *Schundkampf und literarische Jugendpflege* (Berlin: Verlag von Julius Belz, 1932).

Benjamin, Walter, *Lesezeichen* (Leipzig: Reclam, 1970).

Berger, Curt, *Gedanken zur Buchwerbung* (Leipzig: Privatdruck, 1930).

Bernier, Wilhelm, *Die Lebenshaltung, Lohn und Arbeitsverhältnisse von 145 deutschen Landarbeiterfamilien* (Berlin: Enckenhaus, 1931).

Bertholz, Wolfgang, "Das Schund- und Schmutzgesetz in der Praxis," *Die Stimme der Freiheit*, 1 (1929), 173.

Bertkau, Friedrich, and Bömer, Karl, *Der wirtschaftliche Aufbau des Deutschen Zeitungsgewerbes* (Berlin: Carl Duncker Verlag, 1932).

Blau, Albrecht, *Inseratenmarkt der Deutschen Tageszeitung* (Berlin: Junker und Dünnhaupt, 1932).

Blinde, Hans, *Die Zeitung im Dienste der Reklame. Eine Untersuchung über die auf seiten der Zeitung liegenden Bedingungen für die Wirksamkeit der Anzeigenreklame* (Frankfurt a. O: Trowitzsch & Sohn, 1931).

Bockwitz, Hans H. "Deutsche Buchgestaltung," *Archiv für Buchgewerbe und Gebrauchsgraphik* 65 (1928), 599.

Boehm, Wolfgang, "Die Kulturelle Bedeutung des deutschen Buchhandels und seine wirtschaftliche Lage," Ph.D. diss., University of Frankfurt a.M., 1922.

Boesse-Hofmann, Elisa, "Was wir vom Buch erwarten," *Hefte für Büchereiwesen*, 16 (1932), 18–21.

Bömer, Karl, *Bibliographisches Handbuch der Zeitungswissenschaft* (Leipzig: Otto Harrassowitz, 1929).

Borchardt, Rudolf, *Reden* (Stuttgart: Ernst Klett Verlag, 1955).

Borgius, Walter, "Zur Sozialisierung des Buchwesens," in: Beck, Hermann, ed., *Wege und Ziele der Sozialisierung* (Berlin: Verlag neues Vaterland, 1919), 122–161.

Born, Heinz, "Das Anzeigengeschäft der Tagespresse," Ph.D. diss., University of Freiburg i.Br., 1929.

Bosse, Hans, *Das literarische Verständnis der werktätigen Jugend zwischen 14 und 18* (Leipzig: Verlag von Johan Ambrosius Barth, 1923).

Bott, Hans, "Jungbuchhandel, politische Parteien und Gewerkschaften," *Der Neue Stand*, 1 (1932), 229–232.

Botz, Karl, "Zeitungsvertrieb der Deutschen Reichspost," Ph.D. diss., University of Mannheim, 1933.

Braune, Rudolf, "Was sie lesen: Drei Stenotypistinnen," *Frankfurter Zeitung* June 21, 1929.

"Breslauer Haushaltungsrechnungen aus den Jahren 1907 und 1908," *Breslauer Statistik*, XXX (1912), 152–264.

Brieger, Lothar, "Billiges oder Teures Buch?" *Das Heftland* (1922\1924), 89.

Brinkmann, Carl, "Presse und Öffentlichkeit," *Verhandlungen des Siebenten Deutschen Soziologentages vom 28. September bis 1. Oktober 1930 in Berlin* (Berlin J.C.B. Mohr, 1931), 9–31.

Brodführer, Richard, "'Geist und Maschine.' Der erste buchgewerbliche Großfilm Deutschland und die Buchwerbung durch den Film," *Börsenblatt für den Deutschen Buchhandel*, 93 (1926), 1017.

Bruere, Otto, *Das Bücher-Schaufenster* (Berlin: Oldenburg & Co., 1921).

Bry, Christian, *Buchereihen. Fortschritt oder Gefahr für den Buchhandel?* (Gotha: Verlag Friedrich Andreas Pertheas, 1917).

Buch und Gesellschaft. Tagung des Berliner Ausschusses zur Bekämpfung der Schmutz- und Schundliteratur und des Unwesens Kino (Berlin: Hillger Verlag, 1927).

Buchwald, Reinhard, *Die Bildungsinteressen der deutschen Arbeiter* (Tübingen: J.C.B. Mohr, 1934).

Bücher, Karl, *Gesammelte Aufsätze zur Zeitungskunde* (Tübingen: Verlag H. Lauppschen Buchhandlung, 1926).

———, *Die Sozialisierung* (Tübingen: J.C.B. Mohr, 1919).

———, "Haushaltungsbudgets oder Wirtschaftsrechnungen?" *Zeitschrift für die gesamte Staatswissenschaft*, 6 (1906), 686–700.

Bürgel, Bruno, H. *Vom Arbeiter zum Astronom* (Berlin: Ullstein, 1919).

Bunzel, Julius, "Die Sozialisierung des Verlages," in: Ludwig Sinzheimer, ed., *Die geistige Arbeit* (Munich: Duncke & Humbolt, 1922), 415–437.

Burgerdörfer, Friedrich, ed., *Die Statistik in Deutschland nach ihrem heutigen Stand* (Berlin: Paul Schmidt, 1940).

Casson, Herbert N., *Wirksame Werbung* (Berlin: Josef Singer Verlag, 1927).

Cudell, Robert, *Das Buch vom Tabak* (Cologne: Neuenburg Verlag, 1927).

———, "Das Buch als Industrie Werbemittel," *Monatsblätter für Bucheinbände und Handbindekunst* 4 (1928), 7.

de Man, Hendrik, "Verbürgerlichung des Proletariats?" *Neue Blätter für Sozialismus,* 1 (1930), 106–118.

Dette, Walter, *Die Sozialisierung der Buchproduktion und des Buchhandels* (Hannover: Banas & Dette, 1919).

Diederichs, Eugen, "Die Krisis des deutschen Buches," *Die Tat* 21 (1929), 1–4.

Dinse, Robert, *Das Freizeitleben der Großstadtjugend* (Berlin: R. Müller, 1932).

Dovifat, Emil, *Zeitungswissenschaft* (Leipzig: Walter de Gruyter, 1931).

———, "Die Anfänge der Generalanzeigepresse," *Archiv für Buchgewerbe und Gebrauchsgraphik* 65 (1928), 163–184.

Drahn, Ernst, *Geschichte des deutschen Buch- und Zeitschriftenhandels* (Berlin: Central Verein Deutscher Buch und Zeitschriftenhändler, 1914).

———, "Die Bedeutung des Buches und des Zeitschriftenhandels innerhalb des Gesamtbuchhandels," in: idem. *Zwei Vorträge. Bericht über die 44. Mitgliederversammlung des Reichsverbandes Deutscher Buch- und Zeitschriftenhändler 19. und 20. Juni München* (Berlin: Verlag des Reichsverbandes Deutscher Buch und Zeitschriftenhändler, 1932).

300 Haushaltungsrechnungen von Arbeitern der Schuhindustrie und des Schuhmacher-gewerbes in Deutschland (Nürnberg: Zentralverband der Schuhmacher, 1928).

Druckenmüller, Alfred, *Der Buchhandel der Welt* (Stuttgart: C.E. Poeschel Verlag, 1935).

Eckard, Fritz, *Das Besprechungswesen* (Leipzig: Verlag des Börsenvereins der deutschen Buchhändler, 1927).

Ehmcke, Fritz Helmuth, *Persönliches und Sachliches* (Berlin: Verlag Hermann Reckendorg, 1928).

Engel, Ernst, *Rechnungsbuch der Hausfrau und seine Bedeutung im Wirtschaftsleben der Nation* (Berlin: Verlag von Leonard Simon, 1882).

———, *Lebenskosten belgischer Arbeiter Familien* (Dresden: C. Heinrich, 1895).

———, *Wert des Menschen* (Berlin: Verlag von Leonard Simon, 1883).

Epstein, Hans. *Der Detektivroman der Unterschicht* (Frankfurt a.M.: Neuer Frankfurter Verlag, 1930).

d'Ester, Karl, *Das Studium der Zeitungswissenschaft in Deutschland* (Charlottenburg: Verlag Hochschule u. Ausland, 1925).

———, *Zeitung und Lesen* (Leipzig: Harrassowitz, 1941).

———, "Katholische Zeitschrift und ihre Leser," in: Naumann, Wilhelm J. ed. *Die Presse und der Katholik. Anklage und Rechtfertigung* (Augsburg: Haas & Grabherr, 1932).

Eulenburg, Franz, *Kosten der Lebenshaltung in deutschen Großstädten* (Munich: Duncker & Humblot, 1914).

Fink, Erwing, "Die Abonnenten-Versicherung in Deutschland," Ph.D. diss., University of Erlangen, 1917.

Fischer, Samuel, "Bemerkungen zur Bücherkrise," in: Samuel Fischer, "Bemerkungen zur Bücherkrise," in: Friedrich Pfäffin, ed., *S. Fischer Verlag von der Gründung bis zur Rückkehr aus dem Exil* (Marbach: Ausstellungskatalog, 1985), 357–360.

Friedrich, Heinz, "Wie verkaufe ich Romane und Novellen?" *Buchhändlergilde-Blatt,* 10 (1926).

Fromm, Erich, *Arbeiter und Angestellte am Vorabend des Dritten Reiches* (Munich: Dtv, 1983).

Fronemann, Wilhelm, Das Erbe Wolgasts. *Ein Querschnitt durch die heutige Jugendschriftenfrage* (Langensalza: Verlag von Julius Beltz, 1927).

———, *Lesende Jugend* (Langensalza: Verlag von Julius Beltz, 1930).

———, *Kannst du ein Buch empfehlen* (Leipzig: Verlag des Börsenvereins der deutschen Buchhändler, 1928).

———, "Das Buch im Urteil des Kindes und Jugendlichen," *Börsenblatt für den Deutschen Buchhandel* 95 (1928), 1396–1398, and 96 (1929), 9–16.

Fuchs, Karl, "Die gewerberrechtliche Behandlung der Bahnhofsbuchhandlung," Ph.D. diss., University of Cologne, 1936.

Fürth, Henriette, *Ein mittelbürgerliches Budget über einen zehnjärigen Zeitraum* (Jena: Gustav Fischer, 1907).

———, *Die Soziale Bedeutung der Käufersitten* (Jena: Gustav Fischer Verlag, 1917).

———, *Der Haushalt vor und nach dem Krieg. Dargestellt am Hand eines mittelbürgerlichen Budgets* (Jena: Gustav Fischer Verlag, 1922).

Geiger, Theodor, "Zur Kritik der Verbürgerlichung," *Die Arbeit,* 8 (1931), 534–553.

———, "Zur Kritik der arbeiterpsychologischen Forschung," *Die Gesellschaft,* 8 (1932).

Georgii, Erhard, "Über die Grenzen der Zeitungsverbreitung," Ph.D. diss., Humboldt University Berlin, 1932.

Giese-Hüser, Margarte, "Zur Psychologie des Bücherkäufers," *Deutsche Psychologie,* 3 (1921), 1–12.

Glässer, Erich, "Die Rundfunkreklame in Deutschland," Ph.D. diss., University of Nürnberg, 1933.

Goldfriedrich, Johann, *Geschichte des Deutschen Buchhandels* (Leipzig: Verlag des Börsenvereins der Deutschen Buchhändler, 1913).

Groth, Otto, *Die Zeitung* (Mannheim: Benseileimer, 1930).

Grünewald, Max, "Umgang mit Büchern," *Die Büchergilde,* 4 (1928), 153.

Günther, Adolf, Meerwarth, Rudolf, and Zimmermann, Waldemar, *Die Einwirkung des Krieges auf Bevölkerungsbewegung, Einkommen und Lebenshaltung in Deutschland* (Stuttgart: Deutsche Verlag, 1932).

Haas, Willy, "Gibt es eine Krise im deutschen Buchwesen? Gespräche mit bedeutendsten Leipziger Verlagen," *Literarische Welt,* 5 (1929), 135–136, 152, 160, 168.

———, "Bücher, die man nicht heiratet. Zum Niedergang des Broschierten Buches" *Literarische* Welt, 5 (1929), 49–50.

———, "... aber manche Bücher heiratet man doch! Ein paar Betrachtungen zum gebundenen Buch," *Literarische Welt,* 5 (1929), 65–66.

———, "Ein 'Tag des Buches?'," *Literarische Welt,* 5 (1929), 25–26.

Häring, Oskar, ed., *Stilke Georg 1872–1922* (Berlin: Stilke Verlag, 1922).

Hallbauer, Walter, "Die Frau und die volkstümliche Bücherei," *Hefte für Büchereiwesen,* 10 (1925/26), 190–196.

Hamann, Ludwig, *Der Umgang mit Büchern und die Selbstkultur* (Leipzig: Verlag von Ludwig Hamann, 1898).

"Haushaltungsrechnungen und Wohnungsverhältnisse von 10 Bremer Arbeiterfamilien" *Beiträge zur Statistik der Stadt Bremen,* 6 (1909).

Der Haushalt des Kaufmannsgehilfen. 300 Haushaltsrechnungen (Hamburg: Deutschnationaler Handlungsgehilfen-Verband, 1927).

Heenemann, Horst, "Die Auflagenhöhen der deutschen Zeitungen. Ihre Entwicklung und ihre Probleme," Ph.D. diss., University of Leipzig, 1929.

Heide, Walter, ed., *Handbuch der Zeitungswissenschaft* (Leipzig: Verlag Karl Esemann, 1940).

Heidelber, Wilhelm, "Der Vertrieb," *Die Reklame,* 22 (1929), 899–902.

Heigel, Otto, "Untersuchungen über Lesen und Zahlauffassung sowie deren Beeinflussung durch Tee," *Archiv für die gesamte Psychologie,* 64 (1928), 257–299.

Heimann, Eduard, "Sozialisierung," *Neue Blätter für Sozialismus,* 1 (1930), 12–28.

Hellwig, Albert, *Jugendschutz gegen Schundliteratur* (Berlin: Stilke Verlag, 1927).

Herbig, Ernst, "Wirtschaftsrechnungen Saarbrücker Bergleute," *Zeitschrift für das Berg, Hütten und Salinenwesen im Preußischen Staate,* 60 (1912), 451–613.

Heuer, Gerd F. *Entwicklung der Annoncen-Expeditionen in Deutschland* (Frankfurt a.M.: Diesterweg Verlag, 1937).

Heyden, Ludwig, *Wirtschaftsrechnungen von unteren Post- und Telegraphenbeamten* (Berlin: Verband der unteren Telgraphbeamten, 1916).

Hofer, Max, *Die Lebenshaltung des Landarbeiters. Wirtschaftsrechnungen von 130 Landarbeiterfamilien* (Berlin: Landvolk Verlag, 1930).

Hofmann, Walter, *Die Lektüre der Frau. Ein Beitrag zur Leserkunde und Leserforschung* (Leipzig: Quelle & Meyer, 1931).
———, *Buch und Volk. Gesamelte Aufsätze und Reden zur Buchpolitik und Volksbüchereifrage* (Cologne: Verlag der Loewe, 1951).
———, *Das Gedächtnis der Nation. Ein Wort zur Schrifttumspflege in Deutschland* (Jena: Diederichs, 1932).
———, *Der Weg zum Schrifttum. Gedanken und Verwirklichung der deutschen volkstümlichen Bücherei* (Berlin: Verlag d. Arbeitsgemeinschaft, 1922).
———, *Lesetypen innerhalb der erwachsenen männlichen Arbeiterschaft* (Leipzig: Deutsche Zentralstelle für volkstümliches Büchereiwesen, 1928).
———, "Die Organisation des Ausleihedienstes in der modernen Bildungsbibliothek," *Volksbildungsarchiv* (1910) pp. 55–72, 227–344; (1911) pp. 29–131; (1913) pp. 319–374.
——— "Menschenbildung, Volksbildung, Arbeiterbildung in der volkstümlichen Bücherei," *Archiv für Erwachsenenbildung* (1925) pp. 65–104.
Honigsheim, Paul, "Zur Soziologie und Sozialpsychologie der Schundliteratur und des Kinodramas," *Volksbildungsarchiv,* 10 (1923), 124.
Huck, Wolfgang, "Die Kleine Anzeige, ihre Organisation und volkswirtschaftliche Bedeutung," Ph.D. diss., University of Heidelberg, 1914.
Huebner, Friedrich M., "Buchgewerbe und der neue Zeitgeist Grundlage," *Archiv für Buchgewerbe und Gebrauchsgraphik,* 64 (1927), 299–309.
Jaeger, Karl, *Von der Zeitungskunde zur publizistischen Wissenschaft* (Jena: Gustav Fischer, 1926).
Jahn, Franz, "Der deutsche Kolportagebuchhandel," Ph.D. diss., University of Würzburg, 1928.
Jaspers, Karl, *Die geistige Situation der Zeit* (Berlin: Walter de Gruyter, 1931).
Jentsch, Irene, "Zur Geschichte des Zeitungslesens in Deutschland am Ende des 18. Jahrhunderts mit besonderer Berücksichtigung der gesellschaftlichen Formen des Zeitungslesens," Ph.D. diss., University of Leipzig, 1937.
Jeremias, Günther, *Das billige Buch. Entwicklung- und Erscheinungsformen* (Berlin: Triltsch & Huther, 1938).
Kapfinger, Ans, "Der Werbefaktor der Deutschen Zeitungsindustrie," *Die Reklame,* 23 (1930), 622–625.
Karl, von K. "Wirtschaftsrechnungen," *Zeitschrift für die gesamte Staatswissenschaft,* 62 (1906), 710–738.
Kautz, Heinrich, "Die Industriefamilie als Wirtschaftsverband," in: Bauer, Theodor, ed. *Sozialrechtliches Jahrbuch,* vol. 2 (Mannheim: J. Beusheimer, 1931), 183–210.
Kelchner, Mathilde, and Lau, Ernst, *Die Berliner Jugend und die Kriminalliteratur. Eine Untersuchung auf Grund von Aufsätzen Jugendlicher* (Leipzig: Verlag von Johann Ambrosius Barth, 1928).
Kersten, Kurt, "Wirtschaft, Kultur, Intellektuelle," *Die Weltbühne,* 19 (1923), 583–585.
Kiehl, Armin, *Die Eigen-Werbung des Zeitungsverlags* (Eilenburg: C.W. Offenhauer, 1934).
Kirchner, Joachin, *Die Grundlage des deutschen Zeitschriftenwesens* (Leipzig: K.W. Hiersmann, 1928).
Kirschman, August, *Antiqua oder Fraktur?* (Leipzig: Verlag des Deutschen Buchgewerbevereins, 1912).
Klaber, Kurt, "Der proletarische Massenroman," *Linkskurve,* 2 (1930), 22–25.
Klatt, Fritz, "Die Rolle des Buches in der Gegenwart," *Jungbuchhändler-Rundbrief,* 1 (1926), 1.
Kleinberg, Alfred, *Ratschläge für Arbeiterbuchwarte* (Karlsbad: Graphia, 1924).
Kliemann, Horst, *Die Werbung fürs Buch* (Stuttgart: C.E. Poeschel Verlag, 1925).
———, "Die Stellung der Reklame im sozialen und geistigen Geschehen, mit besonderer Berücksichtigung des Buchhandels," *Börsenblatt für den Deutschen Buchhandel,* 91 (1924), 10,755–10,759; 10,847–10,849.
———, "Der Buchreklamefilm," *Börsenblatt für den Deutschen Buchhandel,* 90 (1923), 7176–7177.
———, "Der Börsenverein und seine Werbestelle," *Die Reklame,* 17 (1924), 364–366.
———, "Neuere Motivstatistiken im Buchhandel," *Die Reklame,* 20 (1927), 745–749.
Klotzbach, Rudi, *Deutsche Warenhäuser als Buchhändler* (Leipzig: Verlag der Allgemeinen Vereinigung der Buchhandelsangestellten, 1932).

Kohut, Oswald, *Zeitungen und Zeitschriften als Handelsgut* (Vienna: Verlag Waldheim, 1930).

Kormann, Erich, "Die Verbreitung unzüchtiger Schriften," Ph.D. diss., University of Erlangen, 1931.

Kossow, Karl, "Was liest der deutsche Arbeiter?" *Die Literatur*, 29 (1926/7), 503–504.

Kracauer, Siegfried, *Der Detektiv-Roman. Ein philosophisches Traktat* (Frankfurt a.M.: Suhrkamp, 1979).

———, *Die Angestellte* (Frankfurt a.M.: Suhrkamp, 1971).

———, *Der verbotene Blick* (Leipzig: Reclam, 1992).

Kraziza, Alfons, *259 deutsche Haushaltungsbücher geführt von Abonnenten der Zeitschrift "Nach Feierabend" in den Jahren 1911–1913* (Leipzig: Verlag Bernhard Meyer, 1915).

Krempel, Lore, *Die deutsche Modezeitschrift* (Munich: Tageblatt-Haus, 1935).

Kropff, Hans, and Randolph, Bruno W. *Marktanalyse. Untersuchung des Marktes und Verbreitung der Reklame* (Munich: R. Oldenbourg, 1928).

Ladewig, Paul, *Politik der Bücherei* (Leipzig: Ernst Wiegandt Verlagsbuchhandlung, 1911).

———, *Katechismus der Bücherei* (Leipzig: Wiegandt Verlagbuchhandlung, 1914).

Die Lebenshaltung von 2000 Arbeiter-, Angestellten- und Beamtenhaushaltungen. Erhebung von Wirtschaftsrechnungen im Deutschen Reich vom Jahre 1927/28 Einzelschriften zur Statistik des Deutschen Reiches (Berlin: Hobbing Verlag, 1932).

Die Lebenshaltung des deutschen Reichsbahnpersonals (Berlin: Verlagsgesellschaft deutscher Eisenbahner, 1930).

Die Lebenshaltung der Bauarbeiter nach Wirtschaftsrechnungen aus dem Jahre 1929 (Berlin: Verlag Deutscher Baugewerbesbund, 1931).

Die Lebenshaltung minderbemittelter Familien in Hamburg im Jahr 1925 (Hamburg: Otto Meissner Verlag, 1926).

Lederer, Emil, *Kapitalismus, Klassenstruktur und Probleme der Demokratie in Deutschland 1910–1940*, edited by Jürgen Kocka (Göttingen: Vandenhoeck & Ruprecht, 1979).

Lehmann, Erna, *Die* "Entwicklung und Bedeutung der modernen deutschen Modepresse," Ph.D. diss., University of Heidelberg, 1914.

Lehmann, Ernst H. *Einführung in die Zeitschriftenkunde* (Leipzig: Verlag Karl W. Hiersemann, 1936).

Lehmann, Wilhelm, "Soziale Verfassungskämpfe in der Absatzorganisation des deutschen Buchhandels. Zwischen Buchkonsumentenvereinigungen und regulärem Buchhandel," Ph.D. diss., University of Würzburg, 1922.

Leibel, Richard, "Die geschichtliche Entwicklung des deutschen Bahnhofsbuchhandels," *Der Vertrieb* 24, 25, 26, 37 (1937); 15, 16 (1938); 24 (1939).

Lippert, Elisabeth, *Der Lesestoff der Mädchen in der Vorpubertät* (Erfurt: Verlag Kurt Stenger, 1931).

Lissitzky, El, "Typographische Tatsachen," in: Aloys Leonhard Ruppel, ed. *Gutenberg Festschrift* (Mainz: Verlag der Gutenberg Gesselschaft, 1925).

List, Friedrich, *Grundriß eines Bibliotheksrechts* (Gießen: Verlag von Emil Roth, 1928).

Loele, Kurt, *Neuere deutsche Schaufensterkunst* (Leipzig: Ernst Reil, 1925).

———, "Papierflut," *Der Bahnhofsbuchhandel* (26.3.1930).

Loewenstein, Paul, "Der deutsche Sortimentsbuchhandel. Seine wirtschaftliche Entwicklungsgeschichte," Ph.D. diss., University of Innsbruck, 1921.

Löffler, Otto, "Der Inseratenmarkt der illustrierten Zeitung," Ph.D. diss., University of Heidelberg, 1935.

Lorenz, Erich, "Die Entwicklung des deutschen Zeitschriftwesens," Ph.D. diss., Humboldt University Berlin, 1936.

Lowis, Augusr, "Moderne Deutsche Buchwerbung," *Die Reklame*, 21 (1928), 499–504.

Lueb, Lydia, "Die Freizeit der Textilarbeiterinnen. Eine Untersuchung über die Verwendung der Freizeit der Arbeiterinnen des christlichen Textilarbeitverbandes Bezirk Westfalen," Ph.D. diss., University of Münster, 1929.

Lundeberg, Hildur, "Einige neuere Methoden der Buchpropaganda in der Jugendabteilung der Büchereien," *Bücherei und Bildungspflege*, 13 (1933), 28–32.

Lutz, Norbert, "Welche Menge Schund- und Schmutzliteratur gibt es in Deutschland?" *Börsenblatt für den Deutschen Buchhandel*, 98 (1930), 468.

Lux, Käthe, *Studien über die Entwicklung der Warenhäuser in Deutschland* (Jena: Gustav Fischer Verlag, 1910).

Mann, Heinrich, "Detektiv-Romane," *Die literarische Welt*, 5 (1929), 1– 2.

Mann, Thomas, "Kultur und Sozialismus," in: *Gesammelte Werke*, vol. 12 (Frankfurt a.M.: Fischer Verlag, 1960).

Mataja, Viktor, *Die Reklame. Eine Untersuchung über Ankündigungswesen und Werbetätigkeiten im Geschäftsleben* (Munich: Duncker & Humblot, 1926).

Matz, Elsa, and Seeger, Ernst, *Gesetz zur Bewahrung der Jungend vor Schund- und Schmutzschriften* (Berlin: Karl Heymann Verlag, 1927).

Meiner, Annemarie, *Reclam. Eine Geschichte der Universal-Bibliothek zu ihrem 75jährigen Bestehen* (Leipzig: Verlag von Philipp Reclam, 1942).

Meiner, Felix, *Warum sind die Bücher so teuer? Drei Aufsätze über Buchhandel, Bücherkäfer und Verfasser* (Leipzig: Deutsche Verlagsverein, 1920).

Meißner, Hans-Heinz, "Das Inserat in den großen deutschen politischen Tageszeitungen von 1850 bis 1870," Ph.D. diss., University of Leipzig, 1931.

Meißner, Herbert, "Das Schund- und Schmutzgesetz in seiner strafrechtlichen Bedeutung," Humboldt University Berlin, 1929.

Mennicke, Carl, *Der Buchhandel in der geistigen Lage der Gegenwart* (Potsdam: R. Heidkamp, 1928).

Menz, Gerhard, *Der deutsche Buchhandel der Gegenwart in Selbstdarstellungen* (Leipzig: Verlag von Felix Meiner, 1925).

———, *Der deutsche Buchhandel* (Gotha: Flamberg Verlag, 1925).

———, *Die Zeitschrift. Ihre Entwicklung und ihre Lebensbedingungen* (Stuttgart: C.E. Poeschel Verlag, 1928).

———, *Kulturwirtschaft* (Leipzig: Linder Verlag, 1933).

———, "Zur Frage der Sozialisierung des Buchhandels," *Börsenblatt für den Deutschen Buchhandel*, 87 (1920), 84.

———, "Die Krisis im deutschen Buchhandel," *Börsenblatt für den Deutschen Buchhandel*, 97 (1927), 961–966; 1172–1174.

———, "Das Buch als Ware und Wirtschaftsfaktor," *Archiv für Buchgewerbe und Gebrauchsgraphik*, 67 (1930), 445–459.

Meyer, Erna, "Der Haushalt eines höhere Beamten in den Jahren 1880 bis 1906," in: Frany Eulenberg, ed., *Kosten der Lebenshaltung in deutschen Großstädten* (Munich: Duncker & Humblot, 1915), 1–92.

———, *Der neue Haushalt. Ein Wegweiser zu wirtschaftlicher Hausführung* (Stuttgart: Franckh´sche Verlagshandlung, 1927).

Michael, Oskar, ed. *Handbuch deutscher Zeitungen 1917* (Berlin: Otto Elsner Verlagsgesellschaft, 1917).

Moholy-Nagy, Ladisla, *Malerei, Fotografie, Film* (Munich: Albert Langen Verlag, 1927).

———, "Typo-Foto" *Typographische Mitteilung. Sonderhefte: Elementare Typographie* (1925), 202.

———, "Zeitgemässe Typographie—Ziele, Praxis, Kritik," in: Aloys Leonhard Ruppel, ed., *Gutenberg Festschrift* (Mainz: Verlag der Gutenberg Gesselschaft, 1925).

Molzahn, Johannes, "Nicht mehr lesen! Sehen!" *Das Kunstblatt*, 12 (1928), 78–82.

Moufang, Wilhelm, *Die gegenwärtige Lage des deutschen Buchwesens. Eine Darstellung der Spannug und Reformbewegung am Buchmarkt* (Munich: J. Sweizer Verlag, 1921).

———, "Die kulturpolitische Krisis des deutschen Buches," *Hochland*, 19 (1921/22), 216–227.

Müller, Johannes, *Deutsche Kulturstatistik* (Jena: Verlag von Gustav Fischer, 1928).

Mumm, Reinhard, "Kampf gegen Schund-und Schmutz," *Deutsche Arbeit*, 11 (1926), 28.

Nahnsen, Otto, *Der Straßenhandel mit Zeitung und Druckschriften in Berlin* (Essen: Verlag der Wirtschaftlichen Nachrichten aus dem Ruhrbezirk, 1922).

Naumann, Wilhelm J., ed., *Die Presse und der Katholik. Anklage und Rechtfertigung* (Augsburg: Haas & Grabherr, 1932).

Neckel, Walter, "*Die Kartellformen im Buchhandel,*" Ph.D. diss., University of Munich, 1934.
Niemczyk, Paul, *Die deutsche Abonnentenversicherung unter Reichsaufsicht* (Berlin: Curt Hamelsche, 1932).
Niewöhner, Emil, *Geschichte und Probleme des Zeitschriftenbuchhandels* (Dresden: Zahn & Nasch, 1932).
———, *Der Reise- und Versandbuchhandel* (Dresden: Zahn & Nasch, 1933).
———, *Der deutsche Zeitschriftbuchhandel* (Stuttgart: Poeschel Verlag, 1934).
Nitschmann, Paul, *Die Krisis im Deutschen Buchhandel* (Berlin: Verlag der Deutschen Buchhändler, 1928).
Noack, Reinhard W., *Filmbroschüren. Leitfaden für Film Reklame* (Berlin: Verlag bei Werkunst Fr. K. Koetschau, 1925).
Oldenbourg, Friedrich, *Buch und Bildung* (Munich: Beck, 1925).
———, "Die geistige Krisis und das Buch," *Börsenblatt für den deutschen Buchhandel,* 94 (1927), 1213–1219.
Paneth, Erwin, *Entwicklung der Reklame vom Altertum bis zur Gegenwart* (Munich: R. Oldenbourg, 1926).
Panofski, Lotte, "Die Lebenshaltung der Kohlenbergwerksarbeiter in Deutsch- und Polnisch-Oberschlesien," Ph.D. diss., University of Cologne, 1931.
Pantenburg, Josef, *Die Entwicklung des Anzeigewesens der Berliner Presse von der Aufhebung des Intelligenzszwanges bis zur Generalanzeigen* (Berlin: Triltsch & Hunther, 1938).
Pape, Richard, *Handbuch der Fachpresse* (Berlin: Verlag des 'Archiv für Gewerbepolitik und Volkswirtschaft,' 1926).
———, "Die Deutschen Zeitschriften in ihren Beziehungen zu Wirtschaft und Kultur," *Die Reklame* 21 (1928), 41.
Piper, Reinhard, "Das Buch und der Mensch von heute," *Börsenblatt für den deutschen Buchhandel,* 93 (1926), 1537.
Pollin, Friedrich, "Das Buch in Lichtbild und Film," *Börsenblatt für den deutschen Buchhandel,* 93 (1926), 1014–1017.
Popert, Hermann, *Hamburg und der Schundkampf* (Hamburg: Dichter Gedächtnisstiftung, 1926).
Rau, Christian, "Der strafrechtliche Begriff der unzüchtigen Schrift," Ph.D. diss., University of Leipzig, 1931.
Redlich, Fritz, *Reklame. Begriff—Geschichte—Theorie* (Stuttgart: Fredinand Enke, 1935).
Reisner, Lother, "Die unzüchtige Schrift," Ph.D. diss., University of Würzburg, 1936.
Rennen, Paul, *mechanisierte Graphik* (Berlin: Hermann Verlag, 1931).
———, "Type und Typographie," *Archiv für Buchgewerbe und Gebrauchsgraphik,* 65 (1928), 453–468.
Richter, Kurt, *Der Kampf gegen Schund- und Schmutzschriften in Preußen* (Berlin: Decker Verlag, 1931).
Riebcke, Otto, "Gedanken zur Sozialisierung des Buchwesens," *Börsenblatt für den Deutschen Buchhandel,* 86 (1919), 813–815, 817–820.
Roloff, Hans Paul, *Experimentelle Untersuchung der Werbewirkung von Plakatentwürfen* (Leipzig: Barth, 1927).
Rosenbrock, Edith, *Die Anfänge des Modebildes in deutschen Zeitschriften* (Charlottenburg: Rudolf Lorenz Verlag, 1942).
Ruben, Paul, ed., *Die Reklame und ihre Kunst und Wissenschaft* (Berlin: Hermann Paetel, 1914).
Rumpf, Erich, *Kind und Buch. Das Lieblingsbuch der deutschen Jugend zwischen 9 und 16 Jahren* (Berlin: Dümmels Verlag, 1928).
Rundfunk und Volksbildung (Berlin: Tagung des Berliner Ausschusses zur Bekämpfung der Schund- und Schmutzliteratur, 1926).
Rüttgers, Sevrin, *Literarische Erziehung. Ein Versuch über die Jugendschriftenfrage auf soziologischer Grundlage* (Langensalza: Verlag von Julius Beltz, 1931).
Quitzow, Otto, *Verkaufsgespräche im Sortiment* (Leipzig: Verlag des Börsenvereins der Deutschen Buchhändler, 1925).
Samuleit, Paul, and Brunckhorst, Hans, *Geschichte und Wege der Schundbekämpfung* (Berlin: Carl Heymanns Verlag, 1922).

Schanz, Joachim, "Die Entstehung eines deutschen Presse-Grossverlages," Ph.D. diss., Humboldt University Berlin, 1932.
Scharf, Fritz, "Umfang und Rhythmus der Werbung durch Anzeigen," Ph.D. diss., University of Heidelberg, 1937.
Scheffen, Wilhelm, ed., *Buch und Arbeiter. Grundsätzliches und Praktisches* (Gotha: Verlag Fr. Andreas Perthes, 1924).
Schmidt, Alfred, *Publizistik im Dorf* (Dresden: Verlag M. Ditter, 1939).
Schmidt, Ernst, ed., *Handbuch der Hauszeitschriften* (Cologne: Verlag Gebrüder Brocker, 1933).
Schnabel, Fritz, *Büchertage und Buchwochen* (Leipzig: Verlag des Börsenvereins der deutschen Buchhändler, 1925).
———, "Die Werbung fürs Buch," *Die Reklame,* 17 (1924), 346–348.
Schönfeld, Gerhard, "Die Soziale Frage im Buchhandel," *Jungbuchhändler- Rundbrief,* 4 (1930), 10–22.
——— "Der Untergang der Bildung. Wirtschaft und Bildung," *Die Tat,* 23 (1931), 18–34.
——— "Zur Geschichte des deutschen Jungbuchhandels," *Der neue Stand,* 2 (1932), 34–37.
Schriewer, Franz, "Kampf den Leihbüchereien," *Bücherei und Bildungspflege,* 13 (1933), 110–113.
Schröder, Fritz, "Grundfragen der Verlagsreklame," *Die Reklame,* 17 (1924), 343–345.
Schultze, Ernst, *Die Schundliteratur. Ihr Wesen. Ihre Folgen. Ihre Bäkmpfung* (Halle: Verlag Buchhandlung des Waeisenhauses, 1909).
Schuster, Wilhelm, "Die Soziologie der literarischen Geschmacksbildung und die Volksbücherei," *Bücherei und Bildungspflege,* 11 (1931), 1–8.
Schwegmann, Rudolf, "Experimentelle Untersuchung zur Lesbarkeit von Fraktur und Antiqua und von Groß- und Kleinschreibung," Ph.D. diss., University of Göttingen, 1935.
Semm, Hans, "Einiges über Lehrlingsausbildung," *Buchhändlergilde-Blatt,* 7/8 (1926), 89.
———, "Wie werde ich meinem Kunden gerecht?" *Buchhändlergilde-Blatt,* 7/8 (1926), 33.
———, "Vom Verkaufen im Sortiment," *Buchhändlergilde-Blatt,* 9 (1927), 39.
Seyffert, Rudolf, *Allgemeine Werbelehre* (Stuttgart: C.E. Poeschel, 1929).
Sielaff, Erich, "Was lesen unsere Jungmädchen, und was sollen sie lesen?" *Bücherei und Bildungspflege,* 13 (1933), 1–23.
Siemering, Herta, and Spranger, Eduard, *Weibliche Jugend in unserer Zeit. Beobachtungen und Erfahrungen von Jugendführerinnen* (Leipzig: Quelle & Meyer, 1932).
———, Barschak, Erna, and Gensch, Willy, *Was liest unsere Jugend? Ergebnisse von Feststellungen an Schulen aller Gattungen und Erziehungsanstalten sowie bei Jugendorganisationen und Jugendlichen* (Berlin: Decker's Verlag, 1930).
Simmel, Georg, *Philosophie des Geldes* (Munich: Duncker & Humbolt, 1930).
———, *Das Individuum und die Freiheit* (Frankfurt a.M.: Fischer, 1993).
Sommer, Albrecht, *Lehre vom Privathaushalt* (Berlin: Junker und Dünnhaupt Verlag, 1931).
Sonntag, Kurt, *Das geschichtliche Bewußtsein des Schülers* (Erfurt: Verlag Kurt Stenger, 1932).
Statistische Mitteilungen über den hamburgischen Staat Nr. 26. Die Lebenshaltung der wirtschaftlich schwachen Bevölkerung in Hamburg (Hamburg: Otto Meissners Verlag, 1931).
Stosch-Sarrasani, Hans, *Durch die Welt im Zirkuszelt* (Berlin: Volksverband Bücherfreunde, 1940).
Suhr, Otto, *Die Lebenshaltung der Angestellten* (Berlin: Freier Volksverlag, 1928).
Suhr, Susanne, *Die Weiblichen Angestellten* (Berlin: Zentralverband der Angestellten, 1930).
Tangermann, Fritz, "Die Landgemeinde Belsdorf am Anfang des 20. Jahrhunderts," Ph.D. diss., University of Leipzig, 1905.
Thier, Erich, *Gestaltwandel des Arbeiters im Spiegel seiner Lektüre* (Leipzig: Otto Harrassowitz, 1939).
Thomas, Hans (e.i. Hans Zehrer), "Das Chaos der Bücher," *Die Tat,* 22 (1930/31), 669–679.
Thorner, Hans, "Experimentelle Untersuchungen zur Psychologie des Lesens," *Archiv für die gesamte Psychologie* 64 (1929), 127–184.
Tobis, Hans, "Das Mittelstandsproblem der Nachkriegszeit und seine statistische Erfassung," Ph.D. diss., University of Frankfurt a.M., 1930.
Tönies, Hubert, "Die rechtlichen Grundlagen zur Bekämpfung von Schund-und Schmutz in Schrifttum, Film, Theater und Revuen," Ph.D. diss., University of Hamburg, 1943.

Traub, Hans, *Zeitungswesen und Zeitunglesen* (Dessau: C. Dünnhaupt Verlag, 1928).
———, "Zeitungswissenschaft und Berufsbildung," in: *Jahrbuch der Tagespresse 1930* (Berlin: Duncker Verlag, 1930), pp. III–XIII.
———, "Über die Kritik am Inseratenteil der Zeitung," *Die Reklame,* 22 (1929), 903–908.
Trampler-Steiner, Josefin, "Die Frau als Publizistin und Leserin," Ph.D. diss., University of Munich, 1938.
Tschichold, Jan, *Die Neue Typographie* (Berlin: Verlag des Bildungsverbands des Deutschen Buchdrucks, 1928).
———, *Schriften 1925–1974* (Berlin: Brinkmann & Bose, 1991).
Uderstädt, E.R. "Die Stellung der Annoncen-Expeditionen in der Deutschen Wirtschaft," *Die Reklame,* 22 (1929), 588–592.
Uhlig, Friedrich, *Der Sortimentslehrling* (Leipzig: Verlag des Börsenvereins der Deutschen Buchhändler, 1934).
———, "Der Standort der Verlage im politischen Lebensraum," *Der Neue Stand,* 2 (1932), 128.
——— "Zehn Jahre für Buchhandelsbetriebslehre an der Handelshochschule zu Leipzig," *Börsenblatt für den deutschen Buchhandel,* 102 (1935), 1053–1057.
Umlauff, Ernst, *Beiträge zur Statistik des deutschen Buchhandels* (Leipzig: Verlag des Börsenvereins der Deutschen Buchhändler, 1934).
Victor, Max, "Verbürgerlichung des Proletariats und Proletarisierung des Mittelstandes," *Die Arbeit,* 8 (1931), 17–31.
Volkmann, Wilhelm, *Grundfrage des Vereinsbuchhandels* (Leipzig: Breitkopf & Härtel, 1921).
Waas, Adolf, "Lesekunde," *Volksbildungsarchiv,* 10 (1923), 142–149.
Wagner, Julius, "Experimentelle Beiträge zur Psychologie des Lesens," Ph.D. diss., University of Leipzig, 1918.
Wanart, Stefan, *Um die Zukunft des deutschen Buches* (Freiburg i.Br.: Ernst Günther Verlag, 1920).
Was verbrauchen die Angestellten? (Berlin: Freier Volksverlag, 1931).
Was wir vom Buch erwarten (Leipzig: Verlag des Börsenvereins der Deutschen Buchhändler, 1931).
Watzal, Sebastian, "Wie wir ein Buch verkaufen," *Die Reklame,* 21 (1928), 173.
Weber, Adolf, *Die Großstadt und ihre sozialen Probleme* (Leipzig: Quellen & Mezer, 1908).
Weber, Alfred, *Die Not der Geistigen Arbeit* (Munich: Duncker & Hombolt, 1923).
Weber, Friedrich, "*Schundliteratur und jugendliche Verbrecher,*" Ph.D. diss., University of Munich, 1942.
Das Werk des Volksverbandes der Bücherfreunde (Berlin: Volksverband der Bücherfreunde, 1924).
Weickert, Ilse, *Die Lese-Interessen der werktätigen Mädchen zwischen 14 bis 18* (Bonn: Ludwig Röhrscheid, 1933).
Weise, Leopold v. "Die Sozialisierung des Buchverlags," in: Sinzheimer, Ludwig, ed. *Die geistigen Arbeiter. Freiers Schrifstellertum und Literaturverlag* (Munich: Duncker & Humbolt, 1922).
———, ed., *Soziologie des Volksbildungswesens* (Munich: Duncker & Hubolt, 1921).
Welsche, Gisela, "Studien zur Werbung für die Dichtung in neuerer Zeit," Ph.D. diss., University of Cologne, 1947.
Wesel, Helene, *Lebenshaltung aus Fürsorge und aus Erwerbstätigkeit* (Berlin: R. Müller, 1931).
Wieber, Friedkarl, "Der Zeitungsroman im 20. Jhr. Eine volkskundliche Auseinandersetzung," Ph.D. diss., University of Halle, 1933.
Wieser, Max, "Die geistige Krisis des Buches und die Volksbibliotheken," *Preußische Jahrbücher* 191 (1923), 182–201.
———, "Soziologie des Buches," in: *Buch und Gesellschaft* (Berlin: Hillger Verlag, 1927), 23–25.
———, "Buch und Rundfunk," *Die Tat,* 19 (1929), 737–757.
Wiliams, Walter, "Some Observations on the German Press," *The University of Missouri Bulletin,* 33 (1932), 1–19.
Wingender, Hans, Erfarungen im Kampf gegen Schund- und Schmutzschriften (Düsseldorf: published by the author, 1929).
———, "Bekämpfung von Schmutz-und Schundliteratur," in: *Bewahrung der Jugend vor Schund- und Schmutzschriften* (Düsseldorf: Verlag des Landesjugendamtes, 1928).

———, "Das Schundliteraturgesetz eine Kräftigung des Schundkapitals?" *Die Wohlfahrtspflege der Reihnprovinz,* 3 (1928), 135–138.

Winterhoff, Edmund, *Die Krisis im Deutschen Buchhandel* (Karlsruhe: Verlag G. Braun, 1927).

Wittek, Erhard, *Das Buch als Werbemittel* (Leipzig: Verlag des Börsenvereins der Deutschen Buchhändler, 1926).

———, "Korporative Buchwerbung im Gegenwärtigen Augenblick," *Offset- Buch und Werbekunst,* 3 (1926), 180–182.

Wussow, Max v., *Die deutsche Papierindustrie in Zahlen und Bildern* (Berlin: Kraus & Baumann, 1927).

Zeitler, Julius, "Gebrauchsgraphiker und Buchkünstler," *Die Reklame,* 17 (1924), 373–375.

Zickfeldt, Kurt, "Die Umgestaltung des Buchmarktes durch Buchgemeinschaften und Fachvereinsverlage," Ph.D. diss., University of Freiburg i.Br., 1927.

Zimmerman, Carle C. *Consumption and Standards of Living* (New York: Van Nostrand, 1936).

———, "Ernst Engel's Law of Expenditures for Food," *The Quarterly Journal of Economics,* 47 (1932/33), 78–101.

Secondary literature

Abrams, Lynn, "From control to commercialization: the Triumph of Mass Entertainment in Germany 1900–1925?" *German History,* 8 (1990), 279– 293.

Ackerknecht, Erwing, *Der Kitsch als kultureller Übergangswert* (Bremen: Verein Deutscher Volksbibliothekare, 1950, org. writing in 1934).

Adam, Thomas, *Arbeitermilieu und Arbeiterbewegung in Leipzig 1880 bis 1933* (Cologne: Böhlau, 1999).

Adorno, Theodor W. and Horkheimer, Max, *Dialektik der Aufklärung* (Frankfurt a. M.: Fischer, 1988).

Adrian, Werner, "Frauen im Buchhandel. Eine Dokumentation zur Geschichte einer fast lautlosen Emanzipation," *Archiv für Geschichte des Buchwesens,* 49 (1998), 147–247.

Allen, James Smith, *In the Public Eye: A History of Reading in Modern France 1800–1940* (Princeton: Princeton University Press, 1991).

Altick, Richard D., *The English Common Reader: A Social History of the Mass Reading Public 1800–1900* (Chicago: Chicago University Press, 1957).

Appadurai, Arjun, ed., *The Social Life of Things: Commodities in Cultural Perspective* (Cambridge: Cambridge University Press, 1986).

Arbogast, Hubert, ed. *Über Rudolf Borchardt* (Stuttgart: Klett Cotta, 1977).

Armin, Brend v. and Knilli, Friedrich, *Gewerbliche Leihbüchereien* (Gütersloh: Bertelsmann Verlag, 1966).

Arps, Ludwig, *Auf sicheren Pfeilern. Deutsche Versicherungswirtschaft vor 1914* (Göttingen: Vandenhoeck & Ruprecht, 1965).

———, *Durch Unruhige Zeiten. Deutsche Versicherungswirtschaft seit 1914* (Karlsruhe: Verlag Versicherungswirtschaft, 1976).

Aubach, Christel, *Die Volksbücherei als Bildungsbücherei in der Theorie der deutschen Bücherhallenbewegung* (Cologne: Greven Verlag, 1962).

Aynsley, Jeremy, *Graphic Design in Germany 1890 –1945* (Berkeley: University of California Press, 2000).

Barbian, Jan-Pieter, *Literaturpolitik im Dritten Reich: Institutionen, Kompetenzen, Betätigungsfelder* (Munich: dtv, 1993).

Baumgärtner, Alfred Clemens, ed., *Lesen—Ein Handbuch* (Hamburg: Verlag für Buchhandel Forschung, 1974).

Bausch, Hans, *Rundfunkpolitik in der Weimarer Republik* (Munich: dtv, 1980).

Becker, Frank, *Amerikanismus in Weimar: Sportsymbole und Politische Kultur 1918–1933* (Wiesbaden: DUT, 1993).

Beckmann, Friedrich, "Lektüre als Konsumanreiz? Leserdarstellung in der Mode-Bildwerbung der Gegenwart," *Buchhandelsgeschichte,* 10 (1991/2), 49–69.

Behrnes, Werner, Geiger, Klaus F., Rehermann, Ernst Heinrich, Reidel, Margot, and Schmutzler, Brigitte, "Planskizzen zu einer Sozialgeschichte des Lesens," *Zeitschrift für Volkskunde,* 72 (1976), 1–27.

Berkin, Helmuth, *Masse und Geist. Studien zur Soziologie in der Weimarer Republik* (Berlin: Wav, 1984).

Berman, Russel A. *Modern Culture and Critical Theory: Art, Politics, and the Legacy of the Frankfurt School* (Madison: University of Wisconsin Press, 1989).

———, "Writing for the Book Industry: The Writer under Organized Capitalism," *New German Critique*, 29 (1983), 39–56.

Berminigham, Ann, and Brewer, John, ed., *The Consumption of Culture 1600–1800* (London: Routledge, 1995).

Beutin, Heidi, *"Als eine Frau lesen lernte, trat die Frauenfrage in die Welt"* (Hamburg: Bockel Verlag, 1995).

Bode, Dietrich, ed., *125 Jahre Reclams Universal Bibliothek* (Stuttgart: Reclam, 1992).

Borscheid, Peter, and Wischermann, Clemens, eds., *Bilderwelt des Alltags* (Stuttgart: Franz Steiner Verlag, 1995).

———, *Mit Sicherheit Leben* (Greven: Eggenkampg Verlag, 1989).

Bourdieu, Pierr, *Distinction. A Social Critique of the Judgment of Taste* (Cambridge: Cambridge University Press, 1984).

———, *The Field of Cultural Production* (Oxford: Polity Press, 1993).

Brand, Eva, Brand, Peter, and Schulze, Volker, eds., *Die Zeitungsanzeige* (Aachen: Hahner Verlag, 1990).

Brandes, Helga, *Politische Mythen und Symbole im Mädchenbuch der Gründerzeit* (Oldenburg: Bibliotheksgesellschaft Oldenburg, 1993).

Braun, Rudolf, "Einleitende Bemerkungen zum Problem der historischen Lebensstandartforschung," in: Werner Conze, and Ulrich Engelherdt, eds., *Arbeiter im Industrialisierungsprozeß* (Stuttgart: Klett Cotta, 1979), 128–135.

Breckmann, Warren G., "Dicipling Consumption: The debate about luxury in Wilhelmine Germany 1890–1914," *Journal of Social History*, 24 (1990\91), 485–505.

Bridenthal, Renate; Grossmann, Atina; and Kaplan, Marion, eds., *When Biology becomes Destiny: Women in Weimar and Nazi Germany* (New York: Monthly Review, 1984).

Brewer, John, Mckendrick, Niel, and Plumb, J.H., *The Birth of Consumer Society: The Commercialization of Eighteenth Century England* (Bloomingtone: Indiana University Press, 1982).

———, and Poter, Roy, eds., *Consumption and the World of Goods* (London: Routledge, 1993).

Brohm, Berthold, "Das Buch in der Krise. Studien zur Buchhandelsgeschichte in der Weimarer Republik," *Archiv für Geschichte des Buchwesens*, 51 (1999), 189–331.

Bruchner, Gisela, "Rudolf Borchardt und der Buchhandel. Ein Beitrag zur Literatur des deutschen Buchhandels in den letzten Jahren der Weimarer Republik," *Archiv für Geschichte des deutschen Buchhandels*, 14 (1974), 285–348.

Butsch, Richard, ed., *For Fun and Profit. The Transformation of Leisure into Consumption* (Chapel Hill: University of North Carolina Press, 1991).

Campbel, Colin, *The Romantic Ethic and the Spirit of Modern Consumerism* (Oxford: Basil Blackwell, 1987).

Carter, Erica, *How German is She? Postwar West German Reconstruction and Consuming Women* (Michigan: Michigan University Press, 1997).

Cavallo, Guglielmo, and Chartier, Roger, eds., *A History of Reading in the West*, translated by Lydia G. Cochrane (Amherst: University of Massachusetts Press, 1999).

Chartier, Roger, *The Order of Books* (Stanford: Stanford University Press, 1994).

———, "Ist Geschichte des Lesens möglich? Vom Buch zu lesen: Einige Hypoththesen," in: Brigitte Schlieben-Lange, ed. *Lesen—Historisch* (Göttingen: Vandenhoeck & Ruprecht, 1985), 250–273.

———, "Text, Printing, Reading," in: Hunt, Lynn, ed., *The New Cultural History* (Berkeley: University of California Press, 1987), 154–175.

Conze, Werner, and Kocka, Jürgen, eds., *Bildungsbürgertum im 19. Jahrhundert*, 4 vol. (Stuttgart: Klett-Cotta, 1985ff.).

Cook, Deborah, *The Culture Industry Revised: Theodor W. Adorno on Mass Culture* (London: Rowman & Littlefield Publishers, 1996).

Cook-Gumperz, Jenny, *The Social Constraction of Literacy* (Cambridge: Cambridge University Press, 1986).

Coyner, J. Sandra, "Class Consciousness and Consumption: The New Middle Class during the Weimarer Republic," *Journal of Social History*, 10 (1977), 310–331.

Cross, Gary, *Time and Money: The Making of Consumer Culture* (London: Routledge, 1993).

Dahrendorf, Malte, *Das Mädchenbuch und seine Leserin* (Weinheim: Beltz, 1978).

Dann, Otto, ed., *Lesegesellschaften und bürgerliche Emanzipation* (Munich: Beck Verlag, 1981).

Darnton, Robert, "What is the History of Books?" in: Carpenter, Kenneth E., ed., *Books and Society in History* (New York: R.R. Bowker Co., 1983), 3–29.

———, "History of Reading," in: Burke, Peter, ed., *New Perspectives on Historical Writing* (Oxford: Polity Press, 1986), 140–168.

Denning, Michael, *Dime Novels and Working Class Culture in America* (London: Verso, 1987).

———, "Cheap Stories: Notes on Popular Fiction and Working-class Culture in Nineteenth-century America," *History Workshop*, 22 (1986), 1–18.

Diederichs, Ulf, "Jena und Weimar als verlagerisches Programm. Über die Anfänge des Eugen Diederichs Verlags in Jena," in: John, Jürgen and Wahl, Volker, eds., *Zwischen Konvention und Avantgart: Doppelstadt Jena—Weimar* (Weimar: Böhlau, 1995), 51–81.

Dimpfel, Monika and Jäger, Georg, eds., *Zur Sozialgeschichte der deutschen Literatur im 19. Jahrhundert* (Tübingen: Niemeyer Verlag, 1990).

Diner, Dan, *Verkehrte Welten. Antiamerikanismus in Deutschland* (Frankfurt a.M.: Eichborn, 1993).

Douglas, Mary and Isherwood, Baron, *The World of Goods: Toword an Anthropology of Consumption* (London: Routledge, 1996).

Dowe, Dieter, ed., *Erhebung von Wirtschaftsrechnungen minderbemittelter Familien im Deutschen Reich (1909). 320 Haushaltungsrechnungen von Metallarbeitern (1909)* (Bonn: Dietz, 1981).

———, *Erhebungen von Wirtschaftsrechnungen von Metallarbeiter* (first published 1909) (Bonn: Dietz, 1981).

Du Gay, Paul, ed., *Production of Culture / Cultures of Production* (London: Sage, 1997).

Dupeux, Louis, *Nationalbolschewismus in Deutschland 1919–1933. Kommunistische Strategie und konservative Dynamik* (Frankfurt a.M.: Büchergild Gutenberg, 1985).

Eco, Umberto, *The Role of the Reader* (Bloomington: University of Indiana Press, 1991).

Ehringhaus, Inge, *Die Lektüre unserer Frontsoldaten im Weltkrieg* (Berlin: Junker & Dünnhaupt, 1941).

Eichmann, Herbert, "Darstellung und Analyse der Strukturwandlungen des Massenverbrauchs in Deutschland," Ph.D. diss., University of Münster, 1955.

Elsner, Friedrich, *Beiträge und Dokumente zur Geschichte des werbenden Buches und Zeitschriftenhandels* (Cologne: Verband des werbenden Buch-und Zeitschriftenhandels, 1961–1971).

Engelsing, Rolf, *Zur Sozialgeschichte deutscher Mittel- und Unterschichten* (Göttingen: Vandenhoeck & Ruprecht, 1973).

———, *Analphabetentum und Lektüre. Zur Sozialgeschichte des Lesens in Deutschland zwischen feudaler und industrieller Gesellschaft* (Stuttgart: J.B. Metzler, 1973).

———. *Der Bürger als Leser. Lesergeschichte in Deutschland 1500–1800* (Stuttgart: J.B. Metzlersche, 1974).

———, "Der Bürger als Leser. Die Bildung der protestantischen Bevölkerung Deutschlands im 17. und 18. Jahrhundert am Beispiel Bremens," *Archiv für Geschichte des Buchwesens*, 3 (1961), 205–263.

———, "Das Thema Lesergeschichte," *Jahrbuch für Internationale Germanistik*, 12 (1980), 168–178.

Erman, Hans, *August Scherl. Dämonie und Erfolg in wilhelminischer Zeit* (Berlin: Universitas Verlag, 1954).

Escaprit, Robert, *Das Buch und der Leser. Kunst und Kommunikation* (Cologne: Westdeutscherverlag, 1961).

Faulstich, Werner, *Bestandsaufnahme Bestseller-Forschung. Ansätze—Methoden—Ertraege* (Wiesbaden: Otto Harrassowitz, 1983).

Fauth, Harry, "Zur Geschichte des Jungbuchhandels in Deutschland 1923–1933," in: Kalhöfer, Karl Heinz and Rötzsch, Helmuth, eds., *Beiträge zur Geschichte des Buchwesens*, vol. 4 (Leipzig: VEB Fachverlag, 1969), 163–187.

Feldman, Gerald, *The Great Disorder. Politics, Economics and Society in German Inflation 1914–1924* (Oxford: Oxford University Press, 1997).

———, eds., *Die Anpassung an die Inflationszeit* (Berlin: Walter de Gruzter, 1986).

———, "The Politics of Wissenschaftspolitik in Weimar Germany: A Prelude to the Dilemmas of Twentieth-Century Science Policy," in: Charles Maier, ed., *Changing Boundaries of the Political. Essays on the Evolving Balance Between the State and Society, Public and Private in Europe* (Cambridge: Cambridge University Press, 1987), 255–285.

Felske, Karl, *75 Jahre Verband Deutscher Lesezirkel 1908 bis 1983* (Düsseldorf: Verband Deutscher Lesezirkel, 1983).

———, ed., *Die deutschen Lesezirkel* (Düsseldorf: Verband Deutscher Lesezirkel, 1969).

Fischer, Hans-Ditrich, ed., *Deutsche Presseverleger des 18. und 19. Jahrhunderts* (Pullach: Verlag Dokumentation, 1975).

Fligge, Jörgen and Klotzbücher, Alois, eds., *Stadt und Bibliothek. Literaturversorgung als kommunale Aufgabe im Kaiserreich und in der Weimarer Republik* (Wiesbaden: Harrassowitz, 1997).

Föllmer, Moritz and Graf, Rüdiger, eds., Die Krise der Weimarer Republik: Zur Kritik eines Deutungsmusters (Frankfurt a.M.: Campus Verlag, 2005).

Foucault, Michel, *The History of Sexuality*, Vol. 1 (New York: Vintage Books, 1980).

———, "What is an Author?" *Language, Counter-Memory, Practice*, translated by Donald F. Bouchard (New York: Cornell University Press, 1977), 124–127.

Frevert, Ute, *Women in German History* (Oxford: Berg, 1988).

Friedberg, Anne, *Window Shopping: Cinema and the Postmodern* (Berkeley: University of California Press, 1993).

Fritzsche, Klaus, *Politische Romantik und Gegenrevolution. Fluchwege in der Krise der bürgerlichen Gesellschaft: Das Beispiel des 'Tat-Kreises'* (Frankfurt a.M: Suhrkampf, 1976).

Fritzsche, Peter, *Reading Berlin 1900* (Harvard: Harvard University Press, 1996).

———, "Did Weimar Fail?" *Journal of Modern History*, 68 (1996), 629–656.

Frühwald, Wolfgang, "Büchmann und die Folgen. Zur sozialen Funktion des Bildungszitates in der deutschen Literatur des 19. Jahrhundert," in: Koselleck, Reinhard, ed., *Bildungsbürgertum im 19. Jahrhundert*, vol. 2 (Stuttgart: Klett-Cotta, 1990), 197–219.

Führer, Karl Christian, "Auf dem Weg zur 'Massenkultur'? Kino und Rundfunk in der Weimarer Republik," *Historische Zeitschrift*, 262 (1996), 329–381.

———, "Medium of Modernity? Broadcasting in Weimar Germany 1923–1932," *Journal of Modern History*, 69 (1997), 722–753.

Fullerton, Roland, "Toward a Commercial Popular Culture in Germany: The Development of Pamphlet Fiction, 1871–1914," *Journal of Social History*, 12 (1979), 489–513.

———, "Creating a Mass Book Market in Germany: The Story of the Colporteur Novel 1870–1890," *Journal of Social History*, 11 (1977), 265–284.

Füssel, Stephan, "Vom Schaufenstergesetz zur Bücherverbrennung," *Buchhandelsgeschichte*, 10 (1992), 55–64.

———, "Das Buch in der Medienkonkurenz der zwanziger Jahre," *Gutenberg Jahrbuch*, 71 (1996), 322–340.

Geyer, Martin, *Verkehrte Welt. Revolution, Inflation und Moderne: Munich 1914–1924* (Göttingen: Vandenhoek & Ruprecht, 1998).

Gollbach, Michael, *Die Wiederkehr des Weltkrieges in der Literatur. Zu den Front Romanen der späten zwanziger Jahre* (Kronberg: Scriptor-Verlag, 1978).

Goody, Jack, *Literacy and the Traditional Society* (Cambridge: Cambridge University Press, 1968).

———, *The Domestication of the Savage Mind* (Cambridge: Cambridge University Press, 1977).

Göpfert, G. Herbert, ed., *Buch und Leser* (Hamburg: Ernst Hauswedell & Co., 1977).

———, "Die Buchkrise 1927–1929. Probleme der Literaturvermittlung am Ende der zwanziger Jahre," in: Raabe, Paul, ed., *Das Buch in den zwanziger Jahren* (Hamburg: Hauswedell & Co. Verlag, 1978), 33– 46.

———, "Die Aufgabe der Zeit gegenüber der Literatur. Rudolf Borchardt und der Buchhandel," in: Adrian, Werner, ed., *Das Buch in der dynamischen Gesellschaft. Festschrift für Wolfgang Strauß zum 60. Geburtstag* (Trier: Spee Verlag, 1970), 123–131.

Grenz, Dagmar, *Mädchenliteratur* (Stuttgart: Metzler, 1981).

———, and Wilkending, Gisela, eds., *Geschichte der Mädchenlektüre* (Weinheim: Juveta Verlag, 1997)

Grieser, Thorsten, "Der >>Bücher Streit<< des deutschen Buchhandels im Jahr 1903," *Archiv für Buchhandelsgeschichte,* 48 (1996), 17–28.

Gruppe, Heidemarie, *Volk zwischen Politik und Idylle in der Gartenlaube* (Frankfurt a.M.: Peter Lang, 1976).

Günert, Alexandra, "Die Professionalisierung des Buchhandels im Kaiserreich," *Archiv für Geschichte des Buchwesens,* 47 (1997), 267–350.

Haacke, Wilmont, "Das <<Magazin>>, ein unentdeckter Zeitschrifttypus," *Archiv für Geschichte des Buchwesens,* 11 (1971), 429–448.

Habermas, Jürgen, *Strukturwandel der Öffentlichkeit* (Frankfurt a.M.: Suhrkamp, 1990).

Hack, Bertold, "Marginalien, Nachrichten und Dokumente aus der Geschichte des Bahnhofsbuchhandels bis zum Ersten Weltkrieg," *Der neue Vertrieb,* 386 (1965). 2–15.

———, "Der Bahnhofsbuchhandel vor und im 1. Weltkrieg," *Der neue Vertrieb,* 551 (1972), 1–28.

———, "Vom Bahnhofsbuchhandel unter besonderer Berücksichtigung des Zensurproblems," in: Pflug, Günther, ed., *Bibliothek—Buch—Geschichte* (Frankfurt a.M: Vittorik Klostermann, 1977), 269–279.

Haefs, Wilhelm, "Ästhetische Aspekte des Gebrauchsbuchs in der Weimarer Republik," *Leipziger Jahrbuch zur Buchgeschichte,* 6 (1996), 512– 516.

Hagemann, Karen, *Frauenalltag und Männerpolitik. Alltagsleben und gesellschftliches Handeln von Arbeiterfrauen in der Weimarer Republik* (Bonn: Dietz Verlag, 1990).

Hall, David, "The Use of Literacy in New England 1600–1850," in: idem, Brown, Richard and Hench, John, eds., *Printing and Society in Early America* (Worcester: American Antiquarit Society, 1981), 1–47.

Hanebutt-Benz, Eva-Maria, *Die Kunst des Lesens. Lesemöbel und Leseverhalten vom Mittelalter bis zur Gegenwart* (Frankfurt a.M.: Museum für Kunsthandwerk Frankfurt a.M., 1987).

Hartmann, Silvia, *Fraktur oder Antiqua: Der Schriftstreit von 1881 bis 1941* (Frankfurt a.M.: Peter Lang, 1998).

Haug, Christiane, "Das halbe Geschäft beruht auf Eisenbahnstationen... Zur Entstehungsgeschichte der Eisenbahnbibliotheken im 19. Jahrhundert," *Internationales Archiv für Sozialgeschichte der deutschen Literatur,* 23 (1998), 70–117.

Heidenreich, Frank, *Arbeiterkulturbewegung und Sozialdemokratie in Sachsen vor 1933* (Weimar: Böhlau, 1996).

Heiderhof, Horst, *Antiqua oder Fraktur?* (Wiesbaden: Burgverein e.V Eltville am Reihn, 1971).

Heidler, Irmgard, *Der Verleger Eugen Diederichs und seine Welt 1869–1930* (Wiesbaden: Harrassowitz, 1998).

Heinz, Karen, "Schick, selbst mit beschränkten Mitteln! Die Anteilung zur alltäglichen Distinktion in einer Modezeitschrift der Weimarer Republik," *Werkstatt Geschichte,* 7 (1994), 9–17.

Herf, Jeffery, *Reactionary to Modernism* (Cambridge: Cambridge University Press, 1984).

Hiller, Helmut, *Wörterbuch des Buches* (Frankfurt a.M.: Vittorio Klostermann, 1954).

Hoggart, Richard, *The Uses of Literacy* (London: Chatto & Windus, 1957).

Horowitz, Daniel, *The Morality of Spending. Attitudes Towords the Consumer Society in America* (Baltimore: John Hopkins University Press, 1985).

Hübninger, Gangolf, ed., *Versammlungsort moderner Geist. Der Eugen Diederichs Verlag* (Munich: Diederichs, 1996).

———, "Der Verleger Eugen Diederichs in Jena. Wissenschaftkritik, Lebensreform und völkische Bewegung," *Geschichte und Gesellschaft,* 22 (1996), 31–46.

Hurrelman, Bettina, *Jugendliteratur und Bürgerlichkeit* (Paderborn: Ferdinand Schöning, 1996).

———, "Stand und Aussichten der historischen Kinder und Jugendliteraturforschung," *Interationales Archiv für Sozialgeschichte der deutschen Literatur,* 17 (1992), 105–142.

Jäger, Georg and Schnert, Jörg, eds., *Die Leihbibliothek als Institution des literarischen Lebens im 18. und 19. Jahrhundert* (Hamburg: Ernst Hauswendel, 1980).

———, "Historische Lese(r)forschung," in: Werner, Arnold; Wolfgang, Dittrich, and Bernhard, Zeller, eds., *Die Erforschung der Buch- und Bibliotheksgeschichte in Deutschland* (Wiesbaden: Otto Harrassowitz, 1987), 485–507.

———, *Buchhandel und Wissenschaft* (Siegen: Lumis, 1990).

———, "Der Kampf gegen Schmutz und Schund. Die Reaktion der Gebildeten auf die Unterhaltungsindustrie," *Archiv für Geschichte des Buchwesens,* 31 (1988), 163–191.

———, "Die deutschen Leihbibkiotheken im 19. Jahrhundert. Verbreitung—Organisation—Verfall," *Internationales Archiv für Sozialgeschichte der deutschen Literatur,* 2 (1977), 96–133.

Jaraush, Konrad H. and Michael Geyer, *Shattered Past: Reconstructing German Histories* (Princeton: Princeton University Press, 2003).

———, "Die Krise des deutschen Bildungsbürgertums im ersten Drittel des 20. Jahundert," in: Kocka, Jürgen, ed., *Bildungsbürgertum im 19. Jahrhundert. Politischer Einfluß und gesellschaftliche Formation* (Stuttgart: Klett Cotta, 1989), 180–206.

Jay, Martin, *The Dialectical Imagination: A History of the Frankfurt School and the Institute of Social Research, 1923–1950* (Berkeley: University of California Press, 1996).

Jeismann, Karl-Ernst, and Lundgreen, Peter, eds., *Handbuch der deutschen Bildungsgeschichte 1800–1870* (Munich: C.H. Beck, 1987).

Jordan, John O. and Patten, Robert L., eds., *Literature in the Marketplace. Nineteenth-Century British Publishing and Reading Practices* (Cambridge: Cambridge University Press, 1995).

Kaes, Anton; Martin Jay; and Edward Dimendberg, eds., *The Weimar Sourcebook* (Berkeley: University of California Press, 1994).

———, "Schreiben und Lesen in der Weimarer Republik," in: Weyergraf, Bernard, ed., *Literatur der Weimarer Republik 1918–1933* (Munich: dtv, 1995), 3,865.

Kapr, Albert, *Fraktur. Form und Geschichte der gebrochnen Schriften* (Mainz: Hermann Schmidt, 1993).

Kaschuba, Wolfgang, and Kaspar Maase, eds., *Schund und Schönheit. Populärkultur um 1900* (Cologne: Böhlau, 2001).

Kast, Raimund, "Der deutsche Leihbuchhandel und seine Organisationen im 20. Jahrhundert," *Archiv für Geschichte des Buchwesens,* 36 (1991), 165–349.

Kerbs, Diethart, and Reulecke, Jürgen, eds., *Handbuch der Deutschen Reformbewegung 1880–1933* (Wuppertal: Peter Hammer, 1988).

Killiu, Christina, *Die Antiqua Fraktur Debatte um 1800 und ihre historische Herleitung* (Wiesbaden: Harrassowitz, 1998).

Kirchner, Joachim, *Das deutsche Zeitschriftenwesen: Seine Geschichte und sein Wesen* (Wiesbaden: Harrassowitz, 1962).

Kocka, Jürgen, *Klassengesellschaft im Krieg* (Göttingen: Vandenhoeck & Ruprecht, 1973).

———, ed., *Bürger und Bürgerlichkeit im 19. Jahrhundert* (Göttingen: Vandenhoeck & Ruprecht, 1987).

———, ed., *Bürgertum im 19. Jahrhundert* (Munich: dtv, 1988).

Koegel, Jörgen, ed., *Schriftsteller vor Gericht* (Frankfurt a.M.: Suhrkamp, 1996).

Koselleck, Reinhart, *Vergangene Zukunft* (Frankfurt a.M.: Suhrkamp, 1995).

Köster, Hans, "Jungendbewegung—Lauensteiner Kreis—Anfänge des Jungbuchhandels," *Börsenblatt für den Deutschen Buchhandel,* 29 (1966), 758–763.

Koszyk, Kurt, *Deutsche Presse 1914–1945* (Berlin: Colloquium Verlag, 1972).

———, *Vorläufe der Massenpresse* (Munich: Wilhelm Goldmann Verlag, 1972).

———, "Geschichte des Anzeigenwesens," in: Eva Brand, Peter Brand, and Volker Schulze, eds., *Die Zeitungsanzeige* (Aachen: Hahner Verlag, 1990), 21–31.

Kratzsch, Gerhard, *Kunstwart und Dürerbund. Ein Beitrag zur Geschichte der Gebildeten im Zeitalter des Imperialismus* (Göttingen: Vandenhoeck u. Ruprecht, 1969).

Krieger, Walther, *Unser Weg hinauf. Hedwig Courths-Mahler und ihre Töchter als literarisches Phänomen. Ein Beitrag zur Theorie über den Erfolgsroman des modernen Volksstoffes* (Wien: Stubenrauch, 1954).

Kuhlmann, Hans Joachim, *Anfänge des Richtungsstreits* (Reutlingen: Bücherei u. Bildung, 1961).

Laermans, Rudi, "Learning to Consume: Early Department Stores and the Shaping of Modern Consumer Culture 1860–1914," *Theory, Culture & Society,* 10 (1993), 79–102.

Lamb, Stephan, and Phelan, Antony, "Weimar Culture: The Birth of Modernism," in: Burns, Rob, ed., *German Cultural Studies* (Oxford: Oxford University Press, 1995), 53–99.

Langfeldt, Johannes, ed., *Handbuch des Büchereiwesens* (Wiesbaden: Otto Harrassowitz, 1973).

Langenbucher, "Die Demokratisierung des Lesens in der zweitten Leserevolution," in: Göpfter, Hurbert G., ed., *Lesen und Leben* (Frankfurt a.M.: Buchhändler-Vereinigung, 1975), 12–35.

Langewiesche, Dieter, *Zur Freizeit der Arbeiter* (Stuttgart: Klett Cotta, 1980).

———, and Schönhoven, Klaus, "Arbeiterbibliotheken und Arbeiterlektüre im Wilhelminischen Deutschland," *Archiv für Sozialgeschichte* (1976), 132–204.

Lazarfeld, Paul F., *Radio and the Printed Page* (NewYork: Arno Press, 1971, Org. 1940).

Lenman, Robin J.V., "Art, Society and the Law in Wilhelmine Germany: The Lex Heinze," *Oxford German Studies,* 8 (1973/1974), 86–113.

———, "Mass Culture and the State in Germany 1900–1926," in: Bullen, R.J., Pogge, H. and Polonsky A.B., eds., *Ideas into Politics: Aspects of European History 1880–1950* (London: Crom Helm, 1984), 51–59.

Lüdtke, Alf, Marßolek, Inge and Saldern, Adelheid v. eds., *Amerikanisierung. Traum und Alptraum im Deutschland des 20. Jahrhundert* (Stuttgart: Franz Steiner Verlag, 1996).

Maase, Kaspar, "Der Schundkampfritus," in: Rolf W. Berdnich and Walter Hartinger, eds., *Gewalt in der Kultur* (Passau: Passauer Studien zur Volkskunde, 1994), 511–524.

———, "Kinder als Fremde—Kinder als Feinde. Halbwüchsige, Massenkultur und Erwachsene im wilhelminischen Kaiserreich," *Historische Antropologie,* 4 (1996), 93–126.

———, "Die soziale Konstruktion der Massenkünste: Der Kampf gegen Schmutz- und Schund 1907–1918," in: Papenbrock Martina, ed., *Kunst und Sozialgeschichte* (Pfaffenweiler: Centarus-Verlag, 1995), 262–278.

Martens, Wolfgang, *Die Botschaft der Tugend. Die Aufklärung im Spiegel der deutschen Moralischen Wochenschriften* (Stuttgart J.B. Metzlersche Verlagsbuchhandlung, 1968).

———, "Leserezepte fürs Frauenzimmer. Die Frauenzimmerbibliothek der deutschen moralischen Wochenschriften," *Archiv für Geschichte des Buchwesens,* 15 (1975), 1,143–1,200.

Martino, Alberto, *Die deutsche Leihbibliothek* (Wiesbaden: Harrassowitz, 1990).

Marwinski, Felicitas, *Sozialdemokratie und Volksbildung. Leben und Wirkung Gustav Hennings als Bibliothekar* (Munich: K.G. Saur, 1994).

McCracken, Grant, *Culture and Consumption* (Blommington: Indiana University Press, 1988).

McLuhan, Marshal, *The Gutenberg Galaxy* (Toronto: University of Toronto Press, 1962).

Meindelder, Peter Rudolf, "Die Entwicklung der Arbeiterbuchgemeinschaften in der Weimarer Republik," Ph.D. diss., University of Jena, 1991.

Meiner, Annemarie, *100 Jahre Theodor Ackermann* (Munich: Theodor Ackermann, 1965).

Melis, Urban v. *Die Buchgemeinschaften in der Weimarer Republik: Mit einer Fallstudie über die sozialdemokratische Arbeiterbuchgemeinschaft 'Der Bücherkreis'* (Stuttgart: Hiersemann, 2002).

Mendelsohn, De Peter, *Zeitungsstadt Berlin. Menschen und Mächte in der Geschichte der Deutschen Presse* (Berlin: Ulstein, 1959).

———, *S. Fischer und sein Verlag* (Frankfurt a.M.: Fischer, 1970).

Miller, Daniel, *Material Cultur and Mass Consumption* (Oxford: Basil Blackwel, 1987).

———, ed., *Acknowledging Consumption* (London: Routledge, 1995).

Mirb, Karl Wolfgang, *Pioniere des öffentlichen Bibliothekswesens* (Wiesbaden: Harrassowitz, 1978).

Mohler, Armin, *Die Konservative Revolution* (Darmstadt: Wissenschafliche Buchgesselschaft, 1989).

Möller, Horst, "Bürgertum und bürgerlich-liberale Bewegung nach 1918," in: Gall, Lothar, ed., *Bürgertum und bürgerlich-liberale Bewegung in Mitteleuropa seit dem 18. Jahrhundert.* Historische Zeitschrift—Sonderhefte (Munich: Oldenbourg, 1997), 243–342.

Mommsen, Hans, "Die Auflösung des Bürgertums seit des späten 19. Jahrhunderts," in: Kocka, Jürgen, ed., *Bürger und Bürgerlichkeit im 19. Jahrhundert* (Göttingen: Vandenhoeck & Ruprecht, 1987), 288–315.

Mukerji, Chandra, and Shudson, Michael, eds., *Rethinking Popular Culture* (Berkeley: University of California Press, 1991)._

Müller, Marcel, "Die >>Deutsche Dichter Gedächtnis Stiftung<<," *Archiv für Geschichte des Buchwesens,* 27 (1986), 131–275.

Nies, Fritz, *Bahn und Bett und Blütenduft. Eine Reise durch die Welt der Leserbilder* (Darmstadt: Wissenschaftliche Buchgesellschaft, 1991).

Nipperdey, Thomas, *Nachdenken über die deutsche Geschichte* (Munich: dtv, 1986).

Olsen, David R., *The World on Paper: The Conceptual and Cognitive Implication of Writing and Reading* (Cambridge: Cambridge University Press, 1996).

Ong, Walter, *Orality and Literacy* (London: Metheun, 1982).

Ormrod John, "Bürgerliche Organisation und Lektüre in literarisch-geselligen Vereinen der Restaurationsepoche," in: Günther Höntschel, ed., *Zur Sozialgeschichte der deutschen Literatur von der Aufklärung bis zur Jahrhundertwende* (Tübingen: Niemeyer Verlag, 1985), 123–150.

Petersen, Klaus, *Zensur in der Weimarer Republik* (Stuttgart: Verlag Metzler, 1995).

Peukert, Detlev, *Die Weimarer Republik. Krisenjahre der klassischen Moderne* (Frankfurt a.M.: Suhrkamp, 1987).

———, *Jugend zwischen Krieg und Krise* (Cologne: Bund Verlag, 1987).

———, "Der Schund- und Schmutzkampf als 'Sozialpolitik der Seele'," in: Haarmann, Hermann, ed., *Das war ein Vorspiel nur... Bücher Verbrenung in Deutschland 1933* (Berlin: Akademie Verlag der Künste, 1983), 51–63.

Pfäffing, Friedrich, ed., *100 Jahre S. Fischer Verlag 1886–1986. Über Bücher und ihre äußere Gestalt* (Frankfurt a.M.: S. Fischer, 1986)

Pierenkemper, Toni, ed., *Haushalt und Verbrauch in Historischer Perspektive* (St. Katharina: Scripta Mercaturae Verlag, 1987).

———, "Das Rechnungsbuch der Hausfrau und was wir draus lernen können," *Geschichte und Gesellschaft*, 14 (1988), 38–63.

Popp, Helmoth, *Der Bestseller* (Munich: Oldenbourg, 1975).

Raabe, Paul, *Bücherlust und Lesefreunden. Beiträge zur Geschichte des Buchwesens im 18. und frühen 19. Jahrhunderts* (Stuttgart: J.B. Metzlersche Verlagsbuchhandlung, 1984).

———, ed., *Das Buch in den zwanziger Jahren* (Hamburg: Hauswedell & Co. Verlag, 1978).

Radway, Janice A., *Reading the Romance* (Chapel Hill: University of North Carolina Press, 1984).

Rarisch, Ilsedore, *Industrialisierung und Literatur* (Berlin: Colloquim Verlag, 1976).

Raven, James, Small, Hellen, and Tadmor, Naomi, eds., *The Practice and Representation of Reading in England* (Cambridge: Cambridge University Press, 1996).

———, "New Reading History, Print Culture and Identification of Change: The Case of Eighteenth Century England," *Social History*, 23 (1998), 268–287.

Reinhardt, Dirk, *Von der Reklame zum Marketing. Geschichte der Wirtschaftswerbung in Deutschland* (Berlin: Akademie Verlag, 1993).

Reumann, Kurt, "Entwicklung der Vertriebs- und Anzeigenerlöse im Zeitunggewerbe seit dem 19. Jahrhundert," *Publizistik*, 13 (1968), 226–271.

Reuveni, Gideon, "'Productivist' and 'Consumerist' Narratives Regarding Jews in German History," in: Neil Gregor, Nils Roemer, and Mark Roseman, eds., *German History from the Margins* (forthcoming in Indiana University Press).

Richards, Donald Ray, *The German Bestseller in the 20th Century. A Complete Biography and Analysis 1915–1940* (Bern: Peter Lang, 1967).

Rischk, Anne-Susanne, *Die Lyrik in der Gartenlaube 1853–1903* (Frankfurt a.M.: Peter Lang, 1982).

Rose, Jonathan, "How Historians Study Reader Response: Or, What Did Jo Think of Bleak House," in: Jordan, John O. and Patten, Robert L., eds., *Literature in the Marketplace: Nineteenth-century British Publishing and Reading Practices* (Cambridge: Cambridge University Press, 1995), 195–212.

———, "Re-reading the English Common Reader: A Preface to the History of Audience," *Journal of the History of Ideas*, 53 (1992), 47–70.

Rosenfeld, Hellmut, "Zur Geschichte von Nachdruck und Plagiat. Mit einer chronologischen Bibliographie zum Nachdruck von 1733 bis 1824," *Archiv für Geschichte des Buchwesens*, 11 (1971), 337–372.

Rothbart, Otto-Rudolf, *Bibliothekarische Buchkritik. Bestandsaunahmme und Standortsbestimmung* (Wiesbaden: Otto Harrassowitz, 1992).

Saldern, Adelheid v., "Massenfreizeitkultur im Visier. Ein Beitrag zu den Deutungs- und Einwirkungsversuchen während der Weimarer Republik," *Archiv für Sozialgeschichte* (1993), 2,158.

Sautter, Karl, *Geschichte der Deutschen Post* (Frankfurt a.M.: Bibliothek des Bundespostministerium, 1951).

Scharrenbroich, Wilhelm, *Irreführende und strafbare Werbeanzeigen* (Lübeck: Schmidt Römhild, 1958).

Schauer, Georg Kurt, *Deutsche Buchkunst 1890 bis 1960* (Hamburg: Maximilian Gesellschaft, 1963).

Scheideler, Britta, "Zwischen Beruf und Berufung. Zur Sozialgeschichte der deutschen Schriftsteller 1880–1933," *Archiv für Geschichte des Buchwesens*, 46 (1997), 1–336.

Schenda, Rudolf, *Volk ohne Buch. Studien zur Sozialgeschichte der populären Lesestoffe 1770–1910* (Munich: dtv, 1970).

———, *Die Lesesstoffe der Kleinen Leute. Studien zur populären Literatur im 19. und 20. Jahrhundert* (Munich: C.H. Beck, 1976).

———, "Bilder vom Lesen - Lesen von Bildern," *Internationalarchiv für Sozialgeschichte der deutschen Literatur*, 12 (1987), 82–106.

Schindler, Jeremiah Ronald, *The Frankfurt School Critique of Capitalist Culture: A Critical Theory for Post-Democratic Society and Its Re-Education* (Aldershot: Ashgate, 1996).

Schivelbusch, Wolfgang, *Geschichte der Eisenbahnreise* (Frankfurt a.M.: Fischer, 1981).

Schmiedchen, Johannes, *Geschichte der deutschen Wirtschaftswerbung* (Tübingen: Werking-Verlag, 1953).

Schmitt, Karl, *Unsere Firmengeschichte 1841–1966* (Heidelberg: Schmitt & Co., 1966).

Schneider, Ute, *Der moralische Charakter. Ein Mittel aufklärerischer Menschendarstellung in frühen deutschen Wochenschriften* (Stuttgart: Akademische Verlag, 1976).

———, "Lektürebudges in Privathaushalten der Zwanziger Jahre," *Gutenberg Jahrbuch*, 10 (1996), 341–351.

Schön, Erich, *Der Verlust der Sinnlichkeit oder die Verwandlungen des Lesers* (Stuttgart: Klett-Cotta, 1987).

———, "Mentalitätsgeschichte des Leseglücks," in: Belledaum, Alfred, and Muth, Ludwig, eds., *Leseglück. Eine vergesene Erfahrung* (Opladen: Westdeutscher Verlag, 1996).

Schönhagen, Philomen, *Die Zeitung der Leser* (Munich: Publicom Medienverlag, 1993).

Schottenloher, Karl, and Binkowski, Johanes, *Flugblatt und Zeitung. Ein Wegweiser durch das gedruckte Tagesschriftum* (Munich: Klinkhard & Biermann, 1985).

Schräder, Reinald, *Die Industrialisierung des Buchdruckgewerbes in Deutschland im 19. Jahrhundert und ihre Folgen* (Stuttgart: Verlag Clemens Koechert, 1993).

Schulz, Gerd, "Die Gründung der Werbestelle des Börsenverein," *Börsenblatt für den Deutschen Buchhandel*, 76 (1964), 1869–1871.

———, "Das Klassikerjahr 1867," in: Dietrich Bode, ed., *125 Jahre Reclams Universal-Bibliothek 1867–1992* (Stuttgart: Reclam, 1992), 9–11.

Schulz, Hans, *Das Schiksal der Bücher und der Buchhandel:* System einer Vertriebskunde des Buches (Berlin: Walter de Gruzter, 1960).

Schuster, Gerhard, "Rudolf Brochardt und der Insel-Verlag," *Buchhandelsgeschichte*, 10 (1982), 97–114.

Seidensticker, Mike, *Werbung mit Geschichte* (Cologne: Böhlau, 1995).

Seybold, Annte, "Erzählliteratur in der konservativen Presse 1892–1914," Ph.D. diss., University of Frankfurt a.M., 1987.

Shelley, Donald A., *The Fraktur Writing* (Pennsylvania: The Pennsylvania German Folklore Society, 1961).

Shiach, Morg, *Discourse on Popular Culture* (Cambridge: Polity Press, 1989).

Slater, Don, *Consumer Culture & Modernity* (Cambridge: Polity Press, 1997).

Spree, Reinhard, "Modernisierung des Konsumverhaltens deutscher Mittel- und Unterschichten während der Zwischenkriegseit," *Zeitschrift für Soziologie*, 14 (1985), 400–410.

———, "Klassen und Schichtbildung im Medium des privaten Konsums: vom späten Kaiserreich in die Weimarer Republik," *Historical Social Reseach*, 22 (1997).

Stark, Gary D. *Entrepreneurs of Ideology. Neoconservative Publisher in Germany 1880–1933* (Chapel Hill: The University of North Carolina Press, 1981).

———, "Pornography, Society, and the Law in Imperial Germany," *Central European History*, 14 (1981), 200–229.

Staub, Hermann, "Buchhändlerrische Reklamemarken," *Buchhandelsgeschichte*, 2 (1996), 84–90.

Stearns, Peter N. "Stages of Consumerism: Recent Work on the Issues of Periodization," *Journal of Modern History*, 69 (1997), 102–127.

Steinberg, Hans-Josef, "Was sollten die Arbeiter lesen und was haben sie gelesen? Ein Beitrag zur sozialistischen Arbeiterbildung in Deutschland," *Wolfenbütteler Notizen zur Buchgeschichte*, 21 (1996), 128–132.

Steinberg, Siegfried H. *Die Schwarze Kunst* (Munich: Prestel, 1958).

Stemmle, Erwin, *Das deutsche Buchgewerbe in Konjuktur und Krise* (Zürich: Polzgraphischer Verlag, 1958).

Stieg, Margaret F., "The 1926 German Law to Protect Youth against Trash and Filth: Moral Protectionism in a Democracy," *Central European History*, 23 (1990), 22–56.

Street, Brain, ed., *Cross-Cultural Approaches to Literacy* (Cambridge: Cambridge University Press, 1993).

Stucko-Volz, Germaine, *Der Malik Verlag und der Buchmarkt der Weimarer Republik* (Bern: Peter Lang, 1993).

Suleiman, Susan R. and Crosman, Inge, eds., *The Reader in the Text: Essays on Audience and Interpretation* (Princeton: Princeton University Press, 1980).

Tenfelde, Klaus, and Whler, Hans Ulrich, eds., *Wege zur Geschichte des Bürgertums* (Göttingen: Vandenhoeck & Ruprecht, 1994).

Thauer, Wolfgang, ed., *Die Öffentliche Bücherei der Weimarer Zeit* (Wiesbaden: Otto Harrassowitz, 1984).

———, *Politik der Bücherei. Paul Ladewig und die jüngere Bücherhallenbewegung* (Wiesbaden: Harrassowitz, 1975).

———, and Vodosek, Peter, *Geschichte der Öffentlichen Bücherei in Deutschland* (Wiesbaden: Otto Harrassowitz, 1978).

Thompson, John B., *The Media and Modernity: A Social Theory of the Media* (Stanford: Stanford University Press, 1995).

Tibor, Süle, *Bücherei und Ideologie. Politische Aspekte im Richtungstsreit deutscher Volksbibliothekare* (Cologne: Greven Verlag, 1972).

Tiersten, Lisa, "Redefining Consumer Culture: Recent Literature on Consumption and the Bourgeosie in Western Europe," *Radical History Review*, 57 (1993), 115–159.

Tomicka-Krumrey, Ewa, "Gerhard Menz Buchhandelsbetriebslehre und Wirtschaftsjournalismus an der Handelshochschule Leipzig," *Wissenschaftliche Zeitschrift*, 19 (1992), 104–110.

Tompkins, Jane P., ed., *Reader-Response Criticism: From Formalism to Post-Structuralism* (Baltimore: John Hopkins University Press, 1980).

Triebel, Armin, "*Zwei Klassen und die Vielfalt des Konsums*," Ph.D. diss., Free University of Berlin, 1991.

———, "Variations in patterns of consumption in Germany in the period of the First World War," in: Wall, Richard, and Winter, Jay, eds., *The Upheaval of War: Family, Work and Welfare in Europe 1914–1918* (Cambridge: Cambridge University Press, 1988), 159–195.

———, "Vom Konsum der Klasse zur Vielfalt der Stile: Haushaltbudgetgierung seit der ersten Hälfte des 20. Jahrhunderts," *Historical Social Reaserch* 22 (1997), 81–105.

Uhlig, Friedrich, "Der erste Hochschul-Lehrstuhl für Buchhandelsbetrieblehre," in: idem, ed., *Buchhandel und Wissenschaft* (Gütersloh: Bertelsmann Verag, 1965), 31–73.

Umlauf, Ernst, "Zur Struktur der europäische Kulturwirtschaft. Der deutsche Buchhandel bis 1930," *Kultur Archiv des Europa Archivs*, 2 (1947), 889–902.

Viehöfer, Erich, "Der Verleger als Organisator. Eugen Diederichs und die bürgerlichen Reformbewegungen der Jahrhundertwende," *Archiv für Geschichte des Buchwesens*, 37 (1988), 11–47.

Vincent, David, *Bread, Knowledge & Freedom* (London: Methuen, 1981).

———, *The Rise of Mass Literacy* (Malden: Polity Press, 2000).

Vodosek, Peter, *Arbeitsbibliotheken und öffentliche Bibliotheken* (Berlin: Deutscher Bibliotheksverband, 1975).

———, *Vorformen der öffentlichen Bibliothek* (Wiesbaden: Harrassowitz, 1978).

Vogt-Praclik, Kornelia, *Bestseller in der Weimarer Republik 1925–1930. Eine Untersuchung* (Herzberg: Verlag Traugott Bautz, 1987).

Volkov, Shulamit, "Reflection on the History and Historiography of Antisemitism in Imperial Germany," *Leo Baeck Year Book* 23 (1978), 25–46.

Ward, Janet, *Weimar Surfaces: Urban Visual Culture in 1920s Germany* (Los Angeles: University of California Press, 2001).

Wasem, Erich, *Sammeln von Serienbildchen: Entwicklung und Bedeutung eines beliebten Mediums der Reklame und der Alltagskultur* (Landshut: Trausnitz Verlag, 1981).

———, *Das Serienbild. Medium der Werbung und Alltagskultur* (Dortmund: Harenberg, 1987).

Watt, Ian, *The Rise of the Novel* (London: Penguin, 1957).

Weil, Marianne, ed., *Wehrwolf und Biene Maja. Der deutsche Bücherschrank zwischen den Kriegen* (Berlin: Ästhetik und Kommuniktion, 1986).

Welt, Birgit, "Bücher ins Feld! Literarische Versorgung der Soldaten im Ersten Weltkrieg," *Buchhandelsgeschichte* (1995), 1–16.

Wessel, Wolfram, "Die neuen Medien und die Literatur," in: Wyergraf, Berndhard, ed., *Literatur der Weimarer Republik 1918–1933* (Munich: Hanser Verlag, 1995), 65–98.

Widdig, Bernd, *Culture and Inflation in Weimar Germany* (Berkeley: University of California Press, 2001).

Wiggershaus, Rolf, *The Frankfurt School: Its History, Theories, and Political Significance*, translated by Michael Robertson (Cambridge, Mass.: MIT Press, 1994).

Wildt, Michael, *Am Beginn der Konsumgesellschaft* (Hamburg: Ergebnisse Verlag, 1994).

Wilkending, Gisela, *Literaturpädagogik in der Kaiserzeit* (Paderborn: Schöning, 1982).

———, and Grenz, Dagmar, eds., *Geschichte der Mädchenliteratur* (Weinheim: Juveta Verlag, 1997).

Williams, Raymond, *Problems in materialism and culture* (London: Verso, 1980).

Wittmann, Reinhard, *Geschichte des deutschen Buchhandels. Ein Überblick* (Munich: C.H. Beck, 1991).

———, "Streifzüge zur Geschichte des festen Ladenpreises für Bücher," *Buchhandelsgeschichte,* 11 (1976), 385–392.

———, "Das literarische Leben 1848 bis 1880," in: Bucher, Max, eds., *Realismus und Grüderzeit,* vol. 1 (Stuttgart: J.B. Metzlersche Verlagbuchhandlung, 1976), 163–358.

———, "Was there a Reading Revolution at the End of the Eighteenth Century?" in: Cavallo, Guglielmo, and Chartier, Roger, eds., *A History of Reading in the West* (Amherst: University of Massachusetts Press, 1999), 284–312.

Wolf, Hans-Jürgen, *Geschichte der Druckverfahren* (Elchingen: Historia Verlag, 1992).

Wolter, Hans-Wolfgang, *Generalanzeiger—Das Pragmatische Prinzip* (Bochum: Studienverlag, 1981).

Wulf, Carmen, *Mädchenliteratur und weibliche Sozialisation* (Frankfurt a.M.: Peter Lang, 1996).

Zimmermann, Moshe, "Die 'Judenfrage' als 'die soziale Frage'," in: Dipper, Christoph, and Hudemann, Rainer, eds., *Faschismus und Faschism im Vergleich* (Cologne: SH-Verlag, 1998), 149–163.

Zwahr, Hartmut, "Inszenierte Lebenswelt: Jahrhundertfeiern zum Gedenken an die Erfindung der Buchdruckerkunst. Buchgewerbe, Buchhandel und Wissenschaft," *Geschichte und Gesselschaft,* 22 (1996), 5–19.

Index